GW00778038

INFLUENTIAL PAPERS FROM THE 1940s

PAPERS FROM THE DECADES IN
INTERNATIONAL JOURNAL OF PSYCHOANALYSIS
KEY PAPERS SERIES

Edited by

R. D. Hinshelwood

International Journal of Psychoanalysis Key Papers Series
Series Editors: Paul Williams and Glen O. Gabbard

LONDON   NEW YORK

First published in 2005 by
H. Karnac (Books) Ltd.
6 Pembroke Buildings, London NW10 6RE

Arrangement, Introduction copyright © 2005 Institute of Psychoanalysis;
Parts I–V copyright © 2005 Institute of Psychoanalysis,
republished by permission of the *International Journal of Psychoanalysis*

The right of R. D. Hinshelwood to be identified as the author of this work
has been asserted in accordance with §§ 77 and 78 of the Copyright Design
and Patents Act 1988.

All rights reserved. No part of this publication may be reproduced, stored
in a retrieval system, or transmitted, in any form or by any means,
electronic, mechanical, photocopying, recording, or otherwise, without the
prior written permission of the publisher.

British Library Cataloguing in Publication Data

A C.I.P. for this book is available from the British Library

ISBN 185575 303 0

Edited, designed, and produced by The Studio Publishing Services Ltd,
Exeter EX4 8JN

10 9 8 7 6 5 4 3 2 1

www.karnacbooks.com

INFLUENTIAL PAPERS
FROM THE 1940s

CONTENTS

The International Journal of Psychoanalysis Key Papers Series

The IJP "Key Papers" series brings together the most important psychoanalytic papers in the Journal's eighty-year history, in a series of accessible monographs. The idea behind the series is to approach the IJP's intellectual resource from a variety of perspectives in order to highlight important domains of psychoanalytic enquiry. It is hoped that these volumes will be of interest to psychoanalysts, students of the discipline and, in particular, to those who work and write from an interdisciplinary standpoint. The ways in which the papers in the monographs are grouped will vary: for example, a number of "themed" monographs will take as their subject important psychoanalytic topics, while others will stress interdisciplinary links (between neuroscience, anthropology, philosophy etc., and psychoanalysis). Still others will contain review essays on, for example, film and psychoanalysis, art and psychoanalysis and the worldwide IJP Internet Discussion Group, which debates important papers before they appear in the printed journal (cf. www.ijpa.org). The aim of all the monographs is to provide the reader with a substantive contribution of the highest quality that reflects the principal concerns of contemporary psychoanalysts and those with whom they are in dialogue. This volume is the third within the "Key Papers" series that identifies, reproduces, and discusses the most influential psychoanalytic papers produced in each decade since the *IJP* began. By "influential" we mean papers that not only made an important individual contribution to psychoanalytic knowledge at the time, but also went on to influence the development of psychoanalytic thinking and concepts. The objective of this and future volumes in the "decades" collection will be to provide an overview of the development of psychoanalysis, as articulated through its principal scholarly journal.

We hope you will find this and all the "Key Papers" monographs rewarding and pleasurable to read.

Paul Williams and Glen O. Gabbard
Joint Editors-in-Chief
International Journal of Psychoanalysis
London, 2005

ABOUT THE EDITOR

R. D. Hinshelwood is a Member of the British Psychoanalytic Society, and a Fellow of the Royal College of Psychiatrists. He was previously Clinical Director of The Cassel Hospital and currently is Professor, Centre for Psychoanalytic Studies, University of Essex. He is the author of *A Dictionary of Kleinian Thought* (1989), and *Clinical Klein* (1995). He has written widely on therapeutic communities, and the psychoanalysis of organizations (*Thinking About Institutions* (2001)); and published a book on psychoanalysis and ethics, *Therapy or Coercion* (1997).

Introduction to the Journal in the 1940s

R. D. Hinshelwood

I n September 1939, two momentous events for psychoanalysis occurred. On 3 September, Britain and France declared war on Germany and started the Second World War. On 23 September, Freud died.

The Nazi occupation of central Europe had been more or less a deathblow to German-speaking psychoanalysis; and the invasion of Holland, Belgium, and France in early 1940 spelled out a similar disaster for the western countries of Europe. In fact, only two small societies remained on the continent of Europe—in Switzerland and in Sweden. Britain, despite its empire, was a threatened offshore island in which psychoanalysis, like the rest of British culture, was very dependent on the war effort. The war left its mark on the Journal in a very concrete way. The issues became smaller, with less articles, thinner paper, and smaller type.

The second occurrence, Freud's death, must also have connected with the sense in Europe, and in the European psychoanalysts in America, that psychoanalysis might find it difficult to survive. American psychoanalysis, previously somewhat aloof from European psychoanalysis, had by 1940 absorbed a great many analysts from Europe as refugees. American psychoanalysis of the

1930s was not respected as the inheritor of Freud's mantle (Gay, 1988); and there was a sense in Britain that when the Freud family moved to London (in June 1938) so had the centre of gravity of the movement. Both events overshadowed psychoanalysis as well as the Journal throughout the 1940s.

Jones' magisterial obituary to Freud was published in the first issue of 1940, and in it he foresaw an English translation of all Freud's works, which was realized in James Strachey's *Standard Edition*. He embarked, too, on his own three-volume biography of Freud. The Journal published a number of unpublished, or untranslated, writings of Freud during this decade.

The first half of the decade was occupied with the war, and the survival of psychoanalysis in Europe and the world. The death of Freud left Ernest Jones with no hero to worship, and he had no stomach for the open battles that took place in the British Society during 1943–1944. His activities had always been ones that were much more "behind-the-scenes". He retired from practising psychoanalysis and from active involvement in the organization of the movement in early 1944.[1] The purpose Jones had for the Journal, to represent Freud and his work to the world, was diminished by Freud's death. That event also had the effect of releasing the Journal from responsibility and constraint. In addition, it left Jones without the role he had always set himself. Freud's death meant a time of change and new beginnings, coinciding in the second half of the decade with the reconstruction of Western society in general. Change was not Jones' crusade, and he passed the movement and the Journal over to others, perhaps rather suddenly. James Strachey became Editor in 1940, only a few months after Freud died, but in 1946 he passed on the Editorship again (probably to concentrate on the *Standard Edition*). Adrian Stephen took over, intending to create two Assistant Editors, and, in fact, at that time he asked the American Psychoanalytic Association to appoint one of them. However, the Association was not in a position to do so then.[2] In May, Stephen died and the idea for an American Editor seems to have died too, until recently. John Rickman, Willi Hoffer and W. Clifford M. Scott edited the Journal jointly until 1950.

As it became clear that psychoanalysis would survive, the second half of the decade was a time of freedom of ideas. In 1946, the celebratory "Ernest Jones Lecture" was held, which became an annual event. These lectures were regularly published in the Journal. The first one was given by Lord Adrian, a member of an early generation of neuroscientists. His talk ("On the mental and physical origins of behaviour") treats Ernest Jones to a taste of his immortality. The second of these lectures, included in this book, is much more interesting. In the lecture, given in 1947, the biologist C. H. Waddington, talking after the collapse of the Nazi hegemony and at the beginning of the Soviet–American war of ideologies, interestingly turned to psychoanalysis to understand belief-structures as biological and evolutionary entities (see pp. 25–41).

Some of the great battles that had marked the early years of the Journal were subsiding—child analysis, the disputes with Ferenczi and Rank, the questions of lay analysis and of female sexuality. These are all still there, but the heat has gone out of them. In the 1940s, new issues came to the fore, genuinely post-Freudian issues.

There is a reflective attitude towards psychoanalysis itself, what it is, and where it is going. Of course, this is a necessary result of Freud's death, of the great dislocations and diaspora (Steiner, 2000); but perhaps it is also a matter of time—some half-century after the great discoveries of the 1890s. There is a consciousness of history, and Jones' obituary of Freud (Jones, 1940) is as much a history of psychoanalysis as of Freud, which for Jones completely coincided. It was published as the first article of the whole decade. Immediately following it in the first issue of 1940 was Freud's unfinished "Outline of psychoanalysis". Jones returned to history with his reminiscences on the early years of English-speaking psychoanalysis (Jones, 1945). There is, in this decade, the beginning of personal reminiscences of Freud himself (for instance: Graf, 1942; Sachs, 1944; Simmel, 1940).

Taking off, perhaps, from Freud's own reflective stance in "The outline", there was new debate on the relation between psychoanalysis and philosophy (Brierley, 1947; Horkheimer, 1948; Wisdom, 1943), as well as Wisdom's review of Lewis (Wisdom, 1949).

One of the characteristics of this decade is that there is a plethora of creative ideas coming forward, many of which blossom in later periods; for instance, the development of group therapy, arising out of American social psychology of the 1930s, applied to military needs in the 1940s (Foulkes, 1946, and Beres' 1944 review of Slavson's *Introduction to Group Therapy*). There is a good deal of freedom to review metapsychology, of which we include two basic texts (Bibring, 1941, and Isaacs, 1948; see pp. 53–85 and 87–137, respectively). A number of individuals begin to emerge at this time who will later be of considerable significance in the development of British psychoanalysis and the object-relations school: Ronald Fairbairn, Donald Winnicott, John Bowlby, and Michael and Alice Balint, who brought Ferenczi's views alive in Britain.

Fairbairn published two seminal papers in this decade on his individual approach (Fairbairn, 1941, 1944). Winnicott had his finger on the pulse of psychoanalytic interest in Britain, publishing on the infant and its environment, and also being prescient in his radical discussion of counter-transference (Winnicott, 1949— published in our 1950s book in this series). Bowlby began his child work at this time, though his distinctive biological approach was not apparent until later. In addition, Melanie Klein published her second paper on the depressive position (Klein, 1940), and her paper describing the paranoid–schizoid position (1946).

Michael Balint had brought his loyalty to Ferenczi with him from Budapest, but had at first been somewhat eclipsed by being confined to Manchester during the war (though he was responsible for analysing Esther Bick and Betty Joseph there), before coming to London in 1945. The work of Ferenczi had been somewhat in the shadows before the war. Once settled in London (and at the Tavistock Clinic) Balint began to promote Ferenczi's ideas (Balint, 1949), getting the Editors of the Journal to publish Ferenczi's classic paper on the confusion of tongues (Ferenczi, 1949)[3] in a symposium on Ferenczi in the very last issue of the decade.[4]

Balint's paper from this symposium is published here, and keys with the wide interest in the Journal in the early stages of ego development (see pp. 151–169).

"Early stages of the ego", Fairbairn's paper on endopsychic structure (Fairbairn, 1944; see pp. 171–225), is included in this book. His interest starts with the struggles of the ego to organize itself. For Fairbairn there is from the beginning an organizing principle, the central ego, which pulls together aspects of the personality against a process that splits the ego under the pressure of depriving relations with actual others. The notion of a central organizing element in the ego differs from Glover's (1939) notion of unorganized "ego-nuclei" that are disparate from the beginning. However,

Klein (1946) followed Fairbairn in this respect. The split ego, as Fairbairn conceived it, and its attempts at integration, is an important level of ego functioning typical of hysteria. Fairbairn wanted to move psychoanalysis beyond the depressive focus that arose with Freud's interest in melancholia (Freud, 1917e) and return the focus to its origins in the dissociated states of hysterical patients. He therefore challenged Klein's description of the depressive position (Klein, 1935) as well as Freud's and Abraham's long interest in manic-depressive illnesses.

In contrast to Fairbairn's metapsychological interest, Winnicott and Bowlby are essentially empirical. Both brought their extra-psychoanalytic interests with them into their psychoanalytic contributions and discoveries. Winnicott was originally a paediatrician who became interested in psychoanalysis through the psychology of the infant. The interest of the Psychoanalytic Society, in the 1920s, in early analysis and its theories (for example, Klein 1926; Searl 1924) captured Winnicott's interest too (Winnicott, 1941, 1945; see pp. 227–242 and pp. 279–301, respectively), and he continued to the end in connecting his ideas to Klein's depressive position and internal objects.

Bowlby, a child psychiatrist also attracted to Klein's ideas on children in the 1930s, was at the same time interested in biology. He began his evolutionary contribution to psychoanalytic thinking, and elaborated his understanding of how ethology could inform psychotherapy, later in the 1950s (Holmes, 1993). In the 1940s, he relied on his work in Child Guidance (Bowlby, 1940; see pp. 251–277) as it developed in the 1930s (Bowlby, Miller, & Winnicott, 1939). Bowlby emphasized maternal deprivation (Bowlby, 1951) and this was based on a good deal of work he did with the care of child evacuees displaced and deprived of their parents in the war. Later he co-authored *Deprivation of Mental Health* (World Health Organization Booklet 14, 1952) with Robert Harlow, Margaret Mead, Mary Ainsworth, and others. Harry Harlow later conducted experiments on deprivation in young Rhesus monkeys (Bowlby, 1969–1980).

Both Winnicott and Bowlby were directing attention to the external environment of the developing infant. At this stage they were laying foundations for the distinctive independent (or middle) group of psychoanalysts in the British Psychoanalytical Society, which emerged slowly from 1946 onwards (Raynor, 1991). The contributions here of all four analysts (Balint, Fairbairn, Winnicott, and Bowlby) can be seen as position statements on their independence from the dominance of Klein and of ego-psychology. Zaretsky (1999) has noticed that the interest in the privations and parenting of infants coincided with the dramatic enhancement of the welfare state in Britain—not least the creation of the National Health Service in 1947—later dubbed the "nanny state" by Margaret Thatcher in the 1980s. The psychoanalytic turn towards the mother, as opposed to Freud's emphasis on the father, had been gathering momentum during the 1920s and 1930s, and could be said to be backgrounded by social trends that included women's suffrage. The NHS was never mentioned in the Journal during this decade even though we know it was of some considerable concern to psychoanalysts. The Society in Britain was forming a medical committee to enquire into the implications for psychoanalysis.[5]

The divergence of psychoanalysis on either side of the Atlantic was developing in this decade, and perhaps the place of infancy and motherhood could be said to be one of the defining dimensions in that emerging discrepancy.

Re-establishing psychoanalysis. Papers from American authors are fairly thin on the ground in the Journal. However, Schilder (1941) contributed a metapsychological paper, following up Freud's 1926 paper on "Inhibitions symptoms and anxiety". He categorized the various phantasy fears that beset humans and that can underlie neurosis. Bibring's paper on instincts was published in the Journal in 1941 (see pp. 53–85), when he was in Boston. However, it was a translation of a German-language paper of 1936. Reik's paper, originally published in German in 1937, is an elaboration of Anna Freud's descriptions of the defence, "identification with the aggressor" (Reik, 1941). Jones' policy as Editor had been to include a number of European papers in translation for each issue of the Journal. However, after the exiling of so many European analysts and the destruction of so many European Institutes, these papers dried up and there are only a few hanging over into Strachey's Editorship in the 1940s (Bonaparte, 1940; Reik, 1941).

Oberndorf was the official link the Journal had with America during this time, and he did channel some papers, including a couple by himself (Obendorf, 1943; Obendorf, Greenacre, & Kubie, 1948) on the effectiveness of psychoanalytic therapy. Róheim (1941,

1946) published on social and anthropological topics. None of these is a mainstream paper, however. Kris (1940) and Loewenstein (1944) wrote papers on rather peripheral topics concerned with creativity and expressiveness. No doubt it took a while for the European immigrants to the United States to feel comfortable about publishing in English. The immigration into American psychoanalysis led to disputes over the place of the "anointed" from Vienna, who saw themselves as providing a necessary classical input that indigenous American psychoanalysis had lacked (Kirsner, 2000). Before the founding of the *Journal of the American Psychoanalytic Association* in 1953, there was only the *Psychoanalytic Quarterly* that was respected by IPA analysts in America.

Controversy and subjectivity. The creativeness of British psychoanalysis was not, however, without its own turmoil of a similar kind. The arrival of the Freud family, with many other Viennese analysts into the midst of the "heretical" notions of British psychoanalysts who followed Klein, led to the extraordinarily well-documented scientific debates and controversial discussions of the war years (King & Steiner, 1991). The Journal does not reflect much of the "Controversial Discussions" of the early 1940s. Despite being provoked by the opposition of two Viennese women towards each other, the Controversies were a particularly British affair. The dispute was so much a committee–corridor–common-room war that it did not lend itself so easily to Journal publication. The formal papers given in the series of scientific meetings that the Society arranged in 1943–1944 were published as a book (*Developments in Psychoanalysis*), though not until the 1950s, partly, I believe, because of enduring paper shortages.

In fact, the only evidence in the Journal of these debates was the publication of Susan Isaacs' (1948) seminal paper on phantasy, which we republish here (see pp. 87–137). Susan Isaacs was dying in 1948, which no doubt occasioned the publication of the paper, whereas other papers in the scientific debates were held over to be published in the book (Klein, Heimann, Isaacs, & Riviere, 1952). Isaacs' paper is a modified version of that presented to start the first debate in the scientific controversy (in January 1943). Of all the papers, by a long way, it provoked the most productive discussion, with her serious attempt to grapple with differences between the two sides—classical psychoanalysis on the one hand, and the Klein group on the other. Despite the emotional and political motivations (King & Steiner, 1991) there emerged true gain from the eighteen months of scientific discussions for the Kleinians. The awareness of unconscious phantasy as a (perhaps *the*) fundamental concept in their theories (Hayman, 1994) made Isaacs' paper a fundamental statement of Kleinian metapsychology. Reed and Baudry (1997), however, picked up the debate between Marjorie Brierley and Susan Isaacs[6] concerning the confusion between perceptions as represented by phantasy and conceptions as enshrined in meta-psychology. That is to say, a patient's unconscious phantasy of internalizing an object into his person is at the same time under-stood metapsychologically as the mechanism of introjection. The collapse of experience and concept into one another in this Kleinian approach was opposed by the bemused Viennese. Brierley did her best to clarify what this difference meant, in a series of papers outside the controversies (Brierley, 1941, 1944, 1945, 1947), which became a substantial part of her major work *Trends in Psychoanalysis* (Brierley, 1951; see Hayman 1986).[7]

These issues, so overt in the 1940s debate, implied a turn towards the possibility of psychoanalysis as a "science of subjectiv-ity", as Heimann actually expressed then. This is an incipient devel-opment of the much stronger emphasis, which led to a new view of subjectivity from which grew the modern understanding of counter-transference. This flowering of counter-transference occurred in the 1950s, but it was presaged just prior to that with Winnicott's tough paper on hate in mothers and psychoanalysts (Winnicott, 1949).

The impact of the Viennese arrival in Britain proved to be differ-ent from that in the USA. In Britain, the indigenous psychoanalysts survived better, although the movement split. In the USA, psycho-analysis became dominated for decades by the émigrés. The fruits from the survival of British psychoanalysis is evident in later decades, but the origins of its resistance to being overwhelmed are here in the 1940s. In this decade, the *International Journal* is perhaps less international than at any other period. It indicates just how isolated the backs-to-the-wall attitude of British society and British psychoanalysis had become. The survival of a native psychoanaly-sis in Britain was perhaps as much to do with Melanie Klein person-ally as to any other factor. Klein had a lot to lose personally, but the rigour of her observations and of Susan Isaacs' academic argumentation gave sufficient coherence to offer at least a partial answer to the Viennese, who could claim the full authority of Freud and the Freud family. British psychoanalysis had its own issues in 1938 when Freud arrived, and it continued to pursue these into the 1940s—for instance, the question of the nature of "internal objects" (Matte-Blanco, 1941; Brierley, 1942; Heimann, 1942; Strachey, 1941). This debate stemmed from Melanie Klein's depressive position paper (Klein, 1935), and in this decade Klein made another attempt to explain the depressive position (Klein, 1940). Also, she developed an expansion of her old discovery of the early Oedipus complex (Klein, 1945).[8] But her classic contribution in the 1940s is the introduction of the paranoid–schizoid position, which we publish here (Klein, 1946; see pp. 337–364).

Psychiatry and psychosis. In 1946, Klein plotted a whole new direction for her thinking and her followers. She believed that the ego itself could split up into an internal population of parts, which was a very early experience initiating an alternative developmental path that could lead to schizophrenia. Her analysis of the psychotic boy, Dick (Klein, 1930), and her theories of the origin of manic-depressive illness (1935)[9] directed her attention towards psychosis. Her students began to follow in this direction. She attracted a number of psychiatrists for analytic experience or supervision (John Rickman, Clifford Scott, John Bowlby, Paula Heimann, Hanna Segal, Herbert Rosenfeld, W. R. Bion).[10] In this context Paula Heimann reported the analysis of a psychotic artist. Heimann's aim was to address the nature of internal objects and their implication in the identity of the ego and the nature of sublimation (Heimann, 1942; see pp. 313–335). However, the paper also demonstrated how the concrete experience of internal figures lies at the core of psychosis. It is included here as one of the most precise clinical descriptions of the analysis of a psychotic's experience of identity problems and vulnerability to invasion by bad objects.

However, Klein's paper in 1946 moved the goal posts, and stressed different processes in psychotic experience that resulted from "splitting of the ego" and the projection of the resulting parts of the ego into external objects. This is the origin of a most optimistic phase in psychoanalytic history, which flowered during the 1950s with the work of Segal (1950, 1957), Rosenfeld (1947, 1952,

1954) and Bion (1956, 1957, 1959). Rosenfeld (1947) showed the manoeuvring of parts of the self, as opposed to Heimann's concentration on internal objects.

Psychoanalytic relevance. Psychoanalysis during the First World War gained a huge reputation from being the only psychology to explain war neurosis and to offer a treatment method; but in the Second World War psychoanalysis played a different role. There were, in fact, some papers in the Journal on war neurosis, but they did little to advance knowledge beyond that gained in the First World War. In fact, the pages of the Journal show little interest in the contribution of psychoanalysis to military psychiatry,[11] although Thorner comments in 1946. There are reports of the effects of the war on the civilian population (Glover, 1941, 1942; Money-Kyrle, 1947), and the impact of air-raids (Schmideberg, 1942). Both the Hampstead War Nurseries study by Anna Freud and Dorothy Burlingham (Burlingham & Freud, 1943), and the smaller-scale investigation of nurseries in Cambridge by Susan Isaacs (Isaacs, Brown, & Thouless, 1941), warranted book reviews (Sheehan-Dare, 1945; Stephen, 1942, respectively). So, the Journal is marked by the application of psychoanalysis to the social problems created by the war, rather than to the military effort and military casualties.

The mobilization of the whole nation for the war is an example of social engineering in Britain, almost on the scale of that in Nazi Germany. It is not surprising that there was a general tendency to think socially. This is reflected in more general social thinking in papers by Róheim (1941) and Money-Kyrle (1944) and Jones' concerns about the war (1941, 1943). Up to the mid-1940s, the Journal retained its very wide range of book reviewing, together with the commissioning of review articles on various aspects of psychoanalysis and especially its application. This changed as the Journal issues reduced in size due to paper shortage, and then as editorial policy changed from 1946 onwards. Subsequent Editors lacked the sense of purpose that Jones initiated, and this probably continued until Sandler assumed the Editorship in 1969.

The decade of the 1940s is the first post-Freudian one, and it represents the flowering of ideas, of metapsychology and of a new generation of psychoanalysts, some of whom emerge as characters in the later dramas of psychoanalysis: Fairbairn, Winnicott, Ferenczi (with his important disciple Balint) and Klein, in Britain. In

America, there was still turmoil, the Viennese were solidly battling to establish their version of psychoanalysis over the indigenous developments characterized most pointedly by Harry Stack Sullivan. The peak of the achievement at Chestnut Lodge, inspired by Sullivan, was in the 1940s and 1950s, but this goes unremarked in the Journal. Sullivan's more human approach was relegated to an underground status after 1950, for several decades. Frieda Fromm-Reichman and her work are almost completely absent from the Journal.[12] It is an irony that the quintessential American contribution from Sullivan was unheard in the Journal at a time when the Journal was creating the springboard for developments in counter-transference (see Furman & Levy, 2003).

The aftermath of the turmoil in Europe during the war, and after it in the post-war reconstruction period, allowed a good deal of creative thinking, while at the same time a matching but opposite trend established itself to formalize Viennese and Freud's classical ideas as orthodox ego-psychology. The latter, the traditionalist strain, was much less represented in the Journal. Anna Freud published nothing in it. It was the peak time perhaps for the *Psychoanalytic Quarterly*, an almost exclusive journal for American psychoanalysts. The *Psychoanalytic Quarterly* published Helene Deutsch's (1942) classic paper on the "as if" type of resistance and its relations with schizophrenia, and Frieda Fromm-Reichman's (1947) work on in-patient psychotics in Chestnut Lodge, following Sullivan's views. American psychoanalysis was set on a different course—developing classical psychoanalysis and its metapsychology, ironing out inconsistencies, and exploring new problems by theoretical deductions from accepted theory as left by Freud. In America, émigré Europeans remained suspicious of the British (Bibring, 1947) after the rows between Melanie Klein and Anna Freud, and the inconclusive "exchange lectures", and the schism in the British Psychoanalytical Society after the Controversial Discussions. Americans appear for that reason to have overlooked the Journal for publication of their papers.

This left the papers in this decade of the Journal to forge new theoretical frameworks outside of the classical tradition, often with an emphasis on empirical evidence rather than theoretical deduction. This most British of decades in the Journal covers the most dramatic of events: the mourning of Freud, the obliteration of most psychoanalysis on the continent of Europe, the impact of ego-psychology on America, the impact of the controversies in Britain, and the emerging independence of the truly post-Freudian psycho-analytic world. The Journal only partially represents these things, but how could it truly record them all?

Notes

1. Ernest Jones resigned as President of the IPA in 1949.
2. Clarence Oberndorf, one of the first generation of American psychoan-alysts, was connected with the editorial work of the Journal, from 1921 shortly after the Journal was established, until his death in 1954. He must have had a longer association with the Journal than anyone else in its history (sadly he was not given an obituary).
3. Ferenczi's paper is published in our 1930s book in this series, the decade in which it was first published in German.
4. There were a couple of other papers addressing Ferenczi's technique—de Forest (1942), and Thompson (1943).
5. Bowlby incidentally was secretary of that committee (King & Raynor, 1993).
6. Incidentally, Marjorie Brierley's husband, Professor W.B. Brierley, a botanist, had previously been married to Susan Isaacs.
7. Both Susan Isaacs (1945) and Kurt Eisler (1948) commented on Brierley's notion of personology (derived from Smuts, 1926) which she developed in these papers and which has been thoroughly, but undeservedly, forgotten since then.
8. I have excluded these two papers of Klein's from this collection on the grounds that they are already well enough expressed in previous decades.
9. Scott (1946, 1947) published on manic-depressive illness.
10. Klein's first training analysand was the psychiatrist Clifford Scott, in 1931.
11. Despite the considerable contribution of psychoanalysis to the psychi-atric service to the military in Britain, it was absent from the Journal and celebrated in an issue of the *Bulletin of the Menninger Clinic*, in America, in 1946.
12. There is one brief footnote in Thompson (1943) comparing Fromm-Reichmann briefly but favourably to Ferenczi. And a positive mention of her technique by Payne (1946).

References

Balint, M. (1949). Early developmental states of the ego: primary object love. *International Journal of Psychoanalysis, 30*: 265–273.

Beres, D. (1944). An introduction to group therapy. *International Journal of Psychoanalysis, 25*: 174.

Bibring, E. (1941). The development and problems of the theory of the instincts. *International Journal of Psychoanalysis, 22*: 102–130.

Bibring, E. (1947). The so-called English School of psychoanalysis. *Psychoanalytic Quarterly, 16*: 69–93.

Bion, W. R. (1956). Development of schizophrenic thought. *International Journal of Psychoanalysis, 37*: 344–346.

Bion, W. R. (1957). Differentiation of the psychotic from the non-psychotic personalities. *International Journal of Psychoanalysis, 38*: 266–275.

Bion, W. R. (1959). Attacks on linking. *International Journal of Psychoanalysis, 40*: 308–315.

Bonaparte, M. (1940). Time and the unconscious. *International Journal of Psychoanalysis, 21*: 427–468.

Bowlby, J. (1940). The influence of early environment in the development of neurosis and neurotic character. *International Journal of Psychoanalysis, 21*: 154–178.

Bowlby, J. (1944). Forty-four juvenile thieves: their characters and home-life. *International Journal of Psychoanalysis, 25*: 19–53 & 107–128.

Bowlby, J. (1951). Maternal care and mental health. *Bulletin of the World Health Organisation, 3*: 355–534.

Bowlby, J. (1969–1980). *Attachment and Loss* (3 volumes). London: Hogarth.

Bowlby, J., Miller, E., & Winnicott, D. (1939). Evacuation of small children. *British Medical Journal, (16th Dec)*: 1202–1203.

Brierley, M. (1941). The integration of the personality. *International Journal of Psychoanalysis, 22*: 172–174.

Brierley, M. (1942). "Internal objects" and theory. *International Journal of Psychoanalysis, 23*: 107–112.

Brierley, M. (1944). Notes on metapsychology as process theory. *International Journal of Psychoanalysis, 25*: 97–106.

Brierley, M. (1945). Further notes on the implications of psycho-analysis: metapsychology and personology. *International Journal of Psychoanalysis, 26*: 89–114.

Brierley, M. (1947). Notes on psycho-analysis and integrative living. *International Journal of Psychoanalysis, 28*: 57–105.
Brierley, M. (1951). *Trends in Psychoanalysis.* London: Hogarth.
Burlingham, D., & Freud, A. (1943). *Infants without Families.* London: George Allen & Unwin.
Deutsch, H. (1942). Some forms of emotional disturbance and their relationship to schizophrenia. *Psychoanalytic Quarterly, 11*: 301–321.
De Forest, I. (1942). The therapeutic technique of Sándor Ferenczi. *International Journal of Psychoanalysis, 23*: 120–139.
Eisler, K. (1948). Further notes on the implications of psychoanalysis: metapsychology and personology—Marjorie Brierley. *Psychoanalytic Quarterly, 17*: 420.
Fairbairn, R. (1941). A revised psychopathology of the psychoses and psychoneuroses. *International Journal of Psychoanalysis, 22*: 250–279.
Fairbairn, R. (1944). Endopsychic structure considered in terms of object-relationships. *International Journal of Psychoanalysis, 25*: 70–92.
Ferenczi, S. (1949). Confusion of the tongues between the adults and the child—(the language of tenderness and of passion). *International Journal of Psychoanalysis, 30*: 225–230.
Foulkes, S. (1946). On group analysis. *International Journal of Psychoanalysis, 27*: 46–51.
Freud, S. (1917e). Mourning and melancholia. *S.E., XIV.* London: Hogarth.
Freud, S. (1940e). An outline of psychoanalysis. *International Journal of Psychoanalysis, 21*: 27–84. Reprinted in *S.E., XXIII.* London: Hogarth.
Fromm-Reichman, F. (1947). Problems of therapeutic management in a psychoanalytic hospital. *Psychoanalytic Quarterly, 16*: 325–356.
Furman, A., & Levy, S. (2003). *Influential Papers from the 1950s.* London: IJPA.
Gay, P. (1988). *Freud: A Life for our Time.* London: Dent.
Glover, E. (1939). The concept of dissociation. *International Journal of Psychoanalysis, 24*: 7–13.
Glover, E. (1941). Notes on the psychological effects of war conditions on the civilian population (1). *International Journal of Psychoanalysis, 22*: 132–146.
Glover, E. (1942). Notes on the psychological effects of war conditions on the civilian population (2). *International Journal of Psychoanalysis, 23*: 17–37.
Graf, M. (1942). Reminiscences of Professor Sigmund Freud. *Psychoanalytic Quarterly, 11*: 465–476.

Hayman, A. (1986). On Marjorie Brierley. *International Review of Psychoanalysis*, 13: 383–392.

Hayman, A. (1994). Some remarks about the "Controversial Discussions". *International Journal of Psychoanalysis*, 75: 343–358.

Heimann, P. (1942). A contribution to the problem of sublimation and its relation to processes of internalization. *International Journal of Psychoanalysis*, 23: 8–17.

Holmes, J. (1993). *John Bowlby and Attachment Theory*. London: Routledge.

Horkheimer, M. (1948). Ernst Simmel and Freudian philosophy. *International Journal of Psychoanalysis*, 29: 110–113.

Isaacs, S. (1945). "Notes on metapsychology as process theory": some comments. *International Journal of Psychoanalysis*, 26: 58–62.

Isaacs, S. (1948). The nature and function of phantasy. *International Journal of Psychoanalysis*, 29: 73–97.

Isaacs, S., Brown, S. C., & Thouless, R. (Eds.) (1941). *The Cambridge Evacuation Survey: A Wartime Study in Social Welfare and Education*. London: Methuen.

Jones, E. (1935). Early female sexuality. *International Journal of Psychoanalysis*, 16: 263–273.

Jones, E. (1940). Sigmund Freud 1856–1939. *International Journal of Psychoanalysis*, 21: 2–26.

Jones, E. (1943). "How can civilization be saved?". *International Journal of Psychoanalysis*, 24: 1–7.

Jones, E. (1945). Reminiscent notes on the early history of psychoanalysis in English-speaking countries. *International Journal of Psychoanalysis*, 26: 8–10.

King, P., & Raynor, E. (1993). John Bowlby (1907–1990). *International Journal of Psychoanalysis*, 74: 1823–1828.

King, P., & Steiner, R. (1991). *The Freud–Klein Controversies, 1941–1945*. London: Routledge.

Klein, M. (1926). The psychological principles of infant analysis. *International Journal of Psychoanalysis*, 8: 25–37. Reprinted in *The Writings of Melanie Klein, Volume 1*. London: Hogarth.

Klein, M. (1930). The importance of symbol-formation in the development of the ego. *International Journal of Psychoanalysis*, 11: 24–39. Reprinted in *The Writings of Melanie Klein, Volume 1*. London: Hogarth.

Klein, M. (1935). A contribution to the psychogenesis of manic-depressive states. *International Journal of Psychoanalysis*, 16:145–174.

Republished in *The Writings of Melanie Klein, Volume 1*. London: Hogarth.

Klein, M. (1940). Mourning and its relation to manic-depressive states. *International Journal of Psychoanalysis*, 21: 125–153. Reprinted in *The Writings of Melanie Klein, Volume 1*. London: Hogarth.

Klein, M. (1945). The Oedipus complex in the light of early anxieties. *International Journal of Psychoanalysis*, 26: 11–33. Reprinted in *The Writings of Melanie Klein, Volume 1*. London: Hogarth.

Klein, M. (1946). Notes on some schizoid mechanisms. *International Journal of Psychoanalysis*, 27: 99–110. Reprinted in *The Writings of Melanie Klein, Volume 3*. London: Hogarth.

Klein, M., Heimann, P., Isaacs, S., & Riviere, J. (1952). *Developments in Psychoanalysis*. London: Hogarth.

Kirsner, D. (2000). *Unfree Associations*. London: Process Press.

Kris, E. (1940) Laughter as an expressive process contributions to the psycho-analysis of expressive behaviour. *International Journal of Psychoanalysis*, 21: 14–341.

Lewis, M. M. (1936). *Infant Speech*. London: Kegan Paul.

Matte-Blanco, I. (1941). On introjection and the processes of psychic metabolism. *International Journal of Psychoanalysis*, 22: 17–36.

Money-Kyrle, R. (1944). Some aspects of political ethics from the psycho-analytical point of view. *International Journal of Psychoanalysis*, 25: 166–170.

Money-Kyrle, R. (1947). Insight and personality adjustment. A study of the psychological effects of war. *International Journal of Psychoanalysis*, 28: 53.

Loewenstein, R. (1944). The creative unconscious: studies in the psychoanalysis of art. *International Journal of Psychoanalysis*, 25: 93–94.

Obendorf, C. (1943). Results of psycho-analytic therapy. *International Journal of Psychoanalysis*, 24: 107–114.

Obendorf, C., Greenacre, P., & Kubie, L. (1948). Symposium on the evaluation of therapeutic results. *International Journal of Psychoanalysis*, 29: 7–33.

Payne, S. (1946). Notes on developments in the theory and practice of psycho-analytical technique. *International Journal of Psychoanalysis*, 27: 12–19.

Raynor, E. (1991). *The Independent Mind in British Psychoanalysis*. London: Free Association Books.

Reed, G., & Baudry, F. (1997). The logic of controversy: Susan Isaacs and Anna Freud on f(ph)antasy. *Journal of the American Psychoanalytical Association*, 45: 465–490.

Reik, T. (1941). Aggression from anxiety. *International Journal of Psychoanalysis*, 22: 7–16.

Riviere, J. (1936). On the genesis of psychical conflict in earliest infancy. *International Journal of Psychoanalysis*, 17: 395–422.

Róheim, G. (1941). The psycho-analytic interpretation of culture. *International Journal of Psychoanalysis*, 22: 147–169.

Róheim, G. (1946). Saint Agatha and the Tuesday Woman. *International Journal of Psychoanalysis*, 27: 119–126.

Rosenfeld, H. (1947). Analysis of a schizophrenic state with depersonalization. *International Journal of Psychoanalysis*, 28: 130–139.

Rosenfeld, H. (1952). Notes on the psycho-analysis of the super-ego conflict of an acute schizophrenic patient. *International Journal of Psychoanalysis*, 33: 111–131.

Rosenfeld, H. (1954). Considerations regarding the psycho-analytic approach to acute and chronic schizophrenia. *International Journal of Psychoanalysis*, 35: 135–140.

Sachs, H. (1944). *Freud: Master and Friend*. Cambridge, MA: Harvard University Press.

Schilder, P. (1941). Types of anxiety neuroses. *International Journal of Psychoanalysis*, 22: 209–228.

Schmideberg, M. (1942). Some observations on individual reactions to air raids. *International Journal of Psychoanalysis*, 23: 146–176.

Scott, C. M. (1946). A note on the psychopathology of convulsive phenomena in manic depressive states. *International Journal of Psychoanalysis*, 27: 152–155.

Scott, C. M. (1947). On the intense affects encountered in treating a severe manic-depressive disorder. *International Journal of Psychoanalysis*, 28: 139–145.

Searl, M. (1924). Some analytical illustrations from a child's behaviour. *International Journal of Psychoanalysis*, 5: 358–362.

Segal, H. (1950). Some aspects of the analysis of a schizophrenic. *International Journal of Psychoanalysis*, 31: 268–278.

Segal, H. (1957). Notes on symbol formation. *International Journal of Psychoanalysis*, 38: 39–45.

Sheehan-Dare, H. (1945). Infants without families. *International Journal of Psychoanalysis*, 26: 78–79.

Simmel, E. (1940). Sigmund Freud: the man and his work. *Psychoanalytic Quarterly*, 9: 163–176.

Smuts, J. C. (1926). Holism and evolution. London: Macmillan.

Stephen, A. (1942). Review of *The Cambridge Evacuation Survey: A*

Wartime Study in Social Welfare and Education. Edited by Isaacs et al. *International Journal of Psychoanalysis, 23*: 93–94.

Strachey, A. (1941). A note on the use of the word "internal". *International Journal of Psychoanalysis, 22*: 37–43.

Steiner, R. (2000). *"It is a New Kind of Diaspora"*. London: Karnac.

Thompson, C. (1943). The therapeutic technique of Sándor Ferenczi: A comment. *International Journal of Psychoanalysis, 24*: 64–66.

Thorner, H. (1946). The treatment of psychoneurosis in the British Army. *International Journal of Psychoanalysis, 27*: 52–59.

Waddington, C. H. (1947). Science and belief. *International Journal of Psychoanalysis, 28*: 123–130.

Wälder, R. (1937). The problem of the genesis of psychical conflict in earliest infancy—remarks on a paper by Joan Riviere. *International Journal of Psychoanalysis, 18*: 406–473.

Winnicott, D. W. (1941). The observation of infants in a set situation. *International Journal of Psychoanalysis, 22*: 229–249.

Winnicott, D. W. (1945). Primitive emotional development. *International Journal of Psychoanalysis, 26*:1 37–143.

Winnicott, D. W. (1949). Hate in the countertransference. *International Journal of Psychoanalysis, 30*: 69–74.

Wisdom, J. O. (1943). Determinism and psycho-analysis. *International Journal of Psychoanalysis, 24*: 140–147.

Wisdom, J. O. (1949). Philosophy and psychiatry. *International Journal of Psychoanalysis, 30*: 61.

Zaretsky, E. (1999). "One large secure solid background": Melanie Klein and the origins of the British welfare state. *Psychoanalysis and History, 1*: 136–154.

PART I
CLAIMING AN INTELLECTUAL HERITAGE

Introduction

Claiming an intellectual heritage

C. H. Waddington [Waddington, C. H. (1947). Science and belief. *International Journal of Psychoanalysis*, 28: 123–130]

In 1946, the British Psychoanalytical Society started a series of annual lectures called the Ernest Jones Lecture, in his honour, to present psychoanalytic ideas as relevant to the intellectual world in general. The first lecturer was E. D. Adrian, later Lord Adrian, one of the earliest neuroscientists. It was a laudatory speech, but warning Jones of his immortality

> there are perils in this form of immortality as in the other kinds, and there is much to be said for regulations like that for the Seatonian poem at Cambridge which was to be on one of the attributes of the Divine Being from year to year until such time as the subject should be exhausted. That occurred some years ago, and Dr Ernest Jones may be glad to look forward to the time when his attributes, too, may be taken for granted. [Adrian 1946, p. 1]

More interesting and deserving of the recognition of posterity was the second Ernest Jones Lecture, given by C. H. Waddington in 1947. He was an eminent geneticist, at Edinburgh, responsible for the early steps in developing the science of embryology. His roots in genetics and evolution led him to take a few first steps in what we might call evolutionary psychoanalysis. He had an exceedingly good knowledge of psychoanalysis, having produced a book in 1942 on science and belief, using the notion of the super-ego. In this lecture he summarized these ideas.

He argues that psychoanalysis should not concentrate so completely on the primitive and pathological, but pay more attention to the higher functions of human beings as well. He takes the higher functions to be the social ones, based on the ego-ideal and the super-ego. As a geneticist, he was impressed that the human species has adapted in a way that seems quite contrary to the progress that comes from genes and biological evolution. Human beings advance in the realm of socialization, rather than biology; and in particular our evolutionary advance is to develop a social inhibition of the primitive impulses to action, called the id. The emergent structure for our future evolution, the super-ego has evolved from origins as primitive as the animal impulses it attempts to restrain.

So, writing while still in the shadow of the Nazi period, he was dismayed, in his gentlemanly way, that the social restraining mechanism displays such extremely primitive qualities, so occupied with "war, torture and forced migration". The "belief-structure" impels social progress (as opposed to genetic evolutionary progress), but paradoxically beliefs are outside of rational and reality-based thought. He was concerned about the apparent "hypertrophy" of the super-ego, our belief-systems, and "whether our present development of the super-ego does not represent an over-specialization, comparable to the excessive body-armour of the later Dinosaurs".

He charges psychoanalysts with the task of answering what to do about these higher functions, which seem so easily recruited to the primitive impulses. As the discoverers of this paradox, and working with it every day, a scientist from outside our psychoanalytic world might well ask what we are doing about it. How, Waddington asks, can we deal with excessive belief-structures, which threaten the (social) evolutionary success of human adaptation?

He wrote this immediately after the collapse of the belief-structure of Nazism, and at a time when the excesses of Stalinism were coming to the fore. Today, faced with the over-blown beliefs in global capitalism, centring on the pseudo-Christian notion of an "axis of evil", we can ask the same question as Waddington. For instance, what really would be a psychoanalytically mature challenge to the excessive belief-structures of a resurgent Muslim militancy? Waddington's answer would be that we should not raise an equal and opposite primitive belief-structure. In fact, he counsels us to go instead in search of a more benign ideal, based on inherited wisdom from scientific rationalism and artistic creativity.

Waddington's thinking is interesting in its breadth of scope, taking psychoanalysis as a means of gauging much wider problems elsewhere in our social and political world, and he finds in psychoanalysis a deep dimension that is still relevant for the problems of our civilization today.

References

Adrian, E. (1946). The mental and. the physical origins of behaviour. *International Journal of Psychoanalysis*, 27: 1–6.

Science and belief*

C. H. Waddington

Throughout the whole period of civilization which, one is almost constrained to say, has just ended, matters of belief have been the central focus around which human life has orientated itself. We regard ourselves as the heirs of a Christian civilization, and for centuries it was accepted without question that the fundamental cultural boundary was between the Believers and the Heathen. Within each realm, the differences which divided men into more or less exclusive and often hostile groups were usually expressed in terms of belief in certain formulated doctrines. Some of the most ferocious of all wars have raged between people who considered that their most important characteristic was a belief in Catholicism or Protestantism, in the Divine Right of Kings, in Liberty, Equality and Fraternity, or some other such ideal. Many modern historians would wish to look behind the dividing lines drawn in terms of belief, and claim that one can discover other

* The second Ernest Jones Lecture delivered to the British Psycho-Analytical Society on November 19, 1947. [Reproduced, with permission, from: *International Journal of Psychoanalysis*, 1947; 28: 123–130 © Institute of Psychoanalysis, London, UK]

factors, usually economic in the broad sense, which separated the various groups, and of which, they argue, the consciously held beliefs were mere rationalizations couched in the fashionable religious terminology of the age. That may well be largely true; but it must still be recognized that, as far as an individual man attempted to control his own behaviour, and act as a conscious agent, it was by such beliefs that he was influenced. The religious martyrs did not, consciously, die on behalf of a rising class of entrepreneurs or bourgeois middlemen, but for points of doctrine. And even those who did not in fact believe anything deeply enough to die for it, seem for the most part to have considered beliefs as things to which it was quite proper to give such attachment, were not everyday human nature all too weak for such devotion.

In speaking of beliefs in this way, I am not, of course, referring to comparatively trivial theories concerned with the details of behaviour. A man may believe in the wisdom of the editors of his daily newspaper, in the existence of ghosts, or the value of boarding schools for boys, for any of a number of reasons, most of which are likely to be related to the satisfaction of his conscious or unconscious wishes. Such convictions are not of the first importance even for moulding the believer's own character, let alone for the history of civilization. But a much greater importance must be attached to the ultimate general beliefs or fundamental ideals which provide the guiding principle on which men try, somewhat intermittently perhaps, to direct their lives, and which are the aspiration towards which they feel they ought to strive. It is these major ideals—such things as Christianity, Reason or Communism—that I shall be referring to when I speak of beliefs.

At the present time, a very large and influential body of people within our civilization—perhaps the majority of its members—no longer regard religious dogmas as worthy of complete devotion. In fact, we do not now find it intellectually satisfying to base our actions on any belief, however intensely held, for which objective evidence cannot be produced. But the older attitude of mind persists, not only among those unused to precise thought, but in many places where one would have expected a fuller appreciation of the implications of recent psychological investigation. For instance, a few years ago I wrote an essay which attempted to relate man's ethical ideas to the nature of organic evolution, and particularly to the characteristic human mechanism of evolution. A number of scientists, and others, engaged in a discussion of my thesis. And I was written to by an eminent Cambridge philosopher, of my own generation, who complained bitterly of the slipshod thought of scientists. Why could they not see, he asked, that prior to any question of the relation between ethics and evolution there was a fundamental problem, whose importance had been emphasized by Herbert Spencer in a similar discussion a generation or two ago; and reading further, this fundamental problem turned out to be the query, "Is life worth living?" Not until that had been decided was there, according to my philosopher friend, any ground from which deductions could be drawn.

Surely to anyone brought up in a mental atmosphere tinged with the results of psycho-analytical studies, such a question, far from being of profound importance, must seem a completely trivial intrusion from another world of thought. What can it possibly mean if I say that I believe that life is worth living? Apart altogether from the difficulty of defining any of the terms involved; apart from the fact that, whatever I am prepared to say, I have not yet taken cyanide or a barbiturate; if I say, like a good Anglican Christian, that life is worth living, or, like a Buddhist, deny that statement, I am in either case merely expressing a personal emotional attitude; and this has no more general significance as a basis for deduction, than the stated belief of any other of the infinitude of men past and present. It is merely a rather uninformative piece of evidence as to my mental make-up, since the belief that life is worth living can be combined with almost any other set of beliefs one chooses to name. As evidence for a serious study of the nature of the world, it has no more value than a single line picked out of one of Shakespeare's sonnets—much less value, indeed, as coming from a less profound individual.

To anyone who is not mesmerised by a cultural insistence on the importance of beliefs, a simple common-sense inspection of the behaviour of one's fellows is adequate evidence that even if a man gives as accurate a statement of what he believes as he is capable of formulating, that provides only a very rough and incomplete guide to his character. And at a more critical level of study, psycho-analysts have shown conclusively that consciously held beliefs form only a small part of a much larger complex in the mental structure. Much of this complex normally remains below the level of consciousness, as the greater part of an iceberg is beneath the surface of the sea. Exactly which part floats uppermost, and comes within our vision, is partly a matter of chance. Although there are certain elements of the complex whose nature is such that they tend to be more accessible, the ideas with which these parts become clothed are subject to two sorts of variation, due on the one hand to the nature of the deeper levels on which they are based, and on the other to the particular, rather arbitrarily chosen symbols by which the nature of those levels happens to be expressed in the individual concerned.

The wealth of evidence which modern psychologists, and particularly psycho-analysts, have presented on these matters is such that the intellectual world has been persuaded, for the last twenty years or so, of the general truth of their conclusions, at least in broad outline. Applying such an outlook to one's own thought, as one must, one has to concede that no belief, however firmly held, and no axiom, however self-evident, can provide a basis for deductions about the objective world. The essential conclusion was stated quite clearly by Ernest Jones in the first of his papers on psychoanalysis in a book published over thirty years ago, ". . . whenever an individual considers a given (mental) process as being too obvious to permit of any investigation into its origin, and shows resistance to such an investigation, we are right in suspecting that the actual origin is concealed from him—almost certainly on account of its unacceptable nature. Reflection shows that this criterion applies to an enormous number of our fixed beliefs—religious, ethical, political and hygienic, as well as to a great part of our daily conduct; in other words, the principle above quoted refers to a large sphere of mental processes where we least suspect it." At the time they were written, those sentences must have seemed at best doubtful to most people, and frank heresy to many; today the idea they contain should be one of the central methodological principles in all enquiry into the relations between human beliefs and human behaviour, or between metaphysical systems and the objective world.

It is easy to deduce from such a principle that it is vain to search, as philosophers and metaphysicians and moralists have done for so long, after final truths which may be accepted without question and used as the foundations on which a whole system of thought may be erected. Many philosophers, of course, had already come to a similar conclusion on other grounds. Plato, for instance, states somewhere that the highest truths cannot be expressed as doctrines, but only as myths. And in our own times, Whitehead has insisted that "philosophy is akin to poetry, and both of them seek to express that ultimate good sense which we term civilization" (*Modes of Thought*, p. 238). Other recent philosophers, infected with the mundane climate of thought of our age, would scarcely recognize mere myth and poetry, if that were indeed all that was left of philosophy. Bertrand Russell, for instance, counselled an enlightened scepticism, too brilliantly illuminated by wit to notice such nebulous presences; while Wittgenstein could do no more than recognize them and admit the complete unsuitability of his razor-sharp analytical apparatus for handling their impalpable and Protean nature.

The course of recent history has, however, provided a terrifying exposure of the unacceptableness of a call for scepticism, and the dangers of a high-minded silence about human beliefs. For civilization has obviously been caught on both horns of dilemma. While, on the one side, the intellectual basis for the acceptance of any form of belief has been undermined, on the other, our political development has been distorted by the profound influence of new myths, which have attracted to themselves more fanatical devotion than any other set of beliefs for the last century or more. It is the oldest, most thoroughly tested beliefs which have been given up; not only the ancient elaborately rationalized doctrines such as Christianity, but also the less precisely formulated ideals, such as humanitarianism, liberalism, neighbourliness, which were so influential during the last few centuries. But the place of the former theologies has been taken, and more than filled, by new doctrinal schemes, such as Communism, free enterprise, or the various brands of national socialism and the cruder nationalisms which are qualified by no social aim; while the older values have been replaced by such ideals as efficiency, ruthlessness in attaining a desired end, equalitarianism, or the leadership principle, and whole host of others. I have no wish to claim that all these doctrines or ideals are necessarily unworthy of devotion. Among them are to be found the forces that will shape the future, and, speaking for myself, I can see, clearly enough to feel a moderate optimism, potentialities for a future far preferable to the past. The only point I wish to make here is that these newer doctrines and beliefs, the good and the bad alike, have called forth an intensity of belief which is in flat contradiction to the understanding which we now have of how beliefs are formed and the reasons for which they are held.

There is no need to labour the point and quote more examples. We see clearly that the preliminary analysis of the nature of belief, carried out in the early years of the century, has had consequences of both a negative and a positive kind—negative in that it loosened the hold of the older creeds, and positive by the rather indirect route that it was in actual fact followed by the adoption of a large variety of new doctrines, many of which at least pretended to be "scientific". This evidence is enough to warn us that it is inadequate to draw from the recent analysis merely the pious aspiration that men's conduct should not be affected by any tenet which cannot be proved by the objective criteria of science. There is no doubt that all men's actions (including, let us remember, our own) will continue to be profoundly influenced by beliefs which are held for quite other reasons than the weight of the evidence which supports them.

This need not constrain us to abandon the use of our scientific faculties in discussing human motivation and action. It means that the centre of interest shifts from the nature of the ideal—the particular thing believed—to the mechanisms by which beliefs in general come to be formed, and the part which they play in the functioning of the whole human personality. Already the progress of psychoanalysis, supplemented by the studies of anthropologists and other social scientists, is filling in a picture in whose outlines even the nonexpert can begin to find a fresh and less negative way of criticizing his own and other people's systems of ideals. But there still seems to be a great need for those professionally competent in such matters to discuss explicitly the relation between the detailed technical findings of psychiatrists and the general structure of the human mind as it functions in its highest, and not merely in its lowest, activities. I suppose all scientists are used to outsiders asking them why they concentrate their attention on such apparently trivial matters; I know I have often had to explain at length why I study heredity in fruit-flies, and development in newts' eggs.

Perhaps I am making a similar disingenuous error when I ask psycho-analysts not to concentrate quite so much as they do at present, on the neurotic and pathological. I am very ready to believe that these may be by far the most useful experimental material— that is a technical question of which I cannot judge. But I imagine most psycho-analysts are well aware of the effects of their discoveries on the whole of our philosophy and ethics; and I think one is justified in asking them whether they can truthfully say that they devote enough time to discussing the most fundamental implications of their studies, and make enough investigations specifically directed towards solving the problems that arise.

The conventional views about the origin of man's more deeply-held religious, ethical and political beliefs, have in the past moved between two poles. One was that they had a supernatural origin and were implanted in him independently of any action of his consciousness; the other that they were arrived at by rational thought concerning the nature of the world. The psycho-analytical and sociological investigations have issued in conclusions which are, in some ways, a synthesis of both these. We find that a great part of the belief-structure of an individual has an origin which is independent of his conscious mind in so far that it arises in the very earliest childhood, at a time whose traces are usually almost completely obliterated from later memory; the learning of beliefs is, according to this view, pressed back so far into infancy as to fall, as it were, outside the later conscious personality. On the other hand, the content of belief is dependent on the actual events which the infant experiences. In particular, a major contribution to the underlying factors of all beliefs is made by the social inter-relations between a child and its parents or other early guardians. The formation of beliefs is thus an aspect of the most fundamental biological characteristic of humanity, namely, the development, as the main mechanism for evolutionary change, of a system of learned social behaviour.

One cannot appreciate the fundamental role played by belief in the normal human personality without some idea of the magnitude of this biological revolution of which it is an integral part. A student of the long succession of non-human organisms finds that he can regard them as essentially reducible to the hereditary genes which lie embedded within the nucleus of each cell. Only the most trivial modifications can take place if the genes remain unaltered, and all evolutionary changes are the expressions of changes in the frequency or nature of the genes present in the organisms concerned. In man the situation is totally different. Although individual men and populations of men undoubtedly differ from one another in the genes they contain, it is certain that historical changes of fundamental importance can take place without any closely corresponding genetic alterations. To give one instance, the Maori were within a few decades transformed from a warlike and savage society into peaceful citizens of a modern civilization, and there is no possibility of explaining this by a change in the genetic nature of the population. In general, the progress of civilization—indeed, its very existence—depends not on equipping each individual with a set of genes which gives him the potentiality to develop into a certain kind of person, but on social learning acting within a population all of whom have, throughout all stages of the historical process, essentially similar genetic constitutions. The preeminence of the genetic mechanism, which is the rule throughout the entire non-human world of living organisms, has been superseded by the biologically unparalleled development of the social interactions.

The evolutionary mechanism which man has adopted acts, of course, only in the mental sphere, and leaves his physical structure unchanged. But within its own field of action, it is incomparably more rapid in its effects than the normal biological mechanism of the selection of genes. Even such an "intelligent" animal as the horse differs in mental ability from its ancestors of a few million years ago by only a fraction of the interval which separates a modern farmer from his unlettered Saxon forefathers who lived only a thousand years in the past. The developments of social life must have conferred very great advantages in the struggle for existence on the primitive Hominidae who adopted them; and, by competition between more and less closely integrated groups, the tendency to the formation of societies must have been rapidly strengthened until it came to play something approaching its present fundamental role in determining man's nature.

The formation of any human society is based essentially on some degree of acceptance of authority. The primitive urges to activity, which are probably physiologically inherent in every animal, must be restrained or directed into certain channels if the separate individuals are to live and act together as a community. In the human form of society, this restraint is at least partly conscious. The authority appears within the mind as what I have referred to as "belief-structure"; that is to say, a complex of feelings, images and ideas, partly conscious and partly hidden in the unconscious, which can be grouped together by the fact that they all play the functional role of acting to restrain the primitive urges to activity. Different authorities seem to differ somewhat in their usage of the technical terms, but the complex I am referring to includes the greater parts of the super-ego and ego-ideal, and probably some of what would often be considered as part of the ego.

Psycho-analysis has revealed the previously unsuspected power both of the primitive urges to action (the id) and of the restraining belief-structure. The wars, tortures, forced migrations and other calculated brutalities which make up so much of recent history, have for the most part been carried out by men who earnestly believed that their actions were justified, and, indeed, demanded, by the application of certain basic principles in which they believed. Such events provide, surely, proof enough that the belief-structure, whose function is essentially that of restraining the aboriginal id, has a crude power which may lead it to act quite unlike a gentlemanly and kind policeman. This apparent hypertrophy of the human control mechanism is, perhaps, rather surprising. It may be, of course, that the primitive urges are so strong, and would, if left to themselves, be so incompatible with social existence that a dangerously powerful belief-structure is indispensable before man can reap any evolutionary advantage from living in groups. But it may also be asked whether our present development of the super-ego does not represent an over-specialization, comparable to the excessive body-armour of the later Dinosaurs, or the finicky adaptation of certain parasites which fits them to live on only one host. It would be interesting to know whether the differentiation of the human mind into opposing factions—roughly speaking, into id and super-ego—has increased in modern civilized man as compared with the primitive savages of the still existing Stone Age cultures. Is the apparent prevalence of neurosis in Western civilization a mere consequence of better diagnosis, or the result of the greater strain of industrial civilization, or due to a real over-specialization in the direction of human evolution? If the latter suggestion is true, then the self-destruction of mankind in wars of political religion, which hangs as such an obvious threat over our heads, will be merely one more example in the long tale of evolutionary doom following on over-specialization.

The potential destructiveness of our beliefs has, of course, been recognized by many students of these matters. It has not been so easy to prescribe an antidote. Some have been tempted to suggest a very radical remedy. For instance, in a recent lecture, General Chisholm, a distinguished psychiatrist who was Director-General of Medical Services in the Canadian Army, and is now Executive Secretary of the World Health Organization of the United Nations, went so far as to suggest that we should abolish beliefs, "stop teaching children moralities and rights and wrongs, . . . the poison long ago described and warned against as the fruit of the tree of the knowledge of good and evil". Instead we should "protect their original intellectual integrity". But can we find an original integrity which is independent of the belief-structure mechanism of organizing social life? If I have been on the right lines in the previous discussion, in which I have argued that the setting up of a system of ideals in opposition to the primitive urges is the essential feature of a new evolutionary method, then we cannot merely abolish one half of the dualism, however hypertrophied it may have become.

We need to approach the matter more cautiously and to devote more careful study to the exact nature of the system which we wish to control. What are the broad structural features of that complex of beliefs and their unconscious counterparts which exercises a restraining and directing function within the human mind? And further, since we cannot contemplate the abolition of this complex, we need to enquire what types of internal balance may be set up within such complexes as enable their possessors to live active, creative and co-operative lives. A very great deal more thorough and professional study must still be devoted to such questions. We can as yet give only incomplete and very tentative answers. If I venture on a few suggestions, it must be understood that they are offered out of a background of acknowledged ignorance, and are only put forward in order to provide an example of the kind of working hypothesis which requires investigation.

We may take it that the main element in a belief-structure is the representative of authority. Ultimately this may be regarded as the introjection of a parent or parent-substitute, but in the shifting alchemy of the developing personality, the original human authority may come to be symbolized by many different images and ideas. The function of this element in the complex is to restrain and direct the energies of the primitive physiological urges, and it can only do this by virtue of a measure of love, reverence and submission which is paid to it by the remainder of the self. But this submission cannot be absolute; the primitive urges, and the id which represents them, struggle against restraint; the belief-structure is the subject of hate as well as of love. This sets up a simple duality. Such systems may sometimes come into a balanced equilibrium which remains comparatively stable and unchanging. But they also, and perhaps more frequently, enter on the process which sociologists have spoken of as schismogenesis, that is, an interaction of the two parts which leads to each becoming more extreme and the tension between them more acute. Thus we find often that it is those people with the most deep attachment to an ideal who actually commit the most terrible crimes against it. It was the ultra-nationalists of Germany who showed least respect for the nationalisms of the neighbours, it is the revolutionaries in the name of human brotherhood who root out their enemies like rats.

I should like to put forward the hypothesis that one way, perhaps even the only way, of controlling this tendency to schismogenesis, is to erect a second dualism, as it were, in another dimension to it. If the love of one ideal leads to some degree of attachment to a second ideal, which, while not the diametrical opposite of the first, is yet of a quite different and contrasting kind to it, then the hate directed at the primary symbol can become mutated into the service of the secondary. To give an example, the Christian belief-structure, which lasted for so long, and for much of this period facilitated the growth of a progressive and fairly stable civilization, involved the two ideals of holy humility and the organized Church: Saint Francis and the Popes. A primary attachment to the restraining authority of the Church contained a necessary element of reverence for the very different ideal of brotherly love which the institution was supposed to serve; and the internal forces of hate directed against the organization could take the form of a devotion to this essentially anarchic aspiration. Again, on a some-what lower level, the pre-eminently stable British political system has been based on an acceptance of a social hierarchy, mitigated by a devotion to the principle of equal justice for all men. On the other hand, everyone can see at present the dangers to the whole of civilized life which threaten from an exclusive belief in the virtues of "free enterprise" or in the cause of social organization.

It has, I think, been usual to consider that in a balanced duality of loyalties, the two elements must be of the same nature though opposite in tendency. That is to say, that a belief in the virtues of social organization, for instance, must be countered by a belief in its exact opposite, namely, in social freedom; or a belief in a doctrinaire and hierarchical Church balanced against a belief in the value of the individual conscience. I believe this to be a misinterpretation. A stable mental equilibrium seems to me to be something other than a mere compromise between opposites. It seems rather to involve a relation between two entities of different order. The values of the Sermon on the Mount belong to a different sphere to those of the organized Church; and the balance weight to a belief in social organization is to be found, not in the absence of regulations and planning, but in an insistence on the richness and depth of individual experience. The individual hate directed against the super-ego probably cannot be simply transmuted into love for its opposite, but can, it appears, take the form of an attachment to some ideal totally other to the primary one. I shall not attempt to discuss possible reasons for this, being certainly unqualified to do so; but they must surely be connected with the relations between the conscious and unconscious parts of the mind, and dependent on the difficulty of accommodating within the one field of consciousness two tenets which are clearly opposite to one another. In general, it must be said here, that the extremely simplified sketch which I am offering of the structure of the belief-function of the mind requires supplementing by a much fuller consideration of the mechanism of repression, which introduces still another dualism, that between the conscious and unconscious representatives of the primitive urges and the restraining authority.

The practical conclusion to be drawn from this line of thought is that it is dangerous to allow questions of belief to become concentrated into a single channel. We have to recognize not merely that it is impossible to eliminate beliefs from the human mind, but that a stable and equable personality must be founded, not only on one, but on several ideals. If we see all things in terms of one shibboleth, in monotone, we shall almost certainly come to see them in stark contrasting opposites, in black and white. We need a multidimensional view of the universe.

This conclusion amounts to a denial of the practical value of the philosophers' age-long attempts to reduce the apparent chaos of immediate experience to a single unified and harmonious system of concepts. Of course, in so far as a metaphysical system remains a purely intellectual construction, it does not require criticism on the grounds I have been bringing forward. It would be at least an innocuous component of the mental structure and might even be a useful framework of abstract thought. But so soon as it becomes employed as a guide for action, a metaphysical system must attract to itself some degree of belief; and if, being a comprehensive system, it is taken as the sole guide, it becomes the vehicle for a monotone belief of the kind which, I have argued, is in danger of leading to a destructive schismogenesis. Thus the search for a unified metaphysics remains either an intellectual pastime having no important effects on human action, or it leads belief into the dangerous confinement of a single dimension.

These severe strictures on the elaboration of systems of thought must be counterbalanced by another consideration. Stability is not the only desideratum which we should wish to achieve in the human mind. In fact, if it were not that present-day society is suffering so grievously from mental instability and unbalance, one would probably have been tempted to place much less emphasis on the necessity for a counterbalance of beliefs than I have done in this lecture. From a more general point of view than the purely contemporary, the outstanding characteristic of the human evolutionary mechanism is the width of the field of experience and achievement which it throws open to the individual. The process of social learning offers to him a large part of the thoughts and attainments of his ancestors. A man's life, it may be said, is not restricted to his own existence, as is a dog's. It is primarily on this account that the human method of variation and selection has proved so far more rapid, and to produce such far greater effects, than the normal biological procedure. It is, therefore, obviously a prime requirement of the belief-system that it should not unduly restrict, but should rather enlarge in as great a degree as possible, the breadth and scope of the social heritage which the individual is willing to acknowledge, test, and possibly accept. An ideal, to be worthy of belief, should be on a large scale.

This consideration goes some way to mitigate the apparent particularism of our previous conclusion. It may be easy enough to set up a stable personality on the basis of a belief structure comprising a primary attachment to, say, the cause of the Society for the Prevention of Cruelty to Animals, counterbalanced by a degree of devotion to the exacting, but quite different, God who rules over the game of golf. But these ideals are unduly restricted in their field of application. If mankind in general adopted them as the basis for civilization, we might perhaps be spared the dangers of a destructive schismogenesis, which lead to the committing of terrible crimes in the name of the very ideals which are supposed to prevent such conduct, but it is obvious that the richness and depth of our culture would shrink to pitiful dimensions. It is true, of course, that concentration on a restricted ideal by a given individual may enable him to devote to it sufficient energy to produce a noteworthy result; and to that extent, society may be the gainer from the impoverishment of the beliefs of some of its members. But what may be true of single persons is not necessarily applicable to society as a whole. There can be no doubt that if the generally accepted ideals of belief in a society are narrow in their scope, the richness of civilization must suffer, and the belief-structure partially fail in its function of mediating the acceptance by the individual of the cultural heritage offered him by the past.

This line of thought might at first sight lead to the conclusion that we should, after all, seek an all-embracing ideal. But not only does that seem inevitably to lead, as I have argued above, to an unstable and potentially dangerous internal conflict, but it is also at present intellectually impossible of attainment. No philosophical system yet proposed really accommodates all the values which man has formed from his experience. The acceptance of one system, as the final and comprehensive scheme to which everything may be referred, must lead to an undue restriction of the fullness of civilization even before the schismogenesis to which it will give rise becomes a practical danger. The best we can do is to see that each of the two or more complementary ideals which we adopt is as all-embracing as it can be within the limits of its own field. Thus, if one accepts an attachment to a political ideal formulated in terms of a national loyalty, the larger the national organization chosen, the less likely it is to restrict the range of values which can be appreciated. Similarly, greater scope will be offered if the ideal is formulated in general terms, rather than taken to involve precisely defined and particularized characteristics. A politico-economic belief in, for instance, free trade, or communal ownership, is more limiting than a devotion to the cause of increasing the material standard of living, or enlarging the possibilities for individual development.

The functions proper to the belief-structure of the mind are, potentially, best filled by ideals which are of extremely wide range. The brotherly love of the Christians, the intellectual curiosity and good sense of the Greeks, even the orderly British ideal of conduct appropriate to one's station in life, were beliefs general enough in character to apply to almost all the situations which arise in a full and active life. While representing very clearly the ultimate parental authority on which the whole process of social learning rests, they reflect this as a leading and guiding, rather than a merely restraining influence. The more particular beliefs, such as those in nationalism or free trade, which were mentioned above, can be regarded as incomplete derivatives of one or other of the more general ideals. Unfortunately, there is undoubtedly a strong tendency for such partial ideas to assume a more dynamic role within the personality than the more general ones. The broader and deeper the scope of an idea, the harder it is for the mind to grasp it in its general significance, or to apply it to particular instances. An intellectual formulation of such a belief must, indeed, be of a highly abstract nature, and is beyond the capacity of any but a highly trained mind. Non-intellectual people may, of course, apprehend such ideals; in fact it sometimes appears as if it is easier to attain to a really profound ideal by some unformulated process of an intuitive nature than by close abstract reflection—we must all have met instances of the simple good man. But even these are all too rare. The beliefs one notices as operative in the personalities one meets are usually focussed on some comparatively minor particular, some specific political or religious or ethical point. A devotion which constantly refers back to one of the great large-scale ideals of humanity is something of a rarity in human characters as they are formed by society at the present day. It is surely one of the major tasks of civilization to remedy this, to see that as the child's reverence and love passes on from its parents to some wider authority, it finds itself in the presence not merely of a particular doctrine but directly confronted with the major premises of human society.

There are several current ideals of breadth and scope sufficient to rank among the mainsprings of civilization. Perhaps it is not always realized that science, as it has grown under the co-operative efforts of so many men, has by now become one of the most compelling of the possible candidates for the position of internal authority in the human belief-structure. Its adequacy to this role is often denied, chiefly by those who interpret the scientific ideal in an unduly narrow way. If Christianity meant no more than the strict adherence to the tenets of a particular fervent and narrow-minded sect (say the Fundamentalists of Tennessee) it would seem a poor and dangerous basis on which to try to continue the culture of Western civilization. Equally, if science is thought to mean no more than an exclusive attention to the data of physics, chemistry and physiology, and to demand the dismissal of all other aspects of human experience, it also appears a threadbare and puerile belief. But the scientific attitude of mind is a much more profound embodiment of the human spirit than such a shallow view suggests. I shall not attempt to formulate it in a few words; but psychologists at least have every reason to know that science can approach and discuss even the subtlest problems of human conduct and of the relations between a man and his fellows. I would not say that the scientific ideal alone is a wholly adequate foundation for the good life of the individual, or the highest civilization of society; but my main reason for this is the conviction, the grounds for which I have given earlier, that no single ideal is sufficient. The authority of science gives its sanction to one of the greatest creations of the human mind—the attitude of logical thought continually checked by the empirical appeal to experiment—but it needs, in my view, to be supplemented by the quite different ideal of the creative artist—an ideal which expresses itself in thought-processes which move in a different dimension to the scientific. Perhaps at the end of a discussion on the general topic of beliefs, it may be in order for me to state a belief of my own. That is, that these two types of authority—the scientific and the artistic—

constitute the dualism which is, of all the possible choices open to a child growing up in our time, the most effective in carrying out the functions of the belief-structure of the human mind, namely, of enabling man to use the experience of past generations as an aid in coming to grips with the world as he finds it. In the words of Yeats:

> Civilization is hooped together, brought
> Under a rule, under the semblance of peace
> By manifold illusion; but man's life is thought,
> And he, despite his terror, cannot cease
> Ravening through century after century,
> Ravening, raging, and uprooting that he may come
> Into the desolation of reality.

If we cannot hope to abolish the beliefs or "illusions" on which human social life is based, at least we should choose such as are large enough to accommodate the major part of reality, and are of a kind which facilitate man's gradual approach to it.

PART II
METAPSYCHOLOGY

Introduction

On metapsychology

All through Freud's life psychoanalysis was straining to come apart along its fracture lines. By the time of his death, the fracture lines were increasingly visible. The long-standing suspicion by European psychoanalysts that the "native Americans" were revisionists impelled a particular history when the German-speaking analysts arrived during the 1930s. This caused hardly a ripple in the Journal. The fate of dissension in Britain was different, and did leave some traces.

The Editor, Ernest Jones, had for some time sought to reconcile the differences between British psychoanalysts and the Viennese, by arranging with Paul Federn and Anna Freud a series of exchange lectures between London and Vienna. In fact, because of the crescendo of political troubles in the 1930s, only three of these "Exchange Lectures" were given: Jones, 1935 in Vienna, Wälder, 1935[1] in London, and Riviere, 1936 in Vienna. They achieved little reconciliation, but did clarify many differences. Then, in 1938–1939, when the Viennese arrived in London, they met the much more respected and confident British psychoanalysts. Therefore, the early part of the 1940s saw a psychoanalytic "blitzkrieg" on London, which was partly seen off. Anna Freud herself was anxious not to cause trouble in the host society that had given her, her family, and her colleagues a refuge and new home (Young-Bruehl, 1988). The ultimate result for many reasons was a resigned sense on both sides of having to live together.

From the war, there emerged two more or less clear camps. The bitterness, and indeed much of the substantive issues of the well-documented controversies (King & Steiner, 1991), did not creep visibly into the Journal. Jeanne Lampl-de Groot observed:

> In resuming contact with psycho-analytic writing in other coun-
> tries, after many years of separation enforced by the war, I am
> struck by the varieties of directions in which research work has
> been extended. One line of investigation however seems to me the
> most prevalent: there is an increasing interest in the development
> of the ego and super-ego. [Lampl-de Groot, 1947, p. 7]

This discerns the development of ego-psychology, but characteristically it affects to ignore the emerging object-relations tradition as if it did not exist. This was to be the characteristic mode of dealing with the controversies—to ignore the existence of the other side. However, the Journal did carry two papers that could be considered fundamental statements of the classical and the Kleinian positions—those of Edward Bibring on instincts in 1941 (see pp. 53–85), and of Susan Isaacs on unconscious phantasy in 1948 (see pp. 87–137). Both concern the nature of phantasy as apprehended psychoanalytically. The classical version sticks more closely to the biological impulse and energic quantity, whereas Isaacs' Kleinian notion diverts attention to the narrative, qualitative aspects as instinct is *experienced*.

Note

1. Wälder's lecture was never published but his rebuttal of Riviere's lecture in Vienna in 1936 was (Wälder, 1937).

References

Jones, E. (1935). Early female sexuality. *International Journal of Psychoanalysis, 16*: 263–273.

King, P., & Steiner, R. (1991). *The Freud–Klein Controversies, 1941–1945.* London: Routledge.

Lampl-de Groot, J. (1947). On the development of the ego and super-ego. *International Journal of Psychoanalysis, 28*: 7–11.

Riviere, J. (1936). On the genesis of psychical conflict in earliest infancy. *International Journal of Psychoanalysis, 17*: 395–422.

Wälder, R. (1937). The problem of the genesis of psychical conflict in earliest infancy--remarks on a paper by Joan Riviere. *International Journal of Psychoanalysis, 18*: 406–473.

Young-Bruehl, E. (1988). *Anna Freud: A Biography.* London: Macmillan.

Edward Bibring [Bibring, E. (1941). The development and problems of the theory of the instincts. *International Journal of Psychoanalysis, 22*: 102–130]

Bibring was among the number of Viennese analysts settling in America. The paper published here is an English translation of an earlier paper in German (in 1936). It was published in the Journal for interesting reasons, as an editorial comment makes clear. At that time (1941), Jones in his editorial footnote wrote that the paper "is perhaps the most authoritative account of the various phases of Freud's views upon instincts" (Vol. 22, p. 102), and so it remains today, which is the reason for inclusion in the present volume. One could believe that Jones' inclusion of this paper after its original publication in German is a continuance of his intention to bring the classical tradition and the British views into some kind of dialogue.

Interestingly, another venture in republishing "classic" papers from the Journal was in its fiftieth volume, in 1969. In fact, this paper of Bibring's was one of two chosen for republication then, the other being Strachey's classic "The therapeutic action of interpreta-tion" (originally published in 1934). It is appropriate, therefore, to include Bibring's paper in this collection of classics, but also it is the date that is interesting. 1941 was a year when the controversies in the British Psychoanalytical Society were just brewing up. There-fore, it would appear as a signal from Jones to the British reader-ship of the Journal to take note of the classical Viennese position.

Bibring's paper is about the stages of instinct theory in the course of the development of psychoanalysis. He describes four stages in this historical development. First is Freud's early theory of the contrasting instincts, libido and the ego-instincts, when he was battling to gain acknowledgement and a scientific appraisal of human sexuality, with its component instincts. The economic aspects of the libido were central, and they were, implicitly, biological entities.

Second, this was elaborated with the theory of narcissism, resulting in a monistic theory in which libido had object-libidinal and ego-libidinal forms, according to whether it is directed towards an object or towards the ego. The instincts then vary, not from their separate sources, but from their different directions. However, Freud did not go all the way to this monism and described the ego-instincts as a composite of libidinal and non-libidinal components, the libidinal one coming from the narcissistic turn of libido towards the ego.

In the third step, the non-libidinal element of the ego-instincts was elaborated. The problem of aggression, and especially sadism, remained difficult. So much of the self-preservation impulses had aggressive components. Therefore, aggression (and "sadism") could be viewed as a component of the ego-instincts rather than of the libido, even though it could enter into the service of the libido, a state of fusion between these opposing impulses. Bibring attributes these views to the latter part of Freud's paper on "Instincts and their vicissitudes" in 1915 (Freud, 1915c)..

However, in certain respects the problem of sado-masochism remained unresolved. Bibring points to Freud's (1930a) "Civilization and its discontents", to describe the instinct of aggression, and to assign it independence from the libido and from the ego-instincts. Much of this paper addresses the question of why this fourth step was taken. Bibring concludes that sado-masochism and aspects of the super-ego impel the notion of a death instinct, as well as Freud's reliance on repetition-compulsion. He is at pains to stick with an economic model and biological origin of instincts.

However, he did finally come to the conclusion that the advent of the death instinct radically changed the notion of instinct altogether. Originally instincts were classified according to their source, the erogenous zones, etc. Even when, with step three, instincts also needed to be classified according to aim, Bibring found no real change. But with step four the idea of instinct had to change, as the theory of the life and death instincts implied direction, and mental *qualities* as well as quantities of psychic energy.

The paper is a very clear statement of the evolution of the concept of instinct, and moves carefully between the problems at each historical step, and the solutions which advance the concept to the next step. To a degree, the paper originating in the mid-1930s set out a project and problems that demanded attention from ego-psychology for two or three decades after its transportation to America.

References

Freud, S. (1915c). Instincts and their vicissitudes *S.E., 14*.
Freud, S. (1930a). Civilization and its discontents. *S.E., 21*.
Strachey, J. (1934). The therapeutic action of interpretation. *International Journal of Psychoanalysis, 15*: 127–159.

Susan Isaacs [Isaacs, S. (1948). The nature and function of phantasy. *International Journal of Psychoanalysis, 29*: 73–97]

In January 1943, Susan Isaacs gave a paper to the British Psychoanalytical Society which opened eighteen months of scientific debate, the so-called Controversial Discussions. A committee had been formed (Edward Glover, Marjorie Brierley, and James Strachey) to organize a series of meetings of the Society to discuss scientific differences. This committee invited Isaacs, as a Kleinian, to give a paper on "The role of introjection and projection of objects in the early years of development". This was too big a subject and Isaacs considered that a fundamental issue in this whole topic was the nature of psychic reality and unconscious phantasy, and so she proposed that to the committee. In the event it provoked the greatest interest and the largest discussion of all the four prepared papers by Kleinians.[1]

The paper she actually gave was not published until 1991 (King & Steiner, 1991), but she completely revised and restructured the paper for publication in the Journal in 1948, a few months before she died.[2] We republish the 1948 version (the version also republished in Klein, Heimann, Isaacs, & Riviere, 1952) in which Isaacs is at great pains to establish the method by which one can gain evidence of the very early life of the infant ego. The main methods are (a) direct observational studies, which had been developed aside from psychoanalysis from around 1930 onwards, and (b) the psychoanalytic method. Both required very close attention to detail, and the principle of genetic continuity. This is the principle that whatever is observed has developed from antecedents, and hence allows the possibility of extrapolating back from the present observation of psychoanalysis to a period increasingly distant in time from the present. For instance, the analysis of a child's *pavor nocturnus* at age three will say something significant about the child at the age, maybe nine months, when the panics first occurred. Isaacs' central point, however, is that the evidence from these methods of study resulted in a confirmation of Freud: "[the id] is somewhere in direct contact with somatic processes, and takes over from them instinctual needs and gives them mental expression" (Freud, 1933a). Isaacs then asserts that the "mental expression" Freud refers to is unconscious phantasy; it is ". . . the mental corollary, the psychic representative of instinct. And there is no impulse, no instinctual urge, which is not experienced as [unconscious] phantasy" (in King & Steiner, 1991, p. 277).

This is taken from the original paper in 1943, and is repeated almost word for word in the reconstructed version of the paper in 1948 (pp. 87–137, below). Her claim is that *from the beginning* when instinctual life starts there is a version of the instinct that forms its mental expression,[3] and is experienced as a phantasy of a relationship with an object.

The implications of this view of instincts is then taken up in the rest of the paper. Or rather it is not a completely new view of instincts, since Freud spelled it out. What Isaacs did was to refocus the microscope to peer at the mental representatives of instinct, rather than the somatic source, aim, and intensity of instincts as Bibring classically described. There are many implications that Isaacs did not spell out, which has given rise to an enduring suspicion of Kleinian thought. This is most cogently and starkly put by Glover (1945), who declared this "Klein system" was not psychoanalysis at all. The central point of that critique was that Isaacs' exposition, claiming that there was constant mental activity at this most primitive level of phantasy, ruled out regression if the unconscious is permanently regressed at this primary level. Hence, Glover said there could be no fixation points, no progression, no maturity, sublimation, and so on. Partly due to this critique, the third paper in this series was on regression.[4]

Notes

1. The papers were Susan Isaacs, "The nature and function of phantasy", on 27 January 1943; Paula Heimann "Some aspects of the role of introjection and projection in early development", on 23 June 1943; Paula Heimann and Susan Isaacs "Regression", on 17 December 1943; and Melanie Klein "The emotional life and ego-development of the infant with special reference to the depressive position", on 1 March 1944.
2. Other papers from the Controversial Discussions were collected in a book in 1952 (Klein et al., 1952).
3. In the original 1943 version of the paper, not retained so didactically in the 1948 version, was Isaacs' response to Brierley's (1942) critique that Klein muddles percepts and concepts. What Isaacs wrote about that dispute eventually became another paper (Isaacs, 1945). What Brierley calls a muddle is, in Isaacs' terms, inevitably two sides of the same coin—instincts are biological concepts to be addressed with the economic model, on one hand, and as experienced phantasy on the other. However, more likely is the situation, as Greenberg and Mitchell (1983) noted, that Melanie Klein relinquished the economic model altogether.
4. The paper was by Heimann and Isaacs, and published in an unchanged form in Klein et al., 1952 (King & Steiner, 1991, pp. 687–709).

References

Brierley, M. (1942). The integration of the personality. *International Journal of Psychoanalysis*, 22: 172–174.

Freud, S. (1933a). New introductory lectures. *S.E.*, 22.

Glover, E. (1945). Examination of the Klein system of child psychology. *Psychoanalytic Study of the Child*, 1: 75–118.

Greenberg, J., & Mitchell, S. (1983). *Object Relations in Psychoanalytic*

Theory. Cambridge, MA: Harvard University Press.

Heimann, P., & Isaacs, S. (1952). Regression. In: M. Klein, P. Heimann, S. Isaacs, & J. Riviere (Eds.), *Developments in Psychoanalysis*. London: Hogarth.

Isaacs, S. (1945). "Notes on metapsychology as process theory": some comments. *International Journal of Psychoanalysis, 26*: 58–62.

King, P., & Steiner, R. (1991). *The Freud–Klein Controversies, 1941–1945*. London: Routledge.

Klein, M., Heimann, P., Isaacs, S., & Riviere, J. (1952). *Developments in Psychoanalysis*. London: Hogarth.

The development and problems of the theory of the instincts[1]

Edward Bibring

The following pages set out to give a short and simplified survey of the development of the psycho-analytical theory of the instincts. It is based essentially upon the works of Freud, since, however tempting it may be to take into account the whole of the psycho-analytical literature on the subject, to do so would complicate our exposition too much. . . . The survey follows a chronological order (except in one place, in connection with the fourth step in the history of the theory) but naturally this does not apply to the detailed discussion of certain points.

Before embarking on my actual theme, let me say a few words about the subdivision of the branch of knowledge of which the theory of the instincts is only a part. The psycho-analytical study of the instincts in made up of two main parts, a general theory of the instincts and a specialized one. The general theory includes, besides the *concept* of instinct, the theory of the instincts in the narrower sense, that is, the question of the number and nature of the instincts, the question of the criteria of their classification, and the question of their causation and function; the general theory further includes the theory of instinctual transformation, i.e. the question of the variability of instincts and the laws which such variations (which are in part the same as what are called instinctual vicissitudes) obey; and it includes, finally, the concepts and problems connected with the energic aspect of the instincts. The specialized theory is concerned with the development of the instincts in the individual, together with the working hypotheses which that development entails and the problems to which it gives rise.

In the following pages I shall confine myself to the general theory and in particular to that part of it which is devoted to the theory of the instincts in the narrower sense. This field, too, has been the main subject of psycho-analytical discussions upon the instincts, during the last few years.

Let us begin, for the sake of clarity, with a short sketch of the history of instinctual theory. A theory of the instincts can be monistic, dualistic or pluralistic. . . . Freud's theory was a dualistic one from the beginning, and it remained so, in spite of all the changes that it underwent. What was changed was never the *number* but only the nature of the instincts, or rather the groups of instincts, that were to be distinguished.

The theory of the instincts reached its present position in four steps.

1. The first step was the setting up of two groups of instincts—the sexual and the ego instincts. The sexual instincts were closely studied, whereas the ego instincts remained to begin with a relatively unknown quantity.
2. The second step was an addition to the theory. The introduction of the concept of narcissism into the libido theory led to the postulation of a libidinal component of the ego instincts. Nevertheless Freud held firmly to the view that besides this libidinal component there must exist a primary, non-libidinal component; this he called "interest" in a non-committal way, rather in the sense of non-libidinal egoism.
3. The third step—a step which has for the most part been overlooked in psycho-analytical writings—was that the aggressive trends were ascribed to the ego instincts as being among their essential constituents. This view was set out by Freud in the last sections of his paper on "Instincts and their vicissitudes" (Freud, 1915a, pp. 76–83) and was based upon a discussion of the relation between love and hate, in which he came to the

conclusion that hate was to be regarded as a non-libidinal reaction of the ego.

4. The fourth step was due to a growing knowledge of the structure of the mental apparatus as a whole and its division into a "vital" stratum (the id) and an organized part (the ego), and, more especially, to a study of the unconscious region of the ego, the super-ego. The gist of this view was that the aggressive trends were no longer regarded as primary attributes of the ego instincts but as independently existent instincts of aggression and destruction existing side by side with the sexual instincts in the vital strata of the mind. The ego instincts ceased to be independent entities and were derived partly from the libidinal and partly from the aggressive instincts.

To this fourth step in the development of instinctual theory there was now added a further theory. It postulated the existence of the primal instincts—what are known as the instincts of life and of death. This postulate served to extend the theoretic basis that underlay the fourth step, to solve certain unexplained problems and to bring together and simplify the various theoretical hypotheses that had been so far set up.

I

Let us now proceed to discuss in detail and in due order these four steps in the development of instinctual theory. The first theory made a distinction between sexual and ego instincts and was set up as a result of clinical observation which showed the central importance of mental conflict in the production of neuroses. In support of it Freud adduced the beliefs of popular psychology and, more emphatically, certain biological lines of thought. In view of what will be said further on, it is important to note the following passage in his "Instincts and their vicissitudes" (Freud, 1915c, p. 67): "I am altogether doubtful whether work upon psychological material will afford any decisive indication for the distinction and classification of instincts. Rather it would seem necessary to apply to this material certain definite assumptions in order to work upon it, and we could wish that these assumptions might be taken from some other branch of knowledge and transferred to psychology." Thus, according to him, it is hardly possible to arrive at a classification of the instincts along purely analytical lines.

During the period when this first theory of the instincts held the field, Freud's interest was taken up with developing the sexual theory. His conclusions are mainly to be found in his *Drei Abhandlungen* (Freud, 1905), where they were given progressive formulation. The sexual theory falls naturally into three parts: (1) the thesis of the component instincts, which is linked to the concept of erotogenic zones; (2) the thesis of an ontogenetic development of the sexual instincts taking place in successive stages and following a fixed order prescribed by biological laws; and (3) the libido theory (which amplifies and underpins the first two theses) and also, perhaps, the theory of the transformations of the sexual instincts in general.

It is necessary to enter into the subject of the sexual theory at this point for two reasons. In the first place because the concept of instinct which was arrived at in this field of knowledge and which underlay the sexual theory has been used by many writers to challenge the later hypotheses put forward by Freud; and in the second place because of the quantitative view of the instincts which was held at this time and which gave way later to a qualitative one.

We will first turn to the question of the concept of instinct. According to the most usual definition, instinct is an energy arising from the vital stratum of the mind and having a direction which is determined inherently. Since many facts seem to indicate that instinct originates in organic phenomena, it can be described, with Freud, as being a borderline concept between the mental and the organic spheres. In this way the concept of instinct comes to be classed under the concept of stimulus: instinct is a stimulus of the mind, distinguishable from other kinds of stimuli in that its operation is constant and comes from the interior of the body and not from outside. Thus one can also regard it as "a measure of the demand for work imposed upon the mind in consequence of its connection with the body" (Freud, 1915b, p. 64).

According to this view instinct, whatever may be the form in which it becomes a tension of psychical energy, is always, as being a stimulus, contrasted with the mental apparatus with its postulated methods of functioning. Concerning those methods of functioning themselves some assumptions are necessary, and that necessity, as we know, has led to the laying down of certain principles of mental happening and certain fundamental trends of the mental apparatus. We shall return to this point later; at the moment what we must bear in mind is that the principles or regulative mechanisms regulate the mental apparatus, while the instincts continually impose fresh demands for work upon that apparatus, so regulated. This contrast between instinct and mental activity is perhaps most clearly expressed in a passage in "Instincts and their vicissitudes" (Freud, 1915d, p. 82). There the distinction between sexual and ego instincts is described as an auxiliary construction of a provisional kind, while the thesis that there is a basic trend of the mental apparatus "to abolish stimuli which reach it, or to reduce excitation to the lowest possible level, or even . . . to maintain itself in an altogether unstimulated condition" is laid down as a necessary postulate.

Since the instincts spring from the organic field, the question of their source becomes an important one in their classification. The three characteristics of an instinct as stressed by Freud—its source, aim and object—can be employed as criteria. Of these, the object is the most variable; the aim is less variable, though still somewhat so; but the source is relatively constant and is therefore the best qualified to serve as a basis for a classification of the instincts.

Thus at this stage, in which the sexual theory was being elaborated, the idea of source was the most important criterion of classification. The source of an instinct, being the site of its inception, is from its very nature thought of as linked to an organic event. Such an organic event is in its turn hypothetically regarded, in accordance with the theory of hormones, as a kind of chemical process—as being, possibly, an accumulation of sexual substances or a concentration of chemico-sexual processes which then undergo a fresh distribution or are perhaps dissolved. The organ from which an instinct arises usually coincides with the place at which it obtains satisfaction; or else the place of satisfaction is an organ from which some other component instinct originates.

The differentiation of the separate component instincts is based upon the various organs from which they originate—what are called the erotogenic zones. The aggregation of the component instincts into the homogeneous group of the sexual instincts is based upon their common characteristics and regular relationships.

The concept of erotogenic zones is in the first instance purely descriptive and derived from the oral, anal and genital zones of the body. Their distinctive signs are experimentally verifiable, and are excitation, action and satisfaction; the last of these takes the form of characteristic pleasure-processes, which are different in the case of the oral and anal zones from those in the genital zone.

Instinct, then, is an energy which arises from the vital stratum of the mind, which has a direction that is determined inherently, which presses forward towards a particular aim and is directed somewhat loosely towards things and persons as its object. It is linked to an organ of origin as its source and to a terminal organ as the site of its satisfaction. Its satisfaction consists in the removal of those changes in the zones of excitation which accompany the instinctual tension. Or, to put it more shortly, an instinct is something that "comes from outside", produces energy and is the cause of particular mental processes.

When the component instincts had been aggregated into the homogeneous group of the sexual instincts and had been assigned to predetermined biological stages within the framework of sexual development, it became necessary to set up the libido theory to provide a basis and amplification. According to that theory the instincts are to be regarded as purely quantitative amounts of energy which can be variously localized (displaced) and concentrated. The qualities of the component instincts do not belong to the instincts themselves but are derived from their sources. This hypothesis made it possible to describe in a comparatively simple way the inter-relationships between the erotogenic zones, the transformations of one component instinct into another, and so on. As will be seen presently, the distinction which was afterwards made between the instinctual qualities on the basis of their aim made it impossible to explain those transformations without making certain other assumptions.

Meanwhile the ego instincts were being somewhat neglected. The concept of ego instincts was only a provisional one, as can be seen from Freud's formulations of it at the time. They were of a purely tentative nature; and so, at bottom, was the whole classification of the instincts. This was due partly to historical and partly to practical factors. On the one hand, it was necessary first of all to solve the problem of the structure and development of the sexual instincts—a problem which was the first to offer itself for investigation. On the other, the manifestations of the ego instincts were much more difficult to recognize. The trends emanating from the ego and their modes of expression were much more complicated and consequently harder to understand. But the main reason was that before anything could be learned about them a certain amount had to be known about the libidinal instincts.[2]

It is important to notice that the ego instincts were not regarded as on the same level as the sexual ones. In "Instincts and their vicissitudes" (Freud, 1915c, p. 67) Freud formulated the psychological conflict which can be discovered at the root of every neurosis as a conflict between the demands of sexuality and the demands of the ego. Thus we see that at that time the ego instincts stood for an ego, not as yet accessible to investigation, which was governed by certain tendencies.

The criterion of source which had been used for the classification of the sexual instincts was carried over to the ego instincts, of which the nutritional instincts served as the typical example. They too could be linked with organs of origin and termination, once more with the help of hypothetical chemico-physiological processes.

II

The motive for taking the second step in the development of the theory of the instincts came from the field of psychiatry. New facts appeared which could not be explained by any of the existing ideas and which necessitated a new addition to the libido theory, namely the concept of narcissism.

The concept of narcissism made the first breach in the independent existence of the ego instincts. It included three component parts: (1) A stage was introduced at the beginning of the life of the individual in which his instincts have no object. This stage was called primary narcissism. In it the object-libidinal attitude has not yet been differentiated off, just as there is no proper differentiation between the ego and the external world. The libido is either stored up in some way or other, as it is in sleep or in the embryonic state, and is "quiescent" and perhaps not yet roused to function; or it cannot as yet be distinguished or detached from the energy and functions of the ego—it is only operative, to use Federn's word (Federn, 1931, p. 68), in a "medial" way. (2) The libido, after the separation between the ego and the external world has taken place, can take the subject's own person as its object just as well as any thing belonging to the external world. (3) By means of identification in the ego or the ego ideal, the instinctual energy can be transformed into narcissistic energy. In this case, too, it will act "medially", that is to say, in a secondary way.

The postulation of a libidinal energy operating in the ego necessitated a revision of ideas about the ego instincts. It implied that the energy of the ego instincts was libidinal in origin and that their aims were derived from the aims of narcissistic libido directed to the subject's own self and acting within and upon it. The ego instincts were nothing more than libidinal instincts directed to the ego and hence somewhat differently organized. Just as the reality principle, for instance, was merely a modification of the pleasure principle and yet could turn against it, so the ego instincts seemed to be libido modified in its aims, which was nevertheless able to turn against the true libidinal instincts. This hypothesis is connected with a particular view of the origin of instinctual aims. According to it the general aim of libido appears to be pleasure, but its particular aims are derived from the particular objects to which it is directed. Mental conflict is no longer a conflict between sexual and ego instincts but between parts of the sexual instinct which are directed to the external world and parts which are directed to the ego—between object-libidinal and ego-libidinal trends. This explanation of conflict as a clash between different interests was a possible one, but not easy to maintain; moreover it was too simplified to take all the facts into account.

It seemed inevitable that this undermining of the independent status of the ego instincts should throw doubts upon the dualistic character of the instinctual theory. For there was now only one group of instincts—the libidinal instincts. Instincts were no longer classified with reference to their source but primarily with reference to their relations to various objects, which in their turn seemed to modify the instincts' aim. In essentials this already implied the view that the sexual and the ego instincts were only differentiated products of a common "primal libido".

Nevertheless Freud kept firmly to the idea of the autonomous nature of the ego instincts. This may to a large extent have been because he had classified the instincts in accordance with biological considerations and those considerations were not at first upset by his new discovery of narcissism. The life of the individual seemed to have quite different interests from those concerned with the preservation of the species. Thus it was natural to suppose that different forces were at work. Moreover, the phenomena of sadism in its wider aspects had not as yet been explained. Freud therefore introduced the notion of ego interest in the sense of a non-libidinal egoism; or, to put it more correctly, he asserted that what was known as egoism had two components, a libidinal-narcissistic component and a non-libidinal component. Narcissism, as he wrote (Freud, 1914, p. 31), is only "the libidinal complement to the egoism of the instinct of self-preservation, a measure of which may justifiably be attributed to every living creature." Originally these two components were undifferentiated.

Thus Freud still upheld the view that the nature of the ego instincts was originally non-libidinal. And this view was supported in the first instance by considerations of a theoretical and heuristic kind.

III

Later on, on the strength of empirical observation and theoretical arguments, the non-libidinal portions of the ego instincts were given some additional attributes which tended to confirm their independence of the libido. This constituted the third step in the development of the theory of the instincts, a step which gave the aggressive trends an independent status *vis-à-vis* the libidinal currents and classed them as belonging to the ego instincts.

Let us see what the observations and arguments were which led to this attempt to classify the instincts in this way. The most important reason was that the theory had not, so far, adequately ordered or explained the known facts.

Where the sexual instincts were concerned, it was primarily the position of their sadistic components which still lacked a sound theoretic basis. At first it had seemed as though sadism was erotogenetically bound. Sadistic impulses were to be found on every level, though in a form which apparently varied with the nature of their source or their erotogenic zone. The oral, anal and phallic levels each had their sadistic constituents. As the field of observation widened it seemed more and more probable that sadism was an independent component instinct which permeated every level, was able to ally itself to any other component instinct, had its own vicissitudes and could be regarded, in accordance with the dominant criterion of that time, as linked to the striated muscular system as its "source". Viewed in this way, sadism occupied a more curious position than ever in contrast to the purely libidinal instincts. What was particularly difficult to account for was the contradiction between the *aims* of the two. This contradiction seemed to call for a different genetic history for each. The term "sadism" undoubtedly included all sorts of phenomena, some of them not of an erotic kind, ranging from sexual perversions to impulses of cruelty and harshness which were devoid of any manifest eroticism; and finally it was also employed for certain ego instincts.

As regards the ego instincts, too, various component instincts could be distinguished. In connection with the criterion of source, hunger and thirst seemed to be the appropriate representatives of the ego instincts. But in the course of time they came to lose that position.

Closer inspection of the ego instincts made it possible to introduce a more fundamental classification of them. Impulses to control could be distinguished from defensive impulses; and instincts of power and of self-assertion could be added to them. The impulses to control seemed to be related to the trends of power and neither differed very much from many sadistic manifestations of instinct. The defensive trends, too, which could be sub-divided into impulses to flight and to attack (destructive impulses) exhibited an unmistakable streak of aggressiveness. Thus most of these ego trends had to be credited with an aggressive character; it became necessary to suppose that, in addition to sexual sadism there was a "sadism" of the ego instincts, while they in their turn entered into the service of the libido in the form of instincts of dominance. All this made the situation more than a little complicated. It was precisely this concept of the sadism of the ego instincts that showed clearly what an undue extension the notion of sadism had undergone. The terminology used at that time was the result of the absence of any distinction between the relation on the one hand of sadistic phenomena to libidinal phenomena and on the other hand of aggressive phenomena to sadistic ones.

Since the idea of sadism embraced facts of a disparate kind, the question was, how could the relationship be cleared up between the two sets of instinctual components—between those with aggressive and those with libidinal aims? There is only a limited number of ways in which we can imagine this relationship. Either the libidinal and aggressive instinctual phenomena start from something that is primal and common to both and only become differentiated in the course of development; or they each have a different origin and follow separate though at times intersecting lines of development.

The first of these possible views, namely that they have a common origin, is a monistic one and seeks to regard the libidinal and aggressive phenomena of instinctual life as products of differentiation or modes of the manifestation of one and the same instinct—bipolar phenomena which can replace each other. [Such a view has been maintained in different forms by Reich (1932) and Fenichel (1935).] . . .

The alternative view of the relations between the two groups of instinctual impulses is a purely dualistic one. It assumes the existence of two qualitatively different instincts and endeavours to subsume all the relevant phenomena under them. While the first view draws its support from the existence of phenomena which contain both sets of trends in an undifferentiated state and is met by the problem of accounting for their emergence in a differentiated form, in the second view it is precisely the undifferentiated phenomena which constitute a stumbling-block and have to be accounted for with the help of the theory of fusion.

Before committing himself to the dualistic theory, Freud, as has been seen in the passages referred to in his "Instincts and their vicissitudes", put forward the possibility of a bipolarity of instinct as its ordering principle. But, after having compared the aims of the two groups of instinctual trends and established their disparate character, and after having discussed the question of the "transformation of love into hatred" and denied the possibility of such a thing, he rejected the idea that there was a genetic relationship between the two sets of phenomena.

Thus aggressiveness (including hatred and sadism) and libido differed in regard to aim and origin. But this still left aggressiveness in an uncertain position in the framework of the instinctual theory. Freud's next attempt to solve this point was to ascribe the characteristics of aggressiveness (or "sadism", to use the then current term for the last time) to the ego instincts and to assume that, side by side with an opposition between the sexual and ego (aggressive) instincts, which expresses itself, among other things, in conflict, certain states of fusion between them also occur.

It is important to notice that in this connection Freud did not as yet talk about instincts of aggression as independent entities but only about the aggressive aspect of the ego instincts. This seemed to offer a provisional answer to the question of the relationship between aggressiveness and the ego instincts—namely, whether there are any phenomena of aggression at all outside the field of the ego-preservative functions. (The problem of erotic sadism is not affected by this question.) The question goes back to the empirical fact that aggressiveness appears only or almost only when the life instincts or the ego instincts are exposed to harm. It is a question which will come up again later on.

This third step, then, furnished provisional solutions to a great many problems. In the first place, sadism was taken out of the category of sexual instincts and put among the ego instincts; and in this way the independent character of the ego instincts was asserted. But this amounted only to a reshuffling of the two big groups of instincts, not to a new classification of them. In the second place, the idea of states of fusion threw a little more light upon the situation. The sadism of the sexual instincts would arise from the aggressiveness of the ego instincts and would emerge (Freud, 1915d, p. 82) "when the sexual function is governed by the ego instincts": the latter would "impart to the instinctual aim as well the qualities of hate" (the general name for aggressiveness at that time). Freud attempted to trace the evolution of the influence which the ego instincts have over the sexual instincts, starting from the ambivalence of the oral stage and passing through the sadism of the anal stage to the love belonging to the genital stage, at which love and hate come into direct collision for the first time. Conversely, the ego instincts might themselves receive an admixture from the libidinal side, as in narcissism. In the third place, an alteration in the criterion of the classification of the instincts was thus brought about. The notion of instinctual source gave way to that of instinctual aim. The typical example of the ego instincts was no longer hunger but "hatred", viz. aggression. As we know, the fact of there being different instinctual aims had already led to the problem of the position of sadism. At the same time the question arose whether along with this change of criterion from source to aim there went an alteration in our concept of instinct. As far as the sexual instincts were concerned, this stronger emphasis upon the instinctual aim had entailed no such alteration. It must be remembered, moreover, that instinctual source still retained its significance as a criterion; and so did the theory of energic tension with its chemical foundation. Even if no chemical hypothesis could be formulated for the ego instincts, the general concept of instinct which had been gained from the sexual instincts could nevertheless be carried over to them. They, too, could be regarded as demands for work imposed upon the mental apparatus, as tensions which set going certain activities which procured satisfaction by the attainment of their aim—hunger, for instance, and its resultant impulse to control—, as stimuli which impinged upon the mental apparatus and produced energy.

Thus this third step in the theory of instinct apparently solved a whole number of problems. It seemed to establish the aggressive ego instincts as independent entities; to render plausible the fact that the aim of "sadism" was not purely sexual, by means of the theory of instinctual admixture; and to order and clarify the various manifestations of libidinal and non-libidinal aggressiveness.

IV

The Problem of the Instinct of Aggression.—The need to re-model the theory of the instincts and take another step forward was felt as a consequence partly of research into sado-masochistic phenomena in their widest sense, partly of the fuller knowledge of the structure of the mental apparatus which was obtained as a result of the advance from the study of the repressed forces to that of the repressive ones as well.

In describing this fourth step (which must, in my opinion, be separated into two parts) I shall no longer give a purely historical survey, based upon Freud's works in the order of their appearance, but shall discuss it rather from a systematic standpoint.

The necessity for assuming the existence of an unconscious sense of guilt led to a new conception of the structure of the personality. The ego and the id were contradistinguished, and the ego was looked upon as having arisen out of the id and as being an organized portion of it. The id comprised (1) the vital stratum, in which the instincts had their place of origin and which was in free contact with the ego, (2) the repressed portion of the instincts, which was prevented from having free communication with the ego by anti-cathexes, and (3) the unconscious part of the ego, that is, the super-ego.

The fourth step in the development of the instinctual theory consisted in removing aggressiveness from the ego instincts—i.e. no longer viewing it as a component instinct or as a characteristic of the ego instincts—and in putting it, as an independently subsistent instinctual group with aims of its own, in the vital stratum of the mind. In this way the new theory asserted that there are two groups of instincts in the vital layer—the libidinal and the aggressive (or destructive) group. Each instinctual group moves forward towards satisfaction on its own account; and, partly through a free struggle to obtain it, partly through the influence of an ego which is subjected to the pressure of the external world and of the super-ego, each enters into a great variety of relationships with the other, whether of an associative or an antagonistic kind. Both can easily come into opposition with those trends of the system which operate in a self-preservative sense and which are represented in the ego (the ego instincts). In contradistinction to the instincts of sex and of aggression, which work in the vital layer and are directed to objects, are the ego instincts whose field of operation is the ego.

At this point three questions arise: Why did this fourth step have to be made? What is the advantage of a new instinctual theory which, although dualistic from a genetic point of view, recognizes three sets of instincts? Have the concept of instinct and the criterion for its classification undergone any change?

Since, as we saw from our discussion of the reasons for making the third step in the instinctual theory, it was found necessary to take away the aggressive trends from the sexual instincts and ascribe them to the ego instincts, the whole problem of establishing an instinct of aggression on its own footing is narrowed down to the question of whether aggressive trends of a non-libidinal nature play any role outside the functions of the ego.

There seems to be no doubt that there are in fact aggressive trends which, without betraying any sexual characteristics worth mentioning, do operate outside the field of the self-preservative functions. Moreover, to range aggressiveness completely under the ego instincts is a doubtful proceeding in those cases where its action comes into opposition with those instincts. Manifestations of sexual sadism might possibly be accounted for on the theory of an admixture of the ego instincts; but this is not so easily done with masochistic manifestations. The ego instincts are representatives of the "instinct which constrains every living thing to cling to life" (Freud, 1917, p. 156). That pain, which could only be regarded as a signal acting in the service of this life instinct, should itself become the aim of a masochistic instinct, seemed contrary to the laws of biology, even though the idea of sexualization might offer a possible explanation. But the difficulty became still greater where melancholic depressions exerted a self-destructive power—depressions which Freud described as characterized by "an overthrow, psychologically very remarkable" of the self-preservative instinct (*ibid.*). The same is true of those trends of the super-ego which are turned against the self, as, for instance, in the need for self-punishment, which seems to act like an independent instinct.

These manifestations, against which the ego has to defend itself, just as it has to defend itself against the libidinal impulses, cannot easily be explained as being due to the aggressiveness of the ego instincts. And it is clear that Freud very soon dropped that view. He does not mention it except in the passages from "Instincts and their vicissitudes" which have already been quoted. Nevertheless, the problem of whether manifestations of aggressiveness appear outside the defensive functions of the ego does remain in a sense unsolved, and to that problem belongs also the question of the relationship between the intoxication of omnipotence felt by the ego and the degree of intensity attained by the gratified instincts of aggression.

It was only logical that, when the contrast was made between the ego and the id and it was shown that the ego had to defend itself against the instincts of the id, the aggressive trends should have been placed, as autonomous instinctual forces, in the vital layer of the mental apparatus. To do this was, as Freud says in the sixth chapter of his *Civilization and its Discontents*, not to make any fresh change in the theory of instincts but was "merely a matter of coming to closer quarters with a conclusion to which we long ago committed ourselves and following it out to its logical consequences" (Freud, 1929, p. 94).

The postulation of the existence of an independently subsistent instinct of aggression undoubtedly facilitated a description of the facts in question. The ego was now thought of as being obliged to struggle with aggressiveness exactly as it was obliged to struggle with libido; it could give way to it, sublimate it, repress it, alter it by means of reactive formations, mitigate it by adding libidinal elements to it or offer itself as an object and so direct aggression onto itself (perhaps *via* the super-ego). But of course the mere establishment of such an instinct did not solve everything. The problem had come to be not so much one of destructiveness in its outward operation as of destructive trends turned in upon the self, as they could be observed in melancholia, the need for punishment and the *Schicksalsneurose* or neurosis of fatality. Here it seemed to be a matter of a destructive instinct at work inside the subject himself and this was still more difficult to account for on biological lines than was the existence of pleasure obtained from pain in the narrower field of sexual theory. It looked as though our first investigations of the ego had revealed the existence of what was, phylogenetically speaking, the most recent instinct—an instinct which might have arisen along with the civilization of man.

Primary Destructiveness.—It cannot be doubted that the super-ego exists and that it can, in certain circumstances, carry its punitive trends to the length of destroying the subject himself. Nor can it be doubted that to explain the latter fact as a turning of aggression against the self does not furnish an adequate theoretical account of the phenomenon. Such an explanation is merely the starting point for a discussion of the true problem. How is it possible that the aggressive instincts should be turned against the subject's own person to the point of self-destruction?—that is, how can we explain such a state of things from the hitherto accepted biological standpoint? It will be quite in keeping with the methodological principles of psycho-analysis if we assume the existence of some more fundamental thing in virtue of which this turning of aggression against the ego can take place. This thing can be nothing else than an instinctual trend which somehow has a self-destructive effect but whose manner of working is not visible at the first glance.

The problem was already present in some sense in the sexual theory; and Freud stated it when he asked whether sadism or masochism was the primary phenomenon, viz. the older of the two from a biological point of view. Even at that time he adduced the parallel problems from the development of the purely libidinal instincts and established the fact that in sadism, unlike the other component instincts such as exhibitionism, there did not exist, or could not be shown to exist, a stage that was analogous to the narcissistic stage.

The observation of the clinical phenomena mentioned above, as well as the fundamental methodological need to find an original model[3] in analogy with the parallel hypotheses of the libido theory, made it necessary to assume the existence of a "self-destructive" trend which somehow operated within the self. This trend would be a kind of primary destructiveness and would be analogous to primary narcissism. Aggressiveness directed onto objects would be the counterpart of the object-libidinal trends; and the manifestations of secondary destructiveness would correspond to those of secondary narcissism (Weiss, 1935, p. 393).

This analogy was supported by the observation that similar fluctuations occur between aggressiveness and self-destructiveness as occur between a narcissistic libidinal position and one which is oriented towards objects. Aggressiveness can become directed inwards in the same way that self-destructiveness, if it reaches a dangerous pitch, can find a safety-valve by being turned outwards in the form of aggression.

Here, then, is the problem. If the hypothesis of a primary stage of the destructive instinct is theoretically unavoidable, how can a trend of this kind be formulated? It was in endeavouring to answer this question that Freud opened up those lines of thought which have led to so much misunderstanding and contradiction. . . .

The Theory of the Primal Instincts.—In order to fill in and gather together the theoretical issues involved in the fourth step and in order to solve the problems raised by it, Freud now introduced the theory of the primal instincts. These, according to him, are the life instincts and the death instincts. The theory was not set up on the grounds of any fresh psychological material or indeed of any question of a psycho-logical nature; it was the result of certain theoretical problems which had been raised by previous hypotheses and which it was designed to solve. It was thus in the nature of a theoretical sub-, or rather, superstructure and was a theory of the second order as compared with the instinctual theory which had so far been directly built up upon clinico-psychological data and problems. It was a biological theory of instinct, since it rested almost entirely upon biological considerations. Instincts of life and death are not psychologically perceptible as such: they are biological instincts whose existence is required by hypothesis alone. This being so, it follows that, strictly speaking, the theory of the primal instincts is a concept which ought only to be adduced in a theoretical context and not in discussions of a clinical or empirical character. In them, the idea of aggressive and destructive instincts will suffice to account for all the facts before us.

By drawing this sharp distinction between the two concepts we are more likely, I think, to avoid certain errors and to ensure the clarity of our clinical descriptions.

Some confusion of thought has been created, especially as to the relation between the death instinct and the repetition compulsion, by the manner in which Freud introduced his theory of the death instinct. Let me therefore at once point out that, although he used repetition compulsion as evidence of the existence of the death instinct, the evidence from that source is not to be regarded as indispensable. His writings show in the main two classes of argument in support of the theory of the death instinct. I should like to contrast these with each other under the name of a *speculative* and a *theoretical* line of argument respectively. The speculative line is fully worked out in *Beyond the Pleasure Principle* (Freud, 1920g); the theoretical one is more lightly indicated and is scattered in various places, but it can be collected to form a whole. We will turn our attention to the speculative line first.

The Speculative Basis of the Theory of the Death Instinct.—It would be beyond the scope of this paper to enter into the reasons which led

Freud to the hypothesis of a repetition compulsion and the various problems which are bound up with it. It is enough to say that the result was that he found it necessary to postulate a regulative mechanism which acted independently of the pleasure principle and appeared to be much more primary than it (i.e. earlier from a historical point of view and more elementary), and which must be regarded as a primal principle, a primal characteristic of life, and therefore a characteristic not only of the death instinct but of all instincts.

The concept of repetition compulsion is a complex one and comprises several aspects. (1) Repetition compulsion is an expression of the "inertia" of living matter, of its "disinclination to abandon an old position in favour of a new one" and therefore of a conservative trend which always inclines to maintain the existing state of things. (2) In consequence, there is a tendency to keep to certain forms of adaptation and to certain circuitous routes as a reaction to any disturbance of the usual processes. This may be described as the "impressibility of life". Adaptations once acquired are retained and reproduced. Under this heading may be placed the basic law of biogenesis and the biological concept of reproduction in general. (3) The conservative nature of life, however, does not express itself only in the maintenance and reproduction of already established processes, but also in a backward-looking trend which aims at surmounting or, as it were, throwing off adaptations which have been imposed upon it and at re-instating more primitive situations, that is to say, historically earlier ones. Here inertia and conservatism have become an active "yearning for the past", a regressive trend. (This method of formulation was of importance as a ground for the assumption of the death-instinct.) (4) From the energic point of view repetition compulsion is found to be a special case of the trend towards abreaction. The large quantities of energy released by traumatic stimuli are bound by anticathexes and then gradually, as the traumatic situation is repeated over and over again, discharged in fractional amounts. Under this heading fall the dreams of persons with a neurosis due to an accident, the play of children, the manifestations of the transference situation in analysis, and so on.

As has been indicated above, the historical formulation of the repetition compulsion—as an endeavour to re-establish the *status quo ante* —was used by Freud as a basis for his assumption of the instinct of death. He started from the fact that the earliest moment at which organic life can be said to exist is the moment when it emerges from inorganic, dead matter. The phenomena of inertia in the world of physics, which is no more than an opposition to any change, becomes, as it were, in the realm of biology, an active trend—from the historical standpoint a retrogressive one, and, from the energic standpoint, a trend towards a relaxing of tension, towards absolute rest. But at this point the difficulties involved in this speculative line of argument become evident. Apart from the many handicaps from which it suffers in the hypothetical field, ... there is the further objection that it regards the death instinct as the original one and implies that the life instincts came into existence subsequently as a result of the chances of development. The life instincts are thus subordinated to the death instincts, as is seen when Freud says in *Beyond the Pleasure Principle* that fundamentally the life instincts act in the service of the death instincts. According to this, the life instincts would create tensions of every possible kind only to submit them to the death instinct with its inevitable trend towards relaxation of tension. Freud's speculative effort in this field is indeed a pessimistic one: it affirms that the true essence of life is death.

A subordination of this sort of the life instincts to the death instincts does not seem, however, to be entirely justifiable theoretically. At any rate, the converse of it is quite as possible and arguable. In his *New Introductory Lectures* (1933a) Freud emended this view in so far as he treated the two instincts as synchronous and co-ordinate in their operation: life consists of life and death instincts alike.

The Theoretic Grounds for the Theory of the Death Instinct.—Freud's first suggestion, which seemed so pessimistic, was due to the fact that the need for assuming the existence of instincts of life was not nearly so pressingly felt as the need for assuming the existence of instincts of death. In so far as the existence of the life instincts had to be conceded theoretically, it was done more for biological reasons than for psychological ones. Sexuality as a relationship between germ-cells of different sexes, or rather between the bearers of those cells, does not make its appearance till some way on in the course of phylogenetic evolution. It must, therefore, be either a new acquisition, or, more probably, a modification (made necessary, perhaps, by the need for adaptation) of some older instinct which may have exhibited the most general characteristics of the sexual instincts, such as a trend towards bringing things together or, from the energic aspect, towards creating tensions.

This new conception of the instinctual theory, however, obviously proceeded above all from the necessity for solving the problem of primary destructiveness. We have already seen what considerations led to this problem and need not go into them again; but the question admits of certain further points of discussion.

As we know, psycho-analysis has always had a biological orientation, and the theory of instinct has hitherto rested upon a biological basis. It is therefore quite natural that it should seek to find a preexisting biological model for the destructiveness at work within the individual. The task before it, then, was to formulate the biological model for the primary destructive trend which operates in the mind and whose existence seems so probable on theoretical grounds. Just as it was found earlier that aggressiveness ran counter to the libido in its aims, so now aggressiveness turned against the self must contradict the self-preservative principle of life— unless there was something in life itself which made possible a turning back of this kind.

The questions which we shall now have to discuss are firstly, how is primary destructiveness to be defined? and secondly, how are we to understand the biological "compliance" whose existence has been assumed?

The problem of finding the original model of the self-destructive trends (both primary and secondary) leads inevitably to the subject of death; for the question of the nature of death and its place within the scheme of life is in a sense the same as that problem and should help to solve it. Thus the relationship between life and death, if there is indeed a biological model for self-destruction, must be thought of as more intimate than is usually supposed. In other words an essential characteristic of life must be its relation to death. This statement of the problem leads straight to the sphere of biology and narrows down to two alternatives: is death merely the outcome of an injury from without? or has life a natural end? If the first alternative is true, life is, theoretically, an eternal process which is only terminated by destruction from outside. If the second is true, death is a necessary component of life. Each of these views about the nature of death implies a corresponding view about the nature of life.

It would take us too far afield to bring forward the various relevant biological facts and considerations; we must content ourselves here with answering two questions. The first is the one that has already been asked, and it has been answered by Freud in *Beyond the Pleasure Principle* where he expresses the cautious view that there are a number of facts that speak in favour of the occurrence of natural death and none that definitely exclude it.

The second question is: is natural death, which, as we know, overtakes the soma only and not the germ plasm, a phylogenetic acquisition which has been made possible by the emergence of the multi-cellular organism and which has nothing to do with the essential nature of life? Here also, the answer may be that in the course of phylogenetic evolution something has merely become differentiated which was already an integral part of the unicellular organism—that is, that natural death is an original "character" of life, so that dying, too, is something which instinct strives after.

If this is so, what does it mean in the dynamic sense? If life is regarded as a closed system moving in an orbit, as it were, round a fixed centre of gravity, death must be something that is foreign to that system; it can only be destruction coming from outside. But if life is regarded as proceeding in a linear course, then death is something that is essential to life; it is the goal towards which life is being driven. Living is dying, a process moving towards death, towards zero potential.

But it seems to me that Freud's conception of life is neither of these things, but a third which is a combination of the two. According to him the life system is governed by two trends: it moves towards zero potential but in doing so it creates new tensions. It is, to quote a simile of Aster's, like a self-winding clock. In the individual, life, it would seem, leads inevitably to death; but if life is taken as an integral process including the past and the future and looked at from a larger standpoint than that of individual existence, then Aster's simile holds good. The struggle of the

Titans is constantly creating new forms of life and new deaths in an apparently unending and interminable procession.

The Significance of the Theory of the Death Instinct.—What does the concept of the death instinct do towards clarifying the theoretical problems under consideration and towards unifying the various attempted solutions? Not everything, but a good deal. The biological model of primary destructiveness has been seen to be an instinct of death which can be formulated as a tendency moving towards absolute rest, towards zero potential. From that instinct primary destructiveness and aggressiveness, and all forms of them that turn back upon the self, can be derived. This cannot be done, indeed, without the assistance of certain auxiliary constructions which, though doubtless unsatisfactory in many respects, rest upon certain facts of observation.

To begin with aggressiveness. The fact that aggressiveness can be turned back upon the subject's own self and the equally observable fact that this retroverted destructiveness can once more be turned out upon the external world in the form of aggression make it probable that similar processes and connections occur between primary destructiveness and aggression directed outwards—that is to say that in certain circumstances primary destructiveness is "turned outwards". The findings of crowd psychology, too, speak for this possibility. In this case the individual who is prepared to be aggressive is bound to an organized group and thus his aggression is diverted to a part of the external world which is outside that group, to a so-called "enemy", whether that enemy is a hostile idea or a hostile group of persons. This fact, together with the clinical observation just mentioned, provides us with an *ontogenetic* model (to borrow Kris's words) on the strength of which we can proceed to construct a *phylogenetic* model. According to the latter, the emergence of the multi-cellular organism out of the unicellular one would presumably have the effect of rendering the self-destructiveness of the cells harmless, since they would be bound to one another (perhaps with the help of the libidinal instincts), and of making it in part turn outwards, in some form or other, as an instinct of aggression.

If we now try to tabulate the instinctual classification which we have arrived at in analogy with the parallel concepts of the libido theory, we find the following set of comparisons:

Life Instincts (Eros).	Death Instincts (Primal Sadism, Primal Masochism).
The Sexual Instincts:	The Destructive Instincts:
Primary Narcissism.	Primary Destructiveness.
Object Libido.	Aggressiveness turned against the Object.
Secondary Narcissism.	Aggressiveness turned back against the Self (Secondary Destructiveness).

This symmetrical arrangement is not in any way due to a desire to establish a systematic series, but will be seen to have a role to play when we come to discuss the question of the visible manifestations of the death instincts.

The terms "life instincts" and "sexual instincts" on the one hand and "death instincts" and "destructive instincts" on the other, are used by Freud synonymously and without any distinction. And indeed it does not seem possible to make any sharp division, especially between the second pair. Nevertheless I should like to attempt to trace certain lines of demarcation for heuristic reasons.

The instincts of life and death are purely biological instincts, which operate in the organic sphere but which are reflected in some form or other in the mental sphere as well. The sexual instincts are only a specialized form of the life instincts. The same is true of the concept of the destructive instincts. The two terms are only generalized names for all libidinal phenomena on the one hand and all destructive, or aggressive, phenomena on the other. Thus if we are asked how those instincts manifest themselves we have only to point to all the facts that belong directly or indirectly to the field concerned. The phenomena of the sexual instincts are sufficiently well known; and so are those of aggressiveness, whether turned outwards or back upon the self. All that remains, therefore, is to discover what are the mental representatives of primary destructiveness—these being parallel to the mental representatives of primary narcissism.

Are there any mental phenomena which may be regarded as expressions of this primary destructive trend? The very fact that such a question can be asked at all, and that the existence of a primary destructive trend has had to be deduced in the first instance upon purely theoretical grounds, is tantamount to making the assumption that we are dealing with "silent" instincts. Primary destructiveness must, therefore, be defined in some such way as that it is the destructive energy in virtue of which we grow old and die mentally, to adapt Weiss's phrase (1935, p. 393). . . .

We cannot, then, describe primary destructiveness in any way except by definition. But the question remains, whether, though there are no direct products of it, there may not be some indirect ones? Two facts seem relevant to this question: the need for rest and the need to suffer. I do not think that it would be difficult to show that there is probably such a thing as an instinctual desire for rest. The need for rest comes not only as a result of being tired; it is a phase which alternates naturally with phases of activity or which occurs in the middle of the latter as though it was a primary need that had been neglected and was now demanding to be satisfied. The need for rest seems to govern the psychic apparatus quite as much as the need for pleasure. It is precisely the combined appearance of the two trends in the sexual instincts that led to their being equated in the first place. The instinctual need for sleep, too, or instinctual falling asleep, seems to be an expression of this instinctual need for rest.

A much more difficult task is that of demonstrating the relationship between primary destructiveness and the need to suffer. In this connection Freud has introduced the concept of erotogenic masochism, which can be regarded to a certain extent as a normal phenomenon and which is characterized by having for its aim pleasure in pain, or more generally, a need to suffer. It is assumed that not all primary destructiveness is turned outwards but that some portion of it remains operative within, and, libidinally bound or softened, only emerges in the form of what is called erotogenic masochism; and this assumption is an attempt to establish a direct connection between the postulated primary destructive instinct and the phenomena of masochism. . . .

Thus the need for rest would be a more or less direct reflection in the mind of the death instinct, of primary destructiveness; but the need for suffering would be only indirectly derived from that instinct, with the help of the theory of instinctual admixture. Even pleasure in causing suffering to others is not, according to Freud, an immediate expression of primary destructiveness directed outwards but the result of a state of fusion.

To sum up: With the help of the biological theory of the death instinct it became possible to formulate the nature of primary destructiveness, which was a necessary hypothesis from a theoretical point of view; and furthermore (though not without resorting to various auxiliary hypotheses) to obtain a unified view of destructive and aggressive manifestations. The heuristic advantage of these assumptions is, I think, unquestionable. But this is not all that the theory can accomplish in the direction of unifying the facts.

Instincts and Principles.—In discussing the concept of instinct as implied in the sexual theory we have seen that the instincts were contrasted with the functioning of the mental apparatus. On the one hand the characteristics of the instincts were examined, but it was necessary on the other hand to make certain assumptions about the way in which that apparatus worked: it was presumed to be regulated according to certain trends or principles. What, then, was the relationship between those principles and the instincts? The instincts were regarded as tensions of energy which arise from the organic sphere and act in a "disturbing" way like an external stimulus upon the mental apparatus, and are then dealt with according to the regulative principles governing that apparatus. This is what was meant when instincts were defined as demands for work made upon the mental apparatus. How the disturbing stimuli are to be classified seems a secondary matter compared to the adoption of the view that the mental apparatus has a fundamental method of working in relation to all the stimuli that reach it, whether they come from without or from within.

It must once more be emphasized that in this general view the instincts were not thought of as directing the whole course of mental events, but only as being sources of energy and causes of excitation which set in motion the regulative trends of the mental apparatus.

Freud's basic assumption was that this apparatus is governed by a trend which strives towards a complete relaxation of tension or towards keeping down to the lowest possible level the quantities of incoming stimuli. At first he equated this trend with the pleasure principle, since tension seemed to call out feelings of unpleasure and relaxation of tension feelings of pleasure. Nevertheless there were various facts which could not be made to fit in with this view. The reality principle represented a modification of the pleasure principle according to which pleasure was no longer sought directly and immediately but along devious ways adapted to reality and over an extended passage of time.

But, for reasons which we already know, it proved necessary to detach the pleasure principle from the underlying trend towards relaxing tension and keeping it down to a minimum. Various ideas were put forward about this fundamental trend. It seemed to be a kind of principle of constancy concerned with maintaining tension at a particular level; it was as though, in other words, the individual mental system was regulated at a particular state of equilibrium. Anything which seemed to disturb that balance whether in an upward or a downward direction was brought back by the regulative trend to the normal tension. It was the view which regarded life as something moving in an orbit round a fixed centre of gravity that found expression in the hypothesis of the principle of constancy or stability. It was then possible to define the pleasure principle, which directs mental processes towards an end-state of pleasure, as a modification of the principle of constancy. Everything which led nearer to the constant degree of tension or the state of stability was felt as pleasurable and everything which drew away from them was unpleasurable.

But as soon as the fundamental view of life was changed and it was no longer regarded as moving in an orbit but along a linear course, its basic trend had also to be differently regarded. The principle of constancy was accordingly replaced by the Nirvana principle, the trend of which was to effect a complete levelling down of all difference of potential—to reach zero potential.

Thus, if we leave on one side repetition compulsion,[4] we find that there are three regulative trends directed respectively towards a complete relaxation of tension, towards pleasure and towards adaptation to reality (or the Nirvana principle, the pleasure principle and the reality principle). The reality principle remains, on this view, a modification of the pleasure principle, but the relationship between the Nirvana principle and the pleasure principle becomes a different one from what it was according to the old view, according to which the pleasure principle was regarded as a special form of the principle of constancy. Now each corresponds to a different trend. Desire for pleasure on the one side and desire for rest on the other are the two chief regulative principles of mental life.

It is clear that only a provisional position has been attained by merely contrasting on the one hand the regulative principles of the mental apparatus and, on the other, the instincts which come from the outside and make themselves felt as a demand for work to be done. The heuristic principle, which would lead us to enquire to what extent the entire mental organization and its modes of working are built up upon the instincts, must inevitably raise the question of whether the instincts exert an influence upon the trend of mental processes. But to ask this would be to ask what is the relation between mental principles and instincts.

This question arose all the more easily because the concept of instinct had undergone a change in the course of the development of the instinctual theory. Originally instinct was regarded as an energic tension arising from organic sources and automatically directed towards an inherently determined aim; that aim was attained circuitously *via* an object and consisted ultimately in a modification of the organ of origin of the instinct—in a return of the organ to the state in which it was before the stimulation occurred. It was in conformity with this view that the idea of instinctual source was chosen as a suitable criterion for the classification of the instincts.

The impossibility of discovering sources of this kind for every instinct and the difficulty of constructing them hypothetically, especially in relation to the ego instincts, brought into the foreground the notion of instinctual *aim* as a criterion. This did not necessitate any radical change in the concept of instinct. The aim consisted externally in the carrying out of the purposive act upon the object and internally in the attainment of a relaxation of tension, as, for instance, in the case of the aggressive instincts.

But the theory of the primal instincts (the life and death instincts) was founded upon an essentially changed concept of instinct. According to it, instinct was not a tension of energy which impinged upon the mental sphere, which arose from an organic source and which aimed at removing a state of excitation in the organ from which it originated. It was a directive or directed "something" which guided the life processes in a certain direction. The accent was no longer upon the production of energy but only upon the function determining a direction.

But the mental principles, too, were nothing else than a determining "something" which decided in what direction psychological processes should move. The concepts of "instinct", "principle", "regulation", thus seemed to be very much alike. Just as the instincts regulated the course of biological events, so, naturally, did they regulate the course of mental events. It was no longer possible to maintain a strict contrast between a mental apparatus regulated by principles and instincts pressing in upon it from outside, since the instincts themselves now stood revealed as fundamental principles of life.

This led to the possibility of grouping the principles with the instincts. It would take us too far afield to go into this point in greater detail here. But we know how Freud pictured an arrangement of this sort. He writes: "The Nirvana principle expresses the trend of the death instincts, the pleasure principle represents the claims of the libido [and thus corresponds to the life instincts], while a modification of the latter, the reality principle, represents the influence of the external world" (Freud, 1924, p. 257). The relation between the two main principles was pictured as being that the life instincts effect a modification in the course run by the processes of relaxation of tension, a modification which is associated with the emergence of pleasure. . . .

Let me add a few words upon the question of quantity. So long as the concept of aim was used merely as a criterion for classification, it in no way contradicted the quantitative concept of instinct. But it was otherwise as soon as quality of aim was regarded as a primary characteristic of instincts. To do so involved turning the instincts into mental *qualities* and restricting their *quantitative* aspect to each separate group of them (to the sexual or the aggressive group). There would then be two classes of instinctual energy which would be distinguishable by the quality of their direction, namely, the energy of libido and the energy of aggressiveness—or, as Weiss calls it, "destrudo" (Weiss, 1935; p. 393) —and no exchange of energy could take place between the two. (The problem of *confluence* of aim is on quite a different plane.) Although this view is a consistent one, it brings with it its own difficulties, connected partly

with certain clinical facts and partly with the concept of a narcissistic reservoir of libido. The latter, according to Freud, is "a
displaceable energy, which is in itself neutral, but is able to join
forces either with an erotic or with a destructive impulse, differing
qualitatively as they do, and augment its total cathexis" (Freud,
1923b, p. 61). Freud finds a solution in the supposition that the aim
of the libidinal instincts, which are "more plastic, more readily
diverted and displaced than the destructive ones", can be reduced
to a mere need for "discharge" or relaxation of tension, in which the
object and the paths of discharge are "relegated to a position of no
more than secondary importance". The neutral reservoir of energy
would thus consist of libido sufficiently reduced to be in a position
to make contributions to libidinal and aggressive impulses alike.
Thus a supply of pure energy—i.e. one in which the quality of its
aim is inoperative—would be able to flow only from the libidinal to
the aggressive instincts and only by the way of this undifferentiated
reservoir of libido.

To sum up the discussion. For the sake of greater clarity we have
so far been at pains to make the cleavage between the concepts
under consideration as wide as possible. But I should now like to
narrow the gap once more and to approach the actual structure of
those concepts more closely. On the one hand, the biological life
instincts which create tensions, the sexual instincts, the ego
instincts, with their aim of maintaining life, and the pleasure principle—all these are somehow related to one another; on the other
hand, the death instincts which seek to cancel out tensions, the
instincts of destruction at work within, aggressiveness directed
outwards, the trend towards a state of rest (the Nirvana principle)
and the inclination to suffer—these, also, form a related group.

The "mysterious" instinctual forces, which lie behind all this,
work each in their own direction or against one another or with one
another. They become combined in the form of masochistic pleasure
in suffering, of sadism, of the need for punishment, of self-hatred,
of aggressive ego instincts, and so on.

What we call instinct operates in a directive fashion upon
biological events both in the physical and mental field. Under
certain influences it becomes differentiated and concentrated into
centres of tension which are somehow bound to organic phenomena as sources; it turns outwards upon an object, strives after an

aim which consists externally in a particular kind of behaviour towards that object and towards the subject's own body, and internally in the removal of a state of excitation. How it operates to begin with inside the self is not clear. We can see more easily what it is doing when it is directed towards objects upon which it carries out purposive actions. In order to effect this, something has sometimes to happen to the organ of origin, sometimes only to the object. Satisfaction ensues sometimes in the form of a particular process that is run through, sometimes in a more diffused manner. But the instinct can also take the subject's own self as its object in various ways. It can turn into "motive force" and so increase the energies of the ego. It can enter into a multitude of bypaths and it is so malleable that it can undergo a great variety of changes. We cannot classify it in any single uniform way, but now according to one point of view, now according to another—according to its aim, its object or its source.

All these facts, hypothetical opinions and theories have been formulated in concepts which are often ambiguous and vague. Exact and well-defined notions are not always possible in the region of psychology. But much has been gained if we have been able to advance into a new field and to set up a number of concepts which can shed a mutual light on one another, even if we have done no more than make a first approach to a set of facts which, upon the whole, are still unknown to us.

Notes

1. [Though this paper was published in German some years ago, it seems desirable that it should appear in an English translation, since it presents what is perhaps the clearest and most authoritative account of the various phases of Freud's views upon the instincts. It was based upon two lectures given before the Prague Psycho-Analytical Study Group in November, 1934, and first appeared in *Imago* (1936), 22, 147. A few passages dealing with the views of writers other than Freud have been omitted from the present version. The proposal to make some such omissions was put forward in the first instance by the author himself. Owing to war conditions, however, it has not been possible to obtain his approval in detail of the omissions actually made,

for which, accordingly, the Editor is wholly responsible. They do not, in any case, interrupt the main thread of the paper and the points at which they occur have all been indicated in the text.—ED.]
[Reproduced, with permission, from: *International Journal of Psychoanalysis*, 1941, 22: 102–130 © Institute of Psychoanalysis, London, UK]

2. This applies to the situation as it was then. In the present state of our knowledge it goes without saying that a complete study of the ego presupposes an understanding of both the libidinal and the aggressive instincts.

3. This point is explained and elaborated above, pp. 73–74.

4. Repetition compulsion should also be reckoned among the regulative trends. It is a general regulative principle and serves to bind energies, i.e. to bring them from a state of "flow" to one of "rest". That a regulative trend of this sort does exist seems beyond doubt. The way in which the ego works, too, presupposes this possibility of binding, and of arresting tensions—of making them static. In the same way the repetition compulsion seems to be a *sine qua non* of all the other regulative trends. The quantities of incoming stimuli (in so far as they have not been confined to certain channels in the course of phylogenetic processes of adaptation, or if they have overflowed the capacity of those channels) must be arrested and bound before the other regulative forces can come into play.

References

Federn, P. (1931). Die Wirklichkeit des Todestriebes. *Almanach der Psychoanalyse*, 68.
Fenichel, O. (1935) Zur Kritik des Todestriebes. *Imago, 21*: 458.
Freud, S. (1905). Drei Abhandlungen zur Sexualtheorie, *Gesammelte Schriften V*: 1.
Freud, S. (1914)[Trans. 1925]. On narcissism: an introduction. *Collected Papers IV*: 31.
Freud, S. (1915a)[Trans. 1925]. Instincts and their vicissitudes. *Collected Papers IV*: 76–83.
Freud, S. (1915b). *Collected Papers* 64.
Freud, S. (1915c). *Collected Papers* 67.
Freud, S. (1915d). *Collected Papers* 67 and 63.
Freud, S. (1915e). *Collected Papers* 82.
Freud, S. (1917)[Trans. 1925]. Mourning and melancholia. *Collected Papers IV*: 156.

Freud, S. (1920g)[Trans. 1922]. *Beyond the Pleasure Principle.*

Freud, S. (1923b)[Trans. 1927]. *The Ego and the Id*, p. 61.

Freud, S. (1924)[Trans. 1924]. The economic problem in masochism. *Collected Papers II*: 257.

Freud, S. (1929)[Trans. 1930]. *Civilization and its Discontents*, p. 94.

Freud, S. (1933a)[Trans. 1933]. *New Introductory Lectures on Psycho-Analysis.*

Reich, W. (1932). Der masochistische Charakter. *Int. Z. Psychoanal. 18*: 302.

Weiss, E. (1935). Todestrieb und Masochismus. *Imago, 21*: 393.

The nature and function of phantasy*[1]

Susan Isaacs

Introduction

A survey of contributions to psycho-analytic theory would show that the term "phantasy" has been used in varying senses at different times and by different authors. Its current usages have widened considerably from its earliest meanings.

Much of this widening of the concept has so far been left implicit. The time is ripe to consider the meaning and definition of the term more explicitly.

When the meaning of a technical term does become extended in this way, whether deliberately or insensibly, it is usually for a good reason—because the facts and the theoretical formulations they necessitate require it.[2] *It is the relationships between the facts* which need to be looked at more closely and clarified in our thoughts. This paper is mostly concerned with the definition of "phantasy"; that is

* [Reproduced, with permission, from: *International Journal of Psychoanalysis*, 1948, 29: 73–97 © Institute of Psychoanalysis, London, UK]

to say, with describing the *series of facts* which the use of the term helps us to identify, to organize and to relate to other significant series of facts. Most of what follows will consist of this more careful study of the relationships between different mental processes.

As the work of psycho-analysis has gone on, in particular the analysis of young children, and our knowledge of early mental life has developed, the relationships which we have come to discern between the earliest mental processes and the later more specialized types of mental functioning commonly called "phantasies" have led many of us to extend the connotation of the term "phantasy" in the sense which is now to be developed. (A tendency to widen the significance of the term is already apparent in many of Freud's own writings, including a discussion of unconscious phantasy.)

It is to be shown that certain mental phenomena which have been generally described by various authors, not usually in reference to the term "phantasy", do in fact imply the activity of unconscious phantasies. By correlating these phenomena with the unconscious phantasies with which they are bound up, their true relationships to other mental processes can be better understood, and their function and full importance in the mental life appreciated.

This paper is not primarily concerned to establish any particular content of phantasy. It will deal with the nature and function of phantasy as a whole, and its place in the mental life. Actual examples of phantasy will be used for illustrative purposes, but it is not suggested that these examples cover the field; nor are they chosen systematically. It is true that the very same evidence which establishes the existence of phantasies even at the earliest ages gives us some indication of their specific character; yet to accept the general evidence for the activity of phantasy from the beginning of life and the place of phantasy in the mental life as a whole does not automatically imply accepting any particular phantasy content at any given age. The relation of content to age will be worked out to some extent elsewhere; this paper is intended to pave the way for that by general considerations.

To understand the nature and function of phantasy in the mental life involves the study of the earliest phases of mental development, i.e. during the first three years of life. Scepticism is sometimes expressed as to the possibility of understanding the psychic life at all in the earliest years—as distinct from observing the sequence and development of behaviour. In fact we are far from having to rely upon mere imagination or blind guesswork, even as regards the first year of life. When all the observable facts of behaviour are considered in the light of *analytic* knowledge gained from adults and from children of over two years, and are brought into relation with analytic principles, we arrive at many hypotheses carrying a high degree of probability and some certainties, regarding early mental processes.

Our views about phantasy in these earliest years are based almost wholly upon inference, but then this is true at any age. Unconscious phantasies are always inferred, not observed as such; indeed, the technique of psycho-analysis as a whole is largely based upon inferred knowledge. As has often been pointed out regarding the adult patient too, he does not tell us his unconscious phantasies directly, nor, for that matter, his preconscious resistances. We often observe quite directly emotions and attitudes of which the patient himself is unaware; these and many other observed data (such as those instanced later, on pp. 118–122) make it possible and necessary for us to infer that such and such resistances or phantasies are operating. This is true of the young child as well as of the adult.

The data to be drawn upon here are of three main sorts, and the conclusions to be put forward are based upon a *convergence* of these lines of evidence.

(a) Considerations regarding the relationships between certain established facts and theories, many of which facts and theories, although quite familiar in psycho-analytic thought, have hitherto been dealt with in a relatively isolated way. When considered fully, these relationships require the postulates which will be put forward, and by means of these postulates become better integrated and more adequately understood.

(b) Clinical evidence gained by analysts from the actual analysis of adults and children of all ages.

(c) Observational data (non-analytic observations and experimental studies) of the infant and young child, by the various means at the disposal of the science of child development.

I. Methods of study

A. Observational methods

Before considering our main thesis, it may be useful to survey briefly certain fundamental principles of method which provide us with the material for conclusions as to the nature and function of phantasy, and which are exemplified both in clinical (psychoanalytic) studies and in many of the most fruitful recent researches into the development of behaviour.

A variety of techniques for the study of particular aspects of child development has been evolved in recent years. It is a no table fact that observational researches into the development of personality and social relationships, and especially those which attempt to reach understanding of motives and of mental process generally tend to pay more and more regard to certain methodological principles, now to be discussed. These principles bring them into closer line with clinical studies and thus form a valuable link between observational methods and analytic technique. They are: (a) attention to details; (b) observation of context; (c) study of genetic continuity.

(a) All serious contributions to child psychology in recent years could be instanced as illustration of the growing appreciation of the need to attend to the *precise details* of the child's behaviour, whatever the field of enquiry may be, emotional, social, intellectual, locomotor or manipulative skills, perception and language. The researches of Gesell (1928, 1939, 1940), Shirley (1933), Bayley (1936) and many others into early mental development exemplify this principle. So do the experimental and observational studies of social development, or the researches into infant behaviour by D. W. Winnicott (1941) and M. M. Middlemore (1941). Middlemore's research on the behaviour of infants in the feeding situation, for example, demonstrated how varied and complex even the earliest responses of infants turn out to be when noted and compared in close detail, and how intimately the child's experiences, for example, the way he is handled and suckled, influence succeeding phases of feeling and phantasy and his mental processes generally.

Most advances in observational and experimental technique have been devised to facilitate the precise observation and recording of details of behaviour. We shall later refer to the great importance of this principle in psycho-analytic work and the way in which it helps us to discern the content of early phantasies.

(b) *The principle of noting and recording the context* of observed data is of the greatest importance, whether in the case of a particular instance or sort of social behaviour, particular examples of play, questions asked by the child in the development of speech—whatever the data may be. By "context" is meant, not merely earlier and later examples of the same sort of behaviour, but the whole immediate setting of the behaviour being studied, in its social and emotional situation. With regard to phantasy, for example, we have to note *when* the child says this or that, plays this or that game, performs this or that ritual, masters (or loses) this or that skill, demands or refuses a particular gratification, shows signs of anxiety, distress, triumph, glee, affection, or other emotions; who is present—or absent—at the time; what is his general emotional attitude or immediate feeling towards these adults or playmates; what losses, strains, satisfactions have been recently experienced or are being now anticipated? And so on and so forth.

The importance of this principle of studying the psychological *context* of particular data in the mental life has become increasingly recognized amongst students of children's behaviour, whatever mental process or function of behaviour happens to be the subject of study. Many examples could be given: e.g. the study of temper tantrums, by Florence Goodenough,[3] of the innate bases of fear, by C. W. Valentine[4] (1930); of the development of speech in infancy, by M. M. Lewis[5] (1936); of the development of sympathy in young children, by L. B. Murphy[6] (1937).

Murphy's work, in especial, has shown how indispensable is this principle in the study of social relationships, and how far more fruitful it proves than any purely quantitative or statistical treatment of types of behaviour or traits of personality, made without reference to context.

One of the outstanding examples of the way in which attention to precise details in their total context may reveal the significance of a piece of behaviour in the inner psychic life of the child is Freud's observation of the play of a boy of eighteen months of age. This boy was a normal child, of average intellectual development, and generally well behaved. Freud writes: "He did not disturb his parents at night; he scrupulously obeyed orders about not touching various objects and not going into certain rooms; and above all he never cried when his mother went out and left him for hours together, although the tie to his mother was a very close one: she had not only nourished him herself, but had cared for him and brought him up without any outside help. Occasionally, however, this well-behaved child evinced the troublesome habit of flinging into the corner of the room or under the bed all the little things he could lay his hands on, so that to gather up his toys was often no light task. He accompanied this by an expression of interest and gratification, emitting a loud long-drawn-out 'o-o-o-oh' which in the judgement of the mother (one that coincided with my own) was not an interjection but meant 'gone away' (fort). I saw at last that this was a game, and that the child used all his toys only to play 'being gone' (fortsein) with them. One day I made an observation that confirmed my view. The child had a wooden reel with a piece of string wound round it . . . he kept throwing it with considerable skill, held by the string, over the side of his little draped cot, so that the reel disappeared into it, then said his significant 'o-o-o-oh' and drew the reel by the string out of the cot again, greeting its reappearance with a joyful 'Da' (there). This was therefore the complete game, disappearance and return, the first act being the only one generally observed by the onlookers, and the one untiringly repeated by the child as a game for its own sake, although the greater pleasure unquestionably attached to the second act.

"The meaning of the game was then not far to seek. It was connected with the child's great cultural achievement—the forgoing of the satisfaction of an instinct—as the result of which he could let his mother go away without making any fuss. He compensated himself for this, as it were, by himself enacting the same disappearance and return with the objects within his reach" (1922).

Later on, Freud also noted a further detail in the boy's behaviour: "One day when the mother had been out for some hours she was greeted on her return by the information 'Baby o-o-o-oh' which at first remained unintelligible. It soon proved that during his long lonely hours he had found a method of bringing about his own disappearance. He had discovered his reflection in the long mirror which nearly reached to the ground and had then crouched down in front of it, so that the reflection was 'gone'."

The observation of this detail of the sounds with which the boy greeted his mother's return called attention to the further link of the child's delight in making his own image appear and disappear in the mirror, with its confirmatory evidence of his triumph in controlling feelings of loss, by his play, as a consolation for his mother's absence.

Freud also brought to bear upon the boy's play with the wooden reel other and more remote facts which many observers would not have thought had any relation to it, such as the child's general relationship to his mother, his affection and obedience, his capacity to refrain from disturbing her and to allow her to absent herself for hours together without grumbling or protest. Freud thus came to understand much of the significance of the child's play in his social and emotional life, concluding that in the boy's delight in throwing away material objects and then retrieving them, he enjoyed the phantasied satisfaction of controlling his mother's comings and goings. On this basis he could tolerate her leaving him in actuality, and remain loving and obedient.

The principle of observing context, like that of attention to detail, is an essential element in the technique of psycho-analysis, whether with adults or children.

(c) The principle of Genetic Continuity.

The third fundamental principle, of value both in observational and in analytic studies, is that of *genetic continuity*[7] (Riviere, 1936).

Experience has already proved that throughout every aspect of mental (no less than of physical) development, whether in posture, locomotor and manipulative skill, in perception, imagination, language, or early logic, any given phase develops by degrees out of preceding phases in a way which can be ascertained both in general outline and in specific detail. This established general truth serves as a guide and pointer in further observations. All studies of developmental status (such as those of Gesell and Shirley) rest upon this principle.

It does not mean that development proceeds at an even pace throughout. There are definite crises in growth, and there are integrations which from their nature bring radical changes in experience and further achievement, e.g. learning to walk is such a crisis; but dramatic though it be in the changes it introduces into the child's world, actual walking is but the end-phase of a long series of developing co-ordinations. Learning to talk is another such crisis; but again, one prepared for and foreshadowed in every detail before it is achieved. So true is this that the definition of ability to talk is purely a matter of convention[8] (Hazlitt, 1933). Commonly it is taken to mean the use of two words, an arbitrary standard useful for purposes of comparison, but not intended to blur the continuous course of development. Speech development *begins*, as has often been shown, with the sounds made by the infant when hungry or feeding in the first few weeks of life; and on the other hand, the changes occurring *after* the mastery of the first words are as continuous and as varied and complex as those occurring before this moment.

One aspect of speech development having a special bearing upon our present problems is the fact that *comprehension of words long antedates their use*. The actual length of time during which the child shows that he understands much that is said to him, or spoken in his presence, yet has not come to the point of using any words himself, varies much from child to child. In some highly intelligent children, the interval between comprehension and use of words may be as much as one year. This time lag of use behind comprehension is found generally throughout childhood. Many other intellectual processes, also, are expressed in action long before they can be put into words.

Examples of rudimentary thought emerging in action and in speech from the second year of life are given in the studies of speech development by M. M. Lewis (1937). The experimental studies of the development of logical thinking, by Hazlitt (1933) and others, show the same principle at work in later years.

This general fact of genetic continuity, and its particular exemplifications in speech development, have a specific bearing upon one important question: are phantasies active in the child at the time when the relevant impulses first dominate his behaviour and his experience, or do these become so only in retrospect, when later on he can put his experience into words? The evidence clearly suggests that phantasies are active along with the impulses from which they arise. (This question is bound up with the problem of *regression*, which will be discussed elsewhere.)

Genetic continuity thus characterizes every aspect of development at all ages. There is no reason to doubt that it holds true of phantasy as well as of overt behaviour and of logical thinking. Is it not, indeed, one of the major achievements of psycho-analysis to have shown that the development of the instinctual life, for instance, had a continuity never understood before Freud's work? The essence of Freud's theory of sexuality lies in just this fact of detailed continuity of development.

Probably no psycho-analyst would question the abstract principle, but it is not always appreciated that it is far more than this. The established principle of genetic continuity *is a concrete instrument of knowledge*. It enjoins upon us to accept no particular facts of behaviour or mental processes as *sui generis*, ready-made, or suddenly emerging, but to regard them as items in a developing series. We seek to trace them backwards through earlier and more rudimentary stages to their most germinal forms; similarly, we are required to regard the facts as manifestations of a process of growth, which has to be followed forward to later and more developed forms. Not only is it necessary to study the acorn in order to understand the oak, but also to know about the oak in order to understand the acorn (Freud, 1911).

B. The method of psycho-analysis

These three ways of obtaining evidence of mental process from observation of behaviour: that of noting the context, observing details and approaching any particular data as a part of a developmental process, are essential aspects of the work of psycho-analysis, and most fully exemplified there. They are indeed its breath of life. They serve to elucidate the nature and function of phantasy, as well as of other mental phenomena.

The observation of detail and of context are so intimately bound up in analytic work that they may be briefly dealt with together. With adult patients, as well as children, the analyst not only listens to all the details of the actual content of the patient's remarks and associations, including what is not said as well as what is, but notes also where emphasis is put, and whether it seems appropriate. Repetition of what has already been told or remarked, in its immediate affective and associative context; changes occurring in the patient's account of events in his earlier life, and in the picture he presents of people in his environment, as the work goes on;

changes in his ways of referring to circumstances and to people (including the names he gives them), from time to time, all serve to indicate the character and activity of the phantasies operating in his mind. So do idiosyncrasies of speech, or phrases and forms of description, metaphors and verbal style generally. Further data are the patient's selection of facts from a total incident, and his denials (e.g. of things he has previously said, of states of mind which would be appropriate to the content of what he is saying, of real objects seen or incidents occurring in the analytic room, of facts in his own life which can certainly be inferred from the other known content of his life or family history, of facts known by the patient about the analyst or of happenings in public affairs, such as war and bombs). The analyst notes the patient's manner and behaviour as he enters and leaves the room, as he greets the analyst or parts from him, and while he is on the couch; including every detail of gesture or tone of voice, pace of speaking, and variations in this, idiosyncratic routine or particular changes in mode of expression, changes of mood, every sign of affect or denial of affect, in their particular nature and intensity and their precise associative context. These, and many other such kinds of detail, taken as a context to the patient's dreams and associations, help to reveal his unconscious phantasies (among other mental facts). The particular situation in the internal life of the patient at the moment gradually becomes clear, and the relation of his immediate problem to earlier situations and to actual experiences in his history is gradually made plain.

The third principle, that of genetic continuity, is inherent in the whole approach and the moment-by-moment work of psycho-analysis.

Freud's discovery of the successive phases of libidinal development in the child, and the continuity of the various manifestations of the sexual wishes from infancy to maturity, has not only been fully confirmed with every patient analysed, but, as in the case of every sound generalization of observed facts, has proved to be a reliable instrument for further understanding of new data.

Observations in the analytic field of the development of phantasy and of the continuous and developing interplay between psychic reality and knowledge of the external world, are fully in accordance with the data and generalizations regarding development arrived at in other fields, such as bodily skills, perceptions, speech and logical thinking. As with the external facts of behaviour, so with the development of phantasy, we have to regard each manifestation at any given time and in any given situation as a member of a developing series whose rudimentary beginnings can be traced backwards and whose further, more mature, forms can be followed forward. Awareness of the way in which the content and form of phantasy at any given time are bound up with the successive phases of instinctual development, and of the growth of the ego, is always operating in the analyst's mind. To make this plain (in concrete detail) to the patient is an inherent part of the work.

It was by attending to the details and the context of the patient's speech and manner, as well as of his dreams and associations, that Freud laid bare both the fundamental instinctual drives in the mental life, and the varied processes—the so-called *"mental mechanisms"*—by which impulses and feelings are controlled and expressed, internal equilibrium is maintained and adaptation to the external world achieved. These "mechanisms" are very varied in type and many of them have received close attention. In the view of the present writers, all these various mechanisms are intimately related to particular sorts of phantasy, and at a later point, the character of this relationship will be gone into.

Freud's discoveries were made almost entirely from the analysis of adults, together with certain observations of children. Melanie Klein, in her direct analytic work with children of two years and onwards, developed the full resources of analytic technique by using the children's play with material objects, their games and their bodily activities towards the analyst, as well of course as their mien and manner and signs of feeling and their talk about what they were doing and feeling, or what had been happening in their external lives. The makebelieve and manipulative play of young children exemplify those various mental processes (and therefore, as we shall see, the phantasies) first noted by Freud in the dream life of adults and in their neurotic symptoms. In the child's relationship to the analyst, as with the adult's, the phantasies arising in the earliest situations of life are repeated and acted out in the clearest and most dramatic manner, with a wealth of vivid detail.

Transference situation

It is especially in the patient's emotional relation to the analyst that the study of context, of details and of continuity of development proves fruitful for the understanding of phantasy. As is well known, Freud early discovered that patients repeat towards their analyst situations of feeling and impulse, and mental processes generally, which have been experienced earlier in their relationships to people in their external lives and personal histories. This transference on to the analyst of early wishes, aggressive impulses, fears and other emotions, is confirmed by every analyst.

The personality, the attitudes and intentions, even the external characteristics and the sex of the analyst, *as seen and felt in the patient's mind*, change from day to day (even from moment to moment) according to changes in the inner life of the patient (whether these are brought about by the analyst's comments or by outside happenings). That is to say, *the patient's relation to his analyst is almost entirely one of unconscious phantasy*. Not only is the phenomenon of "transference" as a whole evidence of the existence and activity of phantasy in every patient, whether child or adult, ill or healthy; its detailed changes also enable us to decipher the particular character of the phantasies at work in particular situations, and their influence upon other mental processes. The "transference" has turned out to be the chief instrument of learning what is going on in the patient's mind, as well as of discovering or reconstructing his early history; the unfolding of his transference phantasies, and the tracing of their relation to early experiences and present-day situations, form the chief agency of the "cure".

Repetition of early situations and "acting out" in the transference carry us back far beyond the earliest conscious memories; the patient (whether child or adult) often shows us, with the most vivid and dramatic detail, feelings, impulses and attitudes appropriate not only to the situations of childhood but also to those of the earliest months of infancy. In his phantasies towards the analyst, the patient *is* back in his earliest days, and to follow these phantasies in their context and understand them in detail is to gain solid knowledge of what actually went on in his mind as an infant.

Mental life under two years of age

For the understanding of phantasy and other mental processes in children from the end of the second year onwards, we thus have not only all the evidence of observed behaviour in ordinary life, but also the full resources of the analytic method used directly.

When we turn to children under two years, we bring certain proved instruments of understanding to the study of their responses to stimuli, their spontaneous activities, their signs of affect, their play with people and with material objects, and all the varied aspects of their behaviour. First, we have those principles of observation already outlined—the value of observing context, of noting precise details, and of regarding the data observed at any one moment as being members of a series which can be traced backward to their rudimentary beginnings and forward to their more mature forms. Secondly, we have the insight gained from direct analytic experience into the mental processes so clearly expressed in similar types of behaviour (continuous with these earlier forms) in children of more than two years; above all, the evidence yielded by the repetition of situations, emotions, attitudes and phantasies in the "transference" during analyses of older children and of adults.

Using these various instruments, it becomes possible to formulate certain hypotheses about the earliest phases of phantasy and of learning, of mental development generally, which can be credited with a considerable degree of probability. There are gaps in our understanding, and from the nature of the case, these may take time to remove. Nor are our inferences as certain as those regarding later development. But there is much which is definitely clear, and much more that only awaits further detailed observations, or more patient correlating of the observable facts, to yield a high degree of understanding.

II. The nature and function of phantasy

To turn now to our main thesis:

As has been said, it is on the basis of the convergence of these various lines of evidence that the present-day significance of the concept of phantasy is to be discussed. A consideration of all these sorts of fact and theory calls for a revision of the usages of the term.

Common usages of the term "phantasy"

Among psycho-analytic writers, the term has sometimes referred (in line with everyday language) only to *conscious* "fantasies", of the nature of day-dreams. But Freud's discoveries soon led him to recognize the existence of *unconscious* phantasies. This reference of the word is indispensable. The English translators of Freud adopted a special spelling of the word "phantasy", with the *ph*, in order to differentiate the psycho-analytical significance of the term, i.e. predominantly or entirely unconscious phantasies, from the popular word "fantasy", meaning conscious day-dreams, fictions, and so on. The psycho-analytical term "phantasy" essentially connotes *unconscious* mental content, which may or may not become conscious.

This meaning of the word has assumed a growing significance, particularly in consequence of the work of Melanie Klein on the early stages of development.

Again, the word "phantasy" has often been used to mark a contrast to "reality", the latter word being taken as identical with "external" or "material" or "objective" facts. But when external reality is thus called "objective" reality, this makes an implicit assumption which denies to psychical reality its *own objectivity as a mental fact*. Some analysts tend to contrast "phantasy" with "reality" in such a way as to undervalue the dynamic importance of phantasy. A related usage, very common in patients, is to think of "phantasy" as something "merely" or "only" imagined, as something unreal, in contrast with what is actual, what *happens* to one. This kind of attitude tends towards a depreciation of psychical reality and of the significance of mental processes *as such*.

Psycho-analysis has shown that the quality of being "merely" or "only" imagined is not the most important criterion for the understanding of the human mind. When and under what conditions "psychical reality" is in harmony with external reality is one special part of the total problem of understanding mental life as a whole: a very important part indeed; but, still, "only" one part. (This will be touched upon at various later points, for example p. 132 *et seq.*)

Freud's discovery of *dynamic psychical reality* initiated a new epoch of psychological understanding.

He showed that the inner world of the mind has a continuous living reality of its own, with its own dynamic laws and characteristics, different from those of the external world. In order to understand the dream and the dreamer, his psychological history, his neurotic symptoms or his normal interests and character, we have to give up that prejudice in favour of external reality, and of our conscious orientations to it, that under-valuation of internal reality, which is the attitude of the ego in Western civilized life today.[9]

A further point, of importance in our general thesis, is that unconscious phantasy is fully active in the normal, no less than in the neurotic mind. It seems sometimes to be assumed that only in the "neurotic" is psychical reality (i.e. unconscious phantasy) of paramount importance, and that with "normal" people its significance is reduced to vanishing point. This view is not in accordance with the facts, as they are seen in the behaviour of ordinary people in daily life, or as observed through the medium of psycho-analytic work, notably in the transference. The difference between normal and abnormal lies in the way in which the unconscious phantasies are dealt with, the particular mental processes by means of which they are worked over and modified; and the degree of direct or indirect gratification in the real world and adaptation to it, which these favoured mechanisms allow.

Phantasy as the primary content of unconscious mental processes

Thus far, we have been upon familiar ground. If, however, we bring recent clinical data into closer relation with certain formulations of Freud's, we take a definite step forward in understanding the function of phantasy.

A study of the conclusions arising from the analysis of young children leads to the view that phantasies are the primary content of unconscious mental processes. Freud did not formulate his views on this point in terms of phantasy, but it can be seen that such a formulation is in essential alignment with his contributions.

Freud has said that ". . . everything conscious has a preliminary unconscious stage. . . ."[10] (1932). All mental processes originate in the unconscious and only under certain conditions become conscious. They arise either directly from instinctual needs or in response to external stimuli acting upon instinctual impulses. "We suppose that it (the id) is somewhere in direct contact with somatic processes and takes over from them instinctual needs and gives them *mental expression.*"[11] (1933). (My italics.) "We must say that the Ucs is continued into its so-called derivatives, is accessible to the influence of life, perpetually acts upon the Pcs, and even is, on its part, capable of influence by the latter system"[12] (1915B).

Now in the view of the present writers, this "mental expression" of instinct is unconscious phantasy. Phantasy is (in the first instance) the mental corollary, the psychic representative, of instinct. There is no impulse, no instinctual urge or response which is not experienced as unconscious phantasy.

In the beginning of his researches, Freud was concerned particularly with libidinal desires, and his "mental expression of instinctual needs" would refer primarily to libidinal aims. His later studies, however, and those of many other workers, have required us to include destructive impulses as well.

The first mental processes, the psychic representatives of bodily impulses and feelings, i.e. of libidinal and destructive instincts, are to be regarded as the earliest beginning of phantasies. In the mental development of the infant, however, phantasy soon becomes also a means of defence against anxieties, a means of inhibiting and controlling instinctual urges and an expression of reparative wishes as well. The relation between phantasy and wish-fulfilment has always been emphasized; but our experience has shown, too, that most phantasies (like symptoms) also serve various other purposes as well as wish-fulfilment; e.g. denial, reassurance, omnipotent control, reparation, etc. It is, of course, true that, in a wider sense, all these mental processes which aim at diminishing instinctual tension, anxiety and guilt also serve the aim of wish-fulfilment; but it is useful to discriminate the specific modes of these different processes and their particular aims.

All impulses, all feelings, all modes of defence are experienced in phantasies which give them *mental* life and show their direction and purpose.

A phantasy represents the particular content of the urges or feelings (for example, wishes, fears, anxieties, triumphs, love or sorrow) dominating the mind at the moment. In early life, there is indeed a wealth of unconscious phantasies which take specific form in conjunction with the cathexis of particular bodily zones. Moreover, they rise and fall in complicated patterns according to the rise and fall and modulation of the primary instinct-impulses which they express. The world of phantasy shows the same protean and kaleidoscopic changes as the contents of a dream. These changes occur partly in response to external stimulation and partly as a result of the interplay between the primary instinctual urges themselves.

It may be useful at this point to give some examples of specific phantasies, without, however, discussing the particular age or time relations between these actual examples.

In attempting to give such examples of specific phantasies we are naturally obliged to put them into words; we cannot describe or discuss them without doing so. This is clearly not their original character and inevitably introduces a foreign element, one belonging to later phases of development, and to the preconscious mind. (Later on we shall discuss more fully the relation between phantasies and their verbal expression.)

On the basis of those principles of observation and interpretation, which have already been described and are well established by psycho-analytic work, we are able to conclude that when the child shows his desire for his mother's breast, he *experiences* this desire as a specific phantasy—"I want to suck the nipple". If desire is very intense (perhaps on account of anxiety), he is likely to feel: "I want to eat her all up." Perhaps to avert the repetition of loss of her, or for his pleasure, he may feel: "I want to keep her inside me." If he is feeling fond, he may have the phantasy: "I want to stroke her face, to pat and cuddle her." At other times, when he is frustrated or provoked, his impulses may be of an aggressive character; he will experience these as, e.g.: "I want to bite the breast; I want to tear her to bits." Or if, e.g. urinary impulses are dominant, he may feel: "I want to drown and burn her." If anxiety is stirred by such aggressive wishes, he may phantasy: "I myself shall be cut or bitten up by mother"; and when his anxiety refers to his internal object, the breast which has been eaten up and kept inside, he may want to eject her and feel: "I want to throw her out of me." When he feels loss and grief, he experiences, as Freud described: "My mother has gone for ever." He may feel: "I want to bring her back, I must have her *now*", and then try to overcome his sense of loss and grief and helplessness by the phantasies expressed in auto-erotic satisfactions, such as thumb-sucking and genital play: "If I suck my thumb, I feel she is back here with me, belonging to me and giving me pleasure." If, after having in his phantasy attacked his mother and hurt and damaged her, libidinal wishes come up again, he may feel he wants to restore his mother and will then phantasy: "I want to put the bits together again", "I want to make her better", "I want to feed her as she has fed me"; and so on and so forth.

Not merely do these phantasies appear and disappear according to changes in the instinctual urges stirred up by outer circumstances, they also exist together, side by side in the mind, even though they be contradictory; just as in a dream, mutually exclusive wishes may exist and be expressed together.

Not only so: these early mental processes have an omnipotent character. Under the pressure of instinct-tension, the child in his earliest days not only feels: "I want to", but implicitly phantasies: "I *am* doing" this and that to his mother: "I *have* her inside me", when he wants to. The wish and impulse, whether it be love or hate, libidinal or destructive, tends to be felt as actually fulfilling itself, whether with an external or an internal object. This is partly because of the overwhelmingness of his desires and feelings. In these earliest days, his own wishes and impulses fill the whole world at the time when they are felt. It is only slowly that he learns to distinguish between the wish and the deed, between external facts and his feelings about them. The degree of differentiation partly depends upon the stage of development reached at the time, and partly upon the momentary intensity of the desire or emotion.

This omnipotent character of early wishes and feelings links with Freud's views about hallucinatory satisfaction in the infant.

Hallucination and primary introjection

Freud had been led (by his study of unconscious processes in the minds of adults) to assume that, in the beginning of mental life, ". . . whatever was thought of (desired) was simply imagined in a hallucinatory form, as still happens with our dream-thoughts every night". This he calls the child's "attempt at satisfaction by hallucination" (1911).

What, therefore, does the infant hallucinate? We may assume, since it is the oral impulse which is at work, first, the nipple, then the breast, and later, his mother as a whole person; and he hallucinates the nipple or the breast in order to enjoy it. As we can see from his behaviour (sucking movements, sucking his own lip or a little later his fingers, and so on), hallucination does not stop at the mere picture, but carries him on to what he is, in detail, going to do with the desired object which he imagines (phantasies) he has obtained. It seems probable that hallucination works best at times of less intense instinctual tension, perhaps when the infant half-awakes and first begins to be hungry, but still lies quiet. As tension increases, hunger and the wish to suck the breast becoming stronger, hallucination is liable to break down. The pain of frustration then stirs up a still stronger desire, viz. the wish to take the whole breast into himself and keep it there, as a source of satisfaction; and this in its turn will for a time omnipotently fulfil itself in belief, in hallucination. Thus we must assume that the incorporation of the breast is bound up with the earliest forms of the phantasy life. This hallucination of the internal satisfying breast may, however, break down altogether if frustration continues and hunger is not satisfied, instinct-tension proving too strong to be denied. Rage and violently aggressive feelings and phantasies will then dominate the mind, and necessitate some adaptation.

Let us consider further what Freud has to say about this situation.

He goes on: "In so far as it is auto-erotic, the ego has no need of the outside world, but . . . it cannot but for a time perceive instinctual stimuli as painful. Under the sway of the pleasure principle, there now takes place a further development. The objects presenting themselves, in so far as they are sources of pleasure, are absorbed by the ego into itself, 'introjected' (according to an expression coined by Ferenczi): while, on the other hand, the ego thrusts forth upon the external world whatever within itself gives rise to pain (*v. infra*: the mechanism of projection)" (1915A).

Although in describing primary introjection, Freud does not use the phrase "unconscious phantasy", it is clear that his concept accords with our assumption of the activity of unconscious phantasy in the earliest phase of life.

Difficulties in early development arising from phantasy

Many of the familiar difficulties of the young infant (e.g. in feeding and excreting, or his phobias of strangers and anxiety of being left alone, etc.) can best be integrated with well-established analytic views, and their significance more fully understood, if they are seen as manifestations of early phantasy.

Freud commented on some of these difficulties. E.g. he referred to ". . . the situation of the infant when he is presented with a stranger instead of his mother"; and after speaking of the child's anxiety, added: ". . . the expression of his face and his reaction of crying indicate that he is feeling pain as well. . . . As soon as he misses his mother he behaves as if he were never going to see her again." Freud also referred to "the infant's misunderstanding of the facts. . . ."

Now, by "pain", Freud obviously does not here mean bodily, but *mental* pain; and mental pain has a content, a meaning, and implies phantasy. On the view presented here, "he behaves as if he were never going to see her again" means his phantasy is that his mother has been destroyed (by his own hate or greed) and altogether lost. His awareness of her absence is profoundly coloured by his feelings towards her—his longing and intolerance of frustration, his hate and consequent anxieties. His "misunderstanding of the situation" is that same "subjective interpretation" of his perception of her absence which, as J. Riviere points out, is a characteristic of phantasy.

On another occasion, when speaking of oral frustrations, Freud says: "It looks far more as if the desire of the child for its first form of nourishment is altogether insatiable, and as if it never got over the pain of losing the mother's breast. . . . It is probable, too, that the fears of poisoning are connected with weaning. Poison is the nour- ishment that makes one ill. Perhaps, moreover, the child traces his early illnesses back to this frustration" (1933).

How would it be possible for the child to "trace back his early illnesses to this frustration" unless at the time of the frustration he experienced it *in his mind*, retained it and later on remembered it unconsciously? At the time when he experiences the frustration, there is not merely a bodily happening but also a mental process, i.e. a phantasy—the phantasy of having a bad mother who inflicts pain and loss upon him. Freud says "the fear of poisoning is prob- ably connected with weaning". He does not discuss this connection further; but it implies the existence of phantasies about a poisoning breast, such as Melanie Klein's work has shown (1932).

Again, when Freud speaks of the feelings the little girl has about her mother, he refers to the child's "dread of being killed by the mother".[13]

Now to speak of a "dread of being killed by the mother" is obviously a way of describing the child's phantasy of a murderous mother. In our analytic work, we find that the phantasy of the "murderous" mother supervenes upon that of the mother who is attacked with murderous intent by the child. Sometimes the phantasy of the vengeful mother may come to conscious expression in words later on, as in the small boy reported by Dr Ernest Jones, who said of his mother's nipple when he saw her feeding a younger child: "That's what you bit me with." As we can confirm by analysis of the transference in every patient, what has happened here is that the child has projected his own oral aggressive wishes on to the object of those wishes, his mother's breast. In his phantasy which accompanies this projection, she (the mother or her breast) is now going to bite him to bits as he wanted to do to her.

Phantasies and words

We must now consider very briefly the relation between phantasies and words.

The primary phantasies, the representatives of the earliest impulses of desire and aggressiveness, are expressed in and dealt with by mental processes far removed from words and conscious relational thinking, and determined by the logic of emotion. At a later period, they may under certain conditions (sometimes in children's spontaneous play, sometimes only in analysis) become capable of being expressed in words.

There is a wealth of evidence to show that phantasies are active in the mind long before language has developed, and that even in the adult they continue to operate alongside and independently of words. Meanings, like feelings, are far older than speech, alike in racial and in childhood experience.

In childhood and in adult life, we live and feel, we phantasy and act far beyond our verbal meanings. E.g. some of our dreams show us what worlds of drama we can live through in visual terms alone. We know from dancing, acting, drawing, painting and sculpture and the whole world of art, what a wealth of implicit meaning can reside even in a shape, a colour, a line, a movement, a mass, a composition of form or colour, or of melody and harmony in music. In social life, too, we know from our own ready and intuitive response to other people's facial expression, tones of voice, gestures, etc.,[14] how much we appreciate directly without words, how much meaning is implicit in what we perceive, sometimes with never a word uttered, or even in spite of words uttered. These things, perceived and imagined and felt about, are the stuff of experience. Words are a means of *referring* to experience, actual or phantasied, but are not identical with it, not a substitute for it. Words may evoke feelings and images and actions, and point to situations; they do so by virtue of being signs of experience, not of being themselves the main material of experience.

Freud made quite clear, in more than one passage, his own view that words belong to the conscious mind only and not to the realm of unconscious feelings and phantasies. He spoke, e.g. of the fact that it is real objects and persons which we invest with love and interest, not their names[15] (1915B).

And of visual memory he wrote: ". . . it approximates more closely to unconscious processes than does thinking in words, and it is unquestionably older than the latter, both ontogenetically and phylogenetically."

Perhaps the most convincing evidence of the activity of phantasy without words is that of hysterical *conversion symptoms*.[16] In these familiar neurotic symptoms, ill people revert to a primitive preverbal language, and make use of sensations, postures, gestures and visceral processes to express emotions and unconscious wishes or beliefs, i.e. phantasies. The psychogenic character of such bodily symptoms, first discovered by Freud and followed up by Ferenczi, has been confirmed by every analyst; their elucidation is a commonplace in the work with many types of patient. Each detail of the symptoms turns out to have a specific meaning, i.e. to express a specific phantasy; and the various shifts of form and intensity and bodily part affected reflect changes in phantasy, occurring in response to outer events or to inner pressures.

We are not, however, left to depend upon even such convincing general considerations from adults and older children, but can occasionally gather quite direct evidence from a young child that a particular phantasy may dominate his mind long before its content can be put into words.

As an example: a little girl of one year and eight months, with poor speech development, saw a shoe of her mother's from which the sole had come loose and was flapping about. The child was horrified, and screamed with terror. For about a week she would shrink away and scream if she saw her mother wearing any shoes at all, and for some time could only tolerate her mother's wearing a pair of brightly coloured house shoes. The particular offending pair was not worn for several months. The child gradually forgot about the terror, and let her mother wear any sort of shoes. At two years and eleven months, however (fifteen months later), she suddenly said to her mother in a frightened voice, "Where are Mummy's broken shoes?" Her mother hastily said, fearing another screaming attack, that she had sent them away, and the child then commented: "They might have eaten me right up."

The flapping shoe was thus *seen* by the child as a threatening mouth, and responded to as such, at one year and eight months, even though the phantasy could not be put into words. Here, then, we have the clearest possible evidence that a phantasy can be felt, and felt as real, long before it can be expressed in words.

Phantasies and sensory experience

Words, then, are a late development in our means of expressing the inner world of our phantasy. By the time a child can use words— even primitive words such as "Baby o-o-oh"—he has already gone through a long and complicated history of psychic experience.

The first phantasied wish-fulfilment, the first "hallucination", is bound up with *sensation*. Some pleasurable sensation (organ-pleasure) there must be, very early, if the baby is to survive. E.g. if, for one reason or another, the first sucking impulse does not lead to pleasurable satisfaction, acute anxiety is aroused in the infant. The sucking impulse itself may then tend to be inhibited or to be less well co-ordinated than it should. In extreme cases, there may be complete inhibition of feeding; in less marked instances, "pining" and poor development. If, on the other hand, through a natural unity of rhythm between mother and child, or the skilful handling of any difficulties that may arise, the infant is soon able to receive pleasurable satisfaction at the breast, good co-ordination of sucking and a positive attitude to the suckling process is set up which goes on automatically thereafter, and fosters life and health (Middle-more, 1941). Changes of contact and temperature, the inrush of sound and light stimulation, etc., are manifestly felt as painful. The inner stimuli of hunger and desire for contact with the mother's body are painful, too. But sensations of warmth, the desired contact, satisfaction in sucking, freedom from outer stimulus, etc., soon bring actual experience of pleasurable sensation. At first, the whole weight of wish and phantasy is borne by sensation and affect. The hungry or longing or distressed infant feels actual sensations in his mouth or his limbs or his viscera, which *mean to him* that certain things are being done to him or that he is doing such and such as he wishes, or fears. He *feels as if* he were doing so and so—e.g. reaching or sucking or biting the breast which is actually out of reach, or as if he were being forcibly and painfully deprived of the breast, or as if *it* were biting *him*. And all this at first, probably without visual or other plastic images.

Interesting material bearing upon this point is offered by Middlemore, from the analysis of a girl of two years nine months, who was treated for severe feeding difficulties. In her play, both at home and during her analysis, she was continually biting. "Among other things she pretended to be a biting dog, a crocodile, a lion, a pair of scissors that could cut up cups, a mincing machine and a machine for grinding cement." Her unconscious phantasies and conscious imaginative play were thus of an intensely destructive nature. In actuality, she had from birth refused to suck the breast, and her mother had had to give up the attempt to breast-feed her because of the infant's complete lack of interest and response. When she came to analysis, she was eating very little and never without persuasion. She had thus had no experience of actually "attacking" the breast, not even in sucking, let alone in biting as the animals did whose fierce attacks she played out. Middlemore suggests that the bodily sensations, i.e. the pangs of hunger, which disturbed the infant were the source of these fierce phantasies of biting and being bitten[17] (1941).

The earliest phantasies, then, spring from bodily impulses and are interwoven with bodily sensations and affects. They express primarily an internal and subjective reality, yet from the beginning they are bound up with an actual, however limited and narrow, experience of objective reality.

The first bodily experiences begin to build up the first memories, and external realities are progressively woven into the texture of phantasy. Before long, the child's phantasies are able to draw upon plastic images as well as sensations—visual, auditory, kinæsthetic, touch, taste, smell images, etc. And these plastic images and dramatic representations of phantasy are progressively elaborated along with articulated perceptions of the external world.

Phantasies do not, however, take *origin* in articulated knowledge of the external world; their source is internal, in the instinctual impulses.

E.g. the inhibitions of feeding sometimes appearing in quite young infants, and very commonly in children after weaning and in the second year, turn out (in later analysis) to arise from the anxieties connected with the primary oral wishes of intense greedy love and hate: the dread of destroying (by tearing to bits and devouring) the very object of love, the breast that is so much valued and desired.

It has sometimes been suggested that unconscious phantasies such as that of "tearing to bits" would not arise in the child's mind before he had gained the conscious knowledge that tearing a person to bits would mean killing them. Such a view does not meet the case. It overlooks the fact that such knowledge is inherent in bodily impulses as a vehicle of instinct, in the excitation of the organ, i.e. in this case, the mouth.

The phantasy that his passionate impulses will destroy the breast does not require the infant to have actually seen objects eaten up and destroyed, and then to have come to the conclusion that he could do it too. This aim, this relation to the object, is inherent in the character and direction of the impulse itself, and in its related affects[18] (1915A).

To take another example: the difficulties of children in the control of urination are very familiar. Persistent enuresis is a common symptom even in the middle years of childhood. In the analysis of children and adults it is found that such difficulties arise from particularly powerful phantasies regarding the destructive effect of urine and the dangers connected with the act of urinating. (These phantasies are found in normal people as well, but for particular reasons they have become specially active in incontinent children.) Now in the child's phantasies, urine is very potent for evil. His anxieties thus spring from destructive impulses. It is primarily because he wants his urine to be so very harmful that he comes to believe that it is so, not primarily because his mother gets cross when he wets the bed, and certainly not because he has ever observed that his urine is as harmful as in his phantasies he really believes it to be; nor because he has conscious awareness that people may be drowned and burned in external reality.

The situation goes back to early infancy. In the phantasy: "I want to drown and burn mother with my urine", we have an expression of the infant's fury and aggression, the wish to attack and annihilate mother by means of his urine, partly because of her frustrating him. He wishes to flood her with urine in burning anger. The "burning" is an expression both of his own bodily sensations and of the intensity of his rage. The "drowning", too, expresses the *feeling* of his intense hate and of his omnipotence, when he floods his mother's lap. The infant feels: "I *must* annihilate my bad mother." He overcomes his feeling of helplessness by the omnipotent phantasy: "I can and *will* destroy her"—by whatever means he possesses;[19] and when urinary sadism is at its height, what he feels he can do is to flood and burn her with his urine. Doubtless the "flooding" and "burning" also refer to the way in which he feels *he* is overcome, flooded, by his helpless rage, and burnt up by it. The whole world is full of his anger, and he will himself be destroyed by it if he cannot vent it on his mother, discharging it on her with his urine. The rush of water from the tap, the roaring fire, the flooding river or stormy sea, when these are seen or known as external realities, link up in his mind with his early bodily experiences, instinctual aims and phantasies. And when he is given names for these things, he can *then* sometimes put these phantasies into words.

Similarly with the infant's feelings about his excretions as good things which he wishes to give to his mother. In certain moods and moments he does feel his urine and fæces to be something mother wants and the gift of them is his means of expressing his love and gratitude towards her. Such phantasies of fæces and urine as beneficent are certainly strengthened by the fact that mother is pleased when he gives them at the proper time and place; but his observation of his mother's pleasure is not the primary origin of his feeling of them as good. The source of this lies in his *wish* to give them as good—e.g. to feed his mother as she has fed him, to please her and do what she wants; and in his feeling of the goodness of his organs and of his body as a whole, when he is loving her and feeling her good to him. His urine and fæces are then instruments of his potency in love, just as his voice and smile can also be. Since the infant has so few resources at his command for expressing either love or hate, he has to use all his bodily products and activities as means of expressing his profound and overwhelming wishes and emotions. His urine and fæces may be either good or bad in his phantasy, according to his intentions at the moment of voiding and the way (including at a later period the time and place) in which they are produced.

These feelings and fears about his own bodily products link with the so-called "infantile sexual theories". Freud first drew attention to the fact, since then very widely observed, that young children, consciously as well as unconsciously, form their own spontaneous theories about the origin of babies and the nature of parental sexual intercourse, based upon their own bodily capacities. E.g. babies are made from food, and parental intercourse consists in mutual feeding or eating. Father puts the good food into mother, he feeds her with his genital in return for her feeding him with her breast, and then she has the babies inside her. Or they are made from fæces. Father puts fæces into mother and in so far as the child is loving and able to tolerate the parents' love for each other, he may feel this is good and gives mother life inside her. At other times, when he is feeling full of hate and jealousy and completely intolerant of his parents' intercourse, he wishes father to put bad fæces into mother—dangerous, explosive substances which will destroy her inside; or to urinate into her in a way that will harm her. These infantile sexual theories are obviously not drawn from observation of external events. The infant has never observed that babies are made from food and fæces, nor seen father urinate into mother. His notions of parental intercourse are derived from his own bodily impulses under the pressure of intense feeling. His phantasies express his wishes and his passions, using his bodily impulses, sensations and processes as their material of expression.[20]

These and other specific contents of early phantasies, no less than the ways in which they are experienced by the child and their modes of expression, are in accordance with his bodily development and his capacities for feeling and knowing at any given age.

They are a *part* of his development, and are expanded and elaborated along with his bodily and mental powers, influencing and being influenced by his slowly maturing ego.

The relation of early phantasy to the primary process

The earliest and most rudimentary phantasies, bound up with sensory experience, and being affective interpretations of bodily sensations, are naturally characterized by those qualities which Freud described as belonging to the "primary process": lack of co-ordination of impulse, lack of sense of time, of contradiction, and of negation. Furthermore, at this level, there is no discrimination of external reality. Experience is governed by "all or none" responses and the absence of satisfaction is felt as a positive evil. Loss, dissatisfaction or deprivation are felt in sensation to be positive, painful experiences.

We are all familiar with the feeling of being "full of emptiness". Emptiness is positive, in sensation; just as darkness is felt as an actual thing, not the mere absence of light, whatever we may *know*. Darkness falls, like a curtain or a blanket. When the light comes it drives away the darkness; and so on.

Thus, when we say (justifiably) that the infant feels a mother who does not remove a source of pain to be a "bad" mother, we do not mean that he has a clear notion of the negative fact of his mother's not removing the source of pain. That is a later realization. The pain itself is positive; the "bad" mother is a positive experience, undistinguished at first from the pain. When at six months or so, the infant sits up and *sees* that his mother, as an external object, does not come when he wants her, he may then make the link between what he sees, viz. her not coming, and the pain or dissatisfaction he feels.

When the infant misses his mother and behaves "as if he were never going to see her again", it does not mean that he then has discriminative notions of time, but that the pain of loss is an absolute experience, with a quality of sheer "neverness" about it—until mental development and the experience of time as a slowly built up external reality have brought discriminative perceptions and images.

The "primary process" is, however, not to be regarded as governing the *whole* mental life of the child during any measurable period of development. It might conceivably occupy the main field for the first few days, but we must not overlook the first adaptations of the infant to his external environment, and the fact that both gratification and frustration are experienced from birth onwards. The progressive alterations in the infant's responses during the first few weeks and onwards show that even by the second month there is a very considerable degree of integration in perception and behaviour, with signs of memory and anticipation.

From this time on, the infant spends an increasing amount of time in experimentative play, which is, at one and the same time, an attempt to adapt to reality and an active means of expressing phantasy (a wish-enactment and a defence against pain and anxiety).

The "primary process" is in fact a limiting concept only. As Freud said: "So far as we know, a psychic apparatus possessing only the primary process does not exist, and is to that extent a theoretical fiction."[21] Later on he speaks of the "belated arrival" of the secondary processes, which seems at first sight somewhat contradictory. The contradiction is resolved if we take the "belated arrival" to refer not so much to the *onset* of the secondary processes, their rudimentary beginnings, but rather to their full development. Such a view would best accord with what we can see of the infant's actual development, in adaptation to reality, in control and integration.

Instinct, phantasy and mechanism

We must now consider another important aspect of our problem, that of the relation between instincts, phantasies and mechanisms. A good deal of difficulty and certain confusions on this matter have appeared in various discussions; one of the aims of this section is to clarify the relations between these different concepts.

The distinction between, e.g. the phantasy of incorporation and the mechanism of introjection has not always been clearly observed. For example, in discussions about specific oral phantasies of devouring or otherwise *incorporating* a concrete object, we often meet with the expression: "The *introjected object*". Or people have sometimes spoken of the "introjected breast", again mixing up the concrete bodily phantasy with the general mental process. It is especially with regard to the mechanisms of introjection and projection that these difficulties seem to have arisen, although the problem of the relation between instincts, phantasies and mechanisms can be considered in a more general way, with regard to every variety of mental mechanism.

To consider "introjection" and "projection", in particular: these are abstract terms, the names of certain fundamental mechanisms or methods of functioning in the mental life. They refer to such facts as that ideas, impressions and influences are often taken into the self and become part of it; or that aspects or elements of the self may be disowned and attributed to some person or group of persons, or some part of the external world. These common mental processes, plainly seen in both children and adults, in ordinary social life as well as in the consulting room, are "mechanisms", i.e. particular ways in which mental life operates, as a means of dealing with internal tensions and conflicts.

Now these mental mechanisms are intimately related to certain pervasive phantasies. The phantasies of incorporating (devouring, absorbing, etc.) loved and hated objects, persons or parts of persons, into ourselves are amongst the earliest and most deeply unconscious phantasies, fundamentally oral in character since they are the psychic representatives of the oral impulses. Some of these oral phantasies have been described above (pp. 102–104), for exam-ple: "I want to take and I am taking her (mother or breast) into me." The distinction should be kept clear between a specific phantasy of incorporating an object and the general mental mechanism of intro-jection. The latter has a far wider reference than the former, although so intimately related to it. To understand the relationship between phantasies and mechanisms, we must look more closely at the relation of both to instinct. On our view, phantasy is the opera-tive link between instinct and ego mechanism.

An instinct is conceived of as a border-line psycho-somatic process. It has a bodily aim, directed to concrete external objects. It has a representative in the mind which we call a "phantasy". Every human activity derives from some instinct; it is only through the phantasy of what would fulfil our instinctual needs that we are enabled to attempt to realize them in external reality.

Although themselves psychic phenomena, phantasies are primarily about bodily aims, pains and pleasures, directed to objects of some kind. When contrasted with external and bodily realities, the phantasy, like other mental activities, is a figment, since it cannot be touched or handled or seen; yet it is real in the experience of the subject. It is a true mental function and it has real effects, not only in the inner world of the mind but also in the external world of the subject's bodily development and behaviour, and hence of other people's minds and bodies.

We have already touched incidentally upon many examples of the outcome of particular phantasies; for example, in young children, such difficulties as feeding and excretory troubles and phobias; to these could be added so-called "bad habits", tics, tantrums, defiance of authority, lying and thieving, etc., etc. We have spoken also of hysterical conversion symptoms in people of all ages as being the expression of phantasy (1933). Examples are alimentary disturbances, headaches, susceptibility to catarrh, dysmenorrhoea, and many other psycho-somatic changes. But ordinary bodily characteristics, other than illnesses, such as manner and tone of voice in speaking, bodily posture, gait of walking, mode of handshake, facial expression, handwriting and mannerisms generally, also turn out to be determined directly or indirectly by specific phantasies. These are usually highly complex, related both to the internal and the external worlds, and bound up with the psychical history of the individual.

It is noteworthy how often and to what a degree such bodily expressions of individual phantasies may change, whether temporarily or permanently, during the process of analysis. In moments of depression, for instance, the manner of walking and holding the body, the facial expression and voice, the patient's whole bodily response to the physical world as well as to people, will be different from what it is at times of elation, of defiance, of surrender, of determined control of anxiety, etc., etc. These changes during analysis are sometimes quite dramatic.

In outside life, people may have phases of dropping and breaking or losing things, of stumbling and falling, of a tendency to bodily accidents.[22] One has only to look round at people in ordinary life, in the tube train, the bus or restaurant or family life, to see the endless differentiations of bodily characteristics, e.g. mannerisms, individualities and idiosyncrasies in dress and speech, etc., through which dominant phantasies and the emotional states bound up with them are expressed.

Analytic work brings the opportunity to understand what these varied details signify, what particular changing sets of phantasies are at work in the patient's mind—about his own body and its contents, and about other people and his bodily or social relation to them now or in the past. Many such bodily traits become modified and sometimes considerably altered after the analysis of the underlying phantasies.

Similarly, the broader social expressions of character and personality show the potency of phantasies. E.g. people's attitudes to such matters as time and money and possessions, to being late or punctual, to giving or receiving, to leading or following, to being "in the limelight" or content to work among others, and so on and so forth, are always found in analysis to be related to specific sets of varied phantasies, the development of which can be followed out through their various functions of defence in relation to specific situations, back to their origins in primary instinctual sources.

Freud drew attention to a striking example in his study of "The 'exceptions'", where he discussed the interesting character trait exhibited by quite a number of people, that of proclaiming themselves as exceptions and behaving as such—exceptions from any demands made by particular persons, such as members of the patient's family or the physician, or by reality as a whole. Freud refers to Richard III as a supreme example of this, and in his discussion, he penetrated to some of the phantasies lying behind the apparently simple defiance of Richard on account of his deformity. Freud suggests (1915) that Richard's soliloquy[23] is by no means mere defiance, but signifies an unconscious argument (which we should call a phantasy) as follows: "'Nature has done me a grievous wrong in denying me that beauty of form which wins human love. Life owes me reparation for this, and I will see that I get it. I have a right to be an exception, to overstep those bounds by which others let themselves be circumscribed. I may do wrong myself, since wrong has been done to me.'"

An example which may be quoted from the writer's analytic experience is that of an adolescent boy who came to treatment because of serious difficulties in his home and public school life— e.g. very obvious lying of a sort that was certain to be found out, aggressive behaviour, and a wild untidiness in dress. In general the conduct and attitude of this boy of sixteen years of age were entirely out of keeping with his family traditions; they were those of a social outcast. Even when the analysis had brought sufficient improvement for him to join the Air Force, soon after the outbreak of war, he could not follow the normal course of events for those in his social circumstances. He did brilliant work in the Air Force and built up an excellent reputation, but always refused to accept a commission. At the beginning of the analysis he had been lonely and miserable, and entirely without friends. Later he was able to maintain steady friendships, and was very much liked in the sergeants' mess, but was quite unable to live up to the family social traditions, in which there were distinguished officers.

This boy's illness, as always, was determined by many complex causes of external circumstances and internal response. He had a rich phantasy life, but dominant amongst all other of his phantasies was that the only way of overcoming his aggressiveness towards his younger brother (ultimately, his father) was to renounce all ambition in their favour. He felt it impossible for both himself and his younger brother (a normal, gifted and happy person) to be loved and admired by his mother and father. In bodily terms, it was impossible for them both, himself and his younger brother (ulti-mately himself and his father), to be potent; this notion arose in the depths of his mind from the early phantasies of incorporating his father's genital; he felt that if he himself sucked out father's genital from his mother, swallowed it up and possessed it, then the good genital would be destroyed, his younger brother could not have it, would never grow up, never become potent or loving or wise—indeed, never exist! By electing to renounce everything in favour of his younger brother (ultimately, of his father) the boy modified and controlled his aggressive impulses towards both his parents, and his fears of them.

In this boy, many subsidiary internal processes and external circumstances had served to make this particular phantasy domi-nate his life—the notion that there is only one good thing of a kind— *the* good breast, *the* good mother, *the* good father's penis; and if one person has this ideal object, another must suffer its loss, and thus become dangerous to the possessor. This phantasy is widely found, although in most people it becomes modified and counterbalanced during development, so that it plays a far less dominant part in life.

Similarly, Freud brings out that Richard's claim to be an exception is one which we all of us feel, although in most people it becomes corrected and modified or covered up. Freud remarks: "Richard is an enormously magnified representation of something we may all discover in ourselves"[24] (1915C). Our view that phantasy plays a fundamental and continuous part, not only in neurotic symptoms but also in normal character and personality, is thus in agreement with Freud's comments.

To return to the particular problem of the phantasy of incorporation; the mental process or unconscious phantasy of incorporating is described in abstract terms as the process of introjection. As we have seen, whichever it be called, its real psychic effects follow. It is not an actual bodily eating up and swallowing, yet it leads to actual alterations in the ego. These "mere" beliefs about internal objects, such as, e.g. "I have got a good breast inside me", or, it may be: "I have got a bitten-up, torturing bad breast inside me—I must kill it and get rid of it", and the like, lead to real effects: deep emotions, actual behaviour towards external people, profound changes in the ego, character and personality, symptoms, inhibitions and capacities.

Now the relation between such oral phantasies of incorporation and the earliest processes of introjection has been discussed by Freud in his essay on "Negation". Here he not only states that even the intellectual functions of judgment and reality-testing "are derived from the interplay of the *primary instinctual impulses*" (my italics), and rest upon the *mechanism* of introjection (a point to which we shall return shortly): he also shows us the part played in this derivation by *phantasy*. Referring to that aspect of judgment which asserts or denies that a thing has a particular property, Freud says: "Expressed in the language of the oldest, that is, of the oral instinctual impulses, the alternative runs thus: "I should like to take this into me and keep that out of me." That is to say, it is to be either *inside me* or outside me" (1925). The wish thus formulated is the same thing as a phantasy.

What Freud picturesquely calls here "the language of the oral impulse", he elsewhere calls the "mental expression" of an instinct, i.e. the phantasies which are the psychic representatives of a bodily aim. In this actual example, Freud is showing us the phantasy that is the mental equivalent of an instinct. But he is at one and the same

time formulating the subjective aspect of the *mechanism* of introjection (or projection). Thus *phantasy is the link between the id impulse
and the ego mechanism*, the means by which the one is transmuted
into the other. "I want to eat that and therefore I have eaten it" is a
phantasy which represents the id impulse in the psychic life; it is at
the same time the subjective experiencing of the mechanism or
function of introjection.

The problem of how best to describe the process of introjection
related to the phantasy of incorporation is often dealt with by
saying that what *is* introjected is an image or "imago". This is surely
quite correct; but it is too formal and meagre a statement of a
complex phenomenon to do justice to the facts. For one thing, this
describes only the preconscious processes, not the unconscious.

How does anyone—whether psychologist or other person—
come to know this distinction, to realize that what he has actually
"taken inside", his internal object, is an image and not a bodily
concrete object? By a long and complex process of development.
This, in broad outline, must include the following steps, among
others:

(a) The earliest phantasies are built mainly upon oral impulses,
    bound up with taste, smell, touch (of the lips and mouth),
    kinæsthetic, visceral, and other somatic sensations; these are at
    first more closely linked with the experience of "taking things
    in" (sucking and swallowing) than with anything else. The
    visual elements are relatively small.

(b) These sensations (and images) are a bodily experience, at first
    scarcely capable of being related to an external, spatial object.
    (The kinæsthetic, genital and visceral elements are not usually
    so referred.) They give the phantasy a concrete bodily quality, a
    "meness", experienced in the body. On this level, images are
    scarcely if at all distinguishable from actual sensations and
    external perceptions. The skin is not yet felt to be a boundary
    between inner and outer reality.

(c) The visual element in perception slowly increases, becoming
    suffused with tactile experience and spatially differentiated.
    The early visual images remain largely "eidetic" in quality—
    probably up to three or four years of age. They are intensely
    vivid, concrete and often confused with perceptions. Moreover,

they remain for long intimately associated with somatic responses: they are very closely linked with emotions and tend to immediate action. (Many of the details referred to here so summarily have been well worked out by psychologists.)

(d) During the period of development when the visual elements in perception (and in corresponding images) begin to predominate over the somatic, becoming differentiated and spatially integrated, and thus making clearer the distinction between the inner and the outer worlds, the concrete bodily elements in the total experience of perceiving (and phantasying) largely undergo *repression*. The visual, externally referred elements in phantasy become relatively de-emotionalized, de-sexualized, independent, in consciousness, of bodily ties. They become "images" in the narrower sense, representations "in the mind" (but not, consciously, incorporations in the body) of external objects recognized to be such. It is "realized" that the objects are outside the mind, but their images are "in the mind".

(e) Such images, however, draw their power to affect the mind by being "in it", i.e. their influence upon feelings, behaviour, character and personality, upon the mind as a whole, is founded upon *their repressed unconscious somatic associates* in the unconscious whole of wish and phantasy, which *form the link with the id*; and which do mean, in unconscious phantasy, that the objects to which they refer are believed to be inside the body, to be incorporated.

In psycho-analytic thought, we have heard more of *"imago"* than of *image*. The distinctions between an *"imago"* and *"image"* might be summarized as: (a) *"imago"* refers to an *unconscious* image; (b) *"imago"* usually refers to a person or part of a person, the earliest objects, whilst *"image"* may be of any object or situation, human or otherwise; and (c) *"imago"* includes all the somatic and emotional elements in the subject's relation to the imaged person, the bodily links in unconscious phantasy with the id, the phantasy of incorporation which underlies the process of introjection; whereas in the *"image"* the somatic and much of the emotional elements are largely repressed.

If we pay enough attention to the details of the way in which other mental mechanisms operate in the minds of the patients, every variety of mechanism can be seen to be related to specific phantasies or sorts of phantasy. They are always *experienced* as phantasy. For example, the mechanism of *denial* is expressed in the mind of the subject in some such way as: "If I don't admit it (i.e. a painful fact) it isn't true." Or: "If I don't admit it, no one else will know that it is true." And in the last resort this argument can be traced to bodily impulses and phantasies, such as: "If it doesn't come out of my mouth, that shows it isn't inside me"; or "I can prevent anyone else *knowing* it is inside me." Or: "It is all right if it comes out of my anus as flatus or fæces, but it mustn't come out of my mouth as words." The mechanism of *scotomization* is experienced in such terms as: "What I don't see I need not believe"; or "What I don't see, other people don't, and indeed it doesn't exist."

Again, the mechanism of compulsive confession (which many patients indulge in) also implies such unconscious argument as the following: "If I say it, no one else will", or "I can triumph over them by saying it first, or win their love by at least appearing to be a good boy."[25]

In general it can be said that ego mechanisms are all derived ultimately from instincts and innate bodily reactions. "The ego is a differentiated part of the id" (1926).

Phantasy, memory-images and reality

In quoting just now from Freud's essay on "Negation", we noted his view that the intellectual functions of judgment and reality testing "are derived from the interplay of the primary instinctual impulses". If, then, phantasy be the "language" of these primary instinctual impulses, it can be assumed that phantasy enters into the earliest development of the ego in its relation to reality, and supports the testing of reality and the development of knowledge of the external world.[26]

We have already seen that the earliest phantasies are bound up with sensations and affects. These sensations, no matter how selectively over-emphasized they may be under the pressure of affect, bring the experiencing mind into contact with external reality, as well as expressing impulses and wishes.

The external world forces itself upon the attention of the child, in one way or another, early and continuously. The first psychical experiences result from the massive and varied stimuli of birth and the first intake and expulsion of breath—followed presently by the first feed. These considerable experiences during the first twenty-four hours must already evoke the first mental activity, and provide material for both phantasy and memory. Phantasy and reality-testing are both in fact present from the earliest days.[27]

External perceptions begin to influence mental processes at a certain point (actually from birth on, though at first they are not appreciated as external). At first the psyche deals with most external stimuli, as with the instinctual ones, by means of the primitive mechanisms of introjection and projection. Observation of the infant during the first few weeks shows that in so far as the external world does not satisfy our wishes, or frustrates or interferes with us, it is at once hated and rejected. We may then fear it and watch it and attend to it, in order to defend ourselves against it; but not until it is in some degree libidinized through its connections with oral satisfactions and thus receives some measure of love, can it be played with and learnt about and understood.

We conclude with Freud that the disappointingness of hallucinatory satisfaction is the first spur to some degree of adaptation to reality. Hunger is not satisfied by hallucinating the breast, whether as an external or an internal object, although waiting for satisfaction may be made more tolerable by the phantasy. Sooner or later, hallucination breaks down, and a measure of adaptation to real external conditions (e.g. making demands on the external world by crying, seeking movements, restlessness, etc., and by adopting the appropriate posture and movements when the nipple arrives) is turned to instead. Here is the beginning of adjustment to reality and of the development of appropriate skills and of perception of the external world. Disappointment may be the first stimulus to adaptative acceptance of reality, but the postponement of satisfaction and the suspense involved in the complicated learning and thinking about external reality which the child presently accomplishes—and for increasingly remote ends—can only be endured and sustained when it itself satisfies instinctual urges, represented in phantasies, as well. Learning depends upon interest, and interest is derived from desire, curiosity and fear—especially desire and curiosity.

In their developed forms, phantasy thinking and reality thinking are distinct mental processes, different modes of obtaining satisfaction. The fact that they have a distinct character when fully developed, however, does not necessarily imply that reality thinking *operates* quite independently of unconscious phantasy. It is not merely that they "blend and interweave";[28] their relationship is something less adventitious than this. On our view, *reality-thinking cannot operate without concurrent and supporting unconscious phantasies*. E.g. we continue to "take things in" with our ears, to "devour" with our eyes, to "read, mark, learn and inwardly digest", throughout life.

These conscious metaphors represent unconscious psychic reality. It is a familiar fact that all early learning is based upon the oral impulses. The first seeking and mouthing and grasping of the breast is gradually shifted on to other objects, the hand and eye only slowly attaining independence of the mouth, as instruments of exploration and of knowing the outer world.

All through the middle part of his first year, the infant's hand reaches out to everything he sees in order to put it into his mouth, first, to try and eat it, then at least to suck and chew it, and later to feel and explore it. (Only later do his hand and eye become independent of his mouth.) This means that the objects which the infant touches and manipulates and looks at and explores are invested with oral libido. He could not be interested in them if this were not so. If at any stage he were entirely auto-erotic, he could never learn. The instinctual drive towards taking things into his mind through eyes and fingers (and ears, too), towards looking and touching and exploring, satisfies some of the oral wishes frustrated by his original object. Perception and intelligence draw upon this source of libido, for their life and growth. Hand and eye retain an oral significance throughout life, in unconscious phantasy and often, as we have seen, in conscious metaphor.

In her papers "Infant analysis" (1926) and "The importance of symbol formation in the development of the ego" (1930), Mrs Klein took up Ferenczi's view that (primary) identification, which is the forerunner of symbolism, "arises out of the baby's endeavour to rediscover in every object his own organs and their functioning", and also Ernest Jones's view that the pleasure-principle makes it possible for two separate objects to be equated because of an affective bond of interest. She showed, by means of illuminating clinical material, how the primary symbolic function of external objects enables phantasy to be elaborated by the ego, allows sublimations to develop in play and manipulation, and builds a bridge from the inner world to interest in the outer world and knowledge of physical objects and events. His pleasurable interest in his body, his discoveries and experiments in this direction, are clearly shown in the play of an infant of three or four months. In this play he manifests (among other mechanisms) this process of symbol-formation, bound up with those phantasies which we later discover in analysis to have been operating at the time. *The external physical world is in fact libidinized largely through the process of symbol-formation.*

Almost every hour of free association in analytic work reveals to us something of the phantasies which have promoted (mainly through symbol-formation) and sustained the development of interest in the external world and the process of learning about it, and from which the power to seek out and organize knowledge about it is drawn. It is a familiar fact that, from one point of view, every instance of concern with reality, whether practical or theoretical, is also a sublimation[29] (Sharpe, 1935).

This, in its turn, means that *pari passu* some measure of "synthetic function" is exercised upon instinctual urges, from the beginning. The child could not learn, could not adapt to the external world (physical or human) without some sort and degree of control and inhibition, as well as satisfaction, of instinctual urges, progressively developed from birth onwards.

If, then, the intellectual functions are derived from the interplay of the primary instinctual impulses, we need, in order to understand either phantasy or reality-testing and "intelligence", to look at mental life as a whole and to see the relation between these various functions during the whole process of development. To set them apart and say "this is perception and knowledge, but *that* is something quite different and unrelated, that is mere phantasy", would be to miss the *developmental* significance of both functions.[30]

Certain aspects of the nexus between thought and phantasy were discussed in *Intellectual Growth in Young Children*[29] (Brierley, 1944). From direct records of spontaneous make-believe play among a group of children between two and seven years of age, it was possible to show the various ways in which such imaginative play, arising ultimately from unconscious phantasies, wishes and anxieties, creates practical situations which call for knowledge of the external world. These situations may then often be pursued for their own sake, as problems of learning and understanding, and thus lead on to actual discoveries of external fact or to verbal judgment and reasoning. This does not always happen—the play may for periods be purely repetitive; but at any moment a new line of inquiry or argument may flash out, and a new step in understanding be taken by any or all of the children taking part in the play.

In particular, observation made it clear that spontaneous make-believe play creates and fosters the first forms of "as if" thinking. In such play, the child re-creates selectively those elements in past situations which can embody his emotional or intellectual need of the present, and adapts the details moment-by-moment to the present play situation. This ability to evoke the *past* in imaginative play seems to be closely connected with the growth of the power to evoke *the future* in constructive hypothesis, and to develop the consequences of "ifs". The child's make-believe play is thus significant not only for the adaptive and creative intentions which when fully developed mark out the artist, the novelist and the poet, but also for the sense of reality, the scientific attitude, and the growth of hypothetical reasoning.

The argument of this paper may now be summarized:

1. *The concept of phantasy* has gradually widened in psychoanalytic thought. It now requires clarification and explicit expansion in order to integrate all the relevant facts.
2. On the views here developed:
a. Phantasies are the primary content of unconscious mental processes.
b. Unconscious phantasies are primarily about bodies, and represent instinctual aims towards objects.
c. These phantasies are, in the first instance, the psychic representatives of libidinal and destructive instincts; early in development they also become elaborated into defences, as well as wish-fulfilments and anxiety-contents.
d. Freud's postulated "hallucinatory wish-fulfilment" and his "primary introjection" and "projection" are the basis of the phantasy life.
e. Through external experience, phantasies become elaborated and capable of expression, but they do not depend solely upon external experience for their existence.

f.   Phantasies are not dependent upon words, although they may under certain conditions be capable of expression in words.

g.   The earliest phantasies are experienced in sensations; later, they take the form of plastic images and dramatic representations.

h.   Phantasies have both psychic and bodily effects, e.g. in conversion symptoms, bodily qualities, character and personality, neurotic symptoms, inhibitions and sublimations.

i.   Unconscious phantasies form the operative link between *instincts* and *mechanisms*. When studied in detail, every variety of ego-mechanism can be seen to arise from specific sorts of phantasy, which in the last resort have their origin in instinctual impulses. "The ego is a differentiated part of the id." A mechanism is an abstract general term describing certain mental processes which are experienced by the subject as unconscious phantasies.

j.   Adaptation to reality and reality-thinking require the support of concurrent unconscious phantasies. Observation of the ways in which knowledge of the external world develops shows how the child's phantasy contributes to his learning.

k.   Unconscious phantasies exert a continuous influence throughout life, both in normal and neurotic people, the differences lying in the specific character of the dominant phantasies, the desire or anxiety associated with them and their interplay with each other and with external reality.

Notes

1. A chapter from a book in preparation jointly with Paula Heimann, Melanie Klein and Joan Riviere.

2. In a contribution to the British Psycho-Analytic Society in 1943, Dr Ernest Jones commented with regard to this extension of the meaning of "phantasy": "I am reminded of a similar situation years ago with the word 'sexuality'. The critics complained that Freud was changing the meaning of this word, and Freud himself once or twice seemed to assent to this way of putting it, but I always protested that he made no change in the meaning of the word itself: what he did was to extend the conception and, by giving it a fuller content, to make it more comprehensive. This process would seem to be inevitable in psycho-

analytical work, since many conceptions, e.g. that of conscience, which were previously known only in their conscious sense, must be widened when we add to this their unconscious significance."

3. Goodenough (1931) trained her observers to record not merely the frequency and time distribution of temper tantrums, but also the context of social and emotional situations and physiological conditions in which they occurred. In this way, she was able to elucidate, to a degree which had not been done before, the nature of the situations which give rise to temper tantrums in young children.

4. Repeating Watson's work on the subject of innate fears, Valentine paid attention to the total situation in which the child was placed as well as to the precise nature of the stimuli applied. He concluded that the setting is always a highly important factor in determining the particular response of the child to a particular stimulus. It is a *whole situation* which affects the child, not a single stimulus. The presence or absence of the mother, for example, may make all the difference to the child's actual response.

5. Lewis not only made a complete phonetic record of the development of speech in an infant from birth onwards, but also noted the social and emotional situations in which particular speech sounds and speech forms occurred, enabling us to infer some of the emotional sources of the drive to speech development.

6. Lois Barclay Murphy has made a considerable contribution to problems of social development in a series of careful studies of the personalities of young children and their social relationships. She showed that it is useless to attempt either ratings of personality as a whole, or of particular traits such as sympathy, without having constant regard to the context of the behaviour studied. The social behaviour and personal characteristics of young children vary according to the specific social context. For example, one boy is excited and aggressive when another particular boy is present, but not so when that boy is absent. Murphy's work gives us many such glimpses of the feelings and motives which enter into the development of the child's traits of personality. She sums up her study of "sympathetic behaviour" in young children playing in a group: "the behaviour which constitutes this trait is dependent upon the functional relation of the child to each situation, and when shifts in status give a basis for a changed interpretation of the situation in which the child finds himself, changed behaviour occurs. A significant proportion of the variations in a child's behaviour which we have discussed are related to the child's security, as affected by competitive relations with other children, disapproval by adults, or guilt and self-accusation

in relation to injury to another child," thus emphasising that sympathetic behaviour (as one aspect of personality) cannot be understood apart from the variations in the context in which it is shown.

7. Referred to by Joan Riviere in her paper "On the genesis of psychical conflict in earliest infancy".

8. Hazlitt, in her chapter on "Retention, continuity, recognition and memory" says: "The favourite game of 'peep-bo' which the child may enjoy in an appropriate form from about the third month gives proof of the continuity and retentiveness of the mind of the very young child. If impressions died away immediately and the child's conscious life were made up of a number of totally disconnected moments this game could have no charm for him. But we have ample evidence that at one moment he is conscious of the change in experience, and we can see him looking for what has just been present and is now gone."

Hazlitt's whole treatment of these problems takes the line that explicit memory grows out of early recognition—i.e. "any process of perceiving which gives rise to a feeling of familiarity." She goes on: "In speaking of the month-old child's sucking reaction to the sound of the human voice it has not been assumed that the child recognizes the voices, that there is a conscious experience corresponding to the idea "voices again". There may or may not be such conscious experience. . . . As the weeks go by, however, numberless instances of recognition occur in which the child's expression and general behaviour form a picture so like that which accompanies conscious experience of recognition at the later stages that it is difficult to resist the inference that the child is recognizing in the true sense of the word. Records tell of children from eight weeks onwards appearing to be distressed by strange, and reassured by familiar faces."

Hazlitt also takes the view that even judgment is present, e.g. in the child's adaptive responses, in the third and fourth months. Hazlitt has no doubt that the very earliest responses of the infant show the rudimentary qualities from which memory, imagination, thinking, etc., develop. She says: "Another argument for the view here taken that judgment is present from a very early time is that the expression of surprise at stimuli which are not surprising through their intensity, but from being changed in some way from their usual appearance, is quite common by six months and shows itself every now and then much earlier than this."

Another important field in which this law of genetic continuity operates is that of logical relations. Experimental studies of Hazlitt and others have shown that the child can understand and act upon certain logical relations (such as identity, exception, generalization, etc.) long before he can express these relations in words, and he can understand them in simple concrete terms before he can appreciate them in a more abstract form. E.g. he can act upon the words "all . . . but not . . ." when he cannot yet understand the word "except"; again, he can comprehend and act upon "except" before he can use the word himself.

9. E.g.: "There is a most surprising characteristic of unconscious (repressed) processes to which every investigator accustoms himself only by exercising great self-control; it results from their entire disregard of the reality-test; thought-reality is placed on an equality with external actuality, wishes with fulfilment and occurrence. . . . One must, however, never allow oneself to be misled into applying to the repressed creations of the mind the standards of reality; this might result in undervaluing the importance of phantasies in symptomformation on the ground that they are not actualities; or in deriving a neurotic sense of guilt from another source because there is no proof of actual committal of any crime." (Freud: "Formulations regarding the two principles in mental functioning", 1911.) "An abandonment of the over-estimation of the property of consciousness is the indispensable preliminary to any genuine insight into the course of psychic events. . . ." (Freud: *The Interpretation of Dreams*, 1932, p. 562).

10. *The Interpretation of Dreams*, p. 562.

11. *New Introductory Lectures*, p. 98.

12. *The Unconscious*, p. 122.

13. These occasional references by Freud to phantasies in young children, quoted above, are examples of the way in which the intuitive insight of his genius, perforce scientifically unsupported and unexplained at the time, is being confirmed and made intelligible both by the work of certain of his followers, notably M. Klein, and by observations of behaviour.

14. "When the lady drank to the gentleman only with her eyes, and he pledged with his, was there no conversation because there was neither noun nor verb?"—Samuel Butler.

15. "The system Ucs contains the thing-cathexes of the object, the first and true object-cathexes; the system Pcs originates in a hyper-cathexis of this concrete idea by a linking up of it with the verbal ideas of the words corresponding to it. It is such hyper-cathexes, we may suppose, that bring about higher organization in the mind and make it possible for the primary process to be succeeded by the secondary process which dominates Pcs." ("The Unconscious", *Collected Papers*, IV, pp. 133–134, 1915B).

16. Dr Sylvia Payne pointed out this connection in a discussion on this subject at the B.Ps-An.Soc. January 27, 1943.

17. It was said by Dr Clifford Scott, in a contribution to the discussion on this subject at the B.Ps-An.Soc. on January 27, 1943, that the adult way of regarding the body and the mind as two separate sorts of experience can certainly not hold true of the infant's world. It is easier for adults to observe the actual sucking than to remember or understand what the experience of the sucking is to the infant, for whom there is no dichotomy of body and mind, but a single, undifferentiated experience of sucking and phantasying. Even those aspects of psychological experience which we later on distinguish as "sensation", "feeling", etc. cannot in the early days be distinguished and separated. Sensations, feelings, as such, emerge through development from the primary whole of experience, which is that of sucking–sensing–feeling–phantasying. This total experience becomes gradually differentiated into its various aspects of experience: bodily movements, sensations, imaginings, knowings, and so on and so forth.

    We recall that according to Freud, "The ego is first and foremost a body-ego" (1927). As Dr Scott said, we need to know more about what "the body" means in unconscious phantasy, and to consider the various studies made by neurologists and general psychologists of the "body schema". On this view, the unconscious body-schema or "phantasy of the body" plays a great part in many neuroses and in all psychoses, particularly in all forms of hypochondriasis.

18. The aim of oral love is "incorporating or devouring, a type of love which is compatible with abolition of any separate existence on the part of the object".

19. Grasping, touching, looking and other activities can be felt to be disastrously harmful, as well.

20. Scupin records an instance (of his own boy of eleven and a half months) which illustrates the interpretation of an observed reality in terms of phantasy arising from the infant's own primary instinctual life. "When we (his parents) were fighting in fun, he suddenly uttered a wild scream. To try if it was the noise we made that had frightened him, we repeated the scene in silence; the child looked at his father in horror, then stretched his arms out longingly to his mother and snuggled affectionately up against her. It quite gave the impression that the boy believed his mother was being hurt, and his scream was only an expression of sympathetic fear."

    An example of a child in the second year being comforted by ocular proof that his parents were not fighting was noted by a colleague. His boy suffered from frequent attacks of anxiety, the cause of which was not understood, and he could take comfort from neither parent. Their caresses and soothing voices did not relieve his anxiety. But they found, at first by accident, that when he was in these moods, if they kissed *each other* (not him) in his presence, his anxiety was immediately relieved. It is thus to be inferred that the anxiety was connected with his fear of his parents quarrelling, and his phantasy of their intercourse being mutually destructive, the anxiety being relieved and the child reassured by the visible demonstration that they could love each other and be gentle together in his presence.

21. More fully Freud writes: "When I termed one of the psychic processes in the psychic apparatus the *primary* process, I did so not only in consideration of its status and function, but was also able to take account of the temporal relationship actually involved. So far as we know, a psychic apparatus possessing only the primary process does not exist, and is to that extent a theoretical fiction; but this at least is a fact: that the primary processes are present in the apparatus from the beginning, while the secondary processes only take shape gradually during the course of life, inhibiting and overlaying the primary, whilst gaining complete control over them perhaps only in the prime of life. Owing to this belated arrival of the secondary processes, the essence of our being, consisting of unconscious wish-impulses, remains something which cannot be grasped or inhibited by the preconscious; and its part is once and for all restricted to indicating the most appropriate paths for the wish-impulses originating in the unconscious. . . ."

22. "Accident proneness" has long been recognized among industrial psychologists. The well-known superstition that "if you break one thing you're sure to break three before you've finished", is a strong confirmation of the view that such tendencies spring from phantasies.

23.　　　　But I, that am not shaped for sportive tricks,
　　　　Nor made to court an amorous looking-glass;
　　　　I, that am rudely stamp'd, and want love's majesty
　　　　To strut before a wanton ambling nymph;
　　　　I, that am curtail'd of this fair proportion,
　　　　Cheated of feature by dissembling Nature,
　　　　Deform'd, unfinish'd, sent before my time
　　　　Into this breathing world, scarce half made up,
　　　　And that so lamely and unfashionable,
　　　　That dogs bark at me as I halt by them;
　　　　And therefore, since I cannot prove a lover,
　　　　To entertain these fair well-spoken days,

> I am determined to prove a villain,
> And hate the idle pleasure of these days.

24. Freud writes: ". . . now we feel that we ourselves could be like Richard, nay, that we are already a little like him. Richard is an enormously magnified representation of something we can all discover in ourselves. We all think we have reason to reproach nature and our destiny for congenital and infantile disadvantages; we all demand reparation for early wounds in our narcissism, our self-love. Why did not nature give us the golden curls of Balder or the strength of Siegfried or the lofty brow of genius or the noble profile of aristocracy? Why were we born in a middleclass dwelling instead of in a royal palace? We could as well carry off beauty and distinction as any of those whom now we cannot but envy".

25. In the analysis, a great deal of mocking and triumph and intention to defeat the analyst can often be discerned behind the "goodness" of such compulsive confessions.

> He put in his thumb
> And pulled out a plum,
> And said, "What a good boy am I."

26. ". . . one must not take the difference between ego and id in too hard-and-fast a sense, nor forget that the ego is a part of the id which has been specially modified." (*The Ego and the Id*, 1927, pp. 51–52). Again, ". . . originally, of course, everything was id; the ego was developed out of the id by the continual influence of the external world. In the course of this slow development certain material in the id was transformed into the preconscious state and was thus taken into the ego." ("Outline of psycho-analysis", *International Journal of Psycho-Analysis* (1940e), *21*, p. 43.)

27. An appreciation of what external facts, e.g. the way he is fed and handled in the very beginning, and later the emotional attitudes and conduct of both his parents, or his actual experience of loss or change, *mean* to the child in terms of his phantasy life gives a greater weight to real experiences than would usually be accorded by those who have no understanding of their phantasy value to the child. Such actual experiences in early life have a profound effect upon the character of his phantasies as they develop, and therefore upon their ultimate outcome in his personality, social relationships, intellectual gifts or inhibitions, neurotic symptoms, etc.

28. As Dr Brierley once put it: "phantasy thinking . . . and reality thinking constantly blend and interweave in the patterns of current mental activity"—in adults as well as children.

W. Stern too has written at length (although in reference to the child's conscious fantasies) of "this mutual, intimate intermingling of reality and imagination", which he says is "a fundamental fact" (*Psychology of Early Childhood*, 1930, p. 277, London: George Allen and Unwin).

29. See e.g. E. F. Sharpe's paper on "Similar and divergent unconscious determinants underlying the sublimations of pure art and pure science" (*International Journal of Psycho-Analysis*, 1935, *16*, Part 2).

30. Dr Brierley has written: ". . . the existence of 'internalized object' phantasies would not contravene the memory-trace hypothesis since memories and phantasies have a common trace origin. All images are memory-images, re-activations of past experience. It was suggested that, artificially simplified, the concept of an 'internalized good object' is the concept of an unconscious phantasy gratifying the wish for the constant presence of the mother in the form of a belief that she is literally inside the child. Such an unconscious phantasy would help the child to retain conscious memory of its mother during temporary absences though it might fail to bridge a prolonged absence. A two-year-old child's memory of its mother will not be a simple system but the resultant of two years of life with her. The conscious memory will be the accessible part of a far more extensive unconscious mother-system having its roots in earliest infancy".

References

Baldwin, J. M. (1911). *Genetic Logic*. George Allen.

Bayley, N. (1936). *The California Infant Scale of Motor Development*. University of California Press.

Brierley, M. (1944). Notes on metapsychology as process theory. *International Journal of Psychoanalysis*, 25: 97–106.

Freud, S. (1911). Formulations regarding the two principles in mental functioning. *Collected Papers* 4: 14. London: Hogarth.

Freud, S. (1915A). Instincts and their vicissitudes. *Collected Papers* 4: 78.

Freud, S. (1915B). The unconscious. *Collected Papers* 4: 133–134.

Freud, S. (1915C). Some character types met with in psycho-analytic work. *Collected Papers* 4: 318–344.

Freud, S. (1922). *Beyond the Pleasure Principle*, pp. 11–13. The International Psycho-Analytical Press.

Freud, S. (1925). Negation. *International Journal of Psychoanalysis*. 6: 369.

Freud, S. (1927). *The Ego and the Id*. London: Hogarth.

Freud, S. (1932). *The Interpretation of Dreams*, revised English translation. George Allen and Unwin.

Freud, S. (1933). *New Introductory Lectures on Psycho-Analysis*. London: Hogarth.

Freud, S. (1940e). Outline of psycho-analysis. *International Journal of Psychoanalysis*, 21: 43.

Gesell, A. (1928). *Infancy and Human Growth*. MacMillan.

Gesell, A. (1939). *Biographies of Child Development*. Hamish Hamilton.

Gesell, A. (1940). *The First Five Years of Life*. Methuen.

Goodenough, F. (1931). *Anger in Young Children*. University of Minnesota Press.

Hazlitt, V. (1933). *The Psychology of Infancy*, p. 78. Methuen.

Hazlitt, V. (1930). Children's thinking. *British Journal of Psychology, 20*.

Isaacs, S. (1930). *Intellectual Growth in Young Children*, pp. 99–106. Routledge & Kegan Paul.

Klein, M. (1926). Infant analysis. *International Journal of Psychoanalysis, 7*: 31–63.

Klein, M. (1930). The importance of symbol formation in the development of the ego. *International Journal of Psychoanalysis, 11*: 24–39.

Klein, M. (1932). *The Psycho-Analysis of Children*. London: Hogarth Press.

Klein, M. (1948). *Contributions to Psycho-Analysis 1921–1945*. London: Hogarth Press.

Lewis, M. M. (1936). *Infant Speech*. Kegan Paul.

Lewis, M. M. (1937). The beginning of reference to past and future in a child's speech. *British Journal of Educational Psychology, 7*.

Lewis, M. M. (1938). The beginning and early functions of questions in a child's speech. *British Journal of Educational Psychology, 8*.

Middlemore, M. P. (1941). *The Nursing Couple*. Hamish Hamilton.

Murphy, L. B. (1937). *Social Behaviour and Child Personality*, p. 191. Columbia University Press.

Riviere, J. (1936). On the genesis of psychical conflict in earliest infancy. *International Journal of Psychoanalysis, 17*: 395–422.

Sharpe, E. F. (1935). Similar and divergent unconscious determinants underlying the sublimations of pure art and pure science. *International Journal of Psychoanalysis, 16*: 186–202.

Shirley, M. (1933). *The First Two Years 1, 2, 3*. (A study of the development of twenty-five normal children.) University of Minnesota Press.

Valentine, C. W. (1930). The innate bases of fear. *Journal of Genetic Psychology, 37.*

Winnicott, D. W. (1941). The observation of infants in a set situation. *International Journal of Psychoanalysis, 22:* 229–249.

PART III
THE INDEPENDENT GROUP

Introduction

The Independent group

One feature of the Journal in the latter part of the 1940s was that it provided a platform for the expression of diverse opinions. In this sense, the Journal followed the development occurring specifically in the British Psychoanalytical Society. No doubt the openness to divergence gave rise to caution within American psychoanalysis, which was moving rapidly towards the hegemony of ego-psychology, and caution too among the psychoanalytic societies in Europe re-emerging after the war, who were picking up threads from the 1930s.

In the British Society, however, the enduring impact of child psychoanalysis has continued to point the psychoanalytic finger towards the earliest states of the ego. A number of analysts, including Balint, with his inheritance from Ferenczi, were exploring the possibility of object-relations from birth. Isaacs' paper included in this volume is the Kleinian version of this trend. But there were others whose papers stand out—Ronald Fairbairn, Donald Winnicott, and John Bowlby, who have each bequeathed descendants a coherent account of their ideas.

Some of this was based on empirical observation, as with Winnicott and Bowlby, who observed young children and infants. Balint's views were derived from adult analyses and the experience of Ferenczi. Fairbairn's approach was more systematic, and more challenging of the path that psychoanalysis had been following in the 1920s and 1930s. Altogether this group of people formed a middle group of analysts, freed from coercive allegiances to Freud or to Klein. Of an independent frame of mind, they could explore psychoanalysis independently and formed eventually the Independent group (Raynor, 1991). This "political" development of a separate group began in the late 1940s as an informal alliance of these independent figures.

The outcome of the Controversial Discussions was to accept the divisions between Melanie Klein and her group (reduced then to half a dozen of her followers), and the group of classical analysts, emigrés from Vienna, who clustered around Anna Freud. The majority of the British analysts did not want to take one or other of the two sides, and they opted to form a "buffer-state", as it were, in the middle. Gradually, by the end of the decade they had formed a group in their own right. Most of the Independent group had been influenced by Klein during the 1930s. Prominent in this group was Sylvia Payne, President of the Society after Jones, during this formative period. Michael Balint's was a different tradition, but fitted well with the climate of the British analysts who were forging their independence from the classical tradition (as well as from Klein).[1]

This is the decade when their "manifestos" were appearing in the Journal. The papers are strongly committed to a psychoanalytic understanding of the earliest stages of ego development. They assert the existence of object-relations from the beginning, and thus the ego is a subject also from the beginning. Around this time, there was a great deal of interest in the early condition of the ego, including Freud's posthumous paper on splitting of the ego (see also Fenichel, 1938; Glover, 1943).

Note

1. Edward Glover, a towering figure in British psychoanalysis, never belonged to this group, though his independent spirit might have drawn him there (e.g. Baudry, 1998; Roazen, 2002).

References

Baudry, F. (1998). Kohut and Glover: The role of subjectivity in psycho-analytic theory and controversy. *Psychoanalytic Study of the Child, 53*: 3–24.

Fenichel, O. (1938). Problems of psychoanalytic technique. *Psychoanalytic Quarterly, 7*: 421–442.

Glover, E. (1943). The concept of dissociation. *International Journal of Psychoanalysis, 24*: 7–13.

Raynor, E. (1991). *The Independent Mind in British Psychoanalysis*. London: Free Association Books.

Roazen, P. (2002). *Oedipus in Britain: Edward Glover and the Struggle over Klein*. New York: The Other Press.

Michael Balint's reclamation of Ferenczi [Balint, M. (1949). Early developmental states of the ego: primary object love. *International Journal of Psychoanalysis, 30*: 265–272]

In the fourth part of the Journal in 1949, there was an appreciation of the life and work of Sandor Ferenczi, by Michael Balint (1949). This introduced several papers which the Journal translated and published: two by Ferenczi ("Psychoanalysis and education", 1908, and "Confusion of tongues between adults and the child", 1933) as well as some notes and fragments from two to three years before he died, in 1933, and some of his letters to Freud; then a series of three papers, by Balint and two colleagues, on object-relations at the earliest stage of life. These were by Alice Balint[1] "Love for the mother and mother-love", which was originally published in German in 1939, Endre Petö, "Infant and mother—observations on object-relations in early infancy", originally published in German in 1937, Michael Balint, "Early developmental states of the ego, primary object love", originally published in German in 1937. All this material is a kind of resumé of the work of Hungarian analysts that was interrupted during the Nazi period. It is also a statement of the developments in the Hungarian group after Ferenczi (Harmat, 1987), and before the emigration to Britain.

The crucial paper is Ferenczi's, "Confusion of tongues between adults and the child", and it was clearly seen as inspirational by

Balint. It was written in 1933,[2] and its subtitle "The language of tenderness and passion" is a cue for Balint's own paper ("Early developmental states of the ego: primary object love"). It is selected for the present volume as it summarizes the work of the Hungarians that Balint was re-establishing in Britain. This symposium appears as a statement for resurrecting the Hungarian school in Britain; and the project is an argument for object-relations from the beginning. He draws on colleagues' work (Alice Balint and Imre Hermann), to point out a trajectory originally anticipated by Ferenczi. There is clearly an attempt to keep something alive, the memory of the work with Ferenczi, the memory of his first wife, perhaps, and the work with his colleagues, Imre Hermann and Endre Petö, who stayed in Hungary.[3]

Balint's method is based on genetic continuity, so frequently resorted to at this period, in which he extrapolates back, as did Freud, to the early moments of the ego. Writing this in 1937, he contrasts the work of the London school, exemplified by Joan Riviere's "exchange lecture" (1936), and Robert Wälder's (1937) response. He found both sides of this debate limited in their views of primary narcissism, which he attempted to resolve by his account of primary object love from the beginning. He noticed the uprush of fury on occasions with these patients, and attributed it to the effect of the impassive blank-screen analyst.

His arguments are elegant, and supported by the comparative psychology (now known as ethology) of Imre Hermann (1936) and the comparative pedagogics (ethnology) of Alice Balint (1937). His own results of the genetic method were, he believed, superior to those of the British and the Viennese. He traced all this work back to roots in Ferenczi (1913, 1933).

With this clutch of papers, Balint restored Ferenczi to mainstream psychoanalysis (Haynal, 1988), though the process has taken until the demise of the Soviet domination of Hungary to come to full international recognition. The work in the late 1930s, which spills over into the 1940s decade, was a platform, a statement of the enduring influence of Ferenczi in the form of the Hungarian and British followers.

Notes

1. Michael Balint's first wife, Alice, died in 1939 shortly after they sought exile in Manchester in Britain, after Hungary's alliance to Nazi Germany in 1938, resulting in the institution of legalized anti-semitism.
2. Although not published in the Journal until 1949, Ferenczi's paper will appear in the 1930s book in our series.
3. Both survived the Nazi period.

References

Balint, A. (1949)[1937]. Love for the mother and mother-love. *International Journal of Psychoanalysis*, 30: 251–259.

Ferenczi, S. (1949)[1908]. Psychoanalysis and education. *International Journal of Psychoanalysis*, 30: 220–224.

Ferenczi, S. (1913). Stages in the development of reality. In: *Sandor Ferenczi, First Contributions to Psychoanalysis* [reprinted London: Hogarth, 1952].

Ferenczi, S. (1949)[1933]. Confusion of tongues between adults and the child. *International Journal of Psychoanalysis*.

Harmat, E. (1987). Zsófia Dénes on Freud. *International Review of Psychoanalysis*, 14: 163–167.

Haynal, A. (1988). *The Technique at Issue*. London: Karnac.

Hermann, I. (1936). Sich-Anklammern—Auf-Suche-Gehen. *Int. Z. f. Psa.*, 22: 349–370.

Petö, E. (1949). Infant and mother--observations on object-relations in early infancy. *International Journal of Psychoanalysis*, 30: 260–264.

Riviere, J. (1936). On the genesis of psychical conflict in earliest infancy. *International Journal of Psychoanalysis*, 17: 395–422.

Wälder, R. (1937). The problem of the genesis of psychical conflict in earliest infancy--remarks on a paper by Joan Riviere. *International Journal of Psychoanalysis*, 18: 406–473.

Ronald Fairbairn [Fairbairn, W. R. D. (1944). Endopsychic structure considered in terms of object-relationships. *International Journal of Psychoanalysis, 25*: 70–92]

The paper of Fairbairn's selected for this book (Fairbairn, 1944) summarized his revision of classical libido theory. He examines what changes are necessary if one abandons the economic model and regards impulses as primarily energy to give dynamic charge to structure. He elaborated on a paper where he previously tackled this question (Fairbairn, 1941), and reached a statement that is emblematic of another strand in the group of Independents in the British Psychoanalytical Society.

Fairbairn starts by pointing out that Freud never revised his energy theory after he had moved over to a structural model of the mind in 1923. What would such a revision look like? Fairbairn set out to answer that question, and described a number of far-reaching conclusions. He saw how interpretations, made on the basis of impulses, release a flood of oral-sadistic phantasies.[1] Therefore Fairbairn argued that interpretation of objects had more success. In particular, he advised a return to Freud's early work on hysterics, from which he believed Freud, Abraham, and Klein had all subsequently diverged, concentrating on depressive states. In contrast, Fairbairn argued the need to go back to the splitting that was at the root of hysteria and also schizoid states, including schizophrenia. He made a clear distinction between a depressive phase and an early and more fundamental schizoid phase, anticipating Klein's exposition of the two "positions", depressive and paranoid–schizoid in 1946 (see below).

Fairbairn described splitting, citing a patient who could talk easily about himself as if a "recording agent" of his own phantasies. This is a defence enabling the patient to evade the problems of realizing his phantasies and impulses in reality.[2] These patients, more difficult to approach with a traditional technique, seemed to have become a focus of more attention around this time and to have generated a lot of interest, treatment difficulties, and adaptation of technique ever since. The ego, split between two parts, relates to itself, and presents to view the beginnings of a world of internal relationships. Although Fairbairn related this to the super-ego–ego relationship, he believed that his descriptions underlay Freud's structural model. The triggering situation for the kinds of splitting that he went on to describe is the relationship with a frustrating external object, mother's breast initially. This underlying set of phenomena he believed arose out of problems with object-relations. He described impulse-driven behaviour as a retreat from the ambivalent problems of object-relations, and it is expressed in directionless discharge.

Instead of Freud's structural model, Fairbairn's is an object-relational structure in which (i) the id is a part of the ego, and the ego is not emergent from the id; (ii) an impulse is the energy that charges up a structure within the ego; (iii) the ego relates to objects, but because of the splitting involved in the early defences, the ego can relate to itself, one part to another; (iv) the core problem is one of ambivalent dependence, and not the Oedipus complex; (v) the super-ego is a secondary structure that arises from the hatred that the central ego feels for the split-off needy ego (called the "libidinal ego"); (vi) a new theory of dreams is implied, in which a dream is a snapshot of the internal relations, not the expression of wish-fulfilment, and consequently all figures in a dream represent either parts of the ego, or internal objects related to those parts; (vii) objects and parts of the ego are repressed, impulses are not.

These many results arise, on the whole, deductively in Fairbairn's attempts to improve the coherence and consistency of theory. He tried to bring psychoanalysis up-to-date following Freud's move to a structural model of the mind. His theory is not primarily to make sense of empirically found observations. To a degree, he writes as if he is providing the theory to Klein's observations. However, there are novel ideas of his own; not least is his interpretation of splitting in which different aspects (perhaps functions) of the ego separate from each other but continue in an interrelation; this contrasts with Freud and, especially, Klein, who viewed splitting of the ego as a process in which the subsequent parts do not relate to each other. Fairbairn's complex pattern of intrapsychic (endopsychic, in his terms) structure is then described in aetiological detail. In fact, this paper is a full summary of his mature theory, expressed succinctly but clearly, making this a sort of manifesto that warrants its inclusion here.

Notes

1   Fairbairn is interested in exactly the same phenomenon as Balint's description of similar eruption of violent and sadistic phantasies (see above). In Balint's account, above, this is a result of the analyst's rule of abstinence.

2. Despite the strong echoes of Deutsch's descriptions of the as-if personality, which she was evolving also in the early 1940s (Deutsch, 1942), it is unlikely Fairbairn was influenced by her account.

References

Deutsch, H. (1942). Some forms of emotional disturbance and their rela-
tionship to schizophrenia. *Psychoanalytic Quarterly*, 11: 301–321.
Fairbairn, R. (1941). A revised psychopathology of the psychoses and
psychoneuroses. *International Journal of Psychoanalysis*, 22: 250–279.
Freud, S. (1923). The ego and the id. *S.E., 19*.
Klein, M. (1946). Notes on some schizoid mechanisms. *International
Journal of Psychoanalysis*, 27: 99–110. Reprinted in *The Writings of
Melanie Klein, Volume 3*. London: Hogarth.

Donald Winnicott [Winnicott, D. W. (1945). Primitive emotional
development. *International Journal of Psychoanalysis, 26*: 137–143]

Like Fairbairn, Winnicott a year later (1945) produced his own
outline statement on the earliest phases of ego development. This
paper on primitive emotional states is more empirical, starting with
the observation that there is a palpable change in an infant around
the age of five–six months. At that developmental point there
occurs the experience of having an inside. In parallel is the experience of mother having an inside as well, understanding she has
feelings and moods.[1] The infant develops a concern, as Winnicott
had learned from Klein's depressive position. However, he is interested in the earlier (primitive) emotional period before the change
at six months. Unlike Fairbairn, writing the year before, or Klein a
year after, Winnicott sticks with the depressive position, and argues
that his views are an extension of the Kleinian theory.

His psychology of this earlier phase involves three primary
processes: first, the integration of an ego that is unintegrated at
the outset, upon which, second, the development of a sense of
person, and third, an increasing appreciation of reality (particularly
mother). The first of these processes, the primary unintegration
(contrasted with secondary disintegration), touches on that issue
which Fairbairn and Balint (also Klein) also focused on—the earliest state of the ego. His second process is the sense of person,
and this was later developed in relation to the psychotic's existen-
tial problems as the "continuity of being" (Winnicott, 1962). And
his third process, the dawning reality principle, is a statement
that nearly a decade later (Winnicott, 1953) became his theory of
transitional objects.

Winnicott avoided the temptation of merely making theory. He was steadfastly empiricist in making observations on which his theories could rest,[2] and that could punch holes in his new theories. He is suitably hesitant, and at many points asked for more research. Winnicott's experience was culled from years of consultation work with children and their parents (mother), as well as an attempt at therapy with psychotic patients. He is unapologetic about observation that does not come from the formal and rigorous psychoanalytic setting. He calls for more observational research of this psychoanalytically inspired kind. Like the papers by Balint and Fairbairn, Winnicott here lays out a programme for developing psychoanalytic ideas that have become fused with his name. In a number of respects, therefore, the paper is premonitory of many psychoanalytic developments that will evolve in nearly sixty years since this paper was first published.

Notes

1. This is now termed "mentalization" (Fonagy et al., 2002), rediscovered as it were fifty years later.
2. In fact, another paper—see below.

References

Fonagy, P., Gergely, G., Jurisst, E., & Target, M. (2002). *Affect Regulation, Mentalization, and the Development of the Self*. New York: The Other Press.

Winnicott, D. W. (1953). Transitional objects and transitional phenomena--a study of the first not-me possession. *International Journal of Psychoanalysis, 34*: 89–97.

Winnicott, D. W. (1962). The theory of the parent–infant relationship. *International Journal of Psychoanalysis, 43*: 238–239.

Early developmental states of the ego: primary object love[1]*

Michael Balint

The genetic approach is the principal method we use in our science of psycho-analysis; a mental phenomenon observed in the present is explained by tracing it back to a previous one and by demonstrating how far and by what external and internal influences the previous process was changed into the present one. This crab-like thinking must, however, come to a halt somewhere, i.e. where the previous earlier phenomenon, the original one can no longer be observed but must be inferred from what can be observed. In the early years of psycho-analysis theoretical research reached as far as the Oedipus situation, i.e. to the third to fifth year of life. The theoretical gains thus achieved led to greater power of observation and in turn the better trained observers could verify all the theoretical assumptions.

Naturally research has not come to a standstill and time and again attempts have been made to infer still earlier mental states from observations. This new situation, however, is utterly different from the previous one. Then only one theory, or more correctly, two

* [Reproduced, with permission, from: *International Journal of Psychoanalysis*, 1949, 30: 265–273 © Institute of Psychoanalysis, London, UK]

complementary theories—that of the classic Oedipus situation and that of the polymorph-perverse nature of infantile sexuality—stood to discussion, today we have to deal with several theories, often contradicting one another. Slight differences in theoretical constructions are understandable but we hear and read of theories which diverge considerably and are often diametrically opposite. These differences somehow seem to depend on geography in a way that one is justified in speaking of regional opinions. Probably each one of us will protest against this submerging of his ideas in a regional opinion and will quote sharp controversies within his own group; still the results of his work appear to a distant observer as one or more notes in a regional harmony. Such "regional"—not quite identical but consonant—opinions have been formed during the last years[2] in London, in Vienna and in Budapest.

The word "opinion" is used here intentionally. We must not forget that we are arguing here about theoretical constructions. For we all agree that the earliest state of the human mind is not essentially different in London from what it is in Vienna or in Budapest. Those unpleasantly diverging opinions originate very likely from the fact that the various research workers start from different points of observation and use somewhat different terms. In this paper I shall try to trace back the differences in the theoretical constructions to the different points of view, the different expectations and the different terms used. This, however, does not mean that each point of view and each terminology is equally advantageous. On the contrary, I wish to show that some points of view are linked with certain disadvantages.

I have said that the material from which we have come to such dissimilar conclusions is the same for all of us. To start with I have to choose a description of the infantile mind which will be acceptable to everyone. We need for this purpose a reliable observer who at the same time must be a precise reporter. I quote him (Freud, 1932): "Childish love knows no bounds, it demands exclusive possession, is satisfied with nothing less than all. But it has a second characteristic: It has, besides, no real aim; it is incapable of complete satisfaction and this is the principal reason why it is doomed to end in disappointment and to give place to a hostile attitude" (p. 286). Hence the reproach: "that the mother gave the child too little milk and did not suckle her long enough. Under the conditions of modern civilization this may very often be quite true, but certainly not so often as is maintained in analysis. It would seem rather that this complaint expresses the general dissatisfaction of children . . . as if our children remained for ever unappeased, as if they had never been suckled long enough." "So great is the greed of the childish libido" (pp. 288–289). "In the first phases of the love life ambivalence is evidently the rule" (p. 289). And further: "Those first impulses of libido have an intensity of their own which is greater than anything that comes later and may indeed be said to be incommensurable with any other force" (p. 296). This description by Freud will be acceptable to all of us; it gives only the facts without any theoretical evaluation or attempted explanation.

The Londoners will certainly see in this description nothing but a confirmation of their opinion. The described features of the infant's mental life, such as extravagance, hostility, general discontent, insatiable greed, obvious ambivalence, etc., are the phenomena always emphasized by them. Thus Joan Riviere started her representative lecture in Vienna with the sentence: "My object in this paper is to attempt a short general formulation of the earliest psychical developmental processes in the child, i.e. of the problems of oral sadistic impulses and their attendant anxieties . . ." (Riviere, 1936, p. 395). According to the Londoners: "The baby's mental life in its first weeks is narcissistic in character . . ." (p. 397). Further they assume "that oral and cannibalistic impulses . . . are formed during the actual exercise of the oral function as an object relation"[3] (p. 396). This development has two sources. Sadistic instinctual impulses may arise spontaneously, i.e. without the influence of the external world, as manifestations of the death instinct turned outside. These impulses use above all but not exclusively the oral zone; in addition the muscles, the eyes, breathing, the excretory function, etc., also come into their service. The second—also unavoidable—source of these sadistic impulses is the delaying of gratification. Such a delay causes the child to experience the increased tension as a "traumatic situation" in Freud's sense; he is compelled to give up gradually the security of his narcissistic omnipotence, feels helpless and powerless, at the mercy of evil powers and reacts to all this with hate and aggressiveness. These affects are, either from the very beginning or very soon after, directed towards objects as well as towards the self; as they are intolerable to the weak and undeveloped ego, they are felt as originating from the objects, they are projected on to them. Thus a kind of paranoia (*l.c.* 405) develops, the infant becomes over-sensitive and reacts vehemently to all—however little or unimportant—signs of a negative, careless, or only indifferent, attitude in his environment, everywhere and in everything he sees bad objects. These bad objects engender fear in the infant who then will be afraid of their vengeance. But: "guilt and remorse will also be present to some extent along with these persecutory feelings and will greatly increase the conflict of ambivalence" (*l.c.* 405).[4] Here the struggle begins between the earlier aggressive and the somewhat later developing impulses of tender love which, however, are ultimately based on the original acquisitive impulses with all their tendencies to greed and sadism. Both forms of "love" employ the mechanisms of introjection and projection (as also does hate); mental content in the earliest months consists mainly of phantasies of various physical methods of absorbing, or of expelling (or restoring) good and bad objects (i.e. good and bad aspects of the original object split into two); in addition all other defensive mechanisms, including repression, are already at work in the first months of life. (M. Schmideberg, quoted by Riviere, *l.c.*, p. 398). Two important tendencies are to be mentioned here: the one is an almost spastic effort to keep apart the good objects from the bad ones for fear the good helpful ones might be destroyed by the bad ones; the other is the tendency to repair the effects of one's own sadistic impulses, to change the bad and therefore maltreated objects into good ones.

The subsequent development need not concern us here. I now wish to sum up the most important suppositions which are fundamental for the English point of view: (1) The infant is born in the state of primary narcissism. (2) Vehement sadistic and aggressive impulses appear very early; it remains undecided how much of them is attributable to the archaic death instinct turned towards the external world, and how much to the reactions of hatred caused by the influence of the environment. It seems, however, that the loving impulses appear later and are weaker. (3) The Londoners seem to be uncertain as to when and how reality testing begins;[5] the uncertainty is so great that authors occasionally contradict each other. One instance may be quoted here: J. Riviere reminds us to "keep in mind that this narcissistic world of the psyche is . . . entirely autistic, not only lacking in objectivity, but at first without objects." In the following sentence, however, Glover is quoted who "has empha-sized that even babies have a sense of reality of a kind" (*l.c.*, pp.398–399). (4) Further it is assumed that the infant deals with his primary experiences above all with the help of introjection and projection.

Here the Viennese criticism begins. I am in the fortunate posi-tion—as I was with regard to London—to be able to quote a repre-sentative paper of this school, and so to be very brief Wälder doubts the ubiquity and intensity of the oral sadistic manifestations as described by the Londoners and consequently the validity of the conclusions which were arrived at by generalization from these alleged observations (Wälder, 1937). Further, he criticizes the inex-act, unorthodox use of the concepts of introjection and projection as causing confusion. Equally confusing according to him is the way in which the Londoners describe phantasy and reality, or perhaps more correctly, external and psychic reality. Finally he doubts whether the experiences of the very first developmental stages of the human mind can ever be consciously recollected and even less expressed in words.

Although these objections are very weighty and Wälder's argu-mentation appears to be convincing, the problem remains entire. If one abandons the Londoners' point of view and accepts the Vien-nese, one remains perplexed in face of the infantile phenomena as described by Freud. Why are infants so extravagant, greedy, insati-able, why does hostility appear unavoidably, whence the reproach that mother never fed them rightly, never treated them lovingly? We cannot side with Wälder, i.e. the Viennese without having first found some explanation for the infantile phenomena described by Freud. For it must be admitted, if one accepts the Londoner's assumptions, all these phenomena, observed by all of us, can be explained easily.

The situation is very embarrassing: on the one hand we have a theory which can make understandable very many of the most important phenomena of the infantile mind, the fundamental assumptions of which, however, can hardly stand up to a perfectly justified criticism; on the other hand we have a criticism the conclu-sions of which can hardly be contradicted, but which can teach us almost nothing about the field we are interested in.

The obvious conclusion is that the present material is insuffi-cient to allow of a decision in this issue of paramount importance.

But where can we find new material? I have mentioned that according to Wälder it is hardly to be expected that the experiences of the very early age can ever be recollected consciously. But it is at least equally certain that the experiences of this time are of paramount importance and essentially influence the whole later life of the individual. On this we all agree; but the question arises how one can get reliable data about these experiences. In principle there are—as emphasized by Wälder—two possible ways: direct observation of the infant and reconstruction of infantile behaviour from the data of adult life. If I understood Wälder rightly, the difficulties of a reliable verification of any assumptions are so great that the Viennese consider any assumption in this field with extreme scepticism.

This brings me to Budapest. We have, only recently, it is true, become[6] somewhat less sceptical on this point. Three different trains of thought, independently begun from different angles of approach, have recently led A. Balint, I. Hermann and myself to such converging conclusions that we are practically convinced at least to be going in the right direction. The common principal stimulus to our trains of thought can be traced back to Ferenczi[7] and behind him to Freud. Our common starting point was to consider the formal elements of the analytical situation, more than hitherto customary, as phenomena of transference, hoping that in this way we might obtain valuable data about the individual history of our patients. This hope has been realized; we have even found more, namely that certain features of the analytical situation appear monotonously in every treatment, nay, that they can be observed more and more clearly and frequently as, in the process of analysis, the patient becomes liberated from the defensive mechanisms that he can remember having acquired. Thus we have come to the conclusion that these ever occurring features must be considered as general human quality. There remained, however, to be decided whether these features are determined by the biological nature of man or are precipitates of the earliest psychic experiences.

Independently from each other and without having formulated it explicitly all three of us have chosen the latter of these possibilities as a working hypothesis. We have asked ourselves *how much of these observable, monotonously recurring features of the analytical situation can be traced back to early infantile experiences,* or more correctly *how much of the early infantile mental processes can be inferred from these easily veri-*

fiable observations. We have, in addition, tried to support our conclusions by further material. Here each of us went a different way. Hermann's second source of material was comparative psychology, above all the study of the primates; Alice Balint's a just developing science, comparative pedagogics, while I collected data from the theory of sexuality.

I wish to review the results briefly and shall start with my own investigations.[8] I found that at times, when the analytic work had advanced fairly deeply, my patients expected and often even demanded certain primitive gratifications mainly from their analyst, but also from their environment. If I kept strictly to the rule of analytic passivity, i.e. if these desires for gratification were frustrated automatically by my passivity, phenomena appeared which corresponded in all their essential features to the conception of the infant as put forward by the London analysts. Loss of security, the feeling of being worthless, despair, deeply bitter disappointment, the feeling that one would never be able to trust anyone, etc. Mixed with these came most venomous aggression, wildest sadistic phantasies and orgies depicting the most cunning tortures and humiliations for the analyst. Then again fear of retaliation, the most complete contriteness, because one had spoilt for ever the hope of being loved by the analyst or even merely to be treated by him with interest and kindness; never more could one expect to deserve a good word from him.

If, however—warned by the experiences I have quoted—I later tolerated the satisfaction of those modest wishes we simply went from the frying pan into the fire. An almost manic state broke out. The patients became overblissful; they wanted nothing but to experience again and again the satisfaction of these wishes. All the symptoms disappeared; the patients felt super-healthy as long as they felt secure of obtaining immediately on demand the satisfaction of those extremely important wishes; at such times it was very difficult indeed to keep them at the analytical work. This state very closely resembles that of an addiction or of a severe perversion, even in its lability. At the first serious dissatisfaction or considerable delay of the gratification the whole structure of this enraptured blissfulness breaks down and abruptly the mood changes into the form described previously of despair, hatred and fear of retaliation.

Let us go one step further. What are these dangerous wishes in reality? Rather innocent, naïve one would say. A kind word from the analyst, the permission to call him by his first name or be called by him by one's first name; to be able to see him also outside the analytical session, to borrow something or to get a present from him, even if it be quite insignificant, etc. Very often these wishes do not go further than to be able to touch the analyst, to cling to him, or to be touched or stroked by him. (The latter will lead us into the field of the phenomena of clinging about which more later.)

I must confess that it took me a long time to notice two essential qualities of these wishes. Firstly *without exception they are directed towards an object*, and secondly *they never go beyond the level of fore-pleasure*. That means: firstly, that it is only the external world, the environment that can satisfy them; autoerotic narcissistic satisfaction is never sufficient. Secondly: if the satisfaction arrives at the right moment, and with the right intensity, it causes reactions that are observable only with difficulty because the experience of gratification happens so quietly. Properly this feeling of pleasure could be described as a *tranquil quiet sense of well-being*. If, however, these wishes must remain unsatisfied, their gratification will be demanded very vehemently and an eventual frustration will call forth the most stormy reactions.

Now at last I could explain how the noisy and passionate experiences of satisfaction which perplexed me so much in the beginning have come about. They are not naïve primary reactions but have already a history; they are reactions to frustrations in a similar way as, e.g. compulsory masturbation often luxuriates for quite a long while after some events in the environment—interpreted by the child as a threat of castration. This knowledge enabled me to evaluate these phenomena of the *new beginning* more correctly and to treat them properly. I shall return to these experiences later.

Now it was but a step from here to surmise that our patients have brought these ever recurring forms of reactions from their early infantile stages. I am afraid I shall meet some opposition at this point. It may be admitted that these phenomena repeat certain infantile situations, but why should these be the most primitive ones? I shall deal with this question later when discussing the concept of primary narcissism; for the present, however, I must follow the thread of my argument. In my opinion a very early, most likely the earliest, phase of the extra-uterine mental life is not narcissistic but directed towards objects, but this early object relation is a passive one. Its aim is briefly this: *I shall be loved and satisfied, without being under any obligation to give anything in return.* This is and remains for ever the final goal of all erotic striving. It is the reality that forces us to circuitous ways. One detour is narcissism: if I am not loved sufficiently by the world, not given enough gratification, I must love and gratify myself. The clinically observable narcissism is, therefore, always a protection against the bad or only reluctant object. The other detour is the active object love. We love and gratify our partner, i.e. we conform to his wishes in order to be loved and gratified by him in return.

These observations are well supported by the results of I. Hermann (1933, 1936). As just mentioned, during the period called by me the "new beginning" desires appeared that toook the form of being permitted to touch the analyst or of being touched by him. This instinctual desire for physical contact has occupied Hermann—independently from me—for more than ten years. I can only give here that part of his results which refers to our topic. His theory starts from two observations: (a) The infant of the primates spends the first few months of extrauterine life clinging to its mother's body; (b) the human infant is forcibly separated from the maternal body much too early. The human child has the wish to continue living as a component part of the mother–child-unit (a dual-unit); as this is frustrated—at least in our civilization—by the reality, it develops a number of instinctual substitutive symptoms, such as its sleeping position, a number of reflexes (Moro, etc.), many phenomena of sucking and hand erotism and, last but not least, the general tendency to cling to something in the moment of a threatening danger.

In all these instances we are faced with active behaviour on the part of the infant, even with an activity directed towards an object. The fact must be mentioned also that contrary to common parlance the child is not suckled, indeed it sucks actively.

Sequelæ of this tendency are naturally to be observed in the adult also, in his sexual life, in his neuroses, in his way of associating and in the phenomena of the period of new beginning quoted above. Further I wish to mention the innumerable magic, mystic, or symbolic acts, such as, hand-shake, laying on of hands, touching, clinging, etc., all of which have this tendency as their basis, and show the conscious aim of identifying oneself with the object or asking help from it.

Moreover, Hermann has proved that clinging is the common precursor of a large number of object relations. By attenuating this tendency to touching, stroking, caressing, tenderness develops; in the same way it is possible that frustrations followed by regressive reinforcement may bring forth sadism. Further masochistic tendencies can be traced back to primitive clinging. The importance of clinging in normal sensual sexuality, e.g. embracing, pressing, etc., needs no further proofs.

This theory obtained a still firmer foundation through the research carried out by A. Balint.[9] Hermann and I have examined these phenomena only from the point of view of the patient, i.e. of the child. A woman was needed to illuminate this dual-unit also from the other side, i.e. from the side of the mother. The most important, though not at all unexpected result is that the two parties of this relation are libidinously equal. Libidinally the mother is receiver and giver to the same extent as her child; she experiences her child as part of her own body and yet as something strange and hostile in the same way as the child regards the body of its mother. Often only in phantasy but not so seldom in reality also she does as she likes with her child as if it had no life, no interests on its own. And it is almost with the same words that our Londoner colleagues describe the behaviour of the child *vis-à-vis* its parents.

This primitive—egoistic—form of love works according to the principle: what is good for me, is right for you, i.e. it does not recognize any difference between one's own interests and the interests of the object, it assumes as a matter of fact that the partner's desires are identical with one's own. Claims of the object which go beyond this harmony are intolerable, they call forth anxiety or aggressiveness. The same attitude develops regularly in the course of analytic treatment. Here, in addition to unscrupulous egoism, another quality of this object relation can be observed: paranoid sensitivity. The patient is the pivot of everything, he draws far-reaching conclusions from the minutest details as to whether he is loved, and whether or not he is sufficiently taken into consideration.

It is a commonplace that the ultimate goal of all instincts is the union with the object, the recovery of the ego-object-identity. The adult arrives nearest to this ultimate goal in the orgasm. Coitus, it is true, begins as an altruistic act, but the higher one's excitement grows the less regard is paid to the partner until finally immediately before and during orgasm the partner's interests are completely forgotten, and thus in the safe belief of being united with him (her) in perfect harmony one is able to enjoy together the highest pleasure.

In all these cases we have to do with a faulty or even absent sense of reality with regard to the partner, or the analyst; he is treated as if his desires were truly identical with one's own. His existence, however, is never in doubt. It is legitimate to assume the same primitive form of love in the child. A. Balint was able to support this conclusion by data from comparative pedagogics especially from the different forms of education in primitive tribes.

The results of these three researches can be summed up as follows:

1. The phase of object relation described by all three of us, which could be called primary or primitive object love, must occur very early in life.
2. This phase is unavoidable, a necessary stage of mental development. All later object relations can be traced back to it, i.e. vestiges and remnants of this primitive phase can be demonstrated in all the later ones.
3. This form of object relation is not linked to any of the erotogenic zones; it is not oral, oral-sucking, anal, genital, etc., love but is something on its own as are the other forms of love, such as auto-erotism, narcissism, object love. In my opinion this fact is of paramount importance and I hope that through this strict discrimination it will be possible to disentangle the hopeless confusion brought about by equating both in our theory and in our terminology the development of instinctual aims with the development of instinctual object-relations.
4. The biological basis of this primary object relation is the instinctual interdependence of mother and child; the two are dependent on each other but at the same time they are tuned to each other, each of them satisfies himself by the other without the

compulsion of paying regard to the other. Indeed, what is good for the one, is right for the other. This biological interdependence in the dual unit has been considered hitherto only very superficially; e.g. we thought we had explained it, from the mother's side by a narcissistic identification with her child.

5. This intimate relation is severed by our civilization much too early. Consequences of this early severance are, among others, the well-known tendency to cling, and the general discontent, the insatiable greed of our children.

6. If the instinctual desire is satisfied in time, the pleasure experience never goes beyond the level of forepleasure, i.e. the tranquil, quiet sense of well-being. On the other hand frustration calls forth extremely vehement reactions, and possibly only such misunderstood and consequently misinterpreted environmental influences can cause reactively in the child insatiable cravings, reminiscent of addiction and perhaps also of orgasm-like conditions.

These assumptions perhaps make it possible to understand the disagreement between Vienna and London. Both parties are right and wrong at the same time. The Londoners have studied only the vehement reactions after frustration, but the experience of the tranquil, quiet sense of well-being after proper satisfaction escaped their attention altogether or it has not been appreciated according to its economic importance. The form of appearance drowned the essence: *what presented itself as loud, forceful or vehement, has been valued as important, what happened quietly, as unimportant.* This incomplete description has given rise to a one-sided theory; everything in it is correct, except the proportions. The Viennese have recognized this fault clearly and duly emphasized the incompleteness of the London views; but they were either unable to explain satisfactorily the correctly observed phenomena of the infantile period, such as greed, insatiability, strong ambivalence, etc., or had to resort to ad hoc hypotheses, such as the primary fear of the strength of an instinct.

Thus developed a hopeless polemic. The English felt that they were right in emphasizing the insatiability of the children. However, their thinking got arrested here and they could not go on to view the infantile situation as an instinctual interdependence of mother and child. And the reason for this inability is the fact that they—in the same way as the Viennese—clung desperately to the hypothesis of primary narcissism. This hypothesis bars the assumption of any relation to external objects. This argument from the theory was in fact quoted time and again by the Viennese. To counter it the Londoners could do nothing but stress time and again their rather one-sided clinical material about the aggressive phenomena showing the infantile dissatisfaction: a typical example of talking at cross purposes despite real good will from both sides.

In my opinion it is the hypothesis of primary narcissism that mainly causes the confusion of tongues between Vienna and London. Primary narcissism is a very curious notion, full of meaning and still very poor. If we accept it, the very earliest state of the extra-uterine mental life can be characterized as follows: the infant has no knowledge as yet of the external world, does not yet even perceive it; it has subjectively no relation to the objects and persons of its environment and thus no desires orientated towards the world; it experiences only increase and disappearance of its needs, does not yet connect them with the external world; the observable emotional phenomena, such as crying, whining, scratching, gripping, fidgetting on the one side, smiling, tranquility on the other, are merely abreactions; as the infant does not yet perceive any external objects, it can have no libidinous object-relations as yet, of its libido nothing has yet been turned outwards.

Two objections are to be raised here. One is methodological: all the characteristics of the notion "primary narcissism" are negative and in addition all of them contain the restrictive adverb "as yet". Primary narcissism is, thus, a negative notion; moreover, it gives a description of the real situation only during a very short period. It is extremely difficult to discuss such negative notions as they do not contain anything one can get hold of; they are as slippery as eels. In addition there is that adverb "as yet". Everything and anything that can be stated as counter-argument, can be dealt with schematically without thinking: whatever contradicts the assumption is already a product of development, originally it was not *yet* there.

This is a clear case of extrapolation. It means that primary narcissism is not an observable fact but a hypothesis based on theoretical extrapolation, a point which was time and again duly stressed by Freud himself, e.g.: "The primary narcissism of the child assumed by us, which forms one of the hypotheses in our theory of the libido, is less easy to grasp by direct observation than *to confirm by deduction from another consideration*."[10]

The other objection is this: The two states which come nearest to this assumption and which ever since Freud's basic papers have been quoted as arguments, are the catatonic and the new-born infant. I have not had much experience with psychotics, but experienced and analytically trained psychiatrists have often stated that no catatonic is absolutely unresponsive. With sufficient perseverance proper reactions can be elicited from them, i.e. a proper object-relation can be demonstrated.[11] According to Petö's observations reactions of infants to libidinous environmental influences can be demonstrated indisputably as early as in the first week of their life and certainly in the first month. I am certain that to weaken the force of these observations the two adverbs "already" and "as yet" will be invoked. These observable phenomena are *already* results of development, primary narcissism describes *still* earlier phases, *still* deeper regressions.

To strengthen my thesis I shall quote a few facts about narcissistic states. These facts have been well known for quite a long time but as they were uncomfortable for our theory one pushed them on one side and tried hard not to notice them in their true significance.

1.   Already Freud has emphasized that absolute narcissism in itself is impossible because a living being in this state is not viable. Ever since, following his example, we quote in this connection the nursing environment. It is quite correct to do so. This primary state is only possible in the form of the mother–child unit.

2.   Narcissistic attitude should make one independent of the world. Experience teaches us, however, that this state can be reached only very seldom. (As is well known Buddha himself did not succeed completely.) In general, narcissistic peoples are almost paranoid-hypersensitive, irritable, the slightest unpleasant stimulus may provoke vehement outbursts—they give the impression of an anxiously and painfully counterbalanced enormous lability. The same is true of children's behaviour from the very beginning. This everyday experience can hardly be made to agree with the theory of primary narcissism, on the

other hand it follows naturally from our theory of primary object-relations.

3. The fact that narcissistic people are so difficult to satisfy also belongs here. Whatever one tries to do for them, however considerate one tries to be, it is always wrong, they never have enough. According to the theory of primary narcissism one would expect a sort of indifference towards the world. These people, however, behave as infants. Freud's description quoted in the beginning of this paper is valid for them too.

4. It is generally known that newly born babies cry much more in their first weeks than later. Wälder, too, quotes this observation (*l.c.* p. 412) although it goes against his thesis. If one picks up such a child—which, however, according to most pædiatricians one should not do—it happens fairly regularly, although not always, that it stops crying. To explain this everyday happening the oddest *ad hoc* hypotheses were invented, such as that the mother serves as defence against a possible increase of instinctual excitement, etc., but one would not accept the naïve fact that the crying is the expression of the desire for simple physical contact. The acceptance of such a desire would mean the acceptance of a demonstrable object-relation and with it a serious challenge to primary narcissism.

5. Again it is generally known that the state of primary narcissism cannot ever be observed in a pure form, i.e. without easily demonstrable phenomena of "oral" or "oral-sadistic love". This too follows as self-evident from our theory: oral erotism is in fact one of the most important forms of expression of the primary object love. For the old theory primary narcissism is by definition without any object, therefore all the observed forms of object-relation had to be ascribed to oral erotism, most pregnantly by Abraham in his paper on "The influence of oral-erotism on character formation" (Abraham, 1942) which has fundamentally influenced the development of theory (not only in England). Freud was much more cautious, in his description of 1931, quoted above, "oral love" is not even mentioned, he speaks of the insatiability, greed, dissatisfaction, etc., as of *qualities of the infant*. I wish to add that these are jut the features of the primary object love assumed by us. Oral erotism develops under its domination but so do also other

erotic tendencies, e.g. clinging, the need for physical contact, etc., all of which can be insatiable, greedy, in the same way as oral erotism can be.

Two objections can be expected here. Firstly it will very likely be argued against the assumption of primary object love that the infant does not know of any external world and still less can discriminate objects in the external world; accordingly it is nonsensical to think that it can build up any relation to such objects not yet existing in his mind. As far as I know it is the first time in the history of psycho-analysis that the possibility of an experience (perhaps) not being conscious is used as an argument against its psychological existence. Moreover, how do we know for certain that the infant does not know anything at all of the external world? Certainly not from unchallengeable observations but from theoretical assumptions about the mental life of the infant, i.e. from the assumption of primary narcissism, while it is just this theory that first ought to be proved. And it is remarkable that the very authors who doubt even the possibility of any verifiable assumption about the earliest phases of the mind, claim to know absolutely firmly and safely what *cannot* exist in the infantile mind.

It will be said then, and that is the second objection, that the phenomena quoted above have been known long ago and have nothing to do with the mind, they are simply phenomena of physiological adaptation. Here again one uses as argument the thesis which stands to discussion. Doubtlessly all these are phenomena of adaptation but this statement proves nothing for or against their psychic nature. The infant's sucking is certainly adaptation, but I do not think anyone will deny that sucking plays a very important role in the mind also.

It only shows the overwhelming power of the hypothesis that the whole mind, and with it the Id, could only be thought of as originally narcissistic. It is true, a mind that maintains no relation to the external world, is logically the simplest proposition, but does it follow that the logically simplest form must be in reality the most primitive one? This is a fallacy of which we psycho-analysts are not the only victims. In the same way for quite a long time, the economists put the so-called Robinson Crusoe situation at the beginning of the economic development; in the same way it was assumed that the history of civilization started with logically simple conditions *à la* Rousseau, and in biology the apparently simplest living being, the amoeba, was presented as *primum vivens*. The psychological content of all these assumptions is the narcissistic state totally cut off on all sides, obviously a wish-fulfilment in a sublimated form. More exact research has cleaned up all these assumptions. Thus biology, for instance, had to learn that the logically so simple amoeba is in fact a secondary form: in its individual (not phylogenetic) youth it shows forms which swim freely about like flagellata, have a rather complicated structure, and above all are sexually dimorphous which means that they develop proper object-relations to each other.

I think we find ourselves before a similar change in psychoanalysis. Certainly the logically simplest form of the mind is primary narcissism. This never-observed form was inferred from the clinically easily observable condition of the so-called secondary narcissism by extrapolation. This assumption was eminently useful as long as analysis could not go considerably deeper than the Oedipus situation. Early analyses of children, the recent studies of psychotics and above all the essential improvements of our technical ability, and, with it, the deeper understanding of the transference, have brought more and more material of the pre-oedipal time to light. For the explanation of these new data the theory of primary narcissism proved to be less and less useful.

It must be admitted that the theory of primary object-relations, as proposed here, is based also on extrapolation. But firstly we extrapolate to states much nearer and secondly our theory is anything but a negative notion. Some features of the assumed primary object love were enumerated in this paper, others are to be found in the originals quoted. All of them are verifiable. A further methodological advantage of our theory is that it has no such way of escape as—for the theory of primary narcissism—the play with the adverbs "not yet" and "already". What we ask for is that our theory be examined, above all in the study of the infant and the psychotic. Whether beyond the primary object-relations the way will lead to primary narcissism or not, must remain undecided for the time being. I, for one, do not think so. In my opinion the time has come for us psycho-analysts to follow the biologists in facing the end of the amoeba myth.

Notes

1. Shortened version of a contribution to the First Symposium of the Second "Four Countries" Conference in Budapest, May, 1937. Published in German in Imago, 23, 270–288, 1937.
2. Written in 1937.
3. I noticed only while preparing this translation that the German text of Mrs Riviere's paper omits the words "as an object relation" which are in the original English. The German sentence runs: "dass orale und kannibalistische Triebregungen . . . primär in der Säuge-periode entwickelt werden" (*Int. Z. Psa.*, (1936), **22**, p. 488.)
4. At this point the German translation again deviates from the English original: "Zugleich mit diesen Verfolgungsängsten treten auch schon ansatzweise Schuldgefühle und Sorge für das Objekt auf sobald sich die Liebe zur Brust und zur Mutter geltend macht" (*l.c.*, p. 497). Reference to an early object relation is omitted here from the English version.
5. Apparently the same is true of the beginning of object relations. Cf. the divergencies in the English and German versions of Mrs Riviere's paper.
6. Written in 1937.
7. "Stages in the development of the sense of reality" (1913), "Thalassa: a theory of genitality" (1924), "Confusion of the tongues between the adults and the child" (1933).
8. "The final goal of psychoanalytic treatment', *International Journal of Psycho-Analysis* (1936), *17*: 206–216. (The German original appeared in 1935.) "Zur. Kritik der Lehre von den prägenitalen Libidoorganisationen", *Int. Z. Psa.* (1935), *21*: 525–543. "Eros und Aphrodite", *International Journal of Psycho-Analysis* (1938), *19*: 199–213. (The German original appeared in 1936.)
9. "Handhabung der bertragung auf Grund der Ferenczi'schen Versuche", *Int. Z. f. Psa.* (1937), *22*: 47–58. "Love for the mother and mother's love", *International Journal of Psycho-Analysis*, *30*: 251–259. (Originally appeared in German in 1939.)
10. Freud: *Collected Papers*, fourth impr. 1948, Vol. IV, p. 48. (My italics.)
11. Written in 1937. Cf. *The New Attempts at a Psycho-Theory of Catatonics*, by J. Rosen.

References

Abraham, K. (1942). *Selected Papers*, pp. 393–406. London.

Freud, S. (1932). Female sexuality. *International Journal of Psycho-Analysis*, *13*: 281–297.

Hermann, I. (1933). Zum Triebleben der Primaten. *Imago, 19*: 113, 325.

Hermann, I. (1936). Sich-Anklammern—Auf-Suche-Gehen. *Int. Z. f. Psa., 22*: 349–370.

Riviere, J. (1936). On the genesis of psychical conflict in earliest infancy. *International Journal of Psycho-Analysis, 17*: 395–422.

Wälder, R. (1937). The problem of the genesis of psychical conflict in earliest infancy. *International Journal of Psycho-Analysis. 18*: 416–473.

Endopsychic structure considered in terms of object-relationships*

W. Ronald D. Fairbairn

I n a previous article (1941) I attempted to formulate a new
version of the libido theory and to outline the general features which a systematic psychopathology based upon this
re-formulation would appear to assume. The basic conception
which I advanced on that occasion, and to which I still adhere, is to
the effect that libido is primarily object-seeking (rather than pleasure-seeking, as in the classic theory), and that it is to disturbances
in the object-relationships of the developing ego that we must look
for the ultimate origin of all psychopathological conditions. This
conception seems to me not only to be closer in accord with psychological facts and clinical data than that embodied in Freud's original theory of the libido, but also to represent a logical outcome of
the present stage of psycho-analytical thought and a necessary step
in the further development of psycho-analytical theory. In particular, it seems to me to constitute an inevitable implication of the illuminating conception of internalized objects, which has been so
fruitfully developed by Melanie Klein, but which traces its scientific

* [Reproduced, with permission, from: *International Journal of Psychoanalysis*,
1944, 25: 70–92 © Institute of Psychoanalysis, London, UK]

origin to Freud's theory of the super-ego (an endopsychic structure which was, of course, conceived by him as originating in the internalization of objects).

Quite apart from the considerations advanced in my previous paper or various other considerations which could be adduced, it may be claimed that the psychological introjection of objects and, in particular, the perpetuation of introjected objects in inner reality are processes which by their very nature imply that libido is essentially object-seeking; for the mere presence of oral impulses is in itself quite insufficient to account for such a pronounced devotion to objects as these phenomena imply. A similar implication would appear to arise out of the mere possibility of an Oedipus situation being perpetuated in the unconscious; for unceasing devotion to an object constitutes the very essence of this situation. Nevertheless the conception of internalized objects has been developed without any significant modification of a libido theory with which there is no small reason to think that it is incompatible. Freud himself never saw fit to undertake any systematic re-formulation of his original theory of libido, even after the introduction of his theory of the super-ego. At the same time there are innumerable passages in his works in which it appears to be taken for granted that libido is specifically object-seeking. Indeed it is possible to find passages in which this implicit view becomes explicit—as, for example, when he states quite simply (1929): "Love seeks for objects." This statement occurs in a paragraph in which, referring to his original theory of instincts, he writes as follows: "Thus first arose the contrast between ego instincts and object instincts. For the energy of the latter instincts and exclusively for them I introduced the term libido; an antithesis was then formed between the ego instincts and the libidinal instincts directed towards objects." As Freud proceeds to point out, the distinction between these two groups of instincts was abandoned upon his "introduction of the concept of narcissism, i.e. the idea that libido cathects the ego itself"; but in the light of the passage quoted it would appear no very revolutionary step to claim that libido is primarily object-seeking, especially if, as I have suggested in my previous article, we conceive of narcissism as a state in which the ego is identified with objects.[1]

Nevertheless the ever increasing concentration of psycho-analytical research upon object-relationships has left unmodified the original theory that libido is primarily pleasure-seeking, and with it the related conception that "the course of mental processes is automatically regulated by 'the pleasure principle' " (Freud, 1920g, p. 1). The persistence of this view has raised various problems which might otherwise have proved easier of solution. Prominent amongst these is the problem for which Freud set out to find a solution in *Beyond the Pleasure Principle* (1920g) itself, viz. how it comes about that neurotics cling to painful experiences so assiduously. It was the difficulty of accounting for this phenomenon in terms of the pleasure principle that led Freud to fall back upon the conception of a "repetition compulsion". If, however, libido is regarded as primarily object-seeking, there is no need to resort to this expedient; and in a recent article (1943) I attempted to show how the tendency to cling to painful experiences may be explained in terms of relationships with bad objects. In the same article I also attempted to show how the difficulties involved in the conception of primary "death instincts" (in contrast to the conception of primary aggressive instincts) may be avoided if all the implications of libidinal relationships with bad objects are taken into account.

Impulse psychology and its limitations

In actual fact, the "object-relationship" standpoint which I have now come to adopt has resulted from an attempt, imposed upon me by circumstances, to gain a better understanding of the problems presented by patients displaying certain schizoid tendencies, i.e. a class of individuals for whom object-relationships present an especial difficulty; and here, in parenthesis, I venture to express the opinion that psycho-analytical research in its later phases has suffered from too great a preoccupation with the problems of melancholia. Previous to my reaching the above mentioned standpoint, however, I had already become very much impressed by the limitations of "impulse psychology" in general, and somewhat sceptical of the explanatory value of all theories of instinct in which the instincts are treated as existing *per se*. The limitations of impulse psychology make themselves felt in a very practical sense within the therapeutic field; for, whilst to reveal the nature of his "impulses" to a patient by painstaking analysis is one proposition, to enable him to know what to do with these "impulses" is quite another. What an individual shall do with his "impulses" is clearly a problem of object-relationships. It is equally a problem of his own personality; but (constitutional factors apart) problems of the personality are themselves bound up with object-relationships. These problems are bound up with the relationships of the ego to its internalized objects—or, as I should prefer to say for reasons which will shortly appear, the relationships of various parts of the ego to internalized objects and to one another as objects. In a word "impulses" cannot be considered apart from the endopsychic structures which they energize and the object-relationships which they enable these structures to establish; and, equally, "instincts" cannot profitably be considered as anything more than forms of energy which constitute the dynamic of such endopsychic structures.

From a practical psychotherapeutic standpoint the analysis of impulses considered apart from structures proves itself a singularly sterile procedure, and particularly so in the case of patients with well-marked schizoid tendencies. By means of interpretations couched more or less exclusively in terms of impulses, it is some-times quite easy in such cases to release a flood of associations (e.g. in the form of oral-sadistic phantasies), which appear singularly impressive as manifestations of the unconscious, but which can be maintained indefinitely without any real movement in the direction of integration and without any significant therapeutic develop-ment. The explanation of this phenomenon would appear to be that the ego (or, as I should prefer to say, *the central ego*) does not partici-pate in the phantasies described except as a recording agent. When such a situation arises, the central ego, so to speak, sits back in the dress-circle and describes the dramas enacted upon the stage of inner reality without any effective participation in them. At the same time it derives considerable narcissistic satisfaction from being the recorder of remarkable events and identifying itself with the analyst as observer while asserting a superiority over the analyst as mere observer by reason of the fact that it is not merely observing, but also furnishing the material for observation. This procedure is really a masterpiece of defensive technique—one to which schizoid individuals are only too ready to resort at the best of times, but which constitutes an almost irresistible temptation to them when the analyst's interpretations are couched too exclusively in terms of "impulses". Such a technique provides the best of all means of enabling the patient to evade the central therapeutic problem, viz. how to release those dynamic charges known as "impulses" in the context of reality. This problem is clearly one of object-relationships within the social order.

My point regarding the inadequacy of impulse psychology may be illustrated by a reference to one of the cases in the light of which my present views were developed. This patient was an unmarried woman with schizoid features which were none the less present because the clinical picture was dominated by well-marked phobic and hysterical symptoms, as well as by generalized anxiety. She was repressed in proportion to a high degree of unrelieved libidinal tension. When this libidinal tension rose during a session, it was no uncommon occurrence for her to complain of feeling sick. This sense of nausea was undoubtedly a transference phenomenon based upon an attitude towards her mother and her mother's breast mediated by her father and her father's penis, all as internalized objects; and it readily lent itself to interpretation in terms of oral impulses in so far as her associations had been characterized from the first by a considerable amount of oral material. Nevertheless the chief significance of her nausea seemed to reside, not so much in the oral nature of the reaction as in the influence shown by this reaction to be exercised upon her object-relationships (1) by a libidinal fixation upon her mother's breast, and (2) by an attitude of rejection towards the object of her libidinal need. It was true, of course, that the oral nature of her reaction was related to a severe repression of genital sexuality; and she was probably right when, on more than one occasion, she hazarded the opinion that she would be frigid in intercourse, although the correctness of this surmise had never been put to the test. At the same time, her difficulty in achieving a genital attitude seemed best understood, not in terms of any fixation at an oral stage, but rather in terms of a rejection of her father's penis based partly on an identification of this object with the bad breast, partly on a preferential fixation on the breast, and partly on the emotional "badness" of her father as a whole object. The scales were further weighted against a genital attitude by the fact that an oral attitude involves a lesser degree of commitment to the object whilst conferring a greater measure of power over it. It was not uncommon for the same patient to say during a session: "I want to go the lavatory." In the first instance this statement had quite a literal significance; but later in the analysis it came increasingly to mean that she was experiencing a desire to express libidinal feelings mobilized by the transference situation. Here again, it was not in the nature of the "impulse" considered in terms of phases (this time urinary and anal) that the chief significance of the phenomenon lay. It lay rather in the quality of the object-relationship involved. "Going to the lavatory", like "being sick", undoubtedly signified a rejection of the libidinal object considered as contents. Nevertheless, as compared with "being sick", it signified a lesser measure of rejection; for, although in both cases a cathartic discharge of libidinal tension was also involved, the discharge of contents represented by "going to the lavatory", being a discharge of assimilated contents, indicated a greater willingness to express libidinal feelings *before* an external object, albeit falling short of that direct discharge of feelings towards an object, which characterizes the genital attitude.

The scientific validity of a psychological theory cannot, of course, be assessed solely in terms of psychotherapeutic success or failure; for the scientific significance of therapeutic results can only be judged when it is known exactly how these results are obtained. Impulse psychology cannot be regarded as providing any exception to this general rule; but it is significant that, where psycho-analysis is concerned, it is now generally recognized that therapeutic results are closely related to the phenomenon of transference, i.e. to the establishment of an object-relationship of a special kind with the analyst on the part of the patient. On the other hand, it is an accepted article of the psycho-analytical technique that the analyst should be unusually self-effacing. As we know, there are very good reasons for the adoption of such an attitude on his part; but it inevitably has the effect of rendering the object-relationship between patient and analyst somewhat one-sided from the patient's point of view and thus contributing to the resistance. A certain one-sidedness in the relationship between patient and analyst is, of course, inherent in the analytical situation; but it would appear that, when the self-effacing attitude of the analyst is combined with a mode of interpretation based upon a psychology of impulse, a considerable strain is imposed upon the patient's capacity for establishing satisfactory object-relationships (a capacity which must be regarded as already compromised in virtue of the fact that the patient is a patient at all). At the same time, the patient is placed under a considerable temptation to adopt, among other defences, that to which reference has already been made, viz. the technique of describing scenes enacted on the stage of inner reality without any significant participation on the part of the central ego either in these scenes or in an effective object-relationship with the analyst. One of my patients, who was a past master in this technique, said to me one day, after providing a comprehensive intellecutual description of the state of impulse-tension in which he felt himself to be placed: "Well, what are you going to do about it?" By way of reply I explained that the real question was what he himself was going to do about it. This reply proved highly disconcerting to him, as indeed it was intended to be. It was disconcerting to him because it faced him abruptly with the real problem of the analysis and of his life. How an individual is going to dispose of impulse-tension is clearly a problem of object-relationships: but it is equally a problem of the personality, since an object-relationship necessarily involves a subject as well as an object. The theory of object-relationships thus inevitably leads us to the position that, if impulses cannot be con- sidered apart from objects, whether external or internal, it is equally impossible to consider them apart from ego structures. Indeed it is even more impossible to consider impulses apart from ego struc- tures, since it is only ego structures that can seek relationships with objects. We are thus brought back to the conclusion, already recorded, that "impulses" are but the dynamic aspect of endopsy- chic structures and cannot be said to exist in the absence of such structures, however immature these may turn out to be. Ultimately "impulses" must be simply regarded as constituting the forms of activity in which the life of ego structures consists.

Structure psychology and the repression of structures

Once the position now indicated has been reached, it obviously becomes incumbent upon us to review afresh our theory of the mental apparatus. In particular, it becomes a question how far Freud's description of mental structure in terms of id, ego and super-ego can be retained without modification. The moment this question is raised, it is, of course, plainly in relation to the status of the id that doubts will first arise; for, if it be true that no "impulses" can be regarded as existing in the absence of an ego structure, it will no longer be possible to preserve any psychological distinction between the id and the ego. Freud's conception of the *origin* of the ego as a structure which develops on the surface of the psyche for the purpose of regulating id-impulses in relation to reality will thus give place to a conception of the ego as the source of impulse-tension from the beginning. This inclusion of the id in the ego will, of course, leave essentially unaffected Freud's conception of the *function* served by the "ego" in regulating the discharge of impulse-tension in deference to the conditions of outer reality. It will, however, involve the view that "impulses" are oriented towards reality, and thus to some extent determined by the "reality principle", from the very beginning. Thus, for example, the child's earliest oral behaviour will be regarded as oriented *ab initio* towards the breast. In accordance with this point of view, the pleasure principle will cease to be regarded as the primary principle of behaviour and will come to be regarded as a subsidiary principle of behaviour involving an impoverishment of object-relationships and coming into operation in proportion as the reality principle fails to operate, whether this be on account of the immaturity of the ego structure or on account of a failure of development on its part. Questions regarding the extent to which the reality principle has superseded the pleasure principle will then give place to questions regarding the extent to which an originally immature reality principle has progressed towards maturity; and questions regarding the capacity of the ego to regulate id-impulses in deference to reality will give place to questions regarding the measure in which the ego structure within which impulse-tension arises has been organized in accordance with the reality principle, or, in default of this, has resorted to the pleasure principle as a means of organization.

If, then, "impulse" is to be regarded as inseparably associated with an ego structure from the beginning, what becomes of Freud's conception of repression as a function exercised by the ego in its dealings with impulses originating in the id? I have already elsewhere (1943) considered the implications of my theory of object-relationships for the concept of repression. There I advanced the view that repression is primarily exercised, not against impulses which have come to appear painful or "bad" (as in Freud's final view) or even against painful memories (as in Freud's earlier view), but against *internalized objects* which have come to be treated as bad. I still feel justified in regarding this view as correct; but in certain other respects my views regarding repression have undergone a change. In particular, I have come to regard repression as exercised, not only against internalized objects (which, incidentally, must be regarded as endopsychic structures, albeit not ego structures), but also against parts of the "ego" which seek relationships with these internal objects. Here it may occur to the reader to pass the criticism that, since repression is a function of the "ego", this view involves the anomaly of the ego repressing itself. How, it may be asked, can the ego be conceived as repressing the ego? The answer to this question is that, whilst it is inconceivable that the ego as a whole should repress itself, it is not inconceivable that one part of the "ego" with a dynamic charge should repress another part of the "ego" with a dynamic charge. This is, of course, quite a different proposition from one set of impulses repressing another set—a conception rightly rejected by Freud when engaged in the task of formulating his theory of the mental apparatus. In order to account for repression Freud found himself compelled to postulate the existence of a *structure* capable of instigating repression—viz. the super-ego. It is, therefore, only another step in the same direction to postulate the existence of structures which are repressed. Apart from any theoretical reasons such as those already advanced, there are very good clinical reasons for making such an assumption. Prominent among these is the difficulty experienced in effecting the sublimation of libidinal "impulses". This difficulty cannot be adequately explained as due to an inveterate and inherent obstinacy on the part of "impulses" themselves, especially once we have come to regard "impulses" as just forms of energy at the disposal of the ego structure. On the contrary, it can only be satisfactorily explained on the assumption that the repressed "impulses" are inseparable from an ego structure with a definite pattern. The correctness of this assumption is confirmed by the phenomena of multiple personality, in which the linkage of repressed "impulses" with a submerged ego structure is beyond question; but such a linkage may also be detected in the less extensive forms of dissociation, which are so characteristic of the hysterical individual. In order to account for repression, we thus appear to be driven to the necessity of assuming a certain multiplicity of egos. This should not really prove a particularly difficult conception for any one familiar with the problems presented by schizoid patients. But here, as so often, we are reminded of the limitations imposed upon psycho-analytical theory in some of its later developments by a preoccupation with the phenomena of melancholia.

The schizoid position

That Freud's theory of mental structure is itself based in no small measure upon a consideration of the phenomena of melancholia can hardly escape the notice of any reader of *The Ego and the Id* (1923), the work which contains the classic exposition of the theory; and, in conformity with this fact, it is in his paper entitled "Mourning and melancholia" (1917) that we find the final link in the chain of thought which culminated in the exposition in question. Correspondingly the "depressive position" is accorded a place of central importance in the views of Melanie Klein and her collaborators. Here I must confess that the accordance of such a central place to the depressive position is difficult to reconcile with my own experience. It would be idle, of course, to deny the importance of the depressive position in individuals suffering from true depression or, for that matter, in individuals of a depressive type. So far as my experience goes, however, such individuals do not constitute any appreciable proportion of the analyst's clientèle, although, of course, they are common enough in ordinary psychiatric practice. So far as concerns the usual run of patients suffering from anxiety states, psychoneurotic symptoms and character difficulties, the central position seems to me to be schizoid rather than depressive in the vast majority of those who embark upon and persist in analytical treatment; and it is not very often that I find a patient under analysis displaying what I should regard as an incontrovertibly depressive (i.e. melancholic) reaction. By contrast I find schizoid reactions relatively common.

At this point I feel it necessary to refer to the distinction which I have already drawn (1941) between the characteristically melancholic affect of "depression" and the "sense of futility" which I have come to regard as the characteristically schizoid affect. From the point of view of the observer there is, admittedly, sufficient superficial similarity between the two affects to render the distinction difficult to draw in many cases, especially since the schizoid individual so commonly describes himself as "depressed"; and consequently the familiar term "depressed" is frequently applied in clinical practice to patients who should properly be described as suffering from a sense of futility. In this way a confusion of classification is liable to occur, with the result that a number of patients with psychoneurotic symptoms come to be regarded as belonging to the depressive type when the type to which they belong is really schizoid. Apart from this source of confusion, however, it is a common thing for a basic schizoid position to escape notice in the case of "psychoneurotic" patients owing to the strength of psychoneurotic defences and the resulting prominence of psychoneurotic (e.g. hysterical) symptoms in the clinical picture. Yet, when we consider the cases cited by Janet in illustration of the material upon the basis of which he formulated the conception of hysteria as a clinical entity, it is difficult to avoid concluding that quite a number of the individuals concerned displayed remarkably schizoid characteristics; and indeed it may be surmised that an appreciable proportion would actually be diagnosed as frank schizophrenics if they appeared in a modern psychiatric clinic. Here it may be added that my own investigations of patients with hysterical symptoms leave me in no doubt whatever that the dissociation phenomena of "hysteria" involve a split of the ego fundamentally identical with that which confers upon the term "schizoid" its etymological significance.

"Back to hysteria"

At this point it seems apposite to recall that Freud's earliest researches within the realm of psychopathology were concerned almost exclusively with hysterical (and *not* with melancholic) phenomena, and that it is upon a basis of these phenomena, accordingly, that psycho-analytical theory and practice were originally founded. It would doubtless be idle to speculate to what extent the development of psycho-analytical theory would have pursued a different course if hysterical phenomena had retained the central place which they originally occupied in Freud's researches; but it may at least be surmised that the importance subsequently assumed by the depressive position would have been assumed in large measure by the schizoid position. It was, of course, when Freud turned from the study of the repressed to a study of the agency of repression that the problems of melancholia began to oust problems of hysteria from the central position which the latter had hitherto occupied. That this should have been the case is not difficult to understand in view of (a) the close association which appears to exist between guilt and repression, on the one hand, and (b) the outstanding prominence which guilt assumes in the melancholic state, on the other. Be that as it may, Freud's theory of the super-ego certainly represents an attempt to trace the genesis of guilt and the instigation of repression to a common source in the Oedipus situation. This fact gives rise to a serious incompatibility between Freud's views regarding the origin of repression and Abraham's "phase" theory of libidinal development; for, whilst Freud conceived the Oedipus situation, to which he looked for the rationale of repression, as essentially a genital situation, his account of the origin of the super-ego, which he regarded as the instigator of repression, is conceived in terms of an oral situation, i.e. a situation corresponding to a stage which, according to the "phase" theory, must necessarily be pregenital. Melanie Klein has, of course, come to regard the Oedipus situation as originating at a very much earlier stage than was formerly supposed. Her resolution of the difficulty must accordingly be interpreted as having been achieved at the expense of the "phase" theory. This theory has already been the subject of detailed criticism on my part (1941). At the same time I have now come to look for the source of repression not only beyond the genital attitude, but also beyond the Oedipus situation, and even beyond the level at which the super-ego is established. Thus I not only attempted elsewhere (1943) to show that *repression* originates primarily as a defence against "bad" internalized objects (and not against impulses, whether incestuous in the genital sense or otherwise), but also that *guilt* originates as an *additional* defence against situations involving bad internalized objects. According to this view, *guilt* originates on the principle that the child finds it more tolerable to regard himself as conditionally (i.e. morally) bad than to regard his parents as unconditionally (i.e. libidinally) bad. To describe the process whereby the change from the latter to the former attitude is effected, I introduced the term "moral defence"; and, according to my view, it is only at the instance of the "moral defence" that the super-ego is established.[2] The establishment of the super-ego accordingly represents the attainment of a new level of structural organization, beneath which the old level persists. Thus, in my opinion, beneath the level at which the central ego finds itself confronted with the super-ego as an internal object of moral significance lies a level at which parts of the ego find themselves confronted with internal objects which are, not simply devoid of moral significance, but unconditionally bad from a libidinal standpoint (amoral internal persecutors of one kind or another). Whilst, therefore, the main phenomenon of melancholia may be regarded as receiving a relatively satisfactory explanation at the super-ego level, some of the accompanying phenomena are not so easily explained. Thus the paranoid and hypochondriacal trends which so frequently manifest themselves in melancholics represent an orientation towards internal objects which are in no sense "good", but are unconditionally (i.e. libidinally) bad. The same may be said of the obsessional features which are so characteristic of individuals in the intial stages of depression; for the obsessional defence is not primarily moral. On the contrary, this defence is essentially a defence against the "unlucky", i.e. against situations involving relationships with unconditionally bad (internal) objects. It is equally difficult to find a satisfactory explanation of the symptoms of "hysteria" at the super-ego level—if for no other reason than that in "hysteria" the libidinal inhibitions which occur are out of all proportion to the measure of guilt which is found to be present. Since, therefore, it was in an effort on Freud's part to explain hysterical phenomena that psycho-analysis originated, it may not be without profit to return to a consideration of this material, encouraging ourselves, if encouragement be needed, with the slogan "Back to hysteria".

A multiplicity of egos

Attention has already been drawn to the fact that, whereas the repressed was eventually described by Freud as consisting essentially of impulses, he found it necessary to fall back upon structural conceptions (the ego and the super-ego) when he came to seek an explanation of the agency of repression. Reduced to its simplest terms, Freud's conception of repression is to the following effect:—(a) that the agency of repression is the ego, (b) that repression is instigated and maintained by the pressure of the super-ego (an internalized parental figure) upon the ego, (c) that the repressed consists essentially in libidinal impulses, and (d) that repression arises as a means of defence against impulses involved in the Oedipus situation and treated by the ego as "guilty" in terms of the pressure of the super-ego. That the agent and the instigator of repression should both be regarded as structures whilst the repressed is regarded as consisting of impulses involves a certain anomaly which appears so far to have escaped attention. The extent of this anomaly may perhaps best be appreciated in the light of the fact that the super-ego, which is described as the instigator of repression, is itself largely unconscious; for this raises the difficult question whether the super-ego itself is not also repressed. Freud himself was by no means oblivious to this problem; and he expressly envisages the possibility of the super-ego being in some measure subject to repression. Repression of the super-ego would, of course, represent the repression of a structure. It would thus appear that the general possibility of the repression of a structure is recognized by Freud; and, in the light of the considerations already advanced, it becomes reasonable to ask whether the repressed is not invariably and inherently structural. In this event the anomaly to which I have referred would be avoided.

That the repressed is essentially structural in nature is implicit in the view which I have already advanced (1943) to the effect that repression is primarily directed against internalized objects which are treated as bad; for, unless it is assumed that internalized objects are structures, the conception of the existence of such objects becomes utterly meaningless. In the light of further experience, my view that repression is primarily directed against bad internalized objects has proved to require considerable elaboration in a direction which has eventually led me to a revised conception of psychical structure. What actually provided the occasion of my chief step in this direction was the analysis of a dream recorded by one of my patients. This patient was a married woman who originally came to

me for analysis on account of frigidity. Her frigidity was unquestionably a phenomenon of hysterical dissociation (hysterical anæs-
thesia combined with hysterical paresis of the vagina); but, like all
such phenomena, it represented but one part of a general personality problem. The dream itself was simple enough; but it struck me
in the light of one of those simple manifestations which have so
often in the history of science been found to embody fundamental
truths.

The (manifest) dream to which I refer consisted in a brief scene
in which the dreamer saw the figure of herself being viciously
attacked by a well-known actress in a venerable building which
had belonged to her family for generations. Her husband was looking on; but he seemed quite helpless and quite incapable of protect-
ing her. After delivering the attack the actress turned away and
resumed playing a stage part, which, as seemed to be implied, she
had momentarily set aside in order to deliver the attack by way of
interlude. The dreamer then found herself gazing at the figure of
herself lying bleeding on the floor; but, as she gazed, she noticed
that this figure turned for an instant into that of a man. Thereafter
the figure alternated between herself and this man until eventually
she awoke in a state of acute anxiety.

It came as no great surprise to me to learn from the dreamer's
associations that the man into whom the figure of herself turned
was wearing a suit closely resembling one which her husband had
recently acquired, and that, whilst he had acquired this suit at her
instigation, he had taken "one of his blondes" to the fitting. This
fact, taken in conjunction with the fact that in the dream he was a
helpless spectator of the attack, at once confirmed a natural suspicion that the attack was directed no less against him than against
herself. This suspicion was amply confirmed by further associations
which need not be detailed. The course followed by the associations
also confirmed an additional suspicion that the actress who delivered the attack belonged as much to the personality of the dreamer
as did the figure of herself against which the attack was delivered.
In actual fact, the figure of an actress was well suited to represent a
certain aspect of herself; for she was essentially a shut-in and withdrawn personality who displayed very little genuine feeling
towards others, but who had perfected the technique of presenting
façades to a point at which these assumed a remarkably genuine

appearance and achieved for her a remarkable popularity. Such libidinal affect as she experienced had, since childhood, manifested itself predominantly in a secret phantasy life of masochistic complexion; but in the life of outer reality she had largely devoted herself to the playing of roles—e.g. the roles of good wife, good mother, good hostess and good business woman. From this fact the helplessness attributed to her husband in the dream derived additional significance; for, although she played the role of good wife with conspicuous success, her real personality was quite inaccessible to him and the good wife whom he knew was for the most part only the good actress. This held true not only within the sphere of emotional relationships, but also within the sphere of marital relations; for, whilst she remained frigid during intercourse, she had acquired the capacity of conveying the impression of sexual excitement and sexual satisfaction. Further, as the analysis revealed beyond all question, her frigidity represented not only an attack upon the libidinal component in herself, but also a hostile attitude towards her husband as a libidinal object. It is clear, therefore, that a measure of hidden aggression against her husband was involved in her assumption of the role of actress as this was portrayed in the dream. It is equally clear from the dream that, in a libidinal capacity, she was identified with her husband as the object of her own aggression. At this point, it should be mentioned that, when the dream occurred, her husband was a member of one of the combatant Services and was about to return home on leave. On the eve of his return, and just before the occurrence of the dream, she had developed a sore throat. This was a conjunction of events which had occurred so frequently in the past as to preclude coincidence on this occasion, and which accordingly served to confirm her identification with her husband as the object of her aggression. The situation represented in the dream is thus one in which the dreamer in one capacity, so far unspecified, vents her aggression directly against herself in another capacity, viz., a libidinal capacity, whilst, at the same time, venting her aggression indirectly against her husband as a libidinal object. At a superficial level, of course, this situation readily lent itself to being interpreted in the sense that the dreamer, being ambivalent towards her husband, had diverted the aggressive component in her ambivalent attitude from her husband to herself at the instance of guilt over her aggression in conformity with the melancholic pattern. Nevertheless, during the actual session in which the dream was recorded this interpretation did not commend itself to me as exhaustive, even at a superficial level.

It is obvious, of course, that the situation represented in the dream lent itself to a deeper interpretation than that to which reference has just been made. The situation was described a moment ago as one in which the dreamer in a capacity so far unspecified vented her aggression directly against herself in a libidinal capacity, whilst, at the same time, venting her aggression indirectly against her husband as a libidinal object. This description is, of course, incomplete in that it leaves unspecified the capacity in which she expressed her aggression; and it is when we come to consider the nature of this unspecified capacity that the deeper significance of the dream becomes a matter of moment. According to the manifest content of the dream, it was as an actress that she delivered the attack; and we have already seen how well suited the figure of an actress was to represent an aspect of herself hostile to libidinal relationships. However, abundant material had already emerged during the analysis to make it plain that the figure of an actress was at least equally well suited to represent the dreamer's mother—an artificial woman who had neither displayed any natural and spontaneous affection towards her children nor welcomed any such display on their part towards herself, and for whom the fashionable world provided a stage upon which she had spent her life in playing parts. It was thus easy to see that, in the capacity of actress, the dreamer was closely identified with her mother as a repressive figure. The introduction of her mother into the drama as an apparently "super-ego" figure at once raises the question whether the deeper interpretation of the dream should not be couched in terms of the Oedipus situation; and it becomes natural to ask whether her father is not also represented. In reality her father had been killed on active service during the war of 1914–1918, at a time when she was only six years of age; and analysis had revealed the presence of considerable resentment towards him as a libidinal object who had proved at once exciting and rejecting (this resentment being focussed particularly upon the memory of an early dressing-room scene). If then we are to look for a representation of her father in the dream, our choice is obviously limited to a single figure—the man who alternated with the figure of the dreamer as the object of attack. We have seen, of course, that this figure represented her husband; but analysis had already revealed how closely her husband was identified by transference with her father. For this, as well as for other reasons which need not be detailed, it was safe to infer that the man who was involved in the attack represented her father at the deeper level of interpretation. At this level, accordingly, the dream was capable of being interpreted as a phantasy in which both she and her father were portrayed as being killed by her mother on account of a guilty incestuous relationship. At the same time the dream was equally capable of being interpreted in terms of psychical structure, and thus as representing the repression of her libido on account of its incestuous attachment to her father at the instigation of a super-ego modelled upon her mother. Nevertheless, neither of these interpretations seemed to me to do justice to the material, although the structural interpretation seemed to offer the more fruitful line of approach.

At this point I feel it necessary to make some reference to the development of my own views regarding phantasy in general and dreams in particular. Many years ago I had the opportunity to analyse a most unusual woman whom, in retrospect, I now recognize to have been a schizoid personality, and who was a most prolific dreamer. Among the dreams recorded by this woman were a number which defied all efforts to bring them into conformity with the "wish-fulfilment" theory, and which she herself came to describe quite spontaneously as "state of affairs" dreams, intending by this description to imply that they represented actually existing endopsychic situations. Doubtless this made an impression on me. At any rate, much later, after Freud's theory of psychical structure had become familiar, after Melanie Klein had elaborated the conceptions of psychical reality and internal objects and after I myself had become impressed by the prevalence and importance of schizoid phenomena, I tentatively formulated the view that all the figures appearing in dreams represented either parts of the dreamer's own personality (conceived in terms of ego, super-ego and id) or else identifications on the part of the ego. A further development of this view was to the effect that dreams are essentially, not wish-fulfilments, but snapshots, or rather "shorts" (in the cinematographic sense), of situations existing in inner reality. To the view that dreams are essentially "shorts" of situations existing in inner reality I still adhere in conformity with the general line of thought pursued in this article; but, so far as the figures appearing in dreams are concerned, I have now modified my view to the effect that such figures represent either parts of the "ego" or internalized objects. According to my present view, therefore, the situations depicted in dreams represent relationships existing between endopsychic structures; and the same applies to situations depicted in waking phantasies. This conclusion is the natural outcome of my theory of object-relationships taken in conjunction with a realization of the inescapable fact that internalized objects must be regarded as endopsychic structures if any theoretic significance whatever is to be attached to them.

After this explanatory digression I must return to the specific dream under discussion with a view to giving some account of the conclusions which I subsequently reached, in no small measure as the result of an attempt to solve the theoretic problems which it raised in my mind. As I have already stated, none of the obvious interpretations seemed to me entirely satisfactory, although the structural type of interpretation seemed to offer the most fruitful line of approach. The reader will, of course, bear in mind what I have already said regarding psychical structures; and he will also recall my having already formulated the view that all psychopathological developments originate at a stage antecedent to that at which the super-ego develops and proceed from a level beneath that at which the super-ego operates. Thus no reference will be made in what follows either to the super-ego or to the id as explanatory concepts. On the contrary, whilst adopting a structural approach, I shall attempt to elucidate the significance of the dream quite simply in terms of the data which it itself provides.

In the manifest dream the actual drama involves four figures:— (1) the figure of the dreamer subjected to attack, (2) the man into whom this figure turns, and who then alternates with it, (3) the attacking actress, and (4) the dreamer's husband as a helpless onlooker. In our preoccupation with the actual drama, however, we must not forget our only witness of its occurrence—the dreamer herself, the observing ego. Including her, there are five figures to be reckoned with. At this juncture I venture to suggest that, if the dream had ended a few seconds earlier, there would only have been four figures, even on the assumption that the "I" of the dream is taken into account; for it was only in the fifth act, so to speak, that a man began to alternate with the figure of the dreamer as the object of attack. This is an interesting reflection; for we must conclude that, up to the point of the emergence of this man, the object of attack was a composite figure. The special interest of this phenomenon resides in the fact that, as we have seen, there is good reason to regard a second figure as composite; for the attacking actress undoubtedly represented both another figure of the dreamer and the dreamer's mother. I venture, therefore, to hazard a further suggestion—that, if the dream had lasted a few seconds longer, there might well have been six figures, instead of five. It is safe, at any rate, to infer that there were six figures in the latent content; and this, after all, is what matters for purposes of interpretation. Assuming then that six figures are represented in the dream, let us proceed to consider the nature of these figures. When we do so, our first observation is that the figures fall into two classes—ego structures and object structures. Interestingly enough there are three members of each class. The ego structures are (1) the observing ego or "I", (2) the attacked ego, and (3) the attacking ego. The object structures are (1) the dreamer's husband as an observing object, (2) the attacked object, and (3) the attacking object. This leads us to make a second observation—that the ego structures naturally lend themselves to be paired off with the object structures. There are three such pairs:—(1) the observing ego and the dreamer's husband, who also figured as an observer; (2) the attacking ego and the attacking object representing her mother, and (3) the attacked ego and the attacked object representing her father (for at this point it is to the deeper level of interpretation that we must adhere).

Bearing these two main observations in mind, let us now consider the conclusions to which I was led in an attempt to interpret the dream to my satisfaction. They are as follows. The three ego figures which appear as separate in the dream actually represent separate ego structures in the dreamer's mind. The dreamer's "ego" is therefore split in conformity with the schizoid position; and it is split into three separate egos—a central ego and two other subsidiary egos which are both, relatively speaking, cut off from the central ego. Of these two subsidiary egos, one is the object of aggression on the part of the other. Since the ego which is attacked is closely related to the dreamer's father (and by transference to her husband), it is safe to infer that this ego is highly endowed with libido; and it may thus be appropriately described as a "libidinal ego". Since the attacking ego is closely related to the dreamer's mother as a repressive figure, its behaviour is quite in accord with that traditionally ascribed to the super-ego in the setting of the Oedipus situation. Since, however, the attack bears all the marks of being vindictive, rather than moral, and gives rise to an affect, not of guilt, but of plain anxiety, there is no justification (apart from preconceptions) for equating the attacking ego with the super-ego. In any case, as I have already indicated, there is reason to attach overriding psychopathological importance to a level beneath that at which the super-ego functions. At the same time, it was shown by the circumstances in which the dream occurred that the dreamer's libidinal relationship with her husband was severely compromised; and, so far as the dream is concerned, it is clearly to the operation of the attacking ego that we must look for the compromising factor. Consequently, the attacking ego may perhaps be most appropriately described as an "internal saboteur". In an attempt to discover what this dream was stating and to determine the structural significance of what was stated, I was accordingly led to set aside the traditional classification of mental structure in terms of ego, id and super-ego in favour of a classification couched in terms of an ego-structure split into three separate egos—(1) a central ego (the "I"), (2) a libidinal ego, and (3) an aggressive, persecutory ego which I designate as the internal saboteur. Subsequent experience has led me to regard this classification as having a universal application.

The object-relationships of the central ego and the subsidiary egos

Such being my conclusions regarding the ego structures represented in the dream, let us now pass on to consider my conclusions regarding the object-relationships of these ego structures. As already indicated, each of the three egos in question naturally lends itself to being paired off with a special object. The special object of the central ego was the dreamer's husband; and it is convenient to begin by considering the nature of the attitude adopted by the dreamer's central ego towards him. Since the central ego was the observing "I" of the dream, who was felt to be continuous with the waking "I" by whom the dream was subsequently described, it is safe to infer that this ego is in no small measure preconscious—which is, in any case, what one would naturally expect of an ego deserving the title of "central". This inference gains further support from the fact that the dreamer's husband was a supremely important object in outer reality and was very much in the dreamer's conscious thoughts on the eve of the dream. Although the figure representing him in the dream must be regarded as an internalized object, this object must obviously occupy a much more superficial position in the psyche than the other objects represented (parental objects internalized in childhood); and it must correspond comparatively closely to the relative object in outer reality. Accordingly, the dreamer's attitude to her husband as an external object assumes considerable significance for our present purpose. This attitude was essentially ambivalent, especially where marital relations were concerned. Active manifestations of aggression towards him were, however, conspicuously absent. Equally, her libidinal attachment to him bore the marks of severe repression; and, in associating to the dream, she reproached herself over her lack of deep feeling towards him and her failure to give to him of herself, albeit her conscious capacity to remedy these deficiencies was restricted to an assumption of the role of "good wife". The question therefore arises whether, since her hidden aggression towards him and her hidden libidinal need of him do not declare themselves directly in the dream, they may not manifest themselves in some indirect fashion. No sooner is this question raised than we are at once reminded of the metamorphosis undergone by the figure of the libidinal ego after this was attacked by the figure of the internal saboteur. The libidinal ego changed into, and then began alternating with, a man who, whilst representing the dreamer's father at a deep level, was nevertheless closely associated with her husband. It is thus evident that, instead of being directed against her husband as an external object, a considerable proportion of her aggression was absorbed in an attack directed, not simply against the libidinal ego, but also against an internal object closely connected with the libidinal ego. It is likewise evident that this volume of aggression had come to be at the disposal, not of the central ego, but of the internal saboteur. What then of the libidinal component in her ambivalence? As we have seen, her libidinal attitude to her husband showed signs of considerable impoverishment in spite of good intentions at a conscious level. It is obvious, accordingly, that what held true of her aggression also held true of her libido. A considerable proportion had ceased to be at the disposal of the central ego. The object towards whom this volume of libido is directed can hardly remain in doubt. In terms of the dream, it must surely be the man who alternated with the libidinal self as the object of aggression. Unlike the aggression, however, this libido is not at the disposal of the internal saboteur. On the contrary we must regard it as being at the disposal of the libidinal ego; and indeed it is precisely for this reason that the term "libidinal ego" has come to commend itself to me for adoption. At this point it becomes desirable to formulate a suspicion which must be already present in the mind of the reader—that, although it is represented otherwise in the dream, the attack delivered by the internal saboteur is only secondarily directed against the libidinal ego and is primarily directed against the libidinal object which alternates with this ego. Assuming this suspicion to be correct, we must regard the ordeal to which the libidinal ego is subjected as evidence of a very complete identification with, and therefore a very strong libidinal attachment to, the attacked object on the part of the libidinal ego. It is evidence of the measure of "suffering" which the libidinal ego is prepared to endure out of devotion to its object. The anxiety experienced by the dreamer on waking may be interpreted in a similar sense; and indeed I venture to suggest that this anxiety represented an irruption into consciousness of such "suffering" on the part of the libidinal ego. Here we are at once reminded of Freud's original conception of neurotic anxiety as libido converted into suffering. This is a view which at one time presented the greatest theoretic difficulty to me, but which I have now come to appreciate in the light of my present standpoint, and substantially to accept in preference to the modified view which Freud later (and, as I think, rather reluctantly) came to adopt.

The position regarding the object-relationships of the three egos represented in the dream has now been to some extent clarified; but the process of clarification is not yet complete. Up to date, the position which has emerged would appear to be as follows. The dreamer's preconscious attitude towards her husband is ambivalent; and this is the attitude adopted by her central ego towards its external object, as well as towards the internalized representative of this object. However, both the libidinal and the aggressive components in the object-relationship of the central ego are predominantly passive. On the other hand, a considerable proportion of the dreamer's active libido is at the disposal of the libidinal self and is directed towards an internalized object which, for purposes of nomenclature, may perhaps best be described as "the (internal) needed object". At the same time, a considerable proportion of her aggression is at the disposal of the internal saboteur and is directed (a) towards the libidinal self, and (b) towards the needed object (i.e. towards the object of the libidinal self). It cannot fail to be noticed, however, that this summary of the position leaves out of account certain endopsychic relationships which may be presumed to exist—notably (1) the relationship of the central ego to the other egos, and (2) the relationship of the internal saboteur to the internalized object with which it is so closely associated, and which is represented by the maternal component in the actress figure. Taking the latter relationship first, we have no difficulty in seeing that, since the actress in the dream was a composite figure representing both the dreamer's mother and herself, the internal saboteur is closely identified with its object and must therefore be regarded as bound to this object by a strong libidinal attachment. For purposes of description we must give the object a name; and I propose to describe it as "the (internal) rejecting object". I have chosen this term primarily for a reason which will emerge later; but meanwhile my justification will be that the dreamer's mother, who provided the original model of this internalized object, was essentially a rejecting figure, and that it is, so to speak, in the name of this object that the aggression of the internal saboteur is directed against the libidinal self. As regards the relationship of the central ego to the other egos, our most important clue to its nature lies in the fact that, whereas the central ego must be regarded as comprising preconscious and conscious, as well as unconscious, elements, the other egos must equally be regarded as essentially unconscious. From this we may infer that the libidinal ego and the internal saboteur are both rejected by the central ego; and this inference is confirmed by the fact that, as we have seen, the considerable volume of libido and of aggression which has ceased to be at the disposal of the central ego is now at the disposal of the subsidiary egos. Assuming then that the subsidiary egos are rejected by the central ego, it becomes a question of the dynamic of this rejection. Obviously the dynamic of rejection cannot be libido. So there is no alternative but to regard it as aggression. Aggression must, accordingly, be regarded as the characteristic determinant of the attitude of the central ego towards the subsidiary egos.

I have now completed the account of my attempt to reconstruct, in terms of dynamic structure, the endopsychic situation represented in a patient's dream. The account has been cast in the form of a reasoned statement; and, as such, it should serve to give some indication of what is involved in my view that dreams are essentially "shorts" of inner reality (rather than wish-fulfilments). However, it is not primarily with the aim of substantiating my views on dreams in general that I have claimed so much of the reader's attention for a single dream. On the contrary, it is because the dream in question seems to me to represent an endopsychic situation of a classic order, and indeed of a basic character which entitles it to be regarded as the paradigm of all endopsychic situations. For convenience, the general features of this situation are illustrated in the accompanying diagram.

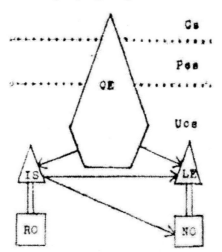

Figure 1   CE, central ego; IS, internal saboteur; LE, libidinal ego; RO, rejecting object; NO, needed object. Cs, conscious; Pcs, preconscious; Ucs, unconscious. →, aggression; =, libido.

The basic endopsychic situation and a revised theory of mental structure founded thereon

I myself feel convinced that the basic endopsychic situation above described is the situation underlying Freud's description of the mental apparatus in terms of ego, id, and super-ego. It is certainly the endopsychic situation upon which I deliberately base the revised theory of mental structure which I now submit, and which is couched in terms of central ego, libidinal ego and internal saboteur. As it would, of course, be natural to expect, there is a general correspondence between Freud's concepts and those which I have now come to adopt. In the case of "the central ego" the correspondence to Freud's "ego" is fairly close from a functional standpoint; but there are important differences between the two concepts. Unlike Freud's "ego", the "central ego" is not conceived as originating out of something else (the "id"), or as constituting a passive structure dependent for its activity upon impulses proceeding from the matrix out of which it originated, and on the surface of which it rests.[3] On the contrary, the "central ego" is conceived as a primary and dynamic structure, from which, as we shall shortly see, the other mental structures are subsequently derived. The "libidinal ego" corresponds, of course, to Freud's "id"; but, whereas according to Freud's view the "ego" is a derivative of the "id", according to my view the "libidinal ego" (which corresponds to the "id") is a derivative of the "central ego" (which corresponds to the "ego"). The "libidinal ego" also differs from the "id" in that it is conceived, not as a mere reservoir of instinctive impulses, but as a dynamic structure comparable to the "central ego", although differing from the latter in various respects, e.g. in its more infantile character, in a lesser degree of organization, in a smaller measure of adaptation to reality and in a greater devotion to internalized objects. The "internal saboteur" differs from the "super-ego" in a number of respects. For one thing it is in no sense conceived as an internal object. It is wholly an ego structure, although, as we have seen, it is very closely associated with an internal object. Actually, the "super-ego" corresponds not so much to the "internal saboteur" as to a compound of this structure and its associated object (like the figure of the actress in the dream). At the same time, the "internal saboteur" is unlike the "super-ego" in that it is conceived as, in itself, devoid of all moral significance. Thus I do not attribute the affect of guilt to its activity, although this activity is unquestionably a prolific source of anxiety. Such anxiety may, of course, merge with guilt; but the two affects are theoretically distinct. Here it should be noted that, whilst introducing the conception of the internal sabo-teur, I am not prepared to abandon the conception of the super-ego as I have now come to abandon that of the id. On the contrary, it seems to me impossible to offer any satisfactory psychological explanation of guilt in the absence of the super-ego; but the super-ego must be regarded as originating at a higher level of mental organization than that at which the internal saboteur operates. Exactly how the activities of the two structures are related must in the meantime remain an open question; but for the most recent expression of my views regarding the origin and the function of the super-ego I must refer the reader to another article (1943).

Splitting of the ego and repression considered as aspects of an identical process operative in both schizoid and hysterical conditions

Before proceeding to consider the origin of what I have called "the basic endopsychic situation", I feel it necessary to record some general conclusions which seem to follow from the inherent nature of the situation itself. The first and most obvious of these conclu-sions is that the ego is split. In this respect, therefore, the basic endopsychic situation which has now emerged conforms to the pattern of the schizoid position—a position which, as already indi-cated, I have come to regard as central (in preference to the depres-sive position). Freud's theory of the mental apparatus was, of course, developed upon a basis of the depressive position; and it is on a similar basis that Melanie Klein has developed her views. By contrast, it is the schizoid position that constitutes the basis of the theory of mental structure which I now advance. It is to be noted, further, that, whilst conforming to the pattern of the schizoid posi-tion, the endopsychic situation revealed in my patient's dream also provided a satisfactory explanation of the dreamer's hysterical frigidity in terms of dynamic structure. Here we are reminded of the common association of hysterical symptoms with an underlying schizoid attitude—an association to which reference has already been made. There would, accordingly, appear to be good grounds for our second conclusion—that hysterical developments are inherently based upon an underlying and fundamental schizoid position. Our third conclusion follows from what has already been said regarding the aggressive attitude of the central ego towards the subsidiary egos. It is to the effect that the splitting of the ego observed in the schizoid position is due to the operation of a certain volume of aggression which remains at the disposal of the central ego. It is this aggression that provides the dynamic of the severance of the subsidiary egos from the central ego. The subsidiary egos are, of course, ordinarily unconscious; and their unconscious status at once raises the suspicion that they are subject to repression. This is obviously so in the case of the libidinal ego (which corresponds to Freud's id); but, if one of the subsidiary ego structures can be repressed, there is no reason for regarding the other as immune from similar treatment at the hands of the central ego. Consequently our fourth conclusion is that the internal saboteur (which largely corresponds to Freud's super-ego in function) is repressed no less than the libidinal ego. This conclusion may at first sight appear to be in conflict with the theory which I previously advanced (1943), to the effect that repression is primarily directed against bad internalized objects. There is no real inconsistency, however; for I regard the repression of the subsidiary egos, which I now envisage, as secondary to the repression of bad internalized objects. Here we find a helpful analogy in the attack of the internal saboteur on the libidinal ego; for, as we have seen, the aggression involved in this attack is primarily directed against the needed object to which the libidinal ego is related, and only secondarily against the libidinal ego itself. Similarly, I regard repression of the libidinal ego on the part of the central ego as secondary to repression of the needed object. Our fifth conclusion needs no elaboration in the light of what precedes. It is to the effect that the dynamic of repression is aggression. Our sixth, and last, conclusion, which follows equally from preceding conclusions, is that splitting of the ego, on the one hand, and repression of the subsidiary egos by the central ego, on the other, constitute essentially the same phenomenon considered from different points of view. Here it is apposite to recall that, whilst the concept of splitting of the ego was formulated by Bleuler in an attempt to explain the phenomena of what was known as "dementia præcox" until he introduced the term "schizophrenia" to take its place, the concept of repression was formulated by Freud in an attempt to explain the phenomena of hysteria. Our final conclusion thus serves to substantiate the view that the position underlying the development of hysterical symptoms is essentially a schizoid position.

The origin of the basic endopsychic situation and of the multiplicity of egos

It is now time for us to turn our attention to questions regarding the origin of the basic endopsychic situation which found a classic expression in my patient's dream. In the light of considerations which have already emerged, it will be obvious that whatever explanation we may reach regarding the origin of this situation will also serve as an explanation of the origin of the schizoid position, the origin of repression and the differentiation of the various fundamental endopsychic structures. As we have seen, the patient whose dream has occupied so much of our attention was essentially ambivalent towards her husband as an external object; and it is from the establishment of a state of ambivalence towards external objects in early life that the basic endopsychic situation springs. The first libidinal object of the infant is, of course, his mother's breast, although there can be no doubt that the form of his mother as a person soon begins to take shape round the original nucleus of this maternal organ. Under theoretically perfect conditions the libidinal relationship of the infant to his mother would be so satisfactory that a state of libidinal frustration could hardly arise; and, as I see it, there would consequently be no ambivalence on the part of the infant towards his object. At this point I must explain that, whilst I regard aggression as a primary dynamic factor in that it does not appear capable of being resolved into libido (as Jung, for example, sought to resolve it), at the same time I regard it as ultimately subordinate to libido, not only metaphysically, but also psychologically. Thus I do not consider that the infant directs aggression spontaneously towards his libidinal object in the absence of frustration; and my observation of the behaviour of animals confirms me in this view. It should be added that in a state of nature the infant would never normally experience that separation from his mother which appears to be imposed upon him increasingly by conditions of civilization. Indeed, it may be inferred that in a state of nature it would be rare for the infant to be deprived of the shelter of his mother's arms and of ready access to her breast until, in the ordinary course of development, he himself became increasingly disposed to dispense with them.[4] Such perfect conditions are, however, only theoretically possible for the human infant born into a cultural group; and in actual fact the libidinal relationship of the infant to his mother is disturbed from the first by a considerable measure of frustration, although, of course, the degree of such frustration varies in different cases. It is the experience of libidinal frustration that calls forth the infant's aggression in relation to his libidinal object and thus gives rise to a state of ambivalence. To content ourselves with saying simply that the infant becomes ambivalent would, however, be to give an incomplete and partial picture of the situation which now arises; for it would be a picture conceived exclusively from the point of view of the observer. From the point of view of the infant himself it is a case of his mother becoming an ambivalent object, i.e. an object which is both good and bad. Since it proves intolerable to him to have a good object which is also bad, he seeks to alleviate the situation by splitting the figure of his mother into two objects. Then, in so far as she satisfies him libidinally, she is a good object, and, in so far as she fails to satisfy him libidinally, she is a bad object. The situation in which he now finds himself placed proves, however, in its turn to be one which imposes a severe strain upon his capacity for endurance and his power of adjustment. Being a situation in outer reality, it is one which he finds himself impotent to control, and which, accordingly, he seeks to mitigate by such means as are at his disposal. The means at his disposal are limited; and the technique which he adopts is more or less dictated by this limitation. He accordingly follows the only path open to him and, since outer reality seems unyielding, he does his best to transfer the traumatic factor in the situation to the field of inner reality, within which he feels situations to be more under his own control. This means that he internalizes his mother as a bad object. Here I would remind the reader that, in my opinion, it is always the bad object (i.e., at this stage, the unsatisfying object) that is internalized in the first instance; for (as already indicated in a footnote) I find it difficult to attach any meaning to the primary internalization of a good object which is both satisfying and amenable from the infant's point of view. There are those, of course, who would argue that it would be natural for the infant, when in a state of deprivation, to internalize the good object on the wish-fulfilment principle; but, as it seems to me, internalization of objects is essentially a measure of coercion and it is not the satisfying object, but the unsatisfying object that the infant seeks to coerce. I speak here of "the satisfying object" and "the unsatisfying object", rather than of "the good object" and "the bad object", because I consider that, in this connection, the terms "good object" and "bad object" tend to be misleading. They tend to be misleading because they are liable to be understood in the sense of "desired object" and "undesired object" respectively. There can be no doubt, however, that a bad object may be desired. Indeed it is just because the infant's bad object is desired as well as felt to be bad that it is internalized. The trouble is that it remains bad after it has been internalized, i.e. it remains unsatisfying. At this point an important consideration arises. Unlike the satisfying object, the unsatisfying object has, so to speak, two facets. On the one hand, it frustrates; and, on the other hand, it tempts and allures. Indeed its essential "badness" consists precisely in the fact that it combines allurement with frustration. Further, it retains both these qualities after internalization. After internalizing the unsatisfying object, accordingly, the infant finds himself in the quandary of "out of the frying-pan into the fire". In his attempts to control the unsatisfying object, he has introduced into the inner economy of his mind an object which not only continues to frustrate his need, but also continues to whet it. He thus finds himself confronted with another intolerable situation—this time an internal one. How does he seek to deal with it? As we have seen, in his attempt to deal with the intolerable external situation with which he was originally faced his technique was to split the maternal object into two objects, (a) the "good" and (b) the "bad", and then proceed to internalize the bad object; and in his attempt to deal with the intolerable internal situation which subsequently arises he adopts a technique which is not altogether dissimilar. He splits the bad internal object into two objects—(a) the tempting or needed object and (b) the frustrating object; and then he represses both these objects (employing aggression, of course, as the dynamic of repression). Here a complication arises, however; for his libidinal attachment to the undivided object is shared, albeit not in equal proportions, by the objects resulting from division. The consequence is that, in the process of repressing the resultant objects, the ego, so to speak, develops pseudopodia by means of which it still maintains libidinal attachments to the objects undergoing repression. The development of these pseudopodia represents the initial stage of a division of the ego. As repression of the objects proceeds, the incipient division of the ego becomes an accomplished fact. The two pseudopodia are rejected by the part of the ego which remains central on account of their connection with the rejected objects; and with their associated objects they share the fate of repression. It is in this way that the two subsidiary egos, the libidinal ego and the internal saboteur, come to be split off from the central ego, and that a multiplicity of egos arises.

The divide et impera technique for the disposal of libido and aggression

It will be noted that the situation resulting from the sequence of processes which has just been described has now assumed the *structural* pattern of what I have called "the basic endopsychic situation". It has also assumed the *dynamic* pattern of this situation except in one important respect—that the aggressive attitude adopted by the internal saboteur towards the libidinal ego and its associated object (the needed object) is still left out of the picture. In order to explain the origin of this feature of the situation, we must return to the original ambivalence of the child towards his mother and consider from a fresh angle what this involves. This time we shall consider the child's reactions, less in their conative, and more in their affective aspect. It is natural for the child, not only to be impulsive, but also to express his feelings in no uncertain terms. Moreover, it is through the expression of his feelings that he makes his chief impression upon his objects. Once ambivalence has been established, however, the expression of feeling towards his mother involves him in a position which must seem to him singularly precarious. Here it must be pointed out that what presents itself to him from a strictly conative standpoint as *frustration* at the hands of his mother presents itself to him in a very different light from a strictly affective standpoint. From the latter standpoint, what he experiences is a sense of lack of love, and indeed emotional *rejection* on his mother's part. This being so, the expression of hate towards her as a rejecting object becomes in his eyes a very dangerous procedure. On the one hand, it is calculated to make her reject him all the more, and thus to increase her "badness" and make her seem *more real* in her capacity of bad object. On the other hand, it is calculated to make her love him less, and thus to decrease her "goodness" and make her seem *less real* (i.e. destroy her) in her capacity of good object. At the same time, it also becomes a dangerous procedure for the child to express his libidinal need, i.e. his nascent love, of his mother in face of rejection at her hands; for it is equivalent to discharging his libido into an emotional vacuum. Such a discharge is accompanied by an affective experience which is singularly devastating. In the older child this experience is one of intense humiliation over the depreciation of his love, which seems to be involved. At a somewhat deeper level (or at an earlier stage) the experience is one of shame over the display of needs which are disregarded or belittled. In virtue of these experiences of humiliation and shame he feels reduced to a state of worthlessness, destitution or beggardom. His sense of his own value is threatened; and he feels bad in the sense of "inferior". The intensity of these experiences is, of course, proportionate to the intensity of his need; and intensity of need itself increases his sense of badness by contributing to it the quality of "demanding too much". At the same time his sense of badness is further complicated by the sense of utter impotence which he also experiences. At a still deeper level (or at a still earlier stage) the child's experience is one of, so to speak, exploding ineffectively and being completely emptied of libido. It is thus an experience of disintegration and of imminent psychical death.

We can understand accordingly how precarious a matter it becomes for the child, when confronted with the experience of rejection by his mother, to express either aggressive or libidinal affect towards her. Reduced to its simplest terms, the position in which he finds himself placed would appear to be one in which, if, on the one hand, he expresses aggression, he is threatened with loss of his good object, and, if, on the other hand, he expresses libidinal need, he is threatened with the loss of his libido (which for him constitutes his own goodness) and ultimately with loss of the ego structure which constitutes himself. Of these two threats by which the child feels menaced, the former (i.e. loss of the good object) would appear to be that which gives rise to the affect of depression, and which provides a basis for the subsequent development of a melancholic state in individuals for whom the disposal of aggression presents greater difficulties than the disposal of libido. On the other hand, the latter threat (i.e. loss of libido and of ego structure) would appear to be that which gives rise to the affect of futility, and which provides a basis for the subsequent development of a schizoid state in individuals for whom the disposal of libido presents greater difficulties than the disposal of aggression.

So far as the ætiology of depressive and schizoid states is concerned, views similar to those just indicated have already been developed by me at some length previously (1941). In the present instance, however, our immediate concern is with the measures adopted by the child to circumvent the various dangers which appear to him to attend the expression of affect, whether libidinal or aggressive, towards his mother when he is faced with the experience of rejection at her hands. As we have already seen, he attempts to deal with the ambivalent situation successively (1) by splitting the figure of his mother into two objects, a good and a bad, (2) by internalizing the bad object in an endeavour to control it, (3) by splitting the bad internalized object in turn into two objects, viz. (a) the tempting or needed object, and (b) the rejecting object, (4) by repressing both these objects and employing a certain volume of his aggression in the process, and (5) by employing a further volume of his aggression in splitting off from his central ego and repressing two subsidiary egos which remain attached to these respective internalized objects by libidinal ties. These various measures, based upon the techniques of internalization and splitting, serve to mitigate the asperities of the situation resulting from the child's experience of frustration in his relationship with his mother and his sense of rejection at her hands; but, except in the most extreme cases, they do not succeed in eliminating the child's need of his mother as an object in outer reality, or in robbing her of all significance—which, after all, is just as well. In conformity with this fact, his libido and his aggression are very far from being wholly absorbed in the processes so far described; and, consequently, the risks involved in the expression of libidinal and aggressive affect towards his mother as a rejecting object still remain to be met. The measures so far described thus require to be supplemented. Actually they are supplemented by a very obvious technique which is closely akin to the well-known principle of "*Divide et impera*". The child seeks to circumvent the dangers of expressing both libidinal and aggressive affect towards his object by using a maximum of his aggression to subdue a maximum of his libidinal need. In this way he reduces the volume of affect, both libidinal and aggressive, demanding outward expression. As has already been pointed out, of course, neither libido nor aggression can be considered as existing in a state of divorce from structure. Accordingly, what remains for us to decide is to which of the ego structures already described the child's excess of libido and excess of aggression are to be respectively allotted. This is a question to which the answer can be in no doubt. The excess of libido is taken over by the libidinal ego; and the excess of aggression is taken over by the internal saboteur. The child's technique of using aggression to subdue libidinal need thus resolves itself into an attack by the internal saboteur upon the libidinal ego. The libidinal ego in its turn directs the excess of libido with which it becomes charged towards its associated object, the needed object. On the other hand, the attack of the internal saboteur upon this object represents a persistence of the child's original resentment towards his mother as a temptress inciting the very need which she fails to satisfy and thus reducing him to bondage—just as, indeed, the attack of the internal saboteur upon the libidinal ego represents a persistence of the hatred which the child comes to feel towards himself for the dependence dictated by his need. It should be added that the processes just described take place simultaneously with those which they are designed to supplement, although, in the interests of clarity of exposition, they have been described separately.

Direct repression, libidinal resistance and indirect repression

Now that the origin of the aggressive attitude adopted by the internal saboteur towards the libidinal ego and the needed object has been described, our account of the processes which determine the dynamic pattern of the basic endopsychic situation is complete. At this point, however, something requires to be added to what has already been said regarding the nature and origin of repression. In terms of the line of thought so far developed, repression is a process originating in a rejection of both the needed object and the rejecting object on the part of the undivided ego. This primary process of repression is accompanied by a secondary process of repression whereby the ego splits off and rejects two parts of itself, which remain attached respectively to one and the other of the repressed internal objects. The resulting situation is one in which the central ego (the residue of the undivided ego) adopts an attitude of rejection, not only towards the needed object and the rejecting object, but also towards the split off and subsidiary egos attached to these respective objects, i.e. the libidinal ego and the internal saboteur. This attitude of rejection adopted by the central ego constitutes repression; and the dynamic of the rejection is aggression. So far so good. But this explanation of the nature and origin of repression is incomplete in so far as it has not yet taken into account what is involved in the technique of reducing the volume of libido and aggression available for expression towards external objects by employing a maximum of aggression to subdue a maximum of libido. As we have seen, this technique resolves itself into a process whereby (a) the excess of aggression is taken over by the internal saboteur and devoted to an attack upon the libidinal ego, and (b) the excess of libido is taken over by the libidinal ego and directed towards the needed object. When the full significance of this process is considered, it becomes at once plain that the relentless attack of the internal saboteur upon the libidinal ego must operate as a very powerful factor in furthering the aims of repression. Indeed, so far as dynamic is concerned, it seems more than likely that this is the most important factor in the maintenance of repression. Obviously it is upon the phenomenon just mentioned that Freud's conception of the super-ego and its repressive functions is based; for the uncompromising hostility which, according to Freud, characterizes the attitude of the super-ego towards id impulses coincides exactly with the uncompromisingly aggressive attitude adopted by the internal saboteur towards the libidinal ego. Similarly, Freud's observation that the self-reproaches of the melancholic are ultimately reproaches directed against the loved object falls readily into line with the aggressive attitude adopted towards the needed object by the internal saboteur.

There is no need at this point to repeat the criticisms already passed upon Freud's conceptions of the super-ego and the id, and upon all that is involved in these conceptions. It does, however, seem desirable to draw attention to the fact that, in his description of repression, Freud left completely out of account all that is involved in the phenomenon which I have described as the attachment of the libidinal ego to the needed object. As we have seen, this attachment comes to absorb a considerable volume of libido. Further, the volume of libido in question is directed towards an object which is both internal and repressed; and, in conformity with this fact, it is inevitably oriented away from outer reality. Such being the case, the object-seeking of the libidinal ego operates as a resistance which powerfully reinforces the resistance directly resulting from repression, and which is thus no less in conflict with therapeutic aims than is the latter resistance. This is a theme which I have already developed, *mutatis mutandis*, elsewhere (1943). I add the proviso "*mutatis mutandis*" here, because, at the time when I wrote the article referred to, I had not yet formulated my present views regarding endopsychic structures; but the effect of these latter views is to give greater point, rather than otherwise, to the original theme. This theme is, of course, in direct conflict with Freud's statement (1920g), (19): "The unconscious, i.e. the 'repressed' material, offers no resistance whatever to curative efforts." It is, however, a theme which develops naturally out of the view that libido is primarily object-seeking, once we come to consider what happens when the object sought is a repressed internal object; and, in terms of my present standpoint, there can be no room for doubt that the obstinate attachment of the libidinal ego to the needed object and its reluctance to renounce this object constitute a particularly formidable source of resistance—and one which plays no small part in determining what is known as the negative therapeutic reaction. The attachment in question, being libidinal in character, cannot, of course, be regarded as in itself a repressive phenomenon; but, whilst itself a resultant of repression exercised by the central ego, it also functions as a powerful aid to this process of repression. The attack of the internal saboteur upon the object of the libidinal ego (the needed object) serves, of course, to perpetuate the attachment of the libidinal ego to its object by virtue of the fact that this object is being constantly threatened. Here we catch a glimpse of the original wolf under its sheep's clothing, i.e. we catch a glimpse of the original ambivalent situation persisting underneath all its disguises; for what the obstinate attachment of the libidinal ego to the needed object and the equally obstinate aggression of the internal saboteur towards the same object really represent is the obstinacy of the original ambivalent attitude. The truth is that, however well the fact may be disguised, the individual is extremely reluctant to abandon his original hate, no less than his original need, of his original objects in childhood. This holds particularly true of psychoneurotic and psychotic individuals, not to mention those who fall into the category of psychopathic personality.

If the attachment of the libidinal ego to the needed object serves as a powerful aid to repression, the same may equally be said of the aggressive attitude adopted towards this internal object by the internal saboteur. So far as the actual process if repression is concerned, however, the latter differs from the former in one important respect; for not only does it forward the aim of repression, but it also actually operates in the same manner as repression. In its attack upon the needed object it performs a function which constitutes it a cobelligerent, albeit not an ally, of the central ego, whose repression of the needed object represents, as we have seen, a manifestation of aggression. The internal saboteur functions further as a cobelligerent of the central ego in respect of its attack upon the libidinal ego—an attack which serves to supplement that involved in the repression of this ego by the central ego. There is a sense, therefore, in which it would be true to say that the attacks of the internal saboteur upon the libidinal ego and upon its associated object represent an *indirect form of repression*, whereby the direct repression of these structures by the central ego is both supplemented and facilitated.

As we have already seen, the subsidiary egos owe their origin to a split of the undivided ego: but, as we have also seen, what presents itself from a topographic standpoint as simply a split of the ego presents itself from a dynamic standpoint as an active rejection and repression of both the subsidiary egos on the part of the central ego. It thus becomes a matter for some comment that, whilst both the libidinal ego and the internal saboteur share a common fate so far as direct repression is concerned, only one of the subsidiary egos, viz. the libidinal ego, should be subjected to the process of indirect repression. When the difference between direct and indirect repression is considered in the light of what has already been said, it is, of course, plain that the process of repression described by Freud corresponds very much more closely to what I have described as indirect repression than to what I have described as direct repression. Nevertheless, when Freud's conception of repression is compared with my conception of the total phenomenon of repression, both direct and indirect, this common feature may be detected—that the libidinal components in the psyche are subjected to a much greater measure of repression than the aggressive components. There can be no doubt, of course, that the repression of aggressive components does occur: but it is difficult to see how this fact can be consistently explained in terms of Freud's theory of the mental apparatus. This theory, conceived as it is in terms of a fundamental divorce between impulse and structure, would appear to permit only of the repression of libido: for, in terms of Freud's theory, the repression of aggression would involve the anomaly of aggression being used to repress aggression. By contrast, if, in conformity with the point of view which I advocate, we conceive of impulse as inseparable from structure and as representing simply the dynamic aspect of structure, the repression of aggressive components in the psyche is no more difficult to account for than the repression of libidinal components. It then becomes a question, not of aggression repressing aggression, but of one ego structure using aggression to repress another ego structure charged with aggression. This being so, my view to the effect that the internal saboteur, no less than the libidinal ego, is repressed by the central ego provides a satisfactory explanation of the repression of aggressive components. At the same time, the fact that libidinal components are subject to a greater measure of repression than aggressive components is satisfactorily explained by means of the conception of indirect repression. The truth would appear to be that, if *the principle of repression* governs the disposal of *excess libido* in greater measure than it governs the disposal of excess aggression, *the principle of topographical redistribution* governs the disposal of excess aggression in greater measure than it governs the disposal of excess libido.

The significance of the Oedipus situation

I have already said enough to indicate that the technique whereby aggression is employed to subdue libido is a process which finds a common place in Freud's conception of "repression" and my own conception of "indirect repression". At the same time, my views regarding the origin of this technique differ from those of Freud. According to Freud, the technique originates as a means of averting the expression of libidinal (incestuous) impulses towards one parent and aggressive (parenticidal) impulses towards the other parent in the setting of the Oedipus situation. According to my view, on the other hand, the technique originates in infancy as a means of averting the expression of both libido and aggression on the part of the infant towards his mother, who at this stage constitutes his only significant object, and upon whom he is wholly dependent. This discrepancy of views will be interpreted, quite correctly, in the sense that I have departed from Freud in my evaluation of the Oedipus situation as an explanatory concept. For Freud, the Oedipus situation is, so to speak, an ultimate cause; but this is a view with which I no longer find it possible to agree. So far from agreeing, I now consider that the role of ultimate cause, which Freud allotted to the Oedipus situation, should properly be allotted to the phenomenon of infantile dependence. In conformity with this standpoint, the Oedipus situation presents itself, not so much in the light of a causal phenomenon as in the light of an end-product. It is not a basic situation, but the derivative of a situation which has priority over it not only in the logical, but also in the temporal sense. This prior situation is one which issues directly out of the physical and emotional dependence of the infant upon his mother, and which declares itself in the relationship of the infant to his mother long before his father becomes a significant object. The present is no occasion for an elaboration of the views which I have now reached regarding the Oedipus situation—views which have been in some measure adumbrated already (1941). Nevertheless, in view of the comparison which I have just drawn between my own conception of repression and Freud's conception, formulated as it is in terms of the Oedipus situation, it seems desirable that I should indicate briefly how I propose to introduce this classic situation into the general scheme which I have outlined. It will hardly be necessary to remind the reader that I have dispensed with the Oedipus situation as an explanatory concept not only in my account of the origin of repression, but also in my account of the genesis of the basic endopsychic situation and in my account of the differentiation of endopsychic structure. These accounts have been formulated exclusively in terms of the measures adopted by the child in an attempt to cope with the difficulties inherent in the ambivalent situation which develops during his infancy in his relationship with his mother as his original object. The various measures which the child adopts in his attempt to deal with this ambivalent situation have all been adopted before the Oedipus situation develops. It is in the setting of the child's relationship to his mother that the basic endopsychic situation is established, that the differentiation of endopsychic structure is accomplished and that repression is originated; and it is only after these developments have occurred that the child is called upon to meet the particular difficulties which attend the Oedipus situation. So far from furnishing an explanatory concept, therefore, the Oedipus situation is rather a phenomenon to be explained in terms of an endopsychic situation which has already developed.

The chief novelty introduced into the child's world by the Oedipus situation, as this materializes in outer reality, is that he is now confronted with two distinct parental objects instead of with only one as formerly. His relationship with his new object, viz. his father, is, of course, inevitably fraught with vicissitudes similar to those which he previously experienced in his relationship with his mother—and, in particular, the vicissitudes of need, frustration and rejection. In view of these vicissitudes, his father becomes an ambivalent object to him, whilst at the same time he himself becomes ambivalent towards his father. In his relationship with his father he is thus faced with the same problem of adjustment as that with which he was originally faced in his relationship with his mother. The original situation is reinstated, albeit this time in relation to a fresh object; and, very naturally, he seeks to meet the difficulties of the reinstated situation by means of the same series of techniques which he learned to adopt in meeting the difficulties of the original situation. He splits the figure of his father into a good and a bad object, internalizes the bad object and splits the internalized bad object into (a) a needed object associated with the libidinal ego and (b) a rejecting object associated with the internal saboteur. It should be added that the new paternal needed object would appear to be partly superimposed upon, and partly fused with the old maternal needed object, and that similarly the paternal rejecting object is partly superimposed upon, and partly fused with the maternal rejecting object.

The adjustment which the child is called upon to make in relation to his father differs, of course, in one important respect from that which he was previously called upon to make in relation to his mother. It differs in the extent to which it has to be achieved upon an emotional plane. The new adjustment must be almost exclusively emotional; for in his relationship with his father the child is necessarily precluded from the experience of feeding at the breast. We are thus introduced to a further important respect in which his adjustment to his father must differ from his previous adjustment to his mother. His father is a man, whereas his mother is a woman. It is more than doubtful, however, whether the child at first appreciates the genital difference between the two parents. It would appear rather that the difference which he does appreciate is that his father has no breasts. His father thus first presents himself to the child as a parent without breasts; and this is one of the chief reasons that his relationship with his father has to be established so much more on an emotional plane than his relationship with his mother. On the other hand, it is because the child does have the experience of a physical relationship with his mother's breast, while also experiencing a varying degree of frustration in this relationship, that his need for his mother persists so obstinately beneath his need for his father and all subsequent genital needs. When the child comes to appreciate, in some measure at least, the genital difference between his parents, and as, in the course of his own development, his physical need tends to flow increasingly (albeit in varying degrees) through genital channels, his need for his mother comes to include a need for her vagina. At the same time, his need for his father comes to include a need for his father's penis. The strength of these physical needs for his parents' genitals varies, however, in inverse proportion to the satisfaction of his emotional needs. Thus, the more satisfactory his emotional relations with his parents, the less urgent are his physical needs for their genitals. These latter needs are, of course, never satisfied, although substitutive satisfactions may be sought, e.g. those of sexual curiosity. Consequently, some measure of ambivalence necessarily develops in relation to his mother's vagina and his father's penis. This ambivalence is reflected, incidentally, in sadistic conceptions of the primal scene. By the time the primal scene is envisaged, however, the relationships of his parents to one another have become a matter of moment for the child; and jealousy of each of his parents in relation to the other begins to assert itself. The chief incidence of his jealousy is, of course, partly determined by the biological sex of the child; but it is also in no small measure determined by the state of his emotional relationships with his respective parents. Be this as it may, the child is now called upon to meet the difficulties of two ambivalent situations at the same time; and he seeks to meet these difficulties by the familiar series of techniques. The result is that he internalizes both a bad maternal genital figure and a bad paternal genital figure and splits each of these into two figures, which are embodied respectively in the structures of the needed object and the rejecting object. It will thus be seen that, before the child is very old, these internal objects have already assumed the form of complex composite structures. They are built up partly on a basis of the superimposition of one object upon another, and partly on a basis of the fusion of objects. The extent to which the internal objects are built up respectively on a basis of layering and on a basis of fusion differs, of course, from individual to individual; and the extent to which either layering or fusion predominates would appear to be a matter of no small importance. Thus, in conjunction with the proportioning of the various component objects, it would appear to play an important part in determining the psycho-sexual attitude of the individual in so far as this is not determined by biological sexual factors. Likewise, in conjunction with the proportioning of the component objects, it would appear to be the chief determining factor in the ætiology of the sexual perversions. We may thus envisage an ætiology of the perversions conceived in terms of object-relationship psychology.

It will be noticed that in the preceding account the personal pronoun employed to indicate the child has been consistently masculine. This must not be taken to imply that the account applies only to the boy. It applies equally to the girl; and the masculine pronoun has been used only because the advantages of a personal pronoun of some kind appear to outweigh those of the impersonal pronoun, however non-committal this may be. It will also be noticed that the classic Oedipus situation has not yet emerged. The stage which was last described was one at which, whilst the relations of his parents with one another had become significant to the child, his position was essentially one of ambivalence towards both parents. We have seen, however, that the child seeks to deal with both ambivalent situations by a series of processes in consequence of which genital figures of each of his parents come to be embodied both in the structure of the needed object and in that of the rejecting object. It must be recognized, of course, that the biological sex of the child must play some part in determining his attitude to his respective parents; but that this is very far from being the sole determining factor is obvious from the frequency of inverted and mixed Oedipus situations. Considered in terms of the views which I have outlined, these inverted and mixed Oedipus situations must necessarily be determined by the constitution of the needed object and the rejecting object. It is, therefore, only taking a further step in the same direction to conclude that the same consideration applies to the positive Oedipus situation. The fact then would appear to be that *the Oedipus situation is not really an external situation at all, but an internal situation*—one which may be transferred in varying degrees to the actual external situation. Once the Oedipus situation comes to be regarded as essentially an internal situation, it is not difficult to see that the maternal components of both the internal objects have, so to speak, a great initial advantage over the paternal components; and this, of course, applies to children of both sexes. The strong position of the maternal components is, of course, due to the fact that the nuclei of both the internal objects are derivatives of the original ambivalent mother and her ambivalent breasts. In conformity with this fact, *of sufficiently deep analysis of the Oedipus situation* invariably reveals that this situation is built up around the figures of an internal needed mother and an internal rejecting mother. It was, of course, on a basis of hysterical phenomena that Freud originally formulated the concept of the Oedipus situation; and according to Abraham's "phase" theory the origin of hysteria is to be traced to a fixation in the genital (phallic) phase. I have already (1941) passed various criticisms on Abraham's "phase" theory; and so I shall be merely passing a further criticism, if only by implication, when I say that I have yet to analyse the hysteric, male or female, who does not turn out to be an inveterate breast-seeker at heart. I venture to suggest that the deep analysis of a positive Oedipus situation may be regarded as taking place at three main levels. At the first level the picture is dominated by the Oedipus situation itself. At the next level it is dominated by ambivalence towards the heterosexual parent; and at the deepest level it is dominated by ambivalence towards the mother. Traces of all these stages may be detected in the classic drama of *Hamlet*; but there can be no doubt that, both in the role of needed and tempting object and in that of rejecting object, the Queen is the real villain of the piece. The position then would appear to be this. The child finds it intolerable enough to be called upon to deal with a single ambivalent object; but, when he is called upon to deal with two, he finds it still more intolerable. He, therefore, seeks to simplify a complex situation, in which he finds himself confronted with two needed objects and two rejecting objects, by converting it into one in which he will only be confronted with a single needed object and a single rejecting object; and he achieves this aim, with, of course, a varying measure of success, by concentrating upon the needed aspect of one parent and the rejecting aspect of the other. He thus, for all practical purposes, comes to equate one parental object with the needed object, and the other with the rejecting object; and by so doing *the child constitutes the Oedipus situation for himself.* Ambivalence to both parents persists, however, in the background; and at rock bottom both the needed object and the rejecting object remain what they originally were, viz. figures of his mother.

Neurotic anxiety and hysterical suffering

I have spoken of the *divide et impera* technique as a means of reducing the volume of affect (both libidinal and aggressive) which demands outward expression; and at this point it would be both relevant and profitable to consider in some detail what happens when the attack of the internal saboteur upon the libidinal ego fails to subdue libidinal need sufficiently to meet the requirements of the central ego, i.e. sufficiently to reduce the volume of available libidinal affect to manageable proportions. It is impossible, however, to embark upon so large a theme on the present occasion. Suffice it to say that, when the technique in question does not succeed in reducing the volume of libidinal affect sufficiently and so fails to fulfil its primary function, it appears to assume a secondary function, in virtue of which it imposes a change of quality upon such libidinal affect as insists upon emerging and thereby disguises the quality of the original affect. Thus, when the dynamic tension within the libidinal ego rises above a certain threshold value and an excess of libidinal need threatens to assert itself, the emergent libidinal affect is converted into (neurotic) *anxiety* by the impact of the aggression which is directed against the libidinal ego by the internal saboteur. When the dynamic tension within the libidinal ego continues to rise until it reaches a further threshold value, it becomes no longer possible for a libidinal discharge to be averted; and the attack of the internal saboteur upon the libidinal ego then has the effect of imparting a *painful* quality to the libidinal affect accompanying the inevitable discharge. Such, at any rate, would appear to be the process involved in the hysterical mode of expressing affect—a process which demands that the expression of libidinal need shall be experienced as suffering.

The psychology of dynamic structure and its general scientific background

In the light of what has just been said regarding the genesis of (neurotic) anxiety, it will be noted that my conception of the nature of anxiety is closely in accord with Freud's original conception, viz. that anxiety is a converted form of undischarged libido. Here we find but one example of the somewhat remarkable fact that, if the general standpoint which I have now come to adopt represents a departure from some of Freud's later views, it has had the effect of revivifying some of Freud's earlier views (views which, in some cases, have latterly been in abeyance). The explanation of this general phenomenon would appear to be that, whilst at every point there is a recognizable analogy between my present views and those of Freud, the development of my views follows a path which diverges gradually from that followed by the historical development of Freud's views. This divergence of paths itself admits of only one explanation—a difference in certain basic theoretic principles. The central points of difference are not difficult to localize. They are two in number. In the first place, although Freud's whole system of thought was concerned with object-relationships, he adhered theoretically to the principle that libido is primarily pleasure-seeking, i.e. that it is directionless. By contrast, I adhere to the principle that libido is primarily object-seeking, i.e. that it has direction. For that matter, I regard aggression as having direction also, whereas, by implication at any rate, Freud regards aggression as, like libido, theoretically directionless. In the second place, Freud regards impulse (i.e. psychical energy) as theoretically distinct from structure, whereas I do not accept this distinction as valid and adhere to the principle of dynamic structure. Of these two central points of difference between Freud's views and those which I have now come to adopt, the latter is the more fundamental; and indeed the former would appear to depend upon the latter. Thus Freud's view that libido is primarily pleasure-seeking follows directly from his divorce of energy from structure; for, once energy is divorced from structure, the only psychical change which can be envisaged as other than disturbing, i.e. as pleasant, is one which makes for the establishment of an equilibrium of forces, i.e. a directionless change. By contrast, if we conceive of energy as inseparable from structure, then the only changes which are intelligible are changes in structural relationships and in relationships between structures; and such changes are essentially directional.

No man, even the greatest and most original, can remain wholly independent of the scientific background of his day; and it cannot be claimed that even Freud provides an exception to this rule. Here we must remind ourselves of the scientific atmosphere of the nineteenth century in which Freud was nurtured. This atmosphere was dominated by the Helmholtzian conception that the physical universe consisted in a conglomeration of inert, immutable and indivisible particles to which motion was imparted by a fixed quantity of energy separate from the particles themselves. The energy in question was conceived as having been, for some unknown reason, unevenly distributed at the beginning and as subsequently undergoing a gradual process of redistribution calculated to lead eventually to an equilibrium of forces and an immobilization of the solid particles. Such being the prevailing conception of the contemporary physicist, it is not difficult to understand how it came about that, when Freud, in advance of his time, set himself the arduous task of introducing order into the hitherto confused realm of psycho-pathology, he should have remained sufficiently under the influence of the scientific atmosphere of his day to conceive impulse (psychical energy) as separate from structure and to cast his libido theory in an equilibrium-seeking mould. In my opinion, however, this feature constitutes a limitation imposed by outside influences upon his thought, which otherwise represented an historic advance upon prevailing conceptions in the psychological field, and which was much more in the spirit of the new scientific outlook at present emerging; for during the twentieth century the scientific conception of the physical universe has already undergone a profound change. The inert and indivisible particles or atoms, of which the physical universe was formerly thought to be composed, are now known to be structures of the greatest complexity embodying almost incredible quantities of energy—energy in the absence of which the structures themselves would be unintelligible, but which is equally difficult to explain in the absence of the structures. This intra-atomic energy has effects which not only determine intra-atomic relationships, but also influence bodies at enormous distances. The most remarkable of these effects is radiation; and it has been found necessary to call in radiation to explain certain of the phenomena of light, which defied explanation on the basis of the wave theory of the previous scientific epoch. Interestingly enough, radiation has proved to possess at least one of the properties formerly regarded as a prerogative of solid matter, viz. mass; and the occurrence of radiation affects the structure of both the emitting and the receiving atoms. Further, the universe itself is conceived as undergoing a process of change other than that involved in the establishment of an equilibrium within a closed system. Thus it would appear that the universe is expanding at a terrific speed. The major forces at work are attraction and repulsion (cf. libido and aggression); but, although attraction has the effect of producing local condensations of matter, the dominant force, at any rate during the present phase, is repulsion. So far from being in process of establishing a non-directional equilibrium, therefore, the universe is in process of expanding towards a limit at which no further expansion will be possible and everything will be so attenuated that no further mutual influences will occur and nothing more will be able to happen. The change which the universe is undergoing is thus a directional change. Such being the general scientific background of the present day, it seems to me a demand of the times, if nothing else, that our psychological ideas should be reformulated in terms of a relationship psychology conceived on a basis of dynamic structure.

The psychology of dynamic structure as an explanatory system

As an explanatory system, the psychology of dynamic structure which I envisage seems to me to have many advantages, among which by no means the least is that it provides a more satisfactory basis than does any other type of psychology for the explanation of group phenomena. However, this is a theme which, like certain others touched upon in this article, must be left for another occasion. It remains for me, in my concluding remarks, to say something regarding the advantages which appear to accrue from the particular theory of mental structure which I have advanced in place of Freud's classic theory. It is obvious, of course, that, from a topographic standpoint, Freud's theory only admits of the operation of three factors (id, ego and super-ego) in the production of the variety of clinical states with which we are familiar. By contrast, my theory admits of the operation of five factors (central ego, libidinal ego, internal saboteur, needed object and rejecting object)—even when the super-ego as I conceive it is left out of account. My theory, accordingly, offers a greater range of ætiological possibilities. In actual practice, the difference between the two theories as regards ætiological possibilities is even greater than at first appears; for, of the three factors envisaged in Freud's theory, only two (the ego and the super-ego) are structures properly speaking—the third (viz. the id) being only a source of energy. The energy proceeding from the id is, of course, conceived by Freud as assuming two forms—libido and aggression. Consequently, Freud's theory admits of the operation of two structural and two dynamic factors in all. Freud's two dynamic factors find a place, of course, in my own theory; but, according to my theory, the number of the structural factors is not two, but five. Thus, with five structural factors and two dynamic factors to conjure with, my theory permits of a much greater range of permutations and combinations than does Freud's theory. Actually, however, the possibilities left open by Freud's theory in the abstract are still further limited by his conception of the function of the super-ego, which he regards not only as characteristically aggressive, but also as characteristically antilibidinal. According to Freud, therefore, the endopsychic drama largely resolves itself into a conflict between the ego in a libidinal capacity and the super-ego in an anti-libidinal capacity. The original dualism inherent in Freud's earliest views regarding repression thus remains substantially unaffected by his subsequent theory of mental structure. Such a conception of the endopsychic drama is unduly limiting, not only so far as its implications for social psychology are concerned (e.g. the implication that social institutions are primarily repressive), but also so far as concerns its explanatory value within the psychopathological and characterological fields. Within these fields explanation reduces itself to an account of the attitudes adopted by the ego in a libidinal capacity vis-à-vis the super-ego. By contrast, my theory possesses all the features of an explanatory system enabling psychopathological and characterological phenomena of all kinds to be described in terms of the patterns assumed by a complex of relationships between a variety of structures. It also possesses the advantage of enabling psychopathological symptoms to be explained directly in terms of structural conformations, and thus of doing justice to the unquestionable fact that, so far from being independent phenomena, symptoms are but expressions of the personality as a whole.

At this juncture it becomes necessary to point out (if indeed it has not already become sufficiently obvious) that the basic endopsychic situation which I have described, and to which I have attached such importance, is by no means conceived as immutable from the economic standpoint. From the topographic standpoint, it must be regarded as relatively immutable, although I conceive it as one of the chief aims of psycho-analytical therapy to introduce some change into its topography by way of territorial adjustment. Thus I conceive it as among the most important functions of psycho-analytical therapy (a) to reduce the split of the original ego by restoring to the central ego a maximum of the territories ceded to the libidinal ego and the internal saboteur, and (b) to bring the needed object and the rejecting object so far as possible within the sphere of influence of the central ego. The extent to which such changes can be effected appears, however, to be strictly limited. In its economic aspect, by contrast, the basic endopsychic situation is capable of very extensive modification. In conformity with this fact, I conceive it as another of the chief aims of psycho-analytical therapy to reduce to a minimum (a) the attachment of the subsidiary egos to their respective associated objects, (b) the aggression of the central ego towards the subsidiary egos and their objects, and (c) the aggression of the internal saboteur towards the libidinal ego and its object. On the other hand, the basic endopsychic situation is undoubtedly capable of considerable modification in a psychopathological direction. As I have already indicated, the economic pattern of the basic endopsychic situation is the pattern which prevails in hysterical states. Of this I have no doubt whatsoever in my own mind. I have, however, come across cases of hysterical individuals who displayed remarkably paranoid traits (even to the point of having been previously diagnosed as paranoid), and who were found, on analysis, to oscillate between paranoid and hysterical attitudes. Such oscillations appeared to be accompanied by changes in the economic pattern of the endopsychic situation—the paranoid phases being characterized by a departure from the economic pattern of what I have called the *basic* endopsychic situation. What economic pattern the endopsychic situation assumes in the paranoid state I do not feel in a position to say; but I do venture to suggest that corresponding to every disinguishable clinical state there is a characteristic pattern of the endopsychic situation. It must be recognized, of course, that various patterns may exist side by side or be superimposed one upon the other. It must also be recognized that patterning of the endopsychic situation may either be rigid or flexible—extreme rigidity and extreme flexibility being alike unfavourable features. At the same time, it must be stressed that the basic (and original) endopsychic situation is that which is found in hysterical states. In conformity with this consideration, I take the view that the earliest psychopathological symptoms to manifest themselves are hysterical in character; and I interpret the screaming fits of the infant in this sense. If I am right in this, Freud showed no mean insight in choosing hysterical phenomena as the material out of which to build the foundations of psycho-analytical theory.

In the light of considerations already advanced it will be understood, of course, that, although the basic endopsychic situation
is the situation underlying hysterical states, it is itself the product
of a split of the original ego and is, therefore, a schizoid phenomenon. Thus, although the earliest psychopathological *symptoms*
are hysterical, the earliest psychopathological *process* is schizoid.
Repression itself is a schizoid process; and splitting of the ego is
a universal phenomenon, although, of course, the degree of such
splitting varies in different individuals. It is not to be inferred,
however, that overt schizoid states are the earliest psychopathological states to develop. On the contrary, the earliest of such states
are hysterical in nature. An actual schizoid state is a much later
development—one which only materializes when the schizoid
process is pushed to a point at which a massive repression of
affect occurs and even an hysterical expression of affect is thereby
precluded. Thus it is only when a massive repression of affect
occurs that the individual becomes unduly detached and experiences a pronounced sense of futility. What is involved in the development of schizoid states cannot, however, be discussed further on
the present occasion.

The dynamic quality of internalized objects

The feature of Freud's theory of the mental apparatus presenting
the greatest anomaly is one to which reference has not yet been
made. It is this—that the only part of the psyche which he describes
in terms at all approximating to those of dynamic structure is the
super-ego. The id is, of course, described as a source of energy without structure; and the ego is described as a passive structure
without energy except such as invades it from the id. By contrast,
the super-ego is described as a structure endowed with a fund of
energy. It is true that the energy in question is conceived as being
ultimately derived from the id; but this in no way alters the fact that
Freud attributes to the super-ego a considerable measure of independent functional activity. So much is this the case that he speaks
of the super-ego and the id as diametrically opposed to one another
in the aims of their activities, and of the ego as buffetted between

these two endopsychic entities. The odd thing about all this is that the super-ego is really only a naturalized alien, as it were, within the realm of the individual mind, an immigrant from outer reality. Its whole significance resides in the fact that it is essentially an internalized object. That the only part of the psyche which Freud treats as a dynamic structure should be an internalized object is, to my mind, an anomaly sufficient in itself to justify my attempt to formulate an alternative theory of psychical structure. It will be observed that, in formulating such an alternative theory, I have so far followed a line opposite to that followed by Freud in that, whereas an internalized object is the only part of the psyche which Freud treats as a dynamic structure, the internalized objects which I envisage are the only parts of the psyche which I have *not* treated as dynamic structures. I have treated the internalized objects simply as *objects* of the dynamic ego structures, i.e. as endopsychic structures which are not themselves dynamic. I have done this deliberately in order to bring into focus the activity of the ego structures which I find it necessary to postulate, and in order to avoid all risk of under-rating the primary importance of this activity; for, after all, it is only through this activity that objects ever come to be internalized. However, in the interests of consistency, I must now draw the logical conclusion of my theory of dynamic structure and acknowledge that, since internal objects are structures, they must necessarily be, in some measure at least, dynamic. In drawing this conclusion and making this acknowledgment, I shall not only be here following the precedent of Freud, but also, it would seem, conforming to the demands of such psychological facts as are revealed, e.g. in dreams and in the phenomena of paranoia. This further step will enhance the explanatory value of my theory of mental structure by introducing additional possibilities into the endopsychic situation by way of permutation and combination. It must be recognized, however, that, in practice, it is very difficult to differentiate between the activity of internalized objects and the activity of the ego structures with which they are associated; and, with a view to avoiding any appearance of demonology, it seems wise to err, if anything, on the side of overweighting the activity of the ego structures rather than otherwise. It remains true, nevertheless, that under certain conditions internalized objects may acquire a dynamic independence which cannot be ignored.

Notes

1. Quite apart from this suggestion, there is no necessary incompatibility between the view that libido is primarily object-seeking and the conception of libido cathecting the ego, since there is always the possibility of one part of the ego structure treating another part as an object—a possibility which cannot be ignored in the light of what follows regarding the splitting of the ego.

2. I should add that, in my opinion, it is always "bad" objects that are internalized in the first instance, since it is difficult to find any adequate motive for the internalization of objects which are satisfying and "good". Thus it would be a pointless procedure on the part of the infant to internalize the breast of a mother with whom he already had a perfect relationship in the absence of such internalization, and whose milk proved sufficient to satify [sic] his incorporative needs. According to this line of thought it is only in so far as his mother's breast fails to satisfy his physical and emotional needs and thus becomes a bad object that it becomes necessary for the infant to internalize it. It is only later that good objects are internalized to defend the child's ego against bad objects which have been internalized already; and the super-ego is a "good object" of this nature.

3. Freud's conception of the ego was, of course, borrowed from Groddeck; but, if there is any truth in the conclusions which will shortly be recorded, it is a conception based upon an endopsychic situation resulting from repression, and therefore is anomalous in terms of Freud's own views, since it implies that repression is responsible for the origin of the ego.

4. It must be recognized, of course, that, under any conditions, a profound sense of separation and loss of security must be experienced by the infant at the time of birth; and it may be presumed that some measure of aggression, in addition to anxiety, is called forth by this experience. There is no reason, however, to think that this experience in itself would give rise to a state of ambivalence in the absence of further experience of libidinal frustration during infancy.

References

Fairbairn, W. R. D. (1941). A revised psychopathology of the psychoses and psychoneuroses. *International Journal of Psychoanalysis, 22:* 250–279.

Fairbairn, W. R. D. (1943). The repression and the return of bad objects *British Journal of Medical Psychology, 19*: 327.

Freud, S. (1917)[(Trans. 1925]. Mourning and melancholia. *Collected Papers IV*: 152.

Freud, S. (1920g)[Trans. 1922]. *Beyond the Pleasure Principle.*

Freud, S. (1923)[Trans. 1927]. *The Ego and the Id.*

Freud, S. (1929)[Trans. 1930]. *Civilization and its Discontents*, 95 f.

Primitive emotional development[1]

D. W. Winnicott

I t will be clear at once from my title that I have chosen a very wide subject. All I can attempt to do is to make a preliminary personal statement, as if writing the introductory chapter to a book.

I shall not first give a historical survey and show the development of my ideas from the theories of others, because my mind does not work that way. What happens is that I gather this and that, here and there, settle down to clinical experience, form my own theories and then last of all interest myself in looking to see where I stole what. Perhaps this is as good a method as any.

About primitive emotional development there is a great deal that is not known or properly understood, at least by me, and it could well be argued that this discussion ought to be postponed five or ten years. Against this there is the fact that misunderstandings constantly recur in the Society's scientific meetings, and perhaps we shall find we do know enough already to prevent some of these misunderstandings by a discussion of these primitive emotional states.

Primarily interested in the child patient, and the infant, I decided that I must study psychosis in analysis. I have had about a dozen psychotic adult patients, and half of these have been rather extensively analysed. This happened in the war, and I might say that I hardly noticed the blitz, being all the time engaged in analysis of patients who are notoriously and maddeningly oblivious of bombs, earthquakes and floods.

As a result of this work I have a great deal to communicate and to bring into alignment with current theories, and perhaps this paper may be taken as a beginning.

By listening to what I have to say, and criticizing, you help me to take my next step, which is the study of the sources of my ideas, both in clinical work and in the published writings of analysts. It has in fact been extremely difficult to keep clinical material out of this paper, which I wished nevertheless to keep short so that there might be plenty of time for discussion.

The following is my highly condensed personal statement.

I

First I must prepare the way. Let me try to describe different types of psycho-analysis. It is possible to do the analysis of a suitable patient taking into account almost exclusively that person's personal relation to people, along with the conscious and unconscious phantasies that enrich and complicate these relationships between whole persons. This is the original type of psycho-analysis. In the last two decades we have been shown how to develop our interest in phantasy, and how the patient's own phantasy about his inner organization and its origin in instinctual experience is important as such.[2] We have been shown further that in certain cases it is this, the patient's phantasy about his inner organization, that is vitally important, so that the analysis of depression and the defences against depression cannot be done on the basis only of consideration of the patient's relations to real people and his phantasies about them. This new emphasis on the patient's phantasy of himself opened up the wide field of analysis of hypochondria in which the patient's phantasy about his inner world includes the phantasy that this is localized inside his own body. It became possible for us to relate, in analysis, the qualitative changes in the individual's inner world to his instinctual experiences. The quality of these instinctual experiences accounted for the good and bad nature, as well as the existence, of what is inside.

This work was a natural progression of psycho-analysis; it involved new understanding but not new technique. It quickly led to the study and analysis of still more primitive relationships, and it is these that I wish to discuss in this paper. The existence of still more primitive object relationships has never been in doubt.

I have said that no modification in Freud's technique was needed for the extension of analysis to cope with depression and hypochondria. It is also true, according to my experience, that the same technique can take us to still more primitive elements, provided of course that we take into consideration the changes in the transference situation inherent in such work.

I mean by this that a patient needing analysis of ambivalence in external relationships has a different phantasy of his analyst and the analyst's work from the one who is depressed. In the former case the analyst's work is thought of as done out of love for the patient, hate being deflected on to hateful things. The depressed patient requires of his analyst the understanding that the analyst's work is to some extent his effort to cope with his own (the analyst's) depression, or shall I say guilt and grief resultant from the destructive elements in his own (the analyst's) love. To progress further along these lines, the patient who is asking for help in regard to his primitive, pre-depressive relationship to objects needs his analyst to be able to see the analyst's undisplaced and co-incident love and hate of him. In such cases the end of the hour, the end of the analysis, the rules and regulations, these all come in as important expressions of hate, just as the good interpretations are expressions of love, and symbolical of good food and care. This theme could be developed extensively and usefully.

II

Before embarking directly on a description of primitive emotional development I should also like to make it clear that the analysis of these primitive relationships cannot be undertaken except as an extension of the analysis of depression. It is certain that these primitive types of relationship in so far as they appear in children and adults come as a flight from the difficulties arising out of the next stages, after the classical conception of regression. It is right for a student analyst to learn first to cope with ambivalence in external relationships and with simple repression and then to progress to the analysis of the patient's phantasy about the inside and outside of his personality, and the whole range of his defences against depression, including the origins of the persecutory elements. These latter things the analyst can surely find in any analysis, but it would be useless or harmful for him to cope with principally depressive relationships unless he was fully prepared to analyse straightforward ambivalence. It is at least as true that it is useless and even dangerous to analyse the primitive pre-depressive relationships, and to interpret them as they appear in the transference, unless the analyst is fully prepared to cope with the depressive position, the defences against depression, and the persecutory ideas which appear for interpretation as the patient progresses.

III

I have more preparatory remarks to make. It has often been noted that, at five to six months, a change occurs in infants which makes it more easy than before for us to refer to their emotional development in the terms that apply to human beings generally. Anna Freud makes rather a special point of this and implies that in her view the tiny infant is concerned more with certain care-aspects than with specific people. Bowlby recently expressed the view that infants before six months are not particular, so that separation from their mother does not affect them in the same way as it does after six months. I myself have previously stated that infants reach something at six months, so that whereas many five months' infants grasp an object and put it to the mouth, it is not till six months that the average infant starts to follow this up by deliberately dropping the object as part of his play with it.

In specifying five to six months we need not try to be too accurate. If in a certain case a baby of three or even two months or even less reaches the stage of development that it is convenient in general description to place at five months, no harm will be done.

In my opinion the stage we are describing, and I think one may accept this description, is a very important one. To some extent it is an affair of physical development, for the infant at five months becomes skilled to the extent that he grasps an object he sees, and can soon get it to his mouth. He could not have done this earlier. (Of course he may have wanted to. There is no exact parallel between skill and wish, and we know that many physical advances, such as the ability to walk, are often held up till emotional development releases physical attainment. Whatever the physical side of the matter, there is also the emotional.) We can say that at this stage a baby becomes able in his play to show that he can understand he has an inside, and that things come from outside. He shows he knows that he is enriched by what he incorporates (physically and psychically). Further, he shows that he knows he can get rid of something when he has got from it what he wants from it. All this represents a tremendous advance. It is at first only reached from time to time, and every detail of this advance can be lost as a regression because of anxiety.

The corollary of this is that now the infant assumes that his mother also has an inside, one which may be rich or poor, good or bad, ordered or muddled. He is therefore starting to be concerned with the mother and her sanity and her moods. In the case of many infants there is a relationship as between whole persons at six months. Now when a human being feels he is a person related to people, he has already travelled a long way in primitive development.

Our task is to examine what goes on in the infant's feelings and personality before this stage which we recognize at five to six months, but which may be reached later or earlier.

There is also this question: how early do important things happen? For instance, does the unborn child have to be considered? And if so, at what age after conception does psychology come in? I would answer that if there is an important stage at five to six months there is also an important stage round about birth. My reason for saying this is the great differences that can be noticed if the baby is pre-mature or post-mature. I suggest that at the end of nine months' gestation an infant becomes ripe for emotional development, and that if an infant is post-mature he has reached this stage in the womb and one is therefore forced to consider his feelings before and during birth. On the other hand a premature infant is not experiencing much that is vital till he has reached the age at which he should have been born, that is to say some weeks after birth. At any rate this forms a basis for discussion.

Another question is: psychologically speaking, does anything *matter* before five to six months? I know that the view is quite sincerely held in some quarters that the answer is "no". This view must be given its due, but it is not mine.

The main object of this paper is to present the thesis that the early emotional development of the infant, before the infant knows himself (and therefore others) as the whole person he is (and they are), is vitally important: indeed that here are the clues to the psychopathology of psychoses.

IV Primary processes

There are three processes which seem to me to start very early: (1) integration, (2) personalization, and (3), following these, the appreciation of time and space and other properties of reality—in short, realization.

A great deal that we tend to take for granted had a beginning and a condition out of which it developed. For instance, many analyses sail through to completion without time being ever in dispute. But a boy of nine who loved to play with Ann, aged two, was acutely interested in the expected new baby. He said: "When the new baby's born will he be born before Ann?" For him time-sense is very shaky. Again, a psychotic patient could not adopt any routine because if she did she had no idea on a Tuesday whether it was last week, or this week, or next week.

The localization of self in one's own body is often assumed, yet a psychotic patient in analysis came to recognize that as a baby she thought her twin at the other end of the pram was herself. She even felt surprised when her twin was picked up and yet she remained where she was. Her sense of self and other-than-self was undeveloped.

Another psychotic patient discovered in analysis that most of the time she lived in her head, behind her eyes. She could only see out of her eyes as out of windows and so was not aware of what her feet were doing, and in consequence she tended to fall into pits and to trip over things. She had no "eyes in her feet". Her personality was not felt to be localized in her body, which was like a complex engine that she had to drive with conscious care and skill. Another patient, at times, lived in a box twenty yards up, only connected with her body by a slender thread. In all practices examples of these failures in primitive development occur daily, and by them we may be reminded of the importance of such processes as integration, personalization and realization.

It may be assumed that at the theoretical start the personality is unintegrated, and that in regressive disintegration there is a primary state to which regression leads. We postulate a primary unintegration.

Disintegration of personality is a well-known psychiatric condition, and its psychopathology is highly complex. Examination of these phenomena in analysis, however, shows that the primary unintegrated state provides a basis for disintegration, and that delay or failure in respect of primary integration predisposes to disintegration as a regression, or result of failure in other types of defence.

In any case, integration starts right away at the beginning of life, and in our work we can never take it for granted. We have to account for it and watch its fluctuations.

An example of unintegration phenomena is provided by the very common experience of the patient who proceeds to give every detail of the week-end and feels contented at the end if everything has been said, though the analyst feels that no analytic work has been done. Sometimes we must interpret this as the patient's need to be known in all his bits and pieces by one person, the analyst. To be known means to feel integrated at least in the person who knows one. This is the ordinary stuff of infant life, and an infant who has had no one person to gather his bits together starts with a handicap in his own self-integrating task, and perhaps he cannot succeed, or at any rate cannot maintain integration with confidence.

The tendency to integrate is helped by two sets of experience: the technique of infant-care whereby an infant is kept warm, handled and bathed and rocked and named, and also the acute instinctual experiences which tend to gather the personality together from within. Many infants are well on the way toward integration during certain periods of the first 24 hours of life. In others the process is delayed or set-backs occur because of early inhibition of making greedy attacks. There are long stretches of time in a normal infant's life in which a baby does not mind whether he is many bits or one whole being, or whether he lives in his mother's face or in his own body, provided that from time to time he comes together and feels something. Later I will try to explain why disintegration is frightening, whereas unintegration is not.

In regard to environment, bits of nursing technique, faces seen and sounds heard, and smells smelt are only gradually pieced together into one being to be called mother. In the transference situation in analysis of psychotics we get the clearest proof that the psychotic states of unintegration had a natural place at a sufficiently primitive stage of the emotional development of the individual.

It is sometimes assumed that in health the individual is always integrated, as well as living in his own body, and able to feel that the world is real. There is, however, much sanity that has a symptomatic quality, being charged with fear or denial of madness, fear or denial of the innate capacity of every human being to become unintegrated, depersonalized, and to feel that the world is unreal. Sufficient lack of sleep produces these conditions in anyone.1

Equally important with integration is the development of the feeling that one's person is in one's body. Again it is instinctual experience and repeated quiet experiences of body-care that gradually build up what may be called satisfactory personalization. And as with disintegration so also the depersonalization phenomena of psychosis relate to early personalization delays.

Depersonalization is a common thing in adults and in children, it is often hidden for instance in what is called deep sleep and in prostration attacks with corpse-like pallor:—"She's miles away," people say, and they're right.

A problem related to that of personalization is that of the imaginary companions of childhood. These are not simple phantasy constructions. Study of the future of these imaginary companions (in analysis) shows that they are sometimes other selves of a highly primitive type. I cannot here formulate a clear statement of what I mean, and it would be out of place for me to explain this detail at length now. I would say, however, that this very primitive and magical creation of imaginary companions is easily used as a defence, as it magically by-passes all the anxieties associated with incorporation, digestion, retention and expulsion.

V Dissociation

Out of the problem of unintegration comes another, that of dissociation. Dissociation can usefully be studied in its initial or natural forms. According to my view there grows out of unintegration a series of what are then called dissociations, which arise owing to integration being incomplete or partial. Take the quiet and the excited states. I think an infant cannot be said to be aware at the start that while feeling this and that in his cot or enjoying the skin stimulations of bathing, he is the same as himself screaming for immediate satisfaction, possessed by an urge to get at and destroy something unless satisfied by milk. This means that he does not know at first that the mother he is building up through his quiet experiences is the same as the power behind the breasts that he has in his mind to destroy.

Also I think there is not necessarily an integration between a child asleep and a child awake. This integration comes in the course of time. Once day-dreams are remembered and even conveyed somehow to a third person, the dissociation is broken down a little; but some people never clearly remember their dreams, and children depend very much on adults for getting to know their dreams. It is normal for small children to have anxiety dreams and terrors. At these times children need someone to help them to remember what they dreamed. It is a valuable experience whenever a dream is both dreamed *and* remembered, precisely because of the breakdown of dissociation that this represents. However complex such a dissociation may be in child or adult, the fact remains that it can start in the natural alternation of the sleeping and awake states, dating from birth.

In fact the waking life of an infant can be perhaps described as a gradually developing dissociation from the sleeping state.

Artistic creation gradually takes the place of dreams or supplements them, and is vitally important for the welfare of the individuals and therefore for mankind.

Dissociation is an extremely widespread defence mechanism, and leads to surprising results. For instance urban life is a dissociation, a serious one for civilization. Also war and peace. The extremes in mental illness are well known. In childhood dissociation appears for instance in such common conditions as somnambulism, incontinence of fæces, in some forms of squinting, etc. It is very easy to miss dissociation when assessing a personality.

VI Reality adaptation

Let us now assume integration. If we do, we reach another enormous subject, the primary relation to external reality. In ordinary analyses we can and do take for granted this step in emotional development, which is highly complex and which, when it is made, represents a big advance in emotional development, yet is never finally made and settled. Many cases that we consider unsuitable for analysis are unsuitable indeed if we cannot deal with the transference difficulties that belong to an essential lack of true relation to external reality. If we allow analysis of psychotics we find that in some analyses this essential lack of true relation to external reality is almost the whole thing.

I will try to describe in the simplest possible terms this phenomenon as I see it. In terms of baby and mother's breast (I am not claiming that the breast is essential as a vehicle of mother-love) the baby has instinctual urges and predatory ideas. The mother has a breast and the power to produce milk, and the idea that she would like to be attacked by a hungry baby. These two phenomena do not come into relation with each other till the mother and child *live an experience together*. The mother being mature and physically able has to be the one with tolerance and understanding, so that it is she that produces a situation which may with luck result in the first tie the infant makes with an external object, that is external to self from the infant's point of view.

I think of the process as if two lines came from opposite directions, liable to come near each other. If they overlap there is a moment of *illusion*—a bit of experience which the infant can take as *either* his hallucination *or* a thing belonging to external reality.

In other language, the infant comes to the breast when excited, and ready to hallucinate something fit to be attacked. At that moment the actual nipple appears and he is able to feel it was that nipple that he hallucinated. So his ideas are enriched by actual details of sight, feel, smell, and next time this material is used in the hallucination. In this way he starts to build up a capacity to conjure up what is actually available. The mother has to go on giving the infant this type of experience. The process is immensely simplified if the infant is cared for by one person and one technique. It seems as if an infant is really designed to be cared for from birth by his own mother, or failing that by an adopted mother, and not by several nurses.

It is especially at the start that mothers are vitally important, and indeed it is a mother's job to protect her infant from complications that cannot yet be understood by the infant, and to go on steadily providing the simplified bit of the world which the infant, through her, comes to know. Only on such a foundation can objectivity be built, or a scientific attitude. All failure in objectivity at whatever date relates to failure in this stage of primitive emotional development. Only on a basis of monotony can a mother profitably add richness.

One thing that follows the acceptance of external reality is the advantage to be gained from it. We often hear of the very real frustrations imposed by external reality, but less often hear of the relief and satisfaction it affords. Real milk is satisfying as compared with imaginary milk, but this is not the point. The point is that in phantasy things work by magic: there are no brakes on magic, and love and hate cause alarming effects. External reality has brakes on it, and can be studied and known, and, in fact, phantasy is only tolerable at full blast when objective reality is appreciated well. The subjective has tremendous value but is so alarming and magical that it cannot be enjoyed except as a parallel to the objective.

It will be seen that phantasy is not something the individual creates to deal with external reality's frustrations. This is only true of phantasying. Phantasy has more title to the word primary than has realization, and its enrichment with the world's riches depends on the moments of illusion that I have described.

It is interesting to examine the individual's relation to the objects in the self-created world of phantasy. In fact there are all grades of development and sophistication in this self-created world according to the amount of illusion that has been experienced, and so according to how much the self-created world has been unable or able to use perceived external world objects as material. This obviously needs a much more lengthy statement in another setting.

In the most primitive state, which may be retained in illness, and to which regression may occur, the object behaves according to magical laws, i.e. it exists when desired, it approaches when approached, it hurts when hurt. Lastly it vanishes when not wanted.

This last is most terrifying, and is the only true annihilation. To not want, perhaps as a result of satisfaction, is to annihilate the object. This is one reason why infants are not always happy and contented after a satisfactory feed. One patient of mine carried this fear right on to adult life and only grew up from it in analysis, a man who had had an extremely good early experience with his mother and in his home.[4]

I realize that this is only the bare outline of the vast problem of the initial steps in the development of a relation to external reality, and the relation of phantasy to reality. Soon we must add ideas of incorporation, but at the start a simple *contact* with external or shared reality has to be made, by the infant's hallucinating and the world's presenting, with moments of illusion for the infant in which the two are taken by him to be identical, which they never in fact are.

For this illusion to be produced in the baby's mind a human being has to be taking the trouble all the time to bring the world to the baby in understandable form, and in a limited way, suitable to the baby's needs. For this reason a baby cannot exist alone, psychologically or physically, and really needs one person to care for him at first.

The subject of illusion is a very wide one that needs study; it will be found to provide the clue to a child's interest in bubbles and clouds and rainbows and all mysterious phenomena, and also to his interest in fluff, which is most difficult to explain in terms of instinct direct. Somewhere here, too, is the interest in breath, which never decides whether it comes primarily from within or without, and which provides a basis for the conception of spirit, soul, anima.

VII Primitive ruthlessness (stage of pre-concern)

We are now in a position to look at the earliest kind of relationship between a baby and his mother.

If one assumes that the individual is becoming integrated and personalized and has made a good start in his realization, there is still a long way for him to go before he is related as a whole person to a whole mother, and concerned about the effect of his own thoughts and actions on her.

We have to postulate an early ruthless object-relationship. This may again be a theoretical phase only, and certainly no one can be ruthless after the concern stage except in a dissociated state. But ruthless dissociation states are common in early childhood, and emerge in certain types of delinquency, and madness, and must be available in health. The normal child enjoys a ruthless relation to his mother, mostly showing in play, and he needs his mother because only she can be expected to tolerate his ruthless relation to her even in play, because this really hurts her and wears her out. Without this play with her he can only hide a ruthless self and give it life in a state of dissociation.[5]

I can bring in here the great fear of disintegration as opposed to the simple acceptance of primary unintegration. Once the individual has reached the stage of concern he cannot be oblivious to the result of his impulses, or to the action of bits of self such as biting mouth, stabbing eyes, piercing yells, sucking throat, etc., etc. Disintegration means abandonment of the whole person-object to his impulses, uncontrolled because acting on their own; and further this conjures up the idea of similarly uncontrolled (because dissociated) impulses directed towards himself.[6]

VIII Primitive retaliation

To go back half a stage: it is usual, I think, to postulate a still more primitive object-relationship in which the object acts in a retaliatory way. This is prior to a true relation to external reality. In this case the object, or the environment, is as much part of the self as the instinct is which conjures it up.[7] In introversion of early origin and therefore of primitive quality the individual lives in this environment which is himself, and a very poor life it is. There is no growth because there is no enrichment from external reality.

IX Thumb-sucking

To illustrate a different method of approach to this subject I add a note on thumb-sucking (including fist and finger sucking). This can be observed from birth onwards, and therefore can be presumed to have a meaning which develops from the primitive to sophistication, and it is important both as a normal activity and as a symptom of emotional disturbance.

We are familiar with the aspect of thumb-sucking which the term auto-erotic covers. The mouth is an erotogenic zone, specially organized in infancy, and the thumb-sucking child enjoys pleasure. He also has pleasurable ideas.

Hate is also expressed when the child damages his fingers by too vigorous or continuous sucking, and in any case he soon adds nail-biting to cope with this part of his feelings. He is also liable to damage his mouth. But it is not certain that all the damage that may be done to a finger or mouth in this way is part of hate. It seems that there is in it the element that something must suffer if the infant is to have pleasure: the object of primitive love suffers by being loved, apart from being hated.

We can see in finger-sucking, and in nail-biting especially, a turning-in of love and hate, for reasons such as the need to preserve the external object of interest. Also we see a turning-in to self, in face of frustration in love of an external object.

The subject is not exhausted by this kind of statement and deserves further study.

I suppose anyone would agree that thumb-sucking is done for consolation, not just pleasure; the fist or finger is there instead of the breast or mother, or someone. For instance, a baby of about four months reacted to the loss of his mother by a tendency to put his fist right down his throat, so that he would have died had he not been physically prevented from acting this way.

Whereas thumb-sucking is normal and universal, spreading out into the use of the dummy, and indeed to various activities of normal adults, it is also true that thumb-sucking persists, in schizoid personalities, and in such cases is extremely compulsive. In one patient of mine it changed at 10 or 11 into a compulsion to be always reading.

These phenomena cannot be explained except on the basis that the act is an attempt to localize the object (breast, etc.), to hold it half-way between in and out; a defence against loss of object in the external world or in the inside of the body. I should say, against loss of control over the object, which occurs in either case.

I have no doubt that normal thumb-sucking has this function too.

The auto-erotic element is not always clearly of paramount importance and certainly the use of dummy and fist soon becomes a clear defence against insecurity feelings and other anxieties of a primitive kind.

Finally, every fist-sucking provides a useful dramatization of the primitive object-relationship in which the object is as much the individual as is the desire for an object, because it is created out of the desire, or is hallucinated, and at the beginning is independent of co-operation from external reality.

Some babies put a finger in the mouth while sucking the breast, thus (in a way) holding on to self-created reality while using external reality.

Conclusion

An attempt has been made to formulate the primitive psychological tendencies which are normal in early infancy, and which appear regressively in the psychoses.

Notes

1. My especial thanks are due to Dr W. Clifford M. Scott for his help both in the work on which this paper is based and in the preparation of the paper itself. Read before the British Psycho-Analytical Society, November 28, 1945. [Reproduced, with permission, from: *International Journal of Psychoanalysis*, 1945, 26: 137–143 © Institute of Psychoanalysis, London, UK]

2. Chiefly through the work of Melanie Klein.

3. Through artistic expression we can hope to keep in touch with our primitive selves. It is from here that the most intense feelings and even fearfully acute sensations derive, and we are poor indeed if we are only sane.

4. I will just mention another reason why an infant is not satisfied with satisfaction. He feels fobbed off. He intended, one might say, to make a cannibalistic attack and he has been put off by an opiate, the feed. At best he can postpone the attack.

5. There is in mythology a ruthless figure—Lilith—whose origin could be usefully studied.

6. Crocodiles not only shed tears when they do not feel sad—pre-concern tears; they also readily stand for the ruthless primitive self. (There is much clinical evidence of this.)

7. This is important because of our relationship to Jung's analytic psychology. We try to reduce everything to instinct, and the analytic psychologists reduce everything to this part of the primitive self which looks like environment but which arises instantly out of instinct (archetypes). We ought to modify our view to embrace both ideas, and to see, if it is true, that in the earliest theoretical primitive state the self has its own environment, self-created, which is as much the self as the instincts that produce it. This is a theme which requires development.

PART IV
INFANT OBSERVATION

Introduction

Infant observation

T he interest in pushing back the understanding of what the earliest ego is like, and how it experiences itself and the world, was at its height in the 1940s. The experience of twenty years of child analysis, in which the results of adult analyses were checked and modified, led to a wish to check (and perhaps modify) the results of child analysis.[1] There was a certain amount of interest in the 1930s (Behn-Eschenberg, 1935; Benedek, 1938; Bernfeld, 1929, 1935; Lampl-de Groot, 1939; Lewis, 1936; Middlemore, 1941; Searl, 1933). But the time was right for more rigorous and systematic observation. The wartime inspired Anna Freud and Susan Isaacs to make observations of children dislocated from their families by the war (Burlingham & Freud, 1943; Isaacs, Brown, & Thouless, 1941).

Both John Bowlby and Donald Winnicott were originally child psychiatrists before becoming psychoanalysts. They were both drawn to psychoanalysis by the results of child analysis reported by Melanie Klein. They were both cautious as well as fascinated by Klein's presentation of the child mind. However, neither was a loyal

Kleinian. Both sought to establish empirically outside the psycho-analytic setting an observational method for understanding the experience of infants. Bick interestingly developed, with Bowlby's encouragement, a psychoanalytic observation method as a learning tool in the training of child psychotherapy trainees (Bick, 1964; Briggs, 2002).

Whereas Isaacs, for instance, particularly relied on "genetic continuity" (see above) as a means of extrapolating back and recon-structing infantile experience, Bowlby and Winnicott called for non-psychoanalytic research, albeit psychoanalytically inspired.[2]

Notes

1. In fact, Freud's observations of his grandson in 1920 were an early inspiration for the possibilities of psychoanalytic observations.
2. Later, Bowlby (1969, 1973, 1980) moved towards ethological observa-tional settings, and has been accused of abandoning psychoanalysis.

References

Behn-Eschenberg, H. (1935). The antecedents of the Oedipus complex. *International Journal of Psychoanalysis, 16*: 175–185.

Benedek, T. (1938). Adaptation to reality in early infancy. *Psychoanalytic Quarterly, 7*: 200–215.

Bernfeld, S. (1929).

Bernfeld, S. (1935). Psychoanalytic psychology of the young child. *Psychoanalytic Quarterly, 4*: 3–14.

Bick, E. (1964). Notes on infant observation in psycho-analytic training. *International Journal of Psychoanalysis, 45*: 558–566.

Bowlby, J. (1969). *Attachment and Loss, Volume 1.* London: Hogarth.

Bowlby, J. (1973). *Attachment and Loss, Volume 2.* London: Hogarth.

Bowlby, J. (1980). *Attachment and Loss, Volume 3.* London: Hogarth.

Briggs, A. (2002). *Surviving Space.* London: Duckworth.

Burlingham, D., & Freud, A. (1943). *Infants without Families.* London: George Allen & Unwin.

Freud, S. (1920g). Beyond the pleasure principle. *S.E., 18.*

Isaacs, S., Brown, S. C., & Thouless, R. (Eds.) (1941). *The Cambridge Evacuation Survey: A Wartime Study in Social Welfare and Education.* London: Methuen.

Lampl-de Groot, J. (1939). Considerations of methodology in relation to the psychology of small children. *International Journal of Psychoanalysis, 20*: 408–417.

Lewis, M. M. (1936). *Infant Speech*. London: Kegan Paul.

Middlemore, M. (1941). *The Nursing Couple*. London: Hamish Hamilton.

Searl, M. (1933). Play, reality and aggression. *International Journal of Psychoanalysis, 14*: 310–320.

John Bowlby [Bowlby, J. (1940). The influence of early environment in the development of neurosis and neurotic character. *International Journal of Psychoanalysis, 21*: 154–178]

Bowlby draws attention to environmental deficits as factors in the development of neurosis. The early part of his paper discusses the effect of major separations between infant and mother in the first year of life—separations of a number of months. He produces evidence that he showed on statistical grounds to be connected with the development of the baby into an affectionless child who pilfered. These observations clearly led to more formal research such as that of Robertson (Bowlby, Robertson, & Rosenbluth, 1952; Robertson, 1962, 1971). However, not all neurotic children have a history of such major separations, and Bowlby then moved on to the possibilities of an inclement emotional atmosphere in the family, or between mother and baby. He postulated the process as numerous incremental effects from small but persistent doses of separation, especially maternal separation, or more commonly of a kind of emotional separation. That cold atmosphere is usually denied by mother, and very often by both parties.

There is an interaction, Bowlby claimed, between the emotional life of the mother and the infant/child. These transactions between them of hostility, and its inhibition, the loading of guilt into the child through projection, and in turn the projective distortions of the mother or both parents, is a complex situation that demands considerable unravelling.

Bowlby took the position of the nurseryman, who recognizes that studying the growth of a plant requires knowledge of the plant, of the soil and of the interaction between the two. Implicitly, he claimed psychoanalysis has concentrated excessively on the first factor to the neglect of the second and third, i.e. a neglect of the external environment. It is a priority that resulted when Freud dropped his seduction theory, it may be claimed. However, as Ernest Jones once argued, "there is no danger of any analysts neglecting external reality, whereas it is always possible for them to underestimate Freud's doctrine of the importance of psychical reality" (Jones, 1935, p. 273). Consequently, some have complained that Bowlby has implicitly challenged the very nature of psychoanalysis.

The setting from which this paper came is a child guidance clinic where direct assessment of the environment of the child—i.e., the mother—can be made. The importance of the environment led Bowlby to call for family assessments; and indeed for some form of family therapy, although such therapy had not been formalized at that stage.

Bowlby argued that, even in adult psychoanalyses, an assessment of the parents is important, and indeed possible. It is true, he admitted, that patients will always give a picture of the parents, and that is always distorted by projections on to them. However, it is likely, indeed almost certain, that the distortions a person makes in his views of his parents are not just to do with the patient, but have origins in something in the parents that can be deduced through psychoanalytic understanding of the interaction between "plant and soil".

Bowlby makes an extremely clear case, with vivid examples. His statement is, like others earlier in this book, a platform on which he intended to build a theoretical structure. Eventually, using comparative animal psychology, Bowlby developed attachment theory (Holmes, 1993). Bowlby is very consistent in developing his system of thought on empirical evidence and, more adventurously, he is quite abandoned in his employment of non-psychoanalytic settings.

References

Bowlby, J., Robertson, J., & Rosenbluth, D. (1952). A two-year-old goes to hospital. *Psychoanalytic Study of the Child*, 7: 82–94.

Holmes, J. (1993). *John Bowlby and Attachment Theory*. London: Routledge.

Jones, E. (1935). Early female sexuality. *International Journal of Psychoanalysis*, 16: 263–273.

Robertson, J. (1962). Mothering as an influence on early development--
a study of well-baby clinic records. *Psychoanalytic Study of the Child*,
17: 245–264.
Robertson, J. (1971). Young children in brief separation—a fresh look.
Psychoanalytic Study of the Child, 26: 264–315.

Donald Winnicott [Winnicott, D. W. (1941). The observation of
infants in a set situation. *International Journal of Psychoanalysis*,
22: 229–249]

Like Bowlby, Winnicott established a greater rigour and detail for
his observations. As in a scientific observation, he designed a set
situation in which infants could be observed and their deviation
from a normal pattern of behaviour could be picked out. Over a
period of twenty years, the reactions of the infant and the reaction
of the mother to the infant showed regularities. He had the opportunity to establish a three-part normal process for an infant, aged
between five and thirteen months, confronted with a shiny metal
spatula on the desk in his consulting room.

In the first stage the infant hesitates, in the second the infant
grasps the spatula and puts it to its mouth, and in the third stage
the infant throws the spatula to the floor. Mother is asked to allow
the infant to play quietly, and any interference of hers points to an
anxious and maybe intrusive mother. Winnicott dwelled on the first
stage of hesitation when the infant notices, and is drawn to, the
shiny object, but then withdraws until sure of the environmental
reaction—or lack of it. It takes the infant time to be reassured about
the acceptability of its fascination. Winnicott explained this as a
super-ego reaction, and also linked it into Freud's theory of anxiety
as fear. Winnicott says that, in the vast majority of cases where the
mother does remain quiet and refrains from prompts and interference, the infant is inhibited not by an external agent, but by the
possible aggression that the infant has in mind. This process of an
internal inhibition, argued Winnicott, endorsed Freud's view of an
internal psychic reality, and Melanie Klein's view of an early super-
ego figure within the infant at this young age.

On these grounds, Winnicott supported the view of phantasy
as an activity of the infant mind from early in the first year of life.
The infant's anxiety is a "fear of something", as Freud said. That

something is an imagined aggression the infant anticipates as a possible reaction to its own impulses and desires. As early as 1941, Winnicott was taking up the issue of phantasy that Isaacs would address in an officially Kleinian way only in 1943. He continued to elaborate on the way the spatula represents figures in the real world, as conceived internally by the infant, figures that might be apprehended by the infant in exaggeratedly good or bad ways. His psychoanalytic understanding of the set situation is based in Kleinian ideas, especially those ideas expressed in her book *The Psychoanalysis of Children* (Klein, 1932).

Winnicott's claim is interesting, as one of his infants, aged seven months, developed asthma, and he could spot the moment when it started in the observation, and also when it disappeared. This is strong evidence in favour of Winnicott's set situation producing convincing empirical evidence of a psychological kind. The question does seem to remain whether evidence of this kind is *psychoanalytic* evidence.

Winnicott argued that on the basis of the standard "set situation" he could make psychoanalytic observations that give empirical data pertinent to infants, just as clinical psychoanalysis does for children and adults. In this way, he aligned himself with Bowlby and others. Agreement on a valid psychoanalytic method usable before the infant can speak has remained elusive, despite claims of the kind that Winnicott and Bowlby made.

References

Klein, M. (1932). *The Psychoanalysis of Children*. London: Hogarth.

The influence of early environment in the development of neurosis and neurotic character*

John Bowlby

T
he material upon which this paper is based is the case-material which I have seen during the past three years at the London Child Guidance Clinic. I have seen there about 150 cases and, although none of the cases has been fully analysed, an immense amount of work has been done, much of it by analytically trained workers, on them. Data regarding the child's past and present environment has been collected by psychiatric social workers[1] and in the huge majority of cases I have personally interviewed the mother and had some opportunity of gauging her character. The material therefore, although far less intensive than that obtained in analysis, is not altogether superficial and contains reliable evidence on issues which are not easily investigated in analysis. In my view there is a vast field of research open to analysts in psychiatric clinics. In those where it is possible to spend a number of hours on each case and the services of a trained psychiatric social worker are available, it is easy to collect detailed clinical material

---

* [Reproduced, with permission, from: *International Journal of Psychoanalysis*, 1940, *21*: 154–178 © Institute of Psychoanalysis, London, UK]

on, analytically speaking, large numbers of cases. It is my belief that this type of research is of much more value in solving certain analytic problems than is research limited to analytic sessions, and the subject of this paper is a conspicuous example of the type of problem which I have in mind. The very meagre attention given to the role of environment in analytic literature seems to me to be due to analysts having in their daily analytic work only very poor opportunities of investigating the problem. Except in the case of child analysts, in fact, first hand observations are impossible. I look forward to the day when analytic research will be pursued vigorously along both the intensive lines of the analytic interview and also the more extensive lines possible in a child guidance clinic or mental hospital.

Perhaps another reason for the neglect of a study of environment has been the gradual recognition that individuals to a great extent choose their environment and so are often the authors rather than the victims of circumstance. Now however true this may be for adults and even adolescents it is far less true for infants and it is with the environment in infancy that I am principally concerned. It seems to me to be as important for analysts to make a scientific study of early environment as it is for the nurseryman to make a scientific study of soil and atmosphere. Psycho-analysts like the nurseryman should study intensively and at first hand (1) the nature of the organism, (2) the properties of the soil and (3) the interaction of the two. Much work has already been done on the study of the organism. This paper is intended as a preliminary survey of the soil conditions with a few suggestions regarding their interaction with the organism.

Naturally familiarity with analytic material is necessary if we are to make use of our extra-analytic opportunities. Many of the observations hitherto made on the environments of neurotic children have been made by workers untrained in analysis. It is not surprising therefore that findings have often been negative. Unless we know the sort of thing which is likely to be significant, we shall not find it. Further, unless we look systematically and are suspicious of general statements that "the environment appears satisfactory", we shall again draw blank. It is surprising what vital facts can be overlooked in a perfunctory interview—the mother being in a T.B. sanatorium for six months when the child was two, the grandmother dying in tragic circumstances in the child's home, the fact that a child was illegitimate and attempts had been made to abort the pregnancy—such facts as these are environmental factors which I believe have great significance but which are often concealed intentionally or unintentionally in a short interview. In a patient whom I am at present treating it was not for two months that I discovered that her mother had never wanted the child and had made a half-hearted attempt at abortion. For these reasons negative evidence that the environment has played no part in the development of a neurosis is worthless, unless it can be shown that a really detailed account of the environment from conception onwards has been obtained and we can satisfy ourselves that our knowledge of the mother's attitude to the child, especially in its unconscious aspects, is adequate.

My own approach to the role of environment in the causation of neurosis has of course been from the analytic angle. For this reason I have ignored many aspects of the child's environment such as economic conditions, housing conditions, the school situation, diet and religious teaching, which some psychiatrists have thought important. Instead I have concentrated my attention upon the emotional atmosphere of the home and the personal environment of the child. In particular I have paid attention to the early environment in which the child has found himself. The numerous studies of the environment of neurotic children published nowadays are woefully lacking in details of early environment, and authors habitually draw from their inadequate observations the most unwarranted conclusions. Thus we find Norwood East and Hubert in their recent study of criminals[2] stating that a certain case showed "no relationship to early or later unsatisfactory environment", despite the fact that the child was illegitimate and had been born in a Salvation Army Home. Although this information is totally inadequate, it is reasonable to suspect that the early environment of this patient was far from satisfactory in a sense which I shall shortly describe in detail.

Because of my belief that the early environment is of vital importance I make careful inquiries into the history of the child's relations to his mother and whether and in what circumstances there have been separations between mother and child. Another general line of inquiry is into the mother's treatment of her child, not merely in its external aspects but also in its deeper emotional quality. In this I always try to obtain some information from which to reconstruct the mother's unconscious attitude towards her child. Finally, I make careful inquiries into illness and death in the family and how it affected the child.

Now I suppose everyone would agree that this personal environment affects every child to some degree. The questions remain, however, to what degree? And in what way?

These questions are inevitably in the front of one's mind when one is working at a child guidance clinic. A child is brought for examination. He is very aggressive and destructive. He bullies his little sister. He suffers from night terrors. At school he is provocative and invites punishment, which he gets. It is clear that there is a serious emotional disturbance, there is a great deal of half-repressed aggression, much anxiety and intense guilt. But what is not clear is why did this child fall ill—why are his instincts so strong?—why has he so much anxiety and guilt?

Amongst many factors there are two which we can always look for—the child's heredity and the personal environment in which he was brought up. These of course are complementary rather than mutually exclusive so that the presence of one need not lead us to dismiss the other as negligible. When I say therefore that a careful survey of the child's past and present environment reveals in the majority of cases conditions which psychologically are patently bad, it should not be assumed that I ignore inherited difficulties, which are almost certainly significant in a large number of cases. Yet it is often doubtful whether a congenital difficulty in coping with instinctual tensions and conflicts would have led to neurosis unless the environment had increased the problems with which the child has had to deal. In my experience it is only in a small minority of children who are sent to a child guidance clinic that the past and present environment appears to be even average from the psychological point of view. Indeed the incidence of certain environmental factors appears so great that it is difficult not to suppose in many cases that without them there would have been no neurosis. In putting forward the following views I am therefore proposing a general theory of the genesis of neurosis.

Environmental factors of a pathogenic character can be divided into two major classes:

A. Those which are operative during the earliest years of life and appear to influence the whole cast of the child's character.

B. Those which occur later in the child's life, say after five years, and appear to act as precipitants. It is my belief that these precipitating factors are pathogenic only when there are already serious emotional conflicts in the child's mind, although traumas such as the tragic death of mother or siblings may, by confirming phantasies of the omnipotent effect of death wishes, have serious effects on even the normal child. The study of precipitating factors is interesting and does much to illuminate the nature of the conflicts which they arouse, but is outside the scope of the present paper.

My concern here is with the environmental factors which are operative during the child's earliest years and which appear so to influence the development of the child's character that they may reasonably be termed factors responsible for neurosis. They are naturally of very many kinds, but can for convenience be classified into two groups:

1. Specific events, such as death of the mother or prolonged separation of the child from his mother.

2. The general colour of the mother's emotional attitude to her child. Under this heading are to be counted her handling of feeding, weaning and toilet-training; for the way in which a mother (or nurse) handles these questions is dependent far more upon her unconscious attitude both to these things in herself and to the child as a person, than upon any conscious method she adopts. The handling of feeding, weaning and habit-training can thus be regarded to a great extent as a function of a mother's character.

In dealing with the specific events first I will discuss by way of example the effects upon a child of being parted for long periods or permanently from his mother.

For a long time broken homes have been suspected of increasing a child's conflicts and making in particular for delinquency. An investigation of this problem has suggested to me that it is not so much the fact of the child's home being broken which is of importance, but the frequent result of this—the separation of the child from his mother. This view is supported by the discovery that children who have been separated in early life, for long periods or permanently, from their mothers or mother-substitutes, whatever the reason, all develop in the same way. Consequently in place of the term "broken home" I prefer to use the more accurate and comprehensive term "broken mother–child relation".

Prolonged breaks during the first three years of life leave a characteristic impression on the child's personality. Clinically such children appear emotionally withdrawn and isolated. They fail to develop libidinal ties with other children or with adults and consequently have no friendships worth the name. It is true that they are sometimes sociable in a superficial sense, but if this is scrutinized we find that there are no feelings, no roots in these relationships. This, I think, more than anything else, is the cause of their hardboiledness. Parents and school-teachers complain that nothing you say or do has any effect on the child. If you thrash him he cries for a bit, but there is no emotional response to being out of favour, such as is normal to the ordinary child. It appears to be of no essential consequence to these lost souls whether they are in favour or out. Since they are unable to make genuine emotional relations, the condition of a relationship at a given moment lacks all significance for them.

Nansi was an example of this sequence. She was nearly eight when first seen. The problem was that she was dishonest and pilfered money, which was usually spent on sweets.

She was the second of five children, all of whom lived with their widowed mother. They were looked after by a decrepit old grandmother because the mother had to work to make a living. The parents' marriage was described as having been "ideally happy". "We never had a single quarrel or cross word, and when he died we were all brokenhearted." The father died when Nansi was five. He had been regarded as highly respectable, and the mother also had a good reputation.

Early history. Birth was normal and the child was bottle-fed like the other children. She appears to have thrived and walked at ten months. At twelve months she fell ill with bronchitis and was in hospital for nine months altogether, having contracted pneumonia and measles whilst away. During all this time she never saw her parents, who were only permitted to visit her when she was asleep. On returning home she was frightened and very babyish and for some months wetted and soiled her bed every night, although previously she had been clean.

Personality. Her mother described the child as always having been the "odd one out". She never wanted to play with either sister or brothers. She appeared quite indifferent to what happened to her and to how she was treated. When her younger brothers were born she treated the event as if it did not concern her and showed no interest. If she wet her knickers she never mentioned it, and showed no shame if it was found out, but preserved her usual detached manner. If given Christmas or birthday presents she either lost them or gave them away.

Her behaviour at school was not so unusual as at home, from the accounts available. She was said to be a bright child who enjoyed her work and played about like any other child. But she was obviously preoccupied with her faults, sometimes going spontaneously to the teacher to say she had been good all the week. She was also a keen Salvationist and had often told her teacher she was saved, "so it will be all right". (Both her parents were Salvationists.)

Pilfering. It was difficult to know for how long the pilfering had been going on, but it had been very persistent during the previous six months. She seems to have taken money from every available source. She had systematically swindled her next brother out of his milk money for a whole term. She had stolen a shilling from her teacher's bag, and the landlady had reported she had found Nansi taking money out of her pocket more than once. She had also taken money from a Salvation Army collecting box, opening it with a knife.

She spent most of her gains on sweets and food. On one occasion she bought fish and chips and fizzy lemonade which she shared with a brother.

When caught she was quite unashamed. Her teacher had known she was light-fingered for some time and had tried hard to break her of the habit both by punishing her and by kindness, but neither had had any effect.

Examination. When examined at the Clinic she was found to have an IQ of 111 and to be a withdrawn, detached and unemotional child, although quite friendly. When it was time for her to go she asked if she might take some toys home "for her little brother" and wanted to take the whole box. Although presented with a cow, it was observed that she secreted a small doll and took that away as well.

In this case the break was nine months in hospital during the second year. But characters similar in all essentials follow if there have been, between the ages of about six months and four years, changes in foster homes, transference of the child to others' care owing to the mother's death or prolonged illness and in some cases where the mother is working and the child is looked after for long periods by strangers.

During the last few years I have seen some sixteen cases of this affectionless type of persistent pilferer and in only two was a prolonged break absent. In all the others gross breaches of the mother–child relation had occurred during the first three years, and the child had become a persistent pilferer. The details were as follows:

1. Girl aged 5.7. Father deserted. Child put in a succession of foster-homes between 7 months and 5 years.
2. Boy aged 10.6. Father deserted. From 2 months to 3 years in foster-home and from 3 years onwards with maternal grandfather.
3. Boy aged 6.3. Mother died at 1.3. Child lived with aunt for 9 months and later with an older sister who was grossly irresponsible.
4. Boy aged 12. Mother died at 12 months. During next 5 years in a succession of foster-homes.
5. Boy aged 9.9. Fell ill at 9 months and in hospital 8 months unvisited.
6. Boy aged 11.6. Illegitimate. With mother 1 month, with great-aunt until she died 18 months later, returned to mother for 1 year, subsequently in foster-home.
7. Girl aged 12.3. Illegitimate. First 20 months unknown. In same foster-home since.
8. Boy aged 12.11. Illegitimate. From 5 months to 3 years in foster-home, then returned to mother.
9. Boy aged 7.8. Mother chronically ill with T.B. and in sanatoria for long periods when boy between 2 and 5. Looked after by a variety of people.

10. Boy aged 6. Fell ill at 18 months and in hospital for 9 months unvisited.
11. Girl aged 7.10. Fell ill at 12 months and in hospital 9 months unvisited. (Patient described above.)
12. Girl aged 3.8. Fell ill at 4 months and in hospital 14 months. Parents visited weekly, but child soon failed to recognize them.
13. Boy aged 9.4. Illegitimate, but looked after by aunt from birth. Fell ill at 3 years and in hospital for long period (dates unknown).
14. Boy aged 11.6. Unwanted and possibly born before parents married. Mother working and boy in various foster-homes for short periods during first 3 years.

The other two children had not been separated, but had nevertheless developed affectionless characters. In one there was bad heredity, the father and grandfather being psychotic. In the other an anxious ambivalent mother and an extremely hostile father seemed to have played a part in causing the condition.

Amongst thirty other children referred for stealing, five had had similar breaks. All five were seriously ill mentally. One was schizophrenic, having previously been a typically affectionless child, one chronically depressed, one a hysterical girl with very pronounced phantasy life and two were defiant and boastful bullies. The latter two had much of the affectionless character about them.

Amongst forty-four unselected child guidance cases who did not steal there were only 3 who had had comparable separations. Two were schizophrenic and one, a girl of 5.4, extremely hysterical in personality, with strong hostility to her foster-mother.

The proportion of cases in which gross breaks in the mother–child relation had occurred can be tabulated thus:

	No.	No. in which mother–child breaks occur
Affectionless thieves	16	14
Other types of thief	30	5
Non-stealing cases	44	3

Since I have had no opportunity of gauging the frequency of this condition amongst normal children conclusions must be tentative. The figures, however, strongly suggest that, whilst an inherited difficulty in maintaining libidinal ties can in certain circumstances be responsible for the development of an affectionless character, it is more frequent for the libidinal inhibition to be brought about by the environmental circumstances in which the child found himself. Moreover there seem grounds for suspecting that this particular environmental influence tends to produce a particular clinical picture. Thus, out of the twenty-two children who had experienced this break, fourteen had become affectionless thieves and three had become schizophrenic (two at least having previously been affectionless). Amongst the sixty-eight who had not experienced such a break, only two were affectionless thieves and three schizophrenic. So frequent therefore is the development of an affectionless and persistent pilferer following an early break that I am tempted to believe that we have here a relation between environmental influence and clinical picture which is relatively specific.

If this view is accepted, a further conclusion seems to me to follow: that minor breaks are likely also to have a damaging effect on a child's development. This of course is much more difficult to investigate than the gross and dramatic breaks which I have been concerned with, but one such case has recently come to my notice.

Sylvia S., aged 2¾ years, was referred for disturbed sleep. She was restless, threw herself from side to side of her cot, rolled her head and talked in her sleep, repeating things she had said during the day. She did not scream or cry. She was in the habit of waking at five o'clock and insisted on playing. Otherwise she was described as a happy normal child who played cheerfully with her dolls, treating them kindly. She was not afraid of the dark or of strangers, although a little shy at first. She ate well and was amenable, provided you were patient. The chief person in her environment, her mother, seemed a pleasant warm-hearted girl who was happily married and fond of the baby. There were no other children.

When the history was gone into it was found that the sleeping difficulties had all come on since Sylvia was in hospital for intussusception at the age of ten months. The mother was not allowed to see the child for the whole of the next week, although the father went daily. He noticed that the child was fretting, and insisted that the mother should be allowed to visit. Finally they removed Sylvia from hospital at the end of the second week against orders, because she was so unhappy. She had never slept well since and when they came to the clinic the mother was very much worried.

A few interviews with the mother and a weekly play-group for Sylvia cleared up the symptoms completely.

Between these two extremes of Nansi, whose personality was very severely disturbed, and Sylvia, who, perhaps largely thanks to particularly sympathetic parents, had not developed more than transient symptoms, there is an endless gradation of cases of children whose emotional difficulties have dated from a break in their relations with their mothers.

Very much more might be said about these gross and dramatic interruptions of the child's emotional development. Such cases are frequently seen in a child guidance clinic and the relation of the mental state to the environmental trauma is not difficult to trace. It will take much more time to work out the psychopathology in detail, and since I hope to make a special study of it I will not go into it further now. I wish instead to proceed to the discussion of the other group, where the ætiological role of the environment is less clear, although in my view just as important.

There are many children who have never suffered any obvious psychological trauma, who have remained in a relatively stable home, looked after by their mothers and well cared for according to ordinary standards. Yet they have developed into neurotic children with great anxiety and guilt and abnormally strong sexual and aggressive impulses. If these cases are carefully investigated, one factor stands out—the personality of the mother and her emotional attitude towards the child. During my child guidance work I have come to recognize certain typical sorts of mothers whose influence has seemed to me to have been injurious to the child through increasing his sexual and aggressive impulses and phantasies, and also his anxiety and guilt.

No doubt fathers are often also of importance, but my information on this score is far less certain owing to fathers never being seen at first hand. In a few cases they appear to have had as much influence on the child as the mother, but in the majority of cases it seems that the influence of fathers is less direct than that of mothers, who of course have far more to do with the children during the first few formative years. A father may, however, considerably influence his wife's handling of the children through his behaviour towards her. He may for instance increase her anxiety and guilt through constant criticism, he may make her miserable and depressed through quarrels and infidelity. On the other hand, by being kind, helpful and sympathetic a husband can ease a wife's feelings and help her to more patience with the children. In this indirect way, it seems to me, fathers play a not inconsiderable role.

Our information regarding the influence of mothers is however far more reliable and can be discussed in detail. A particularly common type of mother to be met with is the one who has a strong unconscious hostility towards her child. Such mothers are by no means always "bad mothers" in the ordinary everyday sense of those words. Indeed many, in over-compensation for their unconscious hostility, have developed a heavily over-protecting attitude, being afraid to let the child out of their sight, fussing over minor illness, worrying lest something terrible should happen to their darlings, doing everything consciously possible to make the child healthy and happy. But despite these sincere and honest attempts to be good mothers such women are commonly very bad mothers. For, as psycho-analytic experience would lead us to expect, in spite of these efforts their hostility does not remain inactive. It comes out in very numerous ways—in unnecessary deprivations and frustrations, in impatience over naughtiness, in odd words of bad temper, in a lack of the sympathy and understanding which the usual loving mother intuitively has. Sometimes of course there are dramatic threats against the child to send it away if it is naughty, but these are not in my view half as important as the myriad of minor pin-pricks and signs of dislike which such women give their children from birth onwards.

I need hardly say that these mothers are neurotic. They almost always have genuine affection for their children, but unconscious hostility makes their attitude ambivalent. This unconscious hostility dates of course from their own childhoods, from ambivalent conflicts in relation to their parents or brothers and sisters.

This type of mother has probably often been recognized before. Melanie Klein in her book[3] describes the mother of Rita, aged 2¾ and suffering from obsessional symptoms, as herself suffering from a severe obsessional neurosis and having had an ambivalent relation towards the child from the first.

Of the very many cases which I have seen I will describe Sheila C., aged 4½, who was referred for screaming-fits and destructiveness. The screaming-fits came on in connection with going to school, which she said she hated. On examination she was found to have a mental age of six years. She had bright ginger hair and red chubby cheeks. At first she was shy and very nervous of leaving her mother, but later she played actively with various toys, although she was unable to settle down to anything and seemed dissatisfied. During her play she squashed a celluloid doll and told me to put it away. The general impression was a peevish and anxious child who was in constant need of reassurance.

The story was that she was the only child of young parents. Her father was a clerk and appeared to be an excellent and loving husband and father. The mother however was of an obviously irritable temperament. She had always looked after Sheila, but now felt quite unable to manage her. She seemed genuinely anxious to do her best for the child, but admitted at once that she was always losing patience, getting irritable and slapping her in temper. She was an intelligent woman and even in the first interview had much insight into the problem. She remarked that the trouble might be because she had never really managed to want the child. She recognized this as a problem and was anxious for help over it.

Mrs C.'s attitude to Sheila had been ambivalent from the first. She became pregnant accidentally very soon after marriage, having intended to spend her first year of married life having a good time. She very much resented being disabled in this way and was frankly jealous of her husband, who went off on Saturdays to play cricket for his firm. When the baby was born she was pleased with it, but at the same time felt it a tie and a nuisance.

One origin of Mrs C.'s hostility to Sheila was not far to seek. She herself had been an only child and her father was killed in the war when she was 6½. She had been attached to her father, but was very happy living alone with her mother after his death. Then, when Mrs C. was eleven, her mother married again and a new baby was born eighteen months later. The new baby was very delicate and consequently had much special attention. The step-father had apparently been extremely strict and this, coupled with his intrusion into the family, had made Mrs C. very hostile to him. Her jealousy and resentment of the baby had moreover been intensified considerably by her having to give up hockey on Saturday mornings to look after it. During this period her feeling for babies apparently changed completely, since previously she had been fond of them but henceforth was indifferent and hostile. Difficulties with her mother and step-father increased as time went on and there was much friction over her engagement.

No doubt an analysis would have given us much more material, especially regarding early ambivalence, but this material gives some impression of her problems. When she came to the Clinic she was very miserable and cried over her lack of affection for her husband and daughter. She felt fond of both, but unable to express her feelings and to respond to her husband. She remarked that her mind seemed to be at war with itself, that she was restless and dissatisfied.

It was clear at the first interview that Sheila was a neurotic child. Further information showed that she was cruel to the cat and was very hostile to her mother. The screaming-attacks at school had come on after she had been called a "bad, naughty girl" and there was much other evidence to show the strong sense of guilt which she was trying to evade and to get reassurance against.

Now it seemed to me then—and many other cases have fortified my belief—that the excess of hostility and guilt found in Sheila was the direct result of her mother's attitude towards her. There must be few children who would not be resentful to a mother who loses her temper, shakes and slaps them when they do not immediately do what is required of them. Constant small frustrations and interferences again are apt to make the best-tempered child furious and bitter. Sheila's hostility is therefore easily explained and no doubt a large measure of her guilt was a direct result of this.

But a further factor came in which is as common in the mothers of neurotic children as the unconscious hostility. Mrs C. was herself a very guilty woman. She was deeply unhappy and miserable about her lack of affection and feeling of jealousy. But although she could at times admit her own faults, she usually projected them on to her daughter and made a scapegoat of her. She would refer to the child as a "horrid little beast", talked bitterly of Sheila's "nasty traits", by which she meant Sheila's desire to be first in everything, her selfishness and greediness. She was specially angry about Sheila's remark—"I want all that pudding—I don't want Daddy to have any." Indeed, Sheila's greediness, selfishness and rudeness were her constant theme in these interviews and she described vividly how she let Sheila know in no uncertain terms how disgusted she was with her.

I arranged to see Mrs C. with a view to helping her to accept these traits in herself in the hope that she would be more tolerant of Sheila and blame her less. It was naturally only after a considerable number of interviews that I could enable her to realize how jealous she had been of her step-father and step-sister, her reaction to the realization being a memory of wanting to hit her own father over the head when he kissed her mother. Her feeling of guilt and self-condemnation about her own jealousy and selfishness were explored and her attitude to Sheila improved very considerably, with the result that Sheila's symptoms almost disappeared.

Of course Sheila remained a neurotic child. She had introjected her mother's condemning attitude very fully, and a modification of the mother's attitude when the child was 4½ was hardly calculated to alter the child's super-ego. Yet it seemed to me probable that a reduction of the maternal condemnation might do something over a period of years to help the child back to normality and at least the situation would be prevented from getting worse.

The two maternal tendencies illustrated in this case, unconscious hostility towards the child and a projection of condemned impulses on to her, are seen extremely commonly in child guidance practice. By way of further examples I will mention two other cases briefly where parental projection is in full swing.

A father brought a child of 2½ for advice on account of alleged masturbation. It appeared that the boy had been seen to touch his genitals on two occasions some months previously. He had immediately been put under the cold tap by his father and since then either his father or his mother had sat by his cot whenever he was in it and not sleeping. In this case it was unnecessary to inquire why such precautions had been taken, for his father began spontaneously to tell at length of his own struggle with masturbation. It had been one of the central issues of his life and he held all the usual views regarding its harmfulness. It was obvious that this father's conflicts had already had a serious influence upon his handling of his son's infantile masturbation and were likely enormously to increase the child's guilt about it.

One feels that without treatment this case might easily develop after the pattern of a case whom Elizabeth Geleerd is at present treating. She is a child of seven years whose principal symptom is open and frequent masturbation. Her mother, it appears, has been in the habit of washing the child's genitals twice a day and inspects them to see whether the child has masturbated or not. This behaviour alone suggests that the mother herself has acute conflicts about masturbation and it seems not unreasonable to suppose that the intensity of the child's conflicts are the result of the mother's attitude.

Finally there is the case of a boy of five, Cyril R., referred for being unmanageable. He is disobedient, destructive, treats his mother like dirt and swears at her. He plays the truant from home and appears to be utterly hard-boiled. When he was 2½ a sister was born. He was jealous and on one occasion took an enamel mug away from her and hit her over the head with it. Soon afterwards the baby died of diarrhoea and vomiting. The father thought Cyril's behaviour had "probably" caused the death, and the mother blamed him openly. The nursery-school, which Cyril was attending at this time, described his mother as being "hateful" to him and openly wishing he was dead after the baby's death. When another baby died a year later, Mrs R.'s resentment against Cyril was reported to have been equally intense. The mother was a neurotic woman and her attitude to Cyril seemed to have been the result of projecting all her guilt about the baby's death on to him. (It is perhaps not without interest that she herself had been left in a railway carriage when she was ten days old and brought up by foster parents. She had always harboured a grudge against her mother for this.)

Now I want to emphasize that the parents of whom I have spoken were very decent people who were honestly intending to do their best for their children. But unconscious resentment dating from their own childhoods had made them impatient and hostile, whilst guilt about jealousy, hatred or masturbation had led them to make scapegoats of their children.

I am inclined to think that much the same factors underlie spoiling. We find a mother who is always looking after her child, fussing about his health, giving him presents in what appears an endless round of protection and love. When we look at things more closely however we find a very different picture. Such a mother behaves in this way in order to compensate for her unconscious hostility to the child, and it is this which I believe damages the child. In one case a mother was so anxious about her boy that when the school had a bun feast and all the children brought buns to put in a common pool, the mother forbade the boy to pool his because she was afraid to let him eat a bun brought by another child. It was not surprising to find a great deal of unconscious hostility behind this obsessional precaution. The boy had developed a great fear of his own aggression as was shown by a tic and a pathetic timidity and it did not seem to me extravagant to suppose that the boy's fear of his own aggression had resulted from his mother's fear and guilt about her own.

Another factor which often appears important in spoiling is the mother's inability to stand hostility or criticism from her child. We may take it for granted that even the most loving children have periods when they hate their parents. Now parents react to this hatred in very different ways. Some take it as a matter of course—an aspect of human life which no one likes but which we have to put up with. But many neurotic parents cannot regard it in this light. Owing to unconscious guilt they must have constant reassurance that they are good mothers, not bad as they fear. Consequently they buy off their children's natural hostility by love and kisses. Some children of course do not respond, but there are many who fall into the trap. Such mothers will go to endless lengths to wheedle affection from their children and to rebuke in a pained way any show of what they call ingratitude. It is perhaps small wonder that the child develops very high ideals of the affection he feels he should give and a horror of his aggressive and greedy impulses which pain his mother so.

The mother of Derek S. was a good example of the person who must see herself as good and cannot bear criticism or hostility. She was a woman of forty-one who brought her boy aged 9½ to the Clinic because of his extreme nervousness, which manifested itself particularly in a refusal to undergo any medical or dental treatment and in his crying "at the least little thing".

When giving a picture of family life to the social worker, she made a point of emphasizing how happy and united the family was, how there was never a cross word and how they all adored each other. Now all this was no doubt true but it was obvious from her very insistence that it was not the whole story. She was clearly afraid of admitting the possibility of any friction or hostility in the family, a view which was confirmed by her husband, who later informed us that a cross word always made Mrs S. ill and that six months previously, after a few words between the two of them, she had had a fit of hysterics and had gone to hospital for three days in a state of collapse.

This little incident well illustrated her pathological fear of conflict and gave some clue as to why she demanded affection and could not tolerate to be seen in any role but that of the good loving mother. Without the knowledge of this incident moreover the unwary might have been led to think that here we were dealing with a normally good mother who could not possibly have had a bad influence on her son. In a recent (unpublished) paper Ignacio Matte Blanco has reported on an adult alcoholic patient whose mother was of this type. He writes:

> As regards the mother, it seems that her own guilt required that she should be considered the perfect mother. She has the reputation of being a saint, and at the beginning of the analysis the patient talked abundantly about it. But it was soon evident that this was only the expurgated edition of a more complex personality. I will quote only one example to show how the mother suppressed the child's criticisms against herself. She used to tell the patient the story of a boy who helped his mother in the work of the house, ran errands for her and did little jobs. One day the boy presented the mother with a bill as follows:

To running errands	2d.
To helping in the work of the house	2d.
Various others	2d.
Total	6d.

> The mother replied with another bill:

To looking after you all these years	Nothing
To loving and cherishing you	Nothing
To feeding and clothing you	Nothing
Total	Nothing

A persistent attitude of this kind will, as Matte Blanco says, effi-
ciently suppress a child's criticism of his mother and canalize all his
feelings into the one permitted expression: love and gratitude. It
will also enormously increase the child's guilt over his selfish,
greedy and hostile impulses.

Of course it is one thing to point to the prevalence of unconscious hostility, guilt, repression, projection and the need for
reassurance amongst the mothers of neurotic children and another
to understand in detail how these factors influence the psychic
development of the child and make him neurotic. Before discussing
this however it may be as well to deal with another question which
is frequently raised. How is it that children of one family can differ
so greatly in their degree of instability?

They are, it might be argued, brought up in the same emotional
atmosphere with the same mother and father, and influences which
affect one child badly should affect the others also: any differences
in the way in which they turn out must therefore be due to inherited disposition. Now it is unquestionably true that children of one
family can vary greatly in their inherited qualities and potentialities, and no doubt this does account for many differences of character within a family. But it must not be allowed to blind us to the
fact that the emotional atmospheres in which the children of one
family grow up are never the same and in some cases bear practically no resemblance to one another. Apart altogether from gross
environmental changes such as hospitalization and visits of parents
abroad which may affect one child and not another at all, the children are bound to be of different ages when the same event occurs.
Thus the mother's absence for six months will affect a child of ten
very differently from a child of two. Position in the family is obviously of significance also, but perhaps even more important are the
parents' feelings towards their several children. One has only to
hear a mother talking about her different children to recognize that
her feelings about them can be as varied as the colours of a rain-
bow. Indeed it is obvious that no mother can feel the same towards
all her children, however much she may try. One child is born when
the parents are radiantly happy together—another when there are
differences and difficulties. One child may be of the right sex,
another a disappointment because it is of the wrong one. One child
may be longed for, another come too soon, yet another be altogether

unwanted. Whilst these variations of feeling are obvious and inevitable even in the normal mother, it seems likely that they are very much exaggerated in the neurotic, whose emotions are always inclined to extremes. A neurotic parent may differentiate extremely between the boys and the girls or again may idolize one child and pour hatred on another who becomes the personification of evil.

As an example of a relatively normal mother who, despite her own wishes, had very different feelings towards her four children as a result of the circumstances of their birth, one might quote the mother of Eric C. He was aged 7.3 and referred for being backward and difficult at school. He was restless, interfering, disobedient and always up to mischief. Although wanting to play with other children, he was so annoying, selfish and spiteful that they soon got sick of him. He was however affectionate and liked very much to be made a fuss of. One of his traits which particularly worried his mother was his inability to ask for anything, his deceitfulness and his fear of owning up to doing wrong—all in marked difference to the elder brother. Eric had a twin sister, who was a persistent masturbator and in other ways very like Eric, a brother one year older and another aged three. His father was a working man who had the reputation of being a good father and a reliable husband. His mother appeared a sensible woman with a kind friendly attitude towards other people and showed a real concern about Eric. In the very first interview she remarked how "she had never felt quite the same affection for the twins as she had for the other two children. She had never wanted to have them on to her knee, and never had any qualms about leaving them in bed and going out when she would always have taken William (the elder brother) with her."

The mother's attitude quite clearly resulted from the circumstances of their birth. In the first place the second pregnancy had begun only nine months after the elder boy was born. Twins had not been predicted and when Eric, who was born second, appeared, he was a very disagreeable surprise. Finally, immediately after the birth the mother developed severe kidney trouble and was kept in hospital. Owing to the mother's condition the twins were taken from her at three weeks and put in another hospital. At four months the mother returned home, having had her kidney out, and the family was reunited. But the mother was hardly fit enough to look after three babies and took the twins in a spirit of self-sacrifice. It was a source of much worry to her that she had never been able to feel affection for the twins as she did for the other two boys, and she realized with remorse that she had treated them coldly and without sympathy all their lives.

Having studied the soil conditions, we may now proceed to the question of how they actually affect the organism and make for maldevelopment. Not having analysed any case fully, I can only give an outline of the ways in which I suppose them to work.

It is not difficult, I think, to understand why the child of an unconsciously hostile mother has abnormally strong id impulses, why he is demanding, jealous and resentful to an abnormal degree. These mothers frustrate their children, not in a few dramatic ways, but persistently and all the time over trifles. When the child wants to run about, the mother stops him, when he wants to play with bricks, she wants him to have his milk, when he wants to have a game with the soap, she wants to get him to bed. All mothers frustrate their children, but the mother of the sort I am describing, having no sympathy or patience, increases the inevitable frustration a hundred or thousand fold. Instead of sympathising with the jealous child she is angry, instead of comforting him when he is miserable she gives him a slap, instead of joining in his play she puts him to bed, instead of taking part in his phantasy life she accuses him of lying. It is not that she uses any particular form of punishment or indulges any special cruelty. It is not that she says or does anything very terrible; but the way in which she does and says the ordinary everyday things of life is what seems to damage the child. When he is treated in this way, it seems to me small wonder that the child develops a greater degree of rage, jealousy and libinal demand than the average.

But we know that it is not merely strong id impulses which make for neurosis, but their conflict and repression by the child's super-ego. Theories of the origin of the super-ego have changed considerably since Freud first described it and there is of course still much controversy about it. Here I shall assume Melanie Klein's theories, which seem to me most easily to fit the facts.

In addition to the introjected elements, the super-ego has an instinctual root in the child's love for his parents. It is because hostility and greed conflict with this love that a part of the child's ego develops to control and repress the unwanted and disturbing impulses. Now it is reasonable to suppose that the stronger these disturbing impulses are, the stronger will the super-ego have to become in order to control them. This seems to me to be one of the factors which lead to the development of severe super-egos in children of unconsciously hostile parents. We have already seen that as a result of frustration and hostility such children develop extremely strong hostile and greedy impulses towards their mothers, impulses which come into direct conflict with their love for them. Some degree of repression of their love is probably always one result, leading in many cases to an assertion of hatred and a denial of love and guilt. The alternative is the overdevelopment of the mechanisms for controlling and coping with unwanted impulses—the super-ego.

But the pattern upon which this simple instinctual institution models itself is of course the parents, both real and imaginary. Much has been written about the introjection of phantastically severe parents, an imaginary severity being itself the product of projection. Less perhaps has been written recently about the introjection of the parents' real characters. Now it is obvious that in so far as these children have unusually strong hostile and greedy impulses, their phantasies of their parents will be cast in unusually lurid colours and their introjected parents correspondingly cruel. But in addition to this there are the characters of their real parents. Sheila's mother regarded the child as a horrid little beast and told her so in the bitterest of tones. She was for ever telling her how disgusted she was by her selfishness, greed and rudeness. Sheila's super-ego not unnaturally came to echo these words. Again and again Mrs C. must have given Sheila the impression that the phantasy bad mother really existed, and so confirmed the child's phantasies. An intolerant and severe super-ego was hardly surprising.

Moreover a vicious circle is soon set up, for the child, feeling guilty, begins to interpret his mother's hostile and condemning attitude as a reaction to his own badness, and so his guilt is increased. This is a familiar mechanism and need not be elaborated.

The explanation of the effect of the "good" spoiling mother on her child may be understood in a slightly different way. Women such as Mrs S., owing to guilt originating in their own childhood, are extremely vulnerable to hostility and criticism. Their whole lives depend upon the reassurance of admiration and affection; hostility therefore causes them real and severe suffering. Now children are very sensitive to the way in which they affect their parents. They want very much to give their mothers pleasure and to see them happy. They are miserable when they have made their mothers miserable. Consequently the children of spiritually fragile mothers suffer particularly. They are always doing things which make their mother unhappy and then regretting it. There is therefore more reason than usual for repressing hostility, a course persistently encouraged by the mother herself, who is of course exploiting her child's conscience and affection to the full. The result is naturally a priggish child who is terrified of his now severely repressed resentment and hostility, or else a child who despairs of doing anything but harm to his mother.

Much more work needs to be done before either the observations or the theories advanced here can be accepted. For instance until a careful statistical comparison is made between the environment of neurotic children and that of normal children, definite scientific conclusions are impossible. I am hoping to undertake some such research. Meanwhile we must be content with clinical impressions. But supposing these clinical impressions are provisionally accepted, what conclusions are to be drawn?

In the first place I think it should make us extremely cautious in recommending small children to be separated from their parents. There are many occasions when separation is unnecessary and many others in which careful arrangements can mitigate the separation. Thus if a child must be in hospital the mother should be encouraged to visit daily, whilst if a mother cannot take her child abroad with her care should be taken to see that the child is looked after by people with whom he is familiar and in familiar surroundings. Great care should even so be exercised when a new baby has just been born. Even a well-arranged separation will be a serious shock to an older child who is left behind if the baby is taken, or even when he is left with the baby. At these times a child's phantasies of being deserted and punished are especially acute and easily inflamed. Of course this does not mean that mothers ought ideally never to be apart from their children. Provided breaks are not too long and continuity is preserved there seems no evidence to suppose that the child who is always with his mother is any better off than the child who only sees her for a few hours a day and not at all for odd holiday weeks. If however it became a tradition that small children were never subjected to complete or prolonged separation from their parents in the same way that regular sleep and orange juice have become nursery traditions, I believe that many cases of neurotic character development would be avoided. That is the most important thing of all.

Unfortunately with neurotic mothers preventive measures are not practicable, short of a prophylactic analysis. But if we hold the view that neurotic mothers have a serious effect upon their children we shall probably pay more attention to treating them, especially when the children are small and the neurotic disturbances not far advanced. Melanie Klein, whilst recognizing the problem, is rather pessimistic in her book as to what can be done. She remarks that giving advice to neurotic mothers only increases their guilt and anxiety, and so makes their attitude to their child even worse. She therefore concludes: "I do not, in the light of my own experiences, put much faith in the possibility of affecting the child's environment. It is better to rely upon the results achieved in the child itself."[4] Now as far as giving advice is concerned I find myself in complete agreement with Mrs Klein's views. Although with the relatively normal mother advice is often of value, with the neurotic mother it is worse than useless. In addition to its being a waste of time to try to change particular things in her handling of her child, by attempting it, as Mrs Klein points out, we increase the mother's guilt and so make the child appear more of a menace in her eyes. An increase of guilt will also increase her tendency to make of the child a scapegoat.

But there are other methods of handling these mothers besides giving them advice. Many of them recognize that it is their whole attitude to their child which is somehow wrong and are prepared to have help in changing it. A weekly interview in which their problems are approached analytically and traced back into their childhood is sometimes remarkably successful. Having once been helped to recognize and recapture the feelings which she herself had as a child and to find that they are accepted tolerantly and understandingly, a mother will become increasingly sympathetic and tolerant towards the same things in her child. It is sometimes possible also to work over unconscious hostility and the guilt associated with it. By these methods the mother's guilt is diminished and her general attitude changed. Naturally it is not possible to work in this way with every mother; some are too ill mentally to be treated once a week; others have too rigid a character for anything but a prolonged analysis to affect it. But there are many young mothers who respond favourably. Naturally one hopes in carrying out this treatment, or a fuller analysis where this is possible, that one may help not merely the one child but also other members of the family.

This procedure is not an alternative to the child being treated. Ideally both mother and child should be seen at the same time by different workers, and this is a procedure I habitually attempt in child guidance work when the child is under six.

So much for the direct approach to the mother. The further question now arises—to what extent is a knowledge of the environmental factor as it affects the child of value in analysing adults? I am aware that this is highly controversial ground and properly needs a paper to itself. But I would like to submit that it is an important problem.

Every patient who comes to us has a distorted view of his parents owing to projection and introjection. Some patients will project all that they feel to be bad in themselves on to their parents and blame and hate their parents. Others will project all the good and idolize their parents. Both attitudes are neurotic and need to be analysed if the patient is to be cured.

Now it may be said that, having no information of the patient's parents except at second-hand, we have no means of judging what the parents really were like. This view seems to me false. Although we must always be cautious in accepting our patients' description of their parents, the little analytic experience which I have had leads me to believe that, through the veil of prejudice and exaggeration woven by our patients, it is almost always possible to get a glimpse of the real personalities of parents with their varying qualities and defects. In giving interpretations of a patient's feelings towards his past or his present love object and also his feelings in the transference, it seems to me to add reality if we relate the origin of his feelings to the actual environmental situation in which he found himself when they began.

For instance if there is reason to believe a mother to have been a prude, this I think should be related to the patient's guilt over sexual problems. If there is reason to suppose that the mother had strong hostility to the child this should be taken into account in analysing the patient's ambivalence towards his mother. If the mother is believed to have demanded great affection and to have been intolerant of hostility, this again must be borne in mind when analysing the patient's guilt about hostility and anxiety about love. Naturally this will apply also in the transference expression of the same feelings. But in saying that these external situations should be taken into account in a full interpretation, it should not be thought that I wish to ignore the spontaneous anxiety and guilt arising internally as a result of conflicting emotions. It is by analysing the interplay between the internal and external forces, I believe, that we help our patients most.

Finally it seems to me that a working knowledge of the characters of a patient's parents helps us in analysing the projections made by him on to his parents. For instance in patients who project all the bad things on to their parents and hate them, I think it often helpful to recognize and accept the really bad aspects of the parents. This strengthens our hand when we wish later to point out the patient's repressed love for the good sides of his parents.

Again, with a patient who idolizes his parents and tells us that his mother was a wonderful woman, it is often necessary, I think, not only to interpret the patient's repressed hatred of her but also, what is much more difficult for many patients to accept, that there really were sides of his mother's character which were not lovable. An inability to admit defects in a loved person is an inability to accept reality. We often see this in the transference. Many patients idealize their analysts and are unable to admit even obvious faults. On one occasion for instance my watch was fast and I dismissed a patient several minutes early, a mistake made easier by the fact that I was in a hurry. She realized that I had given her short measure and mentioned it the next day, but was full of excuses for me—of course it must have been a mistake, and so on. Such patients readily encourage a positive counter-transference and also the analyst's self-conceit, and consequently we have to be on our guard if we are to analyse adequately in the transference a patient's blindness to the real defects of his loved objects. This inhibition is probably always a defence against the fear that the loved object is damaged and angry and is harbouring revengeful and evil feelings. The anxiety is that to admit even one defect may let loose terrifying phantasies which will endanger the whole love relation.

It is probably precisely these mechanisms at work in ourselves which make the scientific evaluation of the environmental factors so difficult. Our own emotional difficulties influence us towards one extreme or the other—either we debase mothers, think of them all as being full of evil wishes which are the cause of our troubles, and are unable even to imagine the benefactions of good mothers; or else we idolize mothers, think of them as being full of good wishes, feel that the cause of our troubles is our own wickedness, and are unable to conceive of bad mothers who do serious harm to their children. It is my belief that both good and bad mothers exist in fact as well as in phantasy, and that a child's emotional development is very dependent upon his mother's unconscious feelings about him. It seems probable that most mothers are reasonably good but that the mothers of neurotic children are frequently bad, in the sense that they have very strong feelings of hatred and condemnation towards their children or else make inordinate demands from them for affection. Such women are no more to be condemned than is any other neurotic person. They are to be pitied. But it would be sentimental to shut our eyes to their existence or to think that they do not have a damaging effect upon their children.

Notes

1. I am particularly indebted to two members of the staff of the London Child Guidance Clinic, Miss C. N. Fairbairn and Miss E. M. Lowden, for the help they have given me.
2. *The Psychological Treatment of Crime* p. 48. HMSO.
3. *The Psycho-Analysis of Children*, p. 24, footnote.
4. *The Psycho-Analysis of Children*, pp. 119–120.

The observation of infants in a set situation*

D. W. Winnicott

For about twenty years I have been watching infants in my clinic at the Paddington Green Children's Hospital, and in a large number of cases I have recorded in minute detail the way infants behave in a given situation which is easily staged within the ordinary clinic routine. I hope gradually to gather together and present the many matters of practical and theoretical interest that can be gleaned from such work, but in this paper I wish to confine myself to describing the set situation and indicating the extent to which it can be used as an instrument of research. Incidentally I cite the case of an infant of seven months who developed and emerged out of an attack of asthma while under observation.

The set situation

I must ask you to let me show you as far as possible the setting of

* Based on a paper read before the British Psycho-Analytical Society, April 23, 1941. [Reproduced, with permission, from: *International Journal of Psychoanalysis*, 1941, 22: 229–249 © Institute of Psychoanalysis, London, UK]

the observations. I want you to know, as far as you can without actually seeing it, what it is that I have become so familiar with: that which I call the "set situation", the situation into which every baby comes who is brought to my clinic for consultation.

In my clinic mothers and their children wait in the passage outside the fairly large room in which I work, and the exit of one mother and child is the signal for the entrance of another. A large room is chosen because so much can be seen and done in the time that it takes the mother and her child to reach me from the door at the opposite end of the room. By the time the mother has reached me I have made a contact with her and probably with the child by my facial expression, and I have had a chance to remember the case if it is not a new patient.

If it is an infant, I ask the mother to sit opposite me with the angle of the table coming between me and her. She sits down with the baby on her knee. I place a right-angled shining tongue-depressor at the edge of the table and I invite the mother to place the child in such a way that, if the child should wish to handle the spatula, this is possible. Ordinarily, a mother will understand what I am about, and it is easy for me gradually to describe to her that there is to be a space of time in which she and I will contribute as little as possible to the situation, so that what happens can fairly be put down to the child's account. You can imagine that mothers show by their ability or relative inability to follow this suggestion something of what they are like at home: if they are anxious about infection, or have strong moral feelings against putting things to the mouth, if they are hasty or move impulsively, these characteristics will be shown up.

It is very valuable to know what the mother is like, but ordinarily she follows my suggestion. Here, therefore, is the child on mother's knee, with a new person (a man, as it happens) sitting opposite, and there is a shining spatula on the table. I may add that if visitors are present, I have to prepare them often more carefully than the mother, because they tend to want to smile and take active steps in relation to the baby—to make love to him, or at least to give the reassurance of friendliness. If a visitor cannot accept the discipline which the situation demands, there is no point in my proceeding with the observation, which immediately becomes unnecessarily complicated.

The infant's behaviour

The baby is inevitably attracted by the shining, perhaps moving, metal object. If other children are present, they know well enough that the baby longs to take the spatula. (Often they cannot bear to see the baby's hesitation when it is pronounced, and take the spatula and shove it into the baby's mouth. This is, however, hastening forward.) Here we have in front of us the baby, attracted by a very attractive object, and I will now describe what, in my opinion, is a normal sequence of events. I hold that any variation from this, which I call normal, is significant.

STAGE I.—The baby puts his hand to the spatula, but at this moment discovers unexpectedly that the situation must be given thought. He is in a fix. Either with his hand resting on the spatula and his body quite still he looks at me and his mother with big eyes, and watches and waits, or, in certain cases, he withdraws interest completely and buries his face in the front of his mother's blouse. It is usually possible to manage the situation so that active reassurance is not given, and it is very interesting to watch the gradual and spontaneous return of the child's interest in the spatula.

STAGE II.—All the time, in "the period of hesitation" (as I call it), the baby holds his body still (but not rigid). Gradually he becomes brave enough to let his feelings develop, and then the picture changes quite quickly. The moment at which this first phase changes into the second is evident, for the child's acceptance of the reality of desire for the spatula is heralded by a change in the inside of the mouth, which becomes flabby, while the tongue looks thick and soft, and saliva flows copiously. Before long he puts the spatula into his mouth and is chewing it with his gums, or seems to be copying father smoking a pipe. The change in the baby's behaviour is a striking feature. Instead of expectancy and stillness there now develops self-confidence, and there is free bodily movement, both general movement and specific, the latter related to manipulation of the spatula.

(I have frequently made the experiment of trying to get the spatula to the infant's mouth during the stage of hesitation. Whether the hesitation corresponds to my normal or differs from it in degree or quality, I find that it is impossible during this stage to get the spatula to the child's mouth apart from the exercise of brute strength. In certain cases where the condition is acute any effort on my part that results in the spatula being moved towards the child produces screaming, mental distress or actual colic.)

The baby now seems to feel that the spatula is in his possession, perhaps in his power, certainly available for the purposes of self-expression. He bangs with it on the table or on a metal bowl which is nearby on the table, making as much noise as he can; or else he holds it to my mouth and to his mother's mouth, very pleased if we pretend to be fed by it. He definitely wishes us to play at being fed, and is upset if we should be so stupid as to take the thing into our mouths and spoil the game as a game.

At this point, I might mention that I have never seen any evidence of a baby being disappointed that the spatula is, in fact, neither food nor a container of food.

STAGE III.—There is a third stage. In the third stage the baby first of all drops the spatula as if by mistake. If it is restored he is pleased, plays with it again, and drops it once more, but this time less by mistake. On its being restored again, he drops it on purpose, and thoroughly enjoys aggressively getting rid of it, and is especially pleased when it makes a ringing sound on contact with the floor.

The end of this third phase[1] is when the baby either wishes to get down on the floor with the spatula, where he starts mouthing it and playing with it again, or else when he is bored with it and reaches out to any other objects that lie at hand.

This is reliable as a description of the normal only between the ages of about five months and thirteen months. After the baby is thirteen months old, interest in objects has become so widened that if the spatula is ignored and the baby reaches out for the blotting-pad, I cannot be sure that there is a real inhibition in regard to the primary interest. In other words, the situation rapidly becomes complicated and approaches that of the ordinary analytic situation which develops in the analysis of a two-year-old child, with the disadvantage (relative to the analytic) that as the infant is too young to speak, material presented is correspondingly difficult to understand. Before the age of thirteen months, however, in this "set situation" the infant's lack of speech is no handicap.

After thirteen months the infant's *anxieties* are still liable to be reflected in the set situation. It is his *positive interest* that becomes too wide for the setting.

(In passing, I would mention the fact that I find therapeutic work can be done in this situation:[2] in fact, the fluidity of the infant's personality and the fact that feelings and unconscious processes are so close to the early stages of babyhood make it possible for changes to be brought about in the course of a few interviews. This fluidity, however, must also mean that an infant who is normal at one year, or who at this age is favourably affected by treatment, is not by any means out of the wood. He is still liable to neurosis at a later stage and to becoming ill if exposed to bad environmental factors. However, it is a good prognostic sign if a child's first year goes well.)

Deviations from the normal

I have said that any variation from that which I have come to regard as the norm of behaviour in the set situation is significant.

The chief and most interesting variation is in the initial hesitation, which may either be exaggerated or absent. One baby will apparently take no interest in the spatula, and will take a long time before becoming aware of his interest or before summoning courage to display it. On the other hand, another will grab it and put it to his mouth in one second. In either case there is a departure from the normal. If inhibition is marked there will be more or less distress, and distress can be very acute indeed.

In another variation from the norm an infant grabs the spatula and immediately throws it on the floor, and repeats this as often as it is replaced by the observer.

In another paper I hope to show that there is a correlation between these and other variations from the norm and the infant's relation to food and to people.

Use of technique illustrated by a case

The set situation which I have described is an instrument which can be adapted by any observer to the observation of any infant that attends his clinic. Before discussing the theory of the infant's normal behaviour in this setting, I will give one case as an illustration, the case of a baby with asthma. The behaviour of the asthma, which came and went on two occasions while the baby was under observation, would perhaps have seemed haphazard were it not for the fact that the baby was being observed as a routine, and were it not for the fact that the details of her behaviour could be compared with that of other children in the same setting. The asthma, instead of having an uncertain relation to the baby's feelings, could be seen, because of the technique employed, to be related to a certain kind of feeling and to a certain clearly defined stage in a familiar sequence of events.

Margaret, a seven-months-old girl, is brought to me by her mother because the night before the consultation she has been breathing wheezily all night. Otherwise she is a very happy child who sleeps well and takes well. Her relations with both parents are good, especially with her father. He is a night worker and sees a lot of her. She already says "Dad-dad", but not "Ma-ma". When I ask: "Whom does she go to when she is in trouble?" the mother says: "She goes to her father; he can get her to sleep." There is a sister sixteen months older who is healthy, and the two children play together and like each other, although the baby's birth did arouse some jealousy in the older child.

The mother explains that she herself developed asthma when she became pregnant with this one, when the other was only seven months old. She was herself bad until a month before the consultation, since when she has had no asthma. Her own mother was subject to asthma, also since the time when she started to have children. The relation between the child and her mother is good, and she is feeding this baby at the breast satisfactorily.

The symptom, asthma, does not come entirely unheralded. The mother reports that for three days Margaret has been stirring in her sleep, only sleeping ten minutes at a time, waking with screaming and trembling. For a month she has been putting her fists to her mouth and this has recently become somewhat compulsive and anxious. For three days she has had a slight cough, but the wheeziness only became definite the night before the consultation.

It is interesting to note the behaviour of the child in the set situation. These are my detailed notes taken at the time. "I stood up a right-angled spatula on the table and the child was immediately interested, looked at it, looked at me and gave me a long regard with big eyes and sighs. For five minutes this continued, the child being unable to make up her mind to take the spatula. When at length she took it, she was at first unable to make up her mind to put it to her mouth, although she quite clearly wanted to do so. After a time she found she was able to take it, as if gradually getting reassured from our staying as we were. On her taking it to herself I noted the usual flow of saliva, and then followed several minutes of enjoyment of the mouth experience." It will be noted that this behaviour corresponded to what I call the normal.

In the second consultation Margaret reached out to take the spatula, but again hesitated, exactly as at the first visit, and again only gradually became able to mouth and to enjoy the spatula with confidence. She was more eager in her mouthing of it than she had been at the previous occasion, and made noises while chewing it. She soon dropped it deliberately and on its being returned played with it with excitement and noise, looking at mother and at me, obviously pleased, and kicking out. She played about and threw down the spatula, put it to her mouth again on its being restored to her, made wild movements with her hands, and then began to be interested in other objects that lay near at hand, which included a bowl. Eventually she dropped the bowl, and as she seemed to want to go down we put her on the floor with the bowl and the spatula, and she looked up at us very pleased with life, playing with her toes and with the spatula and the bowl, but not with the spatula and the bowl together. At the end she reached for the spatula and seemed as if she would bring them together, but she just pushed the spatula right away in the other direction from that of the bowl. When the spatula was brought back she eventually banged it on the bowl, making a lot of noise.

(The main point in this case relevant to the present discussion is contained in the first part of the description, but I have given the whole case-note because of the great interest that each detail could have if the subject under discussion were extended. For instance, the child only gradually came to the placing of the two objects together. This is very interesting and is representative of her difficulty as well as of her growing ability in regard to the management of two people at the same time. In order to make the present issue as clear as possible I am leaving discussion of these points for another occasion.[3]

In this description of the baby's behaviour in the set situation, I have not yet said when it was that she developed asthma. The baby sat on her mother's lap with the table between them and me. The mother held the child round the chest with her two hands, supporting her body. It was therefore very easy to see when at a certain point the child developed bronchial spasm. the mother's hands indicated the exaggerated movement of the chest, both the deep inspiration and the prolonged obstructed expiration were shown up, and the noisy expiration could be heard. The mother could see as well as I did when the baby had asthma. *The asthma occurred on both occasions over the period in which the child hesitated about taking the spatula.* She put her hand to the spatula and then, as she controlled her body, her hand and her environment, she developed asthma, which involves an involuntary control of expiration. At the moment when she came to feel confident about the spatula which was at her mouth, when saliva flowed, when stillness changed to the enjoyment of activity and when watching changed into self-confidence, at this moment the asthma ceased.

A fortnight later the child had had no asthma, except the two attacks in the two consultations.[4] Recently (that is, twenty-one months after the episode I have described), the child had had no asthma, although of course she is liable to it.[5]

Because of the method of observation, it is possible for me to make certain deductions from this case about the asthma attacks and their relation to the infant's feelings. My main deduction is that in this case there was a close enough association between bronchial spasm and anxiety to warrant the postulation of a relationship between the two. It is possible to see, because of the fact that the baby was being watched under known conditions, that for this child asthma was associated with the moment at which there is normally hesitation, and hesitation implies mental conflict. An impulse has been aroused. This impulse is temporarily controlled, and asthma coincides on two occasions with the period of control of the impulse. This observation, especially if confirmed by similar observations, would form a good basis for discussion of the emotional aspect of asthma, especially if taken in conjunction with observations made during the psychoanalytic treatment of asthma subjects.

Discussion of theory

The hesitation in the first place is clearly a sign of anxiety, although it appears normally.

As Freud (1926) said, "anxiety is *about* something". There are two things, therefore, to discuss: the things that happen in the body and mind in a state of anxiety, and the something that there is anxiety about.

If we ask ourselves why it is that the infant hesitates after the first impulsive gesture, we must agree, I think, that this is a super-ego manifestation. With regard to the origin of this, I have come to the conclusion that, generally speaking, the baby's normal hesitation cannot be explained by a reference to the parental attitude. But this does not mean that I neglect the possibility that he does so because he has learned to expect the mother to disapprove or even to be angry whenever he handles or mouths something. The parent's attitude *does* make a difference and can make a lot of difference in certain cases.

I have learned to pick out fairly quickly the mothers who have a rooted objection to the child's mouthing and handling objects, and on the whole I can say that the mothers who come to my clinic do not stop what they tend to regard as an ordinary infantile interest. Amongst these mothers are even some who bring their babies because they have noticed that the infants have ceased to grab things and put them to their mouths, recognizing this to be a symptom.

Further, at this tender age before the baby is, say, fourteen months old, there is a fluidity of character which allows a certain amount of the mother's tendency to prohibit such indulgence to be over-ridden. I say to the mother: "He can do that here if he wants to, but don't actually encourage him to." I have found that in so far as the children are not driven by anxiety they are able to adjust themselves to this modified environment.

But whether it is or is not the mother's attitude that is determining the baby's behaviour, I suggest that the hesitation means that the infant *expects* to produce an angry and perhaps revengeful mother by his indulgence. In order that a baby shall feel threatened, even by a truly and obviously angry mother, he must have in his mind the notion of an angry mother. As Freud (1926) says: "On the other hand, the external (objective) danger must have managed to become internalized if it is to be significant for the ego."

If the mother has been really angry and if the child has real reason to expect her to be angry in the consultation when he grabs the spatula, we are led to the infant's apprehensive phantasies, just as in the ordinary case where the child hesitates in spite of the fact that the mother is quite tolerant of such behaviour and even expects it. The "something" which the anxiety is about is in the infant's mind, an idea of potential evil or strictness, and into the novel situation anything that is in the infant's mind may be projected. When there has been no experience of prohibition the hesitation implies conflict, or the existence in the baby's mind of a *phantasy* corresponding to the other baby's *memory* of his really strict mother. In either case, as a consequence, he has first to curb his interest and desire, and he only becomes able to find his desire again in so far as his testing of the environment affords satisfactory results. I supply the setting for such a test.

It can be deduced, then, that the "something" that the anxiety is about is of tremendous importance to the infant. To understand more about the "something" it will be necessary to draw on the knowledge gained from the analysis of children between two and four years old, particularly between two and three. I mention this age because it has been found by Melanie Klein, and I think by all who have analysed such young children, that there is something in the experience of such analyses which cannot be got from the analyses of even three-and-a-half- and four-year-old children, and certainly not from the analyses of children in the latency period. One of the characteristics of a child at the age of two is that the primary oral phantasies, and the anxieties and defences belonging to them, are clearly discernible alongside secondary and highly elaborated mental processes.

The idea that infants have phantasies is not acceptable to everyone, but probably all of us who have analysed children at two years have found it necessary to postulate that an infant, even an infant of seven months like the asthma baby whose case I have already quoted, has phantasies. These are not yet attached to word-presentations, but they are full of content and rich in emotion, and it can be said that they provide the foundation on which all later phantasy life is built. (Cf. Lowenfeld, 1935.)

These phantasies of the infant are concerned not only with external environment, but also with the fate and inter-relationship of the people and bits of people that are being phantastically taken into him—at first along with his ingestion of food and subsequently as an independent procedure—and which build up the inner reality. A child feels that things inside are good or bad, just as outside things are good or bad. The qualities of good and bad depend on the relative acceptability of aim in the taking-in process. This in turn depends on the strength of the destructive impulses relative to the love impulses, and on the individual child's capacity to tolerate anxieties derived from destructive tendencies. Also, and connected with both of these, the nature of the child's defences has to be taken into account, including the degree of development of his capacity for making reparation. All of which could be summed up by saying that the child's ability to keep alive what he loves and to retain his belief in his own love has an important bearing on how good or bad the things inside him and outside him feel to him to be; and this is to some extent true even of the infant of only a few months. Further, as Melanie Klein has shown, there is a constant interchange and testing between inner and outer reality; the inner reality is always being built up and enriched by instinctual experience in relation to external objects and by contributions from external objects (in so far as such contributions can be perceived); and the outer world is constantly being perceived and the individual's relationship to it being enriched because of the existence in him of a lively inner world.

The insight and conviction gained through the analysis of young children can be applied backwards to the first year of life, just as Freud applied what he found in adults to the understanding of children, and to the understanding not only of the particular patient as a child, but of children in general.

It is illuminating to observe infants directly, and it is necessary for us to do so. In many respects, however, the analysis of two-year-old children tells us much more about the infant than we can ever get from direct observation of infants. This is not surprising; the uniqueness of psycho-analysis as an instrument of research, as we know, lies in its capacity to discover the *unconscious* part of the mind and link it up with the conscious part and thus give us something like a full understanding of the individual who is in analysis.

This is true even of the infant and the young child, though direct observation can tell us a great deal if we actually know how to look and what to look for. The proper procedure is obviously to get all we can both from observation and from analysis, and to let each help the other.

Physiology of anxiety

I now wish to say something about the physiology of anxiety. Is it not holding up the development of descriptive psychology that it is seldom, if ever, pointed out that the physiology of anxiety cannot be described in simple terms, for the reason that it is different in different cases and at different times? The teaching is that anxiety may be characterized by pallor and sweating and vomiting and diarrhoea and tachycardia. I was interested to find in my clinic, however, that there are really several alternative manifestations of anxiety, whatever organ or function is under consideration. An anxious child during physical examination in a heart clinic may have a heart that is thumping, or at times almost standing still, or the heart may be racing away, or just ticking over. To understand what is happening when we watch these symptoms I think we have to know something about the child's feelings and phantasies, and therefore about the amount of excitement and rage that is admixed, as well as the defences against these.

Diarrhoea, as is well known, is not always just a matter of physiology. Analytic experience with children and adults shows that it is often a process accompanying an unconscious fear of definite things, things inside that will harm the individual if kept inside. The individual may know he fears impulses, but this, though true, is only part of the story, because it is also true that he unconsciously *fears specific bad things* which exist somewhere for him. "Somewhere" means either outside himself or inside himself—ordinarily, both outside and inside himself. These phantasies may, of course, in certain cases, be to some extent conscious, and they give colour to the hypochondriac's descriptions of his pains and sensations.

If we are examining the hesitation of an infant in my set situation, we may say that the mental processes underlying the hesitation are similar to the ones that underlie diarrhoea, though opposite in their effect. I have taken diarrhoea, but I might have taken any other physiological process which can be exaggerated or inhibited in accordance with the unconscious phantasy which happens to affect the particular function or organ. In the same way, in consideration of the hesitation of the infant in the set situation, it can be said that even if the baby's behaviour is a manifestation of fear, there is still room for the description of the same hesitation in terms of unconscious phantasy. What we see is the result of the infant's impulse to reach out and take being subjected to control even to the extent of temporary denial of the impulse. To go further and to describe what is in the infant's mind cannot be a matter of direct observation, but, as I have said, this does not mean that there is nothing in the infant's mind corresponding to the unconscious phantasy which through psychoanalysis we can prove to exist in the mind of an older child or of an adult who hesitates in a similar situation.

In my special case, given to illustrate the application of the technique, control includes that of the bronchial tubes. It would be interesting to discuss the relative importance of the control of the bronchus as an organ (the displacement of the control, say, of the bladder) and control of expiration or of the breath that would have been expelled if not controlled. The breathing out might have been felt by the baby to be dangerous if linked to a dangerous idea—for instance, an idea of reaching *in* to take. To the infant, so closely in touch with his mother's body and the contents of the breast, which he actually takes, the idea of reaching in to the breast is by no means remote, and reaching in to the inside of mother's body could easily be associated in the baby's mind with not breathing.[6]

It will be seen that the notion of a dangerous breath or of a dangerous breathing or of a dangerous breathing organ leads us once more to the infant's phantasies.

I am claiming that it could not have been purely by chance that the infant gained and lost asthma so clearly in relation to the control of an impulse on two separate occasions, and that it is therefore very much to the point if I examine every detail of the observations.

Leaving the special case of the asthma infant and returning to the normal hesitation of a baby in taking the spatula, we see that the danger exists in the infant's mind and can only be explained on the supposition that he has phantasies or something corresponding to them.

Now, what does the spatula stand for? The answer to this is complex because the spatula stands for different things.

That the spatula can stand for a breast is certain. It is easy to say that the spatula stands for a penis, but this is a very different thing from saying it stands for a breast, because the baby who is always familiar with either a breast or a bottle has very seldom indeed any real knowledge based on experience of an adult penis. In the vast majority of cases a penis must be the infant's phantasy of what a man might have. In other words, we have said no more by calling it a penis than that the infant may have a phantasy that there is something like a breast and yet different because it is associated more with father than with mother. In his phantasies about this the child is known to draw on his or her own genital sensations and on the results of self-exploration.

However, I think the truth is that what the baby later knows to be a penis, he earlier senses as a quality of mother, such as liveliness, punctuality at feed times, reliability and so on, or else as a thing in her breast equated with its sticking out or its filling up, or in her body equated with her erect posture, or a hundred other things about her that are not essentially herself. It is as if, when a baby goes for the breast and drinks milk, in phantasy he puts his hand in, or dives into, or tears his way into his mother's body, according to the strength of the impulse and its ferocity, and takes from her breast whatever is good there. In the unconscious this is equated with what is later called penis.

Besides standing for breast and penis, the spatula also stands for people, observation having clearly shown that the four-to-five-month infant may be able to take in persons as a whole, through the eyes, sensing the person's mood, approval or disapproval, or distinguishing between one person and another.[7]

(I would point out that in the explanation of the period of hesitation by reference to actual experience of mother's disapproval, an assumption is being made that this infant is normal or developed enough to take in persons as a whole. This is by no means always true, and I could demonstrate to you infants who seem to show an interest in and a fear of the spatula, but who are unable to form an idea of a whole person.)

Everyday observation shows that babies from an age certainly less than the age-group we are discussing (five to thirteen months) ordinarily not only recognize people, but also behave differently towards different people.

In the set situation the infant who is under observation gives me important clues to the state of his emotional development. He may only see in the spatula a thing that he takes or leaves, and which he does not connect with a human being. This means that he has not developed the capacity, or he has lost it, for building up the whole person behind the part object. Or he may show that he sees me or mother behind the spatula, and behave as if this were part of me (or of mother). In this case, if he takes the spatula it is as if he took his mother's breast. Or, finally, he may see mother and me and think of the spatula as something to do with the relation between mother and myself. In so far as this is the case, in taking or leaving the spatula he makes a difference to the relationship of two people standing for father and mother.

There are intermediate stages. For instance, some infants obviously prefer to think of the spatula as related to the bowl, and they repeatedly take it out of the bowl and replace it with evident interest and pleasure and perhaps excitement. They seem to find an interest in two objects simultaneously more natural than an interest in the spatula as a thing that can be taken from me, fed to mother, or banged on to the table.

Only the actual work can do justice to the richness of variation which a number of infants introduce into the simple setting which can so easily be provided.

The infant, if he has the capacity to do so, finds himself dealing with two persons at once, mother and myself. This requires a degree of emotional development higher than the recognition of one whole person, and it is true indeed that many neurotics never succeed in managing a relation to two people at once. It has been pointed out that the neurotic adult is often capable of a good relation with one parent at a time, but gets into difficulties in his relationship with both together. This step in the infant's development, by which he becomes able to manage his relationship to two people who are important to him (which fundamentally means to both his parents), at one and the same time, is a very important one, and until it is negotiated he cannot proceed to take his place satisfactorily in the family or in a social group: According to my observations this important step is first taken within the first year of life.

Before he is one year old the infant may feel that he is depriving others of things that are good or even essential because of the greed roused by his love. This feeling corresponds to his fear, which easily may be confirmed by experience, that when he is deprived of the breast or bottle and of his mother's love and attention, someone else enjoys more of her company. Actually this may be father, or a new baby. Jealousy and envy, essentially oral in their first associations, increase greed but also stimulate genital desires and phantasies, thus contributing to an extension of libidinal desires and love, as well as of hatred. All these feelings accompany the infant's first steps in establishing a relation to both parents—steps which are also the initial stages of his Oedipus situation, the direct and the inverted one. The conflict between love and hatred and the ensuing guilt and fear of losing what is loved, first experienced in relation to the mother only, is carried further into the infant's relation to both parents and very soon to brothers and sisters as well. Fear and guilt stirred by the infant's destructive impulses and phantasies (to which experiences of frustration and unhappiness contribute) are responsible for the idea that if he desires his mother's breast too much he deprives father and other children of it, and if he desires some part of his father's body which corresponds to mother's breast he deprives mother and others of it. Here lies one of the difficulties in the establishment of a happy relation between a child and both parents. I cannot deal with the complicated matter of the interplay of the child's greed and the different ways he has of controlling this greed or of counteracting its results by restoring and reconstructing, but it can readily be seen that these things become complicated where the child's relationship is to two persons instead of to mother alone.

(It will be remembered that in my case-note of the infant with asthma, I referred to the relation between the child's gradual ability to bring the spatula and the bowl together at the end of her game, and the mixtures of wishes and fears in regard to the management of a relation to two people at once. See p. 285.)

Now this situation, in which the infant hesitates as to whether he can or cannot satisfy his greed without rousing anger and dissatisfaction in at least one of the two parents, is illustrated in the set situation of my observations in a way that is plain for all to see. In so far as the baby is normal, one of the main problems before him is the management of two people at once. In this set situation I seem sometimes to be the witness of the first success in this direction. At other times I see reflected in the infant's behaviour the successes and failures he is having in his attempts to become able to have a relation to two people at once at home. Sometimes I witness the onset of a phase of difficulties over this, as well as a spontaneous recovery.[8]

It is as if the two parents allow him the gratification of desires about which he has conflicting feelings, tolerating his expression of his feelings about themselves. In my presence he cannot always make use of my consideration of his interests, or he can only gradually become able to do so.

The experience of daring to want and to take the spatula and to make it his own without in fact altering the stability of the immediate environment acts as a kind of object-lesson which has therapeutic value for the infant. At the age which we are considering and all through childhood such an experience is not merely temporarily reassuring: the cumulative effect of happy experiences and of a stable and friendly atmosphere round a child is to build up his confidence in people in the external world and his general feeling of security. The child's belief in the good things and relationships inside himself is also strengthened. Such little steps in the solution of the central problems come in the every-day life of the infant and young child, and every time the problem is solved something is added to the child's general stability, and the foundation of emotional development is strengthened. It will not be surprising, then, if I claim that in the course of making my observations I also bring about some changes in the direction of health.

What there is of therapeutics in this work lies, I think, in the fact that the full course of an experience is allowed. From this one can draw some conclusions about one of the things that go to make a good environment for the infant. In the intuitive management of an infant a mother naturally allows the full course of the various experiences, keeping this up until the infant is old enough to understand her point of view. She hates to break into such experiences as feeding or sleeping or defæcating. In my observations I artificially give the baby the right to complete an experience which is of particular value to him as an object-lesson.

In psycho-analysis proper there is something similar to this. The analyst lets the patient set the pace and he does the next best thing to letting the patient decide when to come and go, in that he fixes the time and the length of the session, and sticks to the time that he has fixed. Psycho-analysis differs from this work with infants in that the analyst is always groping, seeking his way among the mass of material offered and trying to find out what, at the moment, is the shape and form of the thing which he has to offer to the patient, that which he calls the interpretation. Sometimes the analyst will find it of value to look behind all the multitude of details and to see how far the analysis which he is conducting could be thought of in the same terms as those in which one can think of the relatively simple set situation which I have described. Each interpretation is a glittering object which excites the patient's greed.

Note on the third stage

I have rather artificially divided the observations into three stages. Most of my discussion has concerned the first stage and the hesitation in it which denotes conflict. The second stage also presents much that is of interest. Here the infant feels that he has the spatula in his possession and that he can now bend it to his will or use it as an extension of his personality. In this paper I am not developing this theme. In the third phase the infant practises ridding himself of the spatula, and I wish to make a comment on the meaning of this.

In this the third phase he becomes brave enough to throw the spatula down and to enjoy ridding himself of it, and I wish to show how this seems to me to relate to the game which Freud (1920g) described, in which the boy mastered his feelings about his mother's departure. For many years I watched infants in this setting without seeing, or without recognizing, the importance of the third stage. There was a practical value for me in my discovery of the importance of this stage, because whereas the infant who is dismissed in the second stage is upset at the loss of the spatula, once the third stage has been reached the infant can be taken away and can leave the spatula behind him without being made to cry.

Although I have always known Freud's description of the game with the cotton-reel and have always been stimulated by it to make detailed observations on infant play, it is only in more recent years that I have seen the intimate connection between my third phase and Freud's remarks.

It now seems to me that my observations could be looked at as an extension backwards of this particular observation of Freud's. I think the cotton-reel, standing for the child's mother, is thrown away to indicate a getting rid of the mother because the reel in his possession had represented the mother in his possession. I referred earlier to the infant's phantasies of incorporating his mother's breast, and his father's penis, and whatever he felt had value, all of which was implied in his activities with the spatula in this set situation. Now, having become familiar with the full sequence of incorporation, retention and riddance, I see the throwing-away of the cotton-reel as a part of a game, the rest being implied, or played at an earlier stage. In other words, when the mother goes away this is not only a loss for him of the externally real mother but also a test of his relation to his *inside* mother. This inside mother to a large extent reflects his own feelings, and may be loving or terrifying, or changing rapidly from one attitude to the other. When he finds he can master his relation to his inside mother, including his aggressive riddance of her (Freud brings this out clearly), he can allow the disappearance of his external mother, and not too greatly fear her return.

In particular I have come to understand in recent years the part played in the mind even of the infant of the fear of the loss of the mother or of both parents as valuable internal possessions. When the mother leaves the child he feels that he has lost not only an actual person, but also her counterpart in his mind, for the mother in the external world and the one in the internal world are still very closely bound up with each other in the infant's mind, and are more or less interdependent. The loss of the internal mother, who has acquired for the infant the significance of an inner source of love and protection and of life itself, greatly strengthens the threat of loss of the actual mother. Furthermore, the infant who throws away the spatula—and I think the same applies to the boy with the cotton-reel—not only gets rid of an external and internal mother who has stirred his aggression and is being expelled (and yet can be brought back): in my opinion he also externalizes an internal mother whose loss is feared, so as to demonstrate to himself that this internal mother, now represented through the toy on the floor, has not vanished from his inner world, has not been destroyed by the act of incorporation, is still friendly and willing to be played with. And by all this the child revises his relations with things and people both inside and outside himself.

Thus one of the deepest meanings of the third phase in the set situation is that in it the baby gains reassurance about the fate of his external mother and about her attitude; a depressed mood which accompanies such anxiety is relieved and happiness is regained. These conclusions could of course never be arrived at through observation only, but neither could Freud's profound explanation of the game with the cotton-reel have been arrived at without knowledge gained through analysis proper. In the play-analyses of young children we can see that the destructive tendencies, which endanger the people that the child loves in external reality and in his inner world, lead to fear, guilt and sorrow. Something is missing until the child feels that by his activities in play he has made reparation and revived the people whose loss he fears.

Summary

In this paper I have tried to describe a way by which infants can be observed objectively, a way based on the objective observation of patients in analysis and at the same time related closely to an ordinary home situation. I have described a set situation, and have given what I consider to be a normal (by which I mean healthy) sequence of events in this set situation. In this sequence there are many points at which anxiety may become manifest or implied, and to one of these, which I have called the moment of hesitation, I have drawn special attention by giving a case of a seven-months-old baby girl who developed asthma twice at this stage. I have shown that the hesitation indicates anxiety, and the existence of a super-ego in the infant's mind, and I have suggested that infant behaviour cannot be accounted for except on the assumption that there are infant phantasies.

Other set situations could easily be devised which would bring out other infantile interests and illustrate other infantile anxieties. The setting which I describe seems to me to have the special value that any physician can use it, so that my observations can be confirmed or modified, and it also provides a practical method by which some of the principles of psychology can be demonstrated clinically, and without causing harm to patients.

Notes

1. I will discuss the significance of this phase and link it with Freud's observations on the boy with the cotton-reel, towards the end of this paper (see p. 296).
2. It is not my object in this paper to trace the therapeutic possibilities of this work, but I will remind you in a few words of a case that I published in 1934, in which I committed myself to the belief that such work could be done. In the intervening years I have confirmed my opinion formed then.

    This was the case of a baby girl who had attended from six to eight months on account of feeding disturbance, presumably initiated by infective gastro-enteritis. The emotional development of the child was upset by this illness and the infant remained irritable, unsatisfied and liable to be sick after food. All play ceased, and by nine months not only was the infant's relation to people entirely unsatisfactory, but also she began to have fits. At eleven months fits were frequent.

    At twelve months the baby was having major fits followed by sleepiness. At this stage I started seeing her almost daily and giving her twenty minutes' personal attention, rather in the manner of what I now describe as the set situation, but with the infant on my own knee.

    At one consultation I had the child on my knee observing her. She made a furtive attempt to bite my knuckle. Three days later I had her again on my knee, and waited to see what she would do. She bit my knuckle three times so severely that the skin was nearly torn. She then played at throwing spatulas on the floor incessantly for fifteen minutes. All the time she cried as if really unhappy. Two days later I had her on my knee for half-an-hour. She had had four convulsions in the previous two days. At first she cried as usual. She again bit my knuckle very severely, this time without showing guilt feelings, and then she played the game of biting and throwing away spatulas; *while on my knee she became able to enjoy play*. After a while she began to finger her toes.

    Later the mother came and said that since the last consultation the baby had been "a different child". She had not only had no fits, but had been sleeping well at night—happy all day, taking no bromide. Eleven days later the improvement had been maintained, without medicine;

there had been no fits for fourteen days, and the mother asked to be discharged.

(For further details see original description: Winnicott, 1934.)

I visited the child one year later and found that since the last consultation she had had no symptom whatever. I found an entirely healthy, happy, intelligent and friendly child, fond of play, and free from the common anxieties.

3. I refer to this later, on p. 292.
4. But the mother had re-developed it.
5. The mother again rather made a point that she, however, had been having asthma, as if she felt she had to have it unless the baby had it.
6. At the sight of something particularly wonderful we sometimes say, "It takes my breath away." This and similar sayings, which include the idea of modification of the physiology of breathing, have to be explained in any theory of asthma that is to command respect.
7. As Freud showed, the cotton-reel stood for the mother of the eighteen-months-old boy (see pp. 296–297).
8. I have just watched from start to finish a fortnight's illness in a nine-months-old infant girl. Accompanying earache, and secondary to it, was a psychological disturbance characterized not only by a lack of appetite but also by a complete cessation of handling and mouthing of objects at home. In the set situation the child had only to see the spatula to develop acute distress. She pushed it away as if frightened of it. For some days in the set situation there seemed to be acute pain as if indicating acute colic instead of what is normally hesitation, and it would have been unkind to have kept the child for long at a time in this painful situation. The earache soon cleared up, but it was a fortnight before the infant's interest in objects became normal again. The change occurred gradually except for the last part, which came dramatically when the child was with me. She had become able to catch hold of the spatula and to make furtive attempts to mouth it. Suddenly she braved it, fully accepted it with her mouth and dribbled saliva. Her psychological illness was over and it was reported to me that on getting home she was found to be handling and mouthing objects as she had done before her illness started.

References

Abraham, K. (1924)[Trans. 1927]. The influence of oral erotism on character-formation. *Selected Papers*, 393.

Freud, S. (1920g)[Trans. 1922]. *Beyond the Pleasure Principle*, II ff.
Freud, S. (1926)[Trans. 1936]. *Inhibition, Symptoms and Anxiety*, 158 and 164.
Klein, M. (1932). *The Psycho-Analysis of Children*.
Lowenfeld, M. (1935). *Play in Childhood*, 150.
Winnicott, D. W. (1934). *Clinical Notes on Disorders of Childhood*, 165.

PART V
KLEIN'S REVISION

Introduction

Klein's revision

M elanie Klein not only made revisions in Freud's theories, but she also revised her own. At the start of the decade Klein's concept of the depressive position, and its ancillary concept of the concrete internal object, was widely debated (Hinshelwood, 1997). She contributed to the debate by giving a further paper on the depressive position (Klein, 1940), and her closest followers tried to elucidate the ideas with detailed cases (Heimann, 1942; Isaacs, 1940; Riviere, 1936). Heimann's paper is extremely clear in demonstrating the concreteness of the phenomena that underlie psychosis, and that paper is selected for inclusion here to demonstrate the nature of internal objects as Klein conceived them, or rather as she believed her patients actually experienced them, consciously or unconsciously.

Klein was at this time developing her interest in psychosis. Her boy patient, Dick (Klein, 1930), suggested a link between psychosis and a profound deficit in symbol formation. She explained the boy's predicament as due to a particularly powerful terror and paranoia. She was stimulated by some of her students who were psychiatrists, notably Clifford Scott and Paula Heimann, and during the 1940s she elaborated her further thoughts on the schizoid processes that are central to schizophrenia. She was influenced by the work of Fairbairn (see above) and followed his view that turning back from her concentration on depressive phenomena would allow a deeper understanding of earlier mechanisms in the infant ego. Her thoughts emerged in 1946, undercutting all the efforts that her followers and others had made to grasp the notions of the depressive position and internal objects. She had moved on, and many British psychoanalysts who had previously been willing to follow her evolving thinking now abandoned the effort. Winnicott found it very difficult to give full acknowledgement to her paper in 1946. Later, when her paper on envy was read to the Society in 1955 (Klein 1957), he was openly critical, and sub-sequently concentrated on the development of his own theory of transitional objects. Heimann, too, moved away from Klein's later views.

At this point Klein's own revisions had meant that only her most dogged followers stuck with her, as well as her students in analysis or supervision with her. She had been fortunate in having the most gifted collection of students, who flowered in the 1950s when her new theories were found applicable to understanding psychiatric patients (Bion, 1957; Rosenfeld, 1947; Segal, 1950).

References

Bion, W. R. (1957). Differentiation of the psychotic from the non-psychotic personalities. *International Journal of Psychoanalysis*, 38: 266–275.

Heimann, P. (1942). A contribution to the problem of sublimation and its relation to processes of internalization. *International Journal of Psychoanalysis*, 23: 8–17.

Hinshelwood, R. D. (1997). The elusive concept of "internal objects" (1934–1943): its role in the formation of the Klein group. *International Journal of Psychoanalysis*, 78: 877–897.

Isaacs, S. (1940). Temper tantrums in early childhood in their relation to internal objects. *International Journal of Psychoanalysis*, 21: 280–293.

Klein, M. (1930). The importance of symbol-formation in the development of the ego. *International Journal of Psychoanalysis*, 11: 24–39.

Klein, M. (1940). Mourning and its relation to manic-depressive states. *International Journal of Psychoanalysis*, 21:125–153.

Klein, M. (1957). *Envy and Gratitude*. London: Hogarth.

Riviere, J. (1936). On the genesis of psychical conflict in earliest infancy. *International Journal of Psychoanalysis*, 17: 395–422.

Rosenfeld, H. (1947). Analysis of a schizophrenic state with depersonalization. *International Journal of Psychoanalysis*, 28: 130–139.

Segal, H. (1950). Some aspects of the analysis of a schizophrenic. *International Journal of Psychoanalysis*, 31: 268–278.

Paula Heimann [Heimann, P. (1942). A contribution to the problem of sublimation and its relation to processes of internalization. *International Journal of Psychoanalysis, 23*: 8–17]

Paula Heimann, with Joan Riviere and Susan Isaacs, was part of the formidable group of Kleinians who supported Melanie Klein during the controversies. Apparently Klein and Heimann were drawn together when, in 1934, Melanie Klein's son died in an accident and Klein turned to Heimann as a new arrival in Britain from Berlin (Grosskurth, 1986).

As a result of Klein's paper on the depressive position in 1935, there was considerable discussion in the British Psychoanalytical Society about the validity of her findings. One of the problems was to understand the concrete nature of internal objects, a concept that was at the heart of the depressive position. The paper by Heimann that is presented here was one of the Kleinian attempts to explicate the notion of internal objects. It was given originally as a paper to the British Psychoanalytical Society in 1939, and was her membership paper. However, it appears to have been read to the Society partly as a Kleinian response to Anna Freud's first paper to the Society after the Freud family arrival in Britain. The paper by Anna Freud had been on sublimation, and Heimann followed this topic too (see Hinshelwood, 1997). She argued that the problems of love and hate towards objects that were introjected determined the internal conditions for creative sublimation, or alternatively, the conditions for enslavement to internal objects that demanded merely a recreation of phantasy. Without directly claiming as much, she was giving her own account of Anna Freud's (and Freud's) distinction between enjoying libidinal phantasies, on the one hand, and sublimating libido, on the other.

However, the paper is significant in yet another way, an antici-patory way. Heimann is interested in the psychotic quality of the internal world, which demands attention without recognition of the external world. It is psychotic in that the internal objects override the sense of self and, as it were, dominate that sense of self from inside. This takes Klein's discussion of manic-depressive states further, by describing the psychodynamics of an incipient psycho-sis. The patient was, in Heimann's view, subject to a psychosis, a manic-depressive psychosis, even though she would be diagnosed as neurotic. Severe paranoid anxieties of a psychotic kind formed around a fundamental belief that the self had been invaded and taken over by alien objects, devils. The psychotic level within a personality that would fall within the neurotic range is a sort of "pre-echo" of the later Kleinian work on the psychotic and neurotic parts of the same personality, which Bion, for one, advanced strongly later on (Bion, 1957).

This exposure of the psychotic layer of functioning concerned depressive psychosis, but it anticipated Klein's later paper on schizoid mechanisms that are responsible for the disintegrating loss of self in schizophrenic psychosis. In passing, she clearly described a defence that Klein later named projective identification:

> in the inner drama the objects also display the subject's own impulses. This phenomenon is essentially a defence mechanism against the subject's own evil impulses—a variety of the mecha-nism of projection . . . which can be summed up as methods of divesting the subject of his own evil and aggressiveness and trans-ferring them elsewhere [pp. 319–320, below].

The conformity with Melanie Klein's description of projective identification exemplifies how closely the group of Kleinians worked together at this stage.[1] It suggests this mechanism was being discussed by the Klein group from the early 1940s, or earlier. Heimann's paper is an extremely good example of how Kleinians understood clinical material around this time, and Klein acknow-ledged stimulating discussion with Heimann in connection with the ideas in Klein's paper on schizoid mechanisms. The paper is remarkable; while being her membership paper to the Society, it is a response to Anna Freud, a dissertation on internal objects, and a premonition of Kleinian advances in the future. They were

advances from which Heimann did eventually distance herself dramatically in 1955, when she left the Klein group (see
Tonnesman, 1989).

Note

1. Grosskurth (1986) described an informal "Internal Objects" group,
   which met to discuss the nature of this concept, and it is known that
   around this time Klein and her followers referred repeatedly to each
   other over their papers and publications.

References

Bion, W. R. (1957). Differentiation of the psychotic from the non-
    psychotic personalities. *International Journal of Psychoanalysis, 38*:
    266–275.
Grosskurth, P. (1986). *Melanie Klein: Her World and her Work*. London:
    Hodder & Stoughton.
Hinshelwood, R. D. (1997). The elusive concept of "internal objects"
    (1934–1943): its role in the formation of the Klein group.
    International Journal of Psychoanalysis, 78: 877–897.
Tonnesman, M. (1989). Editor's introduction. In: P. Heimann, *About
    Children and Children-no-Longer*. London: Routledge.

Melanie Klein [Klein, M. (1946). Notes on some schizoid
mechanisms. *International Journal of Psychoanalysis, 27*: 99–110]

Melanie Klein's paper here republished is one of the most important in the canon of her works. It has had a determining effect on
the course of Kleinian thinking ever since, and on those who have
taken her work seriously. It set a new direction for their work.
Following Fairbairn, she heeded his warning that too much emphasis had been placed on depressive phenomena (Fairbairn, 1944—see
above). However, she disagreed with him in a number of respects:
for instance, she explicitly stated that the first introjection was
a good object (not a bad one as Fairbairn equally categorically
claimed); and she pointed out his relative neglect of the rich
vicissitudes of aggression.

The step she took was to move from her observation on children (1932) and the way they split their objects into good and bad ones, to describe a process in which the ego splits itself. This follows Freud's unfinished "Splitting of the ego in the process of defence" (1940e). However, Freud described a split between parts of the ego that used different defences—such as the fetishist, in which one part of the ego uses repression and another denial. Klein described splitting of the ego in terms of separating the impulses, especially hate from love. And, as stated above, Fairbairn thought of the split parts of the ego as retaining a relationship between them, whereas Klein explicitly stated that the parts of the ego were cut off from each other.

Klein's interest was partly that of many others—to discern, by inference, the state of the ego and its anxieties in the very earliest stages of development. She disagreed with Glover's notion of dispersed ego-nuclei (Glover, 1943), and Fairbairn's idea of a central ego with two subsidiaries. She hesitated over Winnicott's idea of primary unintegration (Winnicott, 1945—see above), but finally settled for a hypothesis that she did not in fact infer, but deduced from theory. The earliest anxiety, she believed, derived from the death instinct and the impulsion towards death. This is a fear of annihilation. In response to this the ego falls to bits, in a splitting process that is partly defensive, and achieves a separation from the self-aggression, or splinters it into impotent particles. Splitting is not only defensive but is also partly a satisfaction of the death instinct itself. In other words, the instinct is employed in part as a defence against the fearful impulse. Splitting of the ego is one among a constellation of schizoid defences that includes idealization, denial, projection, and introjection, which correspond to repression at a later stage in development. She did not elaborate on the relation between splitting and repression, but left it for another publication. In fact, she wrote very little indeed on splitting and repression, leaving her account to rather general statements of a maturational change from splitting to repression with a general increase in the communication between the separated parts, from vertical to horizontal, as we might say today (after Kohut).

Splitting combines in many complex and subtle ways with introjection and projection. She described the term "projective identification", for the first time. This paper of Klein's was republished in 1952 in the Kleinian book (which included Isaacs' paper), where she stresses the defence of projective identification by adding a sentence to promote the term from a descriptive one to a technical one. The phantasy is that part of the ego—usually the violent and self-threatening self—is split off and located externally in someone else. That other person is then believed to be that lost part of the ego's identity. In fact, this defence was described without being named by others around this time—Gwen Evans in a paper (unpublished) in January 1946, Clifford Scott, unpublished, in a paper given to the IPA Congress in Paris, 1938. Herbert Rosenfeld's (1947) paper was given to the British Psychoanalytical Society in March 1947, only three months after Melanie Klein's paper was read there. It is clear from Rosenfeld's account of his patient, Mildred, whom he started treating in 1944, that he was beginning to work with this idea before Melanie Klein's paper, and while Rosenfeld was in analysis with Klein. Heimann's paper, published in 1942 (though read in 1939), which is republished above, also described something like projective identification, as I pointed out in the introduction to that paper. It is clear that for a number of years Klein was leading a group of people who were moving towards a conceptualization of the phenomenon of projective identification, which she theorized here.

This defence/phantasy proved a very difficult one for others to grasp, and for a long time the ideas gained a currency only within her small group. In the paper, Klein's notion of splitting of the ego and of projective identification brought in the paranoid–schizoid position, a term which she does not coin here.[1] This is a compound of the "paranoid position", characterized by intense fear and aggression towards objects, which she had used to make a contrast with the depressive position, and Fairbairn's term "schizoid position". From this time on the depressive position and the paranoid–schizoid position are the axes of Klein's theories of development and of clinical work.

She had previously understood how the ego in its earliest stage experiences concrete, motivated objects inside itself—internal objects. Now, she believed these early experiences could engender an aberrant developmental path that led to psychosis, especially depression and paranoia. The paper published here is a landmark paper in defining the Kleinian corpus of ideas, which, though attracting small allegiance then, seems to have steadily expanded in its ability to stimulate psychoanalytic thought and clinical work to the present day.

Note

1. In fact, the first published use of the term "paranoid–schizoid" is in Rosenfeld's paper in 1947.

References

Fairbairn, R. (1944). Endopsychic structure considered in terms of object-relationships. *International Journal of Psychoanalysis, 25*: 70–92.

Freud, S. (1940e). Splitting of the ego in the process of defence. *S.E., 23*.

Glover, E. (1943). The concept of dissociation. *International Journal of Psychoanalysis, 24*: 7–13.

Heimann, P. (1942). A contribution to the problem of sublimation and its relation to processes of internalization. *International Journal of Psychoanalysis, 23*: 8–17.

Klein, M. (1932). *The Psychoanalysis of Children. The Writings of Melanie Klein, Volume 2*. London: Hogarth.

Klein, M., Heimann, P., Isaacs, S., & Riviere, J. (1952). *Developments in Psychoanalysis*. London: Hogarth.

Rosenfeld, H. (1947). Analysis of a schizophrenic state with depersonalization. *International Journal of Psychoanalysis, 28*: 130–139.

Winnicott, D. W. (1945). Primitive emotional development. *International Journal of Psychoanalysis, 26*: 137.

A contribution to the problem of sublimation and its relation to processes of internalization*

Paula Heimann

I n this paper my aim is to point out and discuss certain aspects of the sublimatory processes which in my opinion have not so far been investigated or perhaps sufficiently described. They involve consideration of unconscious phantasies related to internalized objects.

I am taking the artistic productivity of a painter as an example, although I am well aware that in this type of sublimation there are some specific factors operating which are still obscure. I do not aim at dealing exhaustively with the vast subject of sublimation, and the material will illustrate only those important aspects to which I wish to draw attention.

I start from the psycho-analytical conception that sublimation is a form of discharge of the instinctual drive to creation (procreation). I will recall Freud's original concept of sublimation as an activity in which the sexual impulse is deflected from its direct aim but does not succumb to repression, which leads to achievements serving a

* Expanded from a paper read before the British Psycho-Analytical Society, July 5, 1939. [Reproduced, with permission, from: *International Journal of Psychoanalysis*, 1942, 23: 8–17 © Institute of Psychoanalysis, London, UK]

social or higher interest and involves an adaptation to reality, i.e. the progress from the pleasure principle to the reality principle. Gratification on the part of the ego is also an essential element in sublimation; since the ego does not have recourse to repression, it is not restricted and impoverished but enriched by the sublimatory activity. This last point, the conscious gratification, bound up with the experience of expansion and development of the ego, seems to me an important indication that a sublimatory activity is successful, although it may be of short duration only and give way to various forms of discontent, or even to depression and despair. Complete absence of it, however, would suggest to me that there is some serious disturbance in the sublimatory process.

When I use the term "ego", I am not thinking so much of an organization which is firmly established and demarcated in contrast to other parts of the personality—indeed, Freud has warned us against being dogmatic in this matter—but of the sum-total of an individual's feelings, emotions, impulses, wishes, capacities, talents, thoughts and phantasies, in short, all those psychic forces and formations which a person (assuming that his consciousness reached so far as to embrace so much) would identify as his own and which would make him feel: "That is I." Actually most of our patients suffer from not having achieved this experience and I think that it is one of the essential tasks of analysis to help them so to find themselves. This, if successful, goes along with widening the boundaries of the personality and increasing its capacity to tolerate the fight with the inner and outer world.

The patient I am going to describe is a painter in her early thirties, an intelligent and attractive person. She comes of a middle-class family. Her father's profession took him about to sea-port towns and this made a stable home life difficult for the family. The patient has vivid recollections about anxieties in stormy nights on the Scottish coast and of blissful happiness in being beside her mother by a cheerful fireplace. Her one-year-older brother was until puberty her intimate companion and an object of intense feelings of love and hate, domination and jealousy, guilt and envy. Her early sexual games with him, a source of pleasure, guilt and anxiety, proved a lasting influence on her later sexual life. In the analysis her parents were for a long time divided into good and bad objects, in that her father was felt to be entirely good with admirable qualities—intelligence, humour, creativeness—and her mother entirely bad—stupid, dull and narrow-minded. All happy experiences with her, such as that by the fireside, were denied or at least ignored.[1] Only when the anxieties and feelings of guilt, requiring such an extreme separation of love and hate, and leading by such over-simplifications to great distortions of reality, had become allayed, and when the patient became more capable of maintaining feelings of love even to a not perfectly good person, could she admit faults in her father and good qualities in her mother. She then came to see them in a less obsessionally tabulated way and more as real human beings. It turned out then that even the humour of her father, which she had valued so highly, had a very bad aspect; for he had treated her as a funny little thing and refused to take her seriously, whereas her mother to whom she had denied any sense of humour and understanding showed a kindly appreciation of her conflicts.

The family moved about a good deal, but the final blow to security and family unity fell in her early teens when her father left her mother. The standard of the family life changed abruptly. Her mother went to work in a factory to earn a living for herself and the two children. A most painful and dramatic event brought her father back, after he had got into serious trouble from which his wife rescued him. But he was not the same man as before; the relation between the parents was gravely disturbed, and, as it seems, never fully repaired. Her father returned a broken man and became addicted to alcohol, and his death at a comparatively early age appears to have been precipitated by his alcoholism.

The father's desertion of the family led to striking changes in his daughter. She had been a good, though mischievous pupil, but now her achievements in school deteriorated conspicuously, and she became uninterested and restless. After school she attempted various trainings and kinds of work, none of which satisfied or stabilized her. When she came of age she broke away from the family to live independently and lived an unconventional, wild and unhappy life. By chance she was introduced to Freud's works and she read his books with an eager interest which resulted in her coming for analytic treatment herself.

When she came to me she was suffering from intense depression with suicidal tendencies, inhibitions in her work of painting, disturbances in her sexual life and an addiction to morphia, the extent and significance of the symptoms becoming apparent only in the course of analysis.

As a result of analysis all these disturbances have been to a large extent overcome. She has married a man with whom she has a satisfactory relationship in many respects although full sexual gratification has not yet developed. She is infinitely happier than she ever was before; in fact she has learned what it means to be happy. She mixes well with people of different types and has an open and keen interest in actual events. Her capacity for sympathy and helpfulness has developed. She takes a lively part in the world around her, and—what she values most of all—has attained to real creative power in her painting and has made a name for herself in the artistic world.

I shall now describe the course of this analysis with reference only to the connection between her phantasies about internalized objects and her artistic productivity.

The first period of the analysis covered the work of penetrating behind an attitude of dissimulation about the severity of her illness. Above all she tried to gloss over the morphia-addiction, and some time was needed before she gained sufficient confidence in me to enable her to show more freely how much she was really suffering. Thus I did not at once realize the psychotic character of her anxieties, since on the whole she did not give the impression of being a psychotic patient. In my opinion it is one of the great gains of the new research by Melanie Klein (1932, 1935, and 1940) and her school into the processes of internalization that we have become able to discover and analyse psychotic traits in people who are classed as neurotic.

After this first phase, the analysis found access to the full depth of her depressions and her persecutory anxieties, which were intimately bound up with her morphia-addiction. During this period she was mainly engaged in drawing from the model. These drawings showed strong, but rather gross and coarse lines. Without laying claim to an expert understanding of this matter I would say that they definitely showed talent, but perhaps hardly more than that.

When the analysis proceeded to deeper levels it became clear that her depressions were related to a system of phantasies in which she felt herself possessed and inhabited by devils. These devils—at the beginning of the analysis they were innumerable—persecuted her constantly and in ever-varying ways. They roamed about inside her, caused her physical pain and illnesses, inhibited her in all her activities, especially in painting, and compelled her to do things she did not want to do. When she wanted to get up in the morning they moved about violently in her stomach and made her vomit. When she wanted to paint they interfered. They would roar with laughter when she tried to achieve something. They would force her to go to the lavatory constantly, and during a certain period she had to urinate so frequently that it disturbed her work seriously. They had forks with which they prodded and attacked her in the most cruel ways. They would eat her up from inside and force her to take food for them. But she felt she could not eat because they would poison her with their excrement and thus turn the food into poison. Owing to these persecutions she was in agony, especially when painting.

All these phantasies became fully conscious during analysis, in particular through the analysis of the transference-situation, and were intensely real and vivid to the patient. No doubt the fact that she possesses the talent of a painter accounts for the richness and vividness of her phantasies and for the comparative ease with which they could become conscious. There was often not a very clear distinction between conscious and unconscious phantasies. The great drive to paint, inherent in her, in the processes consti-tuting her talent, proved a powerful ally to the analysis and to the endeavour to reach her as yet unpainted internal scenes and situations.[2]

Against these persecutions by the devils she took morphia. Morphia calmed the devils down or put them to sleep or drugged or paralysed them. Morphia also fed and placated them. But they were only temporarily put out of action and with their renewed tormenting the need to take morphia again arose. Gradually the devils became reduced in number and differentiated in type, e.g. "blue painting devils" and "morphia devils". These two types of devils represented her two parents in antagonism to each other carrying out a warlike sexual intercourse inside her, but they were also banded together in a conspiratorial alliance against her. During one period there were three devils of each type.

Phantasies like these which take parental intercourse for a persecutory act arise when the subject stands under the sway of his destructive impulses and his libido is temporarily overpowered. In order to defend himself against the aggressiveness (death instinct) set loose inside himself, the subject directs it outwards, as Freud (1920) has shown, and attributes his own aggressiveness to the object. In this particular situation (that of observing or phantasying parental intercourse), under the impact of jealousy and anxiety the subject's destructive drives become projected on to the parents, so that they are felt to be the agents of destruction. Since in the subject's own processes the fight between the life and the death instinct, love and hate impulses, has entered a phase in which the hate impulses occupy the stronger position, he is unable to perceive parental intercourse as a sexual situation, but interprets, or rather misinterprets, it as a war—war by each partner against the other and against himself. Impotence and frigidity have an important root in such phantasies.

Actual events and childhood memories were interwoven in these devil phantasies and gigantically distorted; and the transference-situation mirrored them. To give one example for many: in her childhood my patient often "dared" her brother to do something and vice versa. Once he "dared" her to prick a pin into a workman's buttocks as he bent down, and she did so. In the devil-phantasies this small mischief became magnified and reversed into attacks by the devils' forks upon herself. She dreaded and hated the devils and she wanted to get rid of them, but she also loved them, was proud of them ("Aren't they brainy to be always finding new ways of tormenting me?") and wanted to keep them. Moreover, she needed them to punish herself for her bad impulses and actions.

Throughout this persecution by devils, however, there had also existed in her mind what she called "the design", and this meant her good parents joined together in harmony with each other and with their children. The design also stood for her own love and creativeness and her capacity to undo the harm she had done to her objects.

Whenever she had some experience of the connection between things—for instance, when the interpretations in analysis joined up various fragments of her associations and made her feel that these associations were not accidental and senseless, but had a deep meaning through which she could appreciate the whole context of the processes in her mind—then she would say: "That fits into the design." After an hour, for instance, in which light had been thrown on important factors in her life, she would experience a blissful state of happiness, about which she said: "I saw my design. It came into me." This made her love me so much that she wanted to rush to me and to give me all her possessions; on that day she had no need for morphia. The design represented love and creativeness. It was the principle which binds together, and which turns chaos into cosmos. It was an ideal of perfection. When she realized, however, on one occasion that by saying the design comprises everything, good and bad, she used it to justify her bad feelings to herself and to carry out destructive actions, the design was felt to be destroyed and lost, and a deep depression resulted from this experience. Gradually the design became more and more established, and she developed a firm faith in its existence, and was no longer dependent on getting constant visible proofs of it. The working of her design could be applied more and more to her painting, and her pictures became more and more manifestations of the design.

To return to the devil phantasies. The devils represented the objects of her instinctual drives, both libidinal and aggressive, that is to say, they stood primarily for her parents and her brother, but also for people in her actual surroundings, including myself; and all these objects could be both parts of persons and also whole persons. Moreover, the devils were a cover for her own sadistic and destructive impulses, which she disowned and personified in them.

I will now endeavour to explain how this world full of devils inside her had come about.

The memory-traces of psychical experience, past and present, are not static imprints like photographs, but moving and living dramas, like never-ending scenes on a stage. These inner dramas are composed of the subject and her instinctual impulses towards her original objects (father, mother, brother and their later substitutes, up to and including the analyst), who are seen as they had been felt and are felt to be under the impact of her impulses; in addition, the objects also display her own impulses. Moreover, all the protagonists in the drama, herself and her objects, her own impulses and their responses, derive some features from the actual setting and events of childhood: her own physical and emotional personality during childhood and that of the persons around her, and the things, places and events of that life. Features of the world in which and towards which her instinctual impulses were originally directed, dating from the period of time and the actual occasions in which they were originally felt (and were more or less expressed or denied) become woven into the inner drama played out by her impulses and their objects.

In this way the drama of the internal world took shape originally; and it continues a ceaseless activity throughout life, all subsequent experiences after the original ones providing new scenes, mostly on the pattern of the earliest. Conversely also, the drama of the internal world colours the subject's perception of the external world and lends features of internal phantasy and memory to experiences with present-day external objects. The sense of reality often suffers considerably from this admixture.

I said above that in the inner drama the objects also display the subject's own impulses. This phenomenon is essentially a defence-mechanism against the subject's own evil impulses—a variety of the mechanism of projection and turning outward of aggressiveness (death instinct) discussed by Freud (1920). The object which has been internalized in hate and greed becomes the internal carrier of these very impulses. This comes about by way of many phantasies, which can be summed up as methods of divesting the subject of his own evil and aggressiveness and transferring them elsewhere, thus relieving the subject of anxiety and also of the guilt resulting from his aggressiveness towards his objects.

At this stage, therefore, the internal drama tells a story of the subject's innocence; its purpose is achieved only when the subject arrives at a point where he no longer feels guilty. My patient's impulses have been projected on to the objects of her internal world: hate and greed actuate them on the stage of her inner drama; *they* are bad, *they* are devils—no blame could be attached to *her*. In thus disowning guilt, however, and denying all responsibility, she is adopting a passive position; she can only feel helpless and persecuted, a victim of all the evil taking place inside her—she has no say in the matter, as it were. Now she has got into a cleft stick, an *impasse* from which there is no way out; since she disowns responsibility, her own capacities are rendered impotent, she can do nothing. One consequence of this is that since her own efforts, the efforts of a human being, can achieve nothing, magic must be introduced, and a magic means from outside must come to her help—morphia.

Moreover, the feeling of being inhabited by persecuting creatures (people, animals and things) necessitates energetic defences aimed at destroying these persecutors. But since these defences consist of attacking the persecutors inside the self, they are of no avail as a solution, for they involve the subject at the same time as her objects. The battlefield is in the home country, not on enemy territory. A vicious circle is thus set up and a perpetual warfare ensues which is played out in the subject's internal world—always affecting her external life and often expressed in terms of physical symptoms.[3]

In this way the patient's objects had become devils to her, because she had been a devil to them. A ceaseless war was going on inside her between them and her, or between their allies and hers. Analysis was able to break up this vicious circle by bringing home to the patient her responsibility for her internal objects, their origin in her own impulses which had been active in her relation to her external objects, and the manifold aspects of her motives in regard to external events and her responses to "real situations", as they are called. Only when the experience of analysis brings home to the patient his own impulses and his responsibility for them (when he is enabled to endure guilt and grief as such and comes to dispense with defending himself against these experiences by persecutory systems) can the internal world become modified, can "past experiences", "unconscious memories", be transformed so that they lose their hold over the patient.

Thus a fuller understanding of the internalisation processes shows us in detail the facts implied in Freud's early statement (1910) that "hysterics suffer from reminiscences". These memories are not, however, exact replicas in the child's mind of people and events he encountered, but a complicated summation and interweaving of external and internal experiences with live persons in action, as I tried to show above when I described how my patient's world of devils had come about. We must not conceive of the child's mind as if it were a blank photographic film which reflects external scenes exactly and faithfully; it is a film on which the child's instinctual impulses and defences (unconscious and also conscious phantasies) have already taken shape before it is exposed to a given external reality. So that the outcome we call memory is in fact a composite superimposed picture of two worlds in one. What we call a memory-trace would be felt subjectively from one point of view as a situation involving "internal objects". A person re-experiences the past in his analysis, because he still carries this past as a living world inside him; and he perceives present reality in a way that is both restricted in quantity and altered in quality by the influence which his "past"—his internal world—exerts upon him. We find the access to this past—the drama that is perpetually being acted out inside him—through the transference-situation, which enables us to evaluate the interplay between the environmental ("objective") and the subjective factors in the composite picture. However, I cannot attempt here to discuss in detail the way in which our technique of analysis operates in enabling us to come to grips with the patient's internal objects. But I can say that analysis cures the illness caused by "unconscious memories" in that it deals with these memories in the way they are experienced by the patient, namely, as an internal world of intense actual reality.

It was through the analysis of her devil-phantasies that the patient's whole childhood history was recaptured. The multiple aspects in which she had seen and felt her parents and her brother, and the complicated relationship between each of them, and between them and herself, were faithfully acted out by the devils inside her.

I hope I have succeeded in conveying the feeling of absolute reality which the patient experienced in these phantasies about the devils, and in picturing the intense anxiety states into which these devils threw her. Severe depression, the feeling of absolute unworthiness and suicidal states of despair ensued from this situation of having active devils inside her.

With the analysis of her childhood situation and especially of her penis-envy and her earliest oral anxieties relating to breast and penis, which she dreaded to find destroyed by her insatiable greed, the force of these devils inside her diminished. She came to understand that the devils were her parents and her brother whom she had distorted in this extensive manner by investing them with her own greedy, soiling, persecuting impulses and whom she had devoured and incorporated under the impact of her destructive impulses; that she had created these devils to personify the badness which she could not bear to acknowledge as her own, as part of herself. She gradually realized this, as she became more able to tolerate feelings of guilt and pain; she then no longer felt inhabited by persecuting devils and this type of phantasy practically ceased to exert any influence over her. Included in this process was the development of a greater tolerance towards aggressiveness, her own and other people's. And the greater tolerance enabled her to react with less anxiety towards aggressive situations and to avoid the vicious circle in which aggressiveness increases anxiety and anxiety increases aggressiveness.

Concurrently with the process of understanding her internal world in childhood and its relation to the external world, the craving for morphia diminished. She arrived at a "gentleman's agreement" with herself of a monthly allowance of four morphia tablets, usually taking part of them during her intense menstruation pains, the other part a fortnight after the menstruation. I cannot here go into the problems relating to the menstruation pains and the phantasies determining their gravity; they were principally determined by cruel and frightening phantasies connected with her penis-envy. She eventually gave up morphia altogether; the menstrual pains became so much reduced that she could go about as usual and even dance during the period.

During the phase I have just described (when her life was dominated by the devils inside her) she proceeded from drawing to painting. The subjects were at first somewhat coarsely symbolical representations, and she showed the urgency of her need to restore her objects by painting huge fathers and huge penises, huge mothers and mother symbols. The first picture painted without her having to take morphia during her work represented this kind of wholesale and massive attempt at restoring the destroyed internal objects. It was in some ways primitive and clumsy; there were very few objects, and an absence of elaboration, differentiation, and movement.[4]

In the later part of this period, when the devils began to reveal their human origin and when her childhood history was being translated from the "devil-language", she proceeded to paint Victorian family scenes showing certain of her childhood situations. Here phantasies were worked out more fully; more objects and more events occurred, and details which offered a possibility of variation and differentiation supplied more life and movement.

The painter derived great relief and pleasure from these pictures; she made her name by them in the artistic world, and she even set a fashion. But there was an obsessional element in this form of restoration which interfered with its sublimatory value. She herself became aware of it as an anxiety that she might not be able to paint in any other manner but this and that if she was compelled to go on with this type of painting her possibilities of self-expression would be gravely restricted; if she had no other function in life but that of restoring her childhood objects, she would not attain the full range of a boundless territory in which to develop herself.

The next phase in her analysis was characterized by the disappearance of persecution by devils and also of her very severe depressions and suicidal impulses. There were still anxieties of a persecutory nature, relating to the doings of people she felt were inside her, but they were people and not devils; there were also milder depressions and fewer obsessional features in her relation to painting.

The significance of her striving to paint, moreover, gradually developed into a desire to express herself and to *improve* her internal objects, as distinguished from a compulsion to save them from unutterable destruction.

Ernest Jones (1937) has pointed out the great significance of the difference between doing something out of love or out of a sense of duty. To my mind the biggest advance in the development of the patient's personality was shown, not only when she became capable of restoring her objects out of love instead of from compulsive necessity, but when she began to struggle to do something for herself at the same time. She could then attempt this not in her old way, in which whatever her mother gained she lost and *vice versa*, but in such a way that she could—to some extent—rest assured that she was not still devouring and destroying her objects and need not therefore sacrifice herself utterly and completely for them, but could afford to aim also at the widest possible unfolding and expansion of herself. This in turn would then also enlarge her capacity to restore and benefit her objects.

I do not wish to convey the impression that everything was all right with the patient at this time. She was not yet well and I could enumerate a number of symptoms which showed her neurosis. This holds good also to some degree even for the present phase of analysis. In the phase I am describing she proceeded from painting pictures of Victorian life to painting life of the present day; and the boundless territory she had sought for her activities was reached in that anything and everything was capable of inspiring her. The pictures of this period show a great advance in colour and composition. During this period her internal objects (previously represented by the devils) appeared frequently in the form of artistic problems. Her interest was thus not only more objective, but far richer and comprehending far more varied details. Her internal conflicts were objectified in terms of æthetic and technical problems. Instead of suffering from the torments of a devilish father and mother, she struggled with the problems of "human interest" and "æthetic interest" in painting.

I will now refer to a recent session with the patient, though I shall not give a full account of the hour and of the analytic work done in it. To make the situation clear it is necessary for me to describe the setting of the transference which forms the context of the hour. Two recent events had characterized the tone of the transference:

1. I had surmised correctly from her associations an external factor belonging to a very important event in her past life and she felt that I had made a discovery. It concerned an exceedingly painful experience of her father's when he had left the family.
2. She had come into contact with a man whom she connected with me, and she suspected that I used him to spy on her and to relate to me facts in her life which would enable me to deprive her of her pleasures and of all her good internal possessions.

A third point worth mentioning is that in her painting at this time the technical problem of "joining up" was absorbing her interest. She reacted to my discovery about the very painful incident concerning her father with great relief, which showed itself in an increase of activities and in a liberation of sexual feelings, leading to a sexual intercourse with her husband after many months of complete abstinence. She felt very grateful to me and admired me, but at the same time her persecutory anxieties and suspicions about my finding out about everything in order to take everything away from her were greatly stimulated.

On that particular day she began the hour thus: "I am fed up. My mouth is full of ulcers." She then told me a story of what had happened to her car that day. She said: "A fool of a man drove into it. Would you believe it? All the scratches on my car have been made by other people." She then proceeded to describe in a very emotional way another unpleasant experience she had had that morning. When she was going along in her car, after all her excitement and anger about the man driving into it, another car exceeding the speed limit drove up on her wrong side. "Of course", she said, "it was a woman driver." In front there was a lorry which gave a sign and turned to the right into a side turning. Immediately after that the woman on her left, without giving any sign, turned to the right also, passing in front of my patient's car, and in order to avoid a collision she herself quickly swerved her own car into the same right-hand turning, although she had intended to go straight on. She was "livid with anger" (I am trying as far as possible to repeat her own words) and now took her revenge on the woman by getting in front of her and crawling along at five miles an hour and making it impossible for the woman behind to pass. Presently they came to red traffic lights. The woman pulled up and was now on the same level as my patient, who poked her head out of the window and said: "That was the worst piece of road-hogging I have ever seen. Do you know that by cutting-in in front of me from the wrong side you forced me to turn to the right so as to avoid a collision, though I wanted to go straight on?" The woman, who had a red beery face, gave a shrug and a laugh and said: "What do I care?" My patient was furious and sat trying to think of a most scathing remark. Finally she found it: "On second thoughts", she said, "there is an excuse for you. I can see that you are well beyond your prime. You should leave driving to women who are younger and more intelligent than yourself." The woman gasped, but before she could reply the traffic lights changed and my patient drove off. She was very pleased with herself.

I omit my interpretations and add only some more of the material pertaining to our problem.

My patient now drove to her art school and started on a sketch to a given theme; this theme had to do with stealing. She started the sketch, but found that there was something wrong with her drawing, both while she was working on it and when she had finished and hung it up on the wall. She could not find out what it was, and she said to me: "That was the most awful thing about it." When the artist who criticized the sketches came to hers, he said in surprise: "Good God, what has happened to you? This looks like a drawing out of a Victorian family album." My patient now realized what it was she had felt to be wrong with it. She said: "It looked like a drawing that had been done fifty years ago." She felt so awful about this that she had to go and have three sherries. Later she noticed the ulcers in her mouth. I may say here that she never drinks when level-headed. In fact, one of her great anxieties is that she might become addicted to alcohol as her father was.

I will now summarize these points. The patient started by mentioning that she was fed up and her mouth was full of ulcers. Then she proceeded to tell me the events of the day preceding the ulcers, that is to say, the history of the ulcers.

1.   A "fool of a man" had scratched her car.
2.   She had made scathing remarks to a bad woman.
3.   She hurt the woman by a reference to her age and by demanding that she should yield up driving to herself (the younger and more intelligent woman).
4.   The woman had a red "beery" face (was drunk).
5.   My patient was very pleased with her scathing remark to the woman.
6.   Something was wrong with her drawing, that is to say, a sublimatory activity was impaired. She did not know what was wrong with it and this was "the most awful thing" in the situation. She had to go to a public house and have three sherries.
7.   Later she found ulcers in her mouth.

It is important to know that the fault of her drawing was that "it looked as though it was fifty years old", "out of a Victorian family album".

It seems to me that the various symptoms,

1.   the unintentionally old-fashioned painting,
2.   the need to drink alcohol,
3.   the appearance of the ulcers,

point clearly to what had been going on in the patient's unconscious. She had carried out her impulse to hurt the woman and was
consciously pleased with her success. But unconsciously—as the
woman stood for me and her mother, towards whom she had love
impulses as well as hostile ones—she could not bear the injuries she
had inflicted on her nor could she remain at a distance from her. She
had immediately internalized this mother-figure and she had internalized her in the injured condition for which she felt responsible
and guilty, namely, as a worn-out, fifty-year-old, decrepit, incom-
petent and useless person; and then she herself became changed,
for she was necessarily affected by the injuries and faults of the
internalized object.

The ulcers corresponded to the feeling that she had treated the
woman scathingly by her sneering remarks; the out-of-date, inadequate drawing corresponded to her having deprived the woman of
her prime; and the need to drink reflected the red "beery" face of
the woman. There were of course more determinants for the various symptoms, of which I will only mention some. Thus the ulcers
expressed the need to punish the organ which was the instrument
of the criminal impulse in a manner that fitted the crime; and they
were further related to the phantasies which the scratches on her
car had aroused. The experience with the "fool of a man" and the
later encounter with the beery-faced woman had stimulated phantasies about her parents in their persecutory intercourse, phantasies
of the kind I described earlier. In her unconscious mind her father
had injured her (the car with the scratches) at the command of her
hostile jealous mother. (Just as I—in her phantasies—had sent the
man whom she connected with me to spy on her and report her
doings to me.)

The persecution by the woman driver, "the road-hog", assumed
such an intensity, moreover, because the woman with her red
"beery" face also reminded my patient of her father, whom she had
often seen in an intoxicated state.

Along with the conscious feeling of triumph at having successfully attacked the bad woman went an unconscious feeling of guilt.

This woman who was her rival and who compelled her to follow a way she did not want to go—to the "right"—is also identified with her mother and me whom she, at the same time, loved and admired. Unconsciously she was admitting that the wrong way the woman made her take was the right and good way which her mother (and analysis) showed her. She had indeed felt a great relief when I had discovered the painful incident in her father's life which had oppressed her so much, and she acknowledged the help analysis had given her, although her admiration for me stimulated her feelings of rivalry, owing to which she turned me again into an interfering and hostile mother. She was able to deny her anxiety and her guilt and to feel only triumph about her scathing remarks because other mechanisms, namely, self-punishment and the restoration of the injured object, were also at work (the ulcers, the old-fashioned drawing, and the urge to drink).

It is important to see that the atonement for guilt is here carried out by internalizing the attacked external object and restoring it after the internalization in a specific manner in which every detail of the crime has to be dealt with and which corresponds to the subject's conception of the object's character and qualities. The patient felt that the mother-figure to whom she had made the scathing remarks, out of whose hands she had torn the driving wheel and the capacity to steer her way through life, was now inside herself; and in order to restore the destroyed mother-figure she had to take on to herself the condition resulting from the scathing treatment (the ulcers) and to yield up to the mother-figure the steering wheel (the crayons) and her own capacity, the artist's skill. The woman inside her had drawn the sketch, while she herself was poisoned and sore; she had become the mother-figure she had attacked.

We can see that the internal object exerted an influence on the patient's sublimation in that the sketch bore the imprint of the internal object and not that of the subject, and that, in this way, the sublimatory activity was impaired. We did not hear that the sketch was badly drawn, or that the design or the technique was faulty, but that it did not reflect the patient's personality, that it was an inadequate expression of her intention (she had not set out to paint in a Victorian fashion) and that it was alien to her understanding. The experience of self-expression and development with its accompanying conscious gratification was completely absent in this impaired sublimation. This is really the point I wish to illustrate, for it is related to those aspects of the problem of sublimation with which I am here concerned and which have so far not found sufficient recognition. I refer to the element of *internal freedom and independence* which I consider to be an essential condition for successful sublimation.

The child who avoids dirtying or does his homework well because he is afraid of being punished by his mother, or because he has to placate her in order to secure her love and good gifts, has not achieved sublimation in the full sense of the word; he is not carrying out an activity which enables him to express his personality, the wishes, impulses, and inclinations he feels to be his own. In a similar manner the work of an adult who is compulsively dominated by his internal objects has not the character of a full and true sublimation either.

We know that the impulse to restore is a most fundamental factor in sublimation and creative production. But if guilt and anxiety are overstrong they interfere with the successful functioning of the impulse to restore, because they lead to the employment of various mechanisms for *magical control* of the internal persecutors. This control, however, in its turn keeps the ego under control and interferes with the independent ego-expanding activities which are implied in successful sublimation.

I referred to the arousing of anxieties in my patient related to phantasies about the combined parental figures—the parents inside engaged in a warlike intercourse. In such a state the subject is compelled to save the parents and himself from their mutually destructive doings; he is bound to separate them in their disastrous union[5] and to do whatever serves this end, and he is therefore hampered in the expression of his own impulses, wishes and talents.

Fear of persecution and distrust of the internal objects necessitate defence, just as the supreme purpose in a war is to secure and safeguard vital issues, and this pushes all other tasks into the background. The productive capacity becomes overwhelmed by the subject's frantic efforts at saving his life and the lives of his internal objects whom he feels to be one with him. Whilst thus the dangers from the persecutory actions of the combined parents inside him urge the subject to separate them, their separation brings about new dangers, for they are now felt to be in a hopeless state of aphanisis;[6] moreover, the subject becomes impoverished and impotent on account of having only aphanitic parents inside him. Between the Scylla of persecutorily combined parents and the Charybdis of guiltily destroyed parents the subject is caught in hopeless despair.

The acute anxieties attaching to the primitive combined parental figure lead to severe restriction of the subject's activities and inner freedom. When the subject distorts the parent's sexuality into destructiveness, he is thereby inhibited from obtaining gratifications for himself, whether of a direct or of a sublimated nature. My patient could not enjoy the symbolic intercourse with her crayons nor give birth to a child-picture, because her fear and guilt about her ageing and deprived mother were too intense. There is a great difference between wanting to paint Victorian family scenes and being unconsciously compelled (by an internal Victorian mother) to paint in a Victorian fashion. Indeed she had felt it as awful—as the most awful thing—that, certain though she was that something was wrong with the drawing, she did not know what it was. She did not know her own creation.[7]

My experience has convinced me that the kind of restoration in which the injured object is felt to be snatching away the subject's good possessions leads to an impaired sublimation; because this type of restoration has too much the character of revenge and punishment by the objects, a penal servitude, an utter sacrifice on the part of the subject. In it the relation between subject and object is too much on the basis of oral sadism and too far from co-operation and mutual give-and-take.[8]

All these anxiety-situations are well known and have often been described. But I contend that the anxieties resulting from a *compulsion* to look after the good internal objects, to preserve them in a good condition, to subordinate all activities to their well-being and to watch them constantly also constitutes a danger to the success of a sublimation. The anxieties relating to bad and good internal objects which interfere with the subject's internal freedom are bound to arise when the internalized parents are felt as foreign bodies embedded in the self.

I think that the independence which is an important factor in successful sublimation and productive activity is achieved through a process which I like to call the "assimilation" of the internal objects, by which the subject acquires and absorbs those qualities of his internal parents which are suitable and adequate to him.[9] As Goethe says:

> Was Du ererbt von Deinen Vätern hast, Erwirb es, um es zu besitzen.
> [What you inherited from your fathers, You must acquire yourself in order to possess it.]

This process presupposes a diminution of aggressiveness (greed) and anxiety and thus involves a breaking up of the vicious circle. The subject withdraws the extreme features which he has superimposed on his external objects by his own sadism, guilt and anxiety, when he can accept them as his own. Thus his internal objects become more human, less like monsters, less like saints; and the subject can admit and accept his own bad and good qualities and those of his internalized parents. These assume more the character which the external parents had and the subject in his phantasy feels that he is creating his parents rather than swallowing them— the child is father to the man—and with this diminution of greed he acquires the right to absorb their good qualities.

This process also contributes to the setting free of forces which the subject can employ for his own benefit in a free choice of activity and for the development of his talents. This will result in an increase of productive capacities directed towards actual reality and aiming at a truer expression of the self and in an increase of the gratification experienced through his sublimatory activities.

I do not mean that the assimilation of the internal objects leads to a static condition in which the conflicts cease to exist. As I have said, the inner world is a never-ending drama of life and action. Life is bound up with the dynamic processes set up by aggression, guilt, anxiety and grief about the internal objects, and by the impulses of love and restoration; Love and Hate are urging the subject to strive for sublimation. The internal freedom to which I refer is a relative, not an absolute fact; it does not abolish conflicts, but it enables the subject to enlarge and unfold his ego in his sublimations.

Notes

1. It will be seen later that, although this view of the father as good and the mother as bad is part and parcel of the familiar Oedipus attitude,

such an exaggerated, uncompromising and compulsive form of it is no simple and direct expression of Oedipus feelings. It is rather a complicated outcome of phantasies concerning both libidinal and aggressive wishes for and against both parents, and defences against these, i.e. the separation of the parents was the essential aim in it, as an expression of the patient's necessity to keep her own love for them separate and unaffected by her hate for them in her inner world.

2. I believe that the analysis can count on the patient's support where there exists a more or less definite channel for sublimatory activities, especially when these amount to real creativeness. The ego sets great store by its creative abilities. My impression is that this support is greater in artists than, for instance, in scientists. It may be because the scientist knows that his production will not last in the form he gives it, that his own contribution creates the very means for its being surpassed by the advance of knowledge at which he aims, whereas the artist can feel that his creation is potentially immortal.

3. Cf. (pp. 326–329) the ulcers which she produced on a certain occasion.

4. The primitive character of this first picture painted without morphia, its lack of detail and imagination, expressed the extreme urgency of the danger in which she felt her good objects to be. She had as it were to apply every energy to the single attempt to save their existence and rescue them from a condition of most critical extremity. At such a moment no question arises of comforting such almost lifeless persons by minor arrangements having no bearing on the main dangers: just as it would never occur to one to put flowers in the sickroom of someone whose life was at that instant threatened by a hæmorrhage. All minor considerations cease to exist when a life-saving operation is a matter of moments.

5. Cf. note 1, pp. 332–333.

6. Ernest Jones (1927) introduced the term "aphanisis". This concept seems to me to constitute a step forward in our understanding of the fear of castration; for it shows that the experience is not simply that of losing an organ which produces gratification, but that a totality of experience is in question, a threat of the loss of all capacities for ever experiencing any gratification of the libido and thus of all capacity for establishing a "good" relation to an object. This concept to my mind approaches very nearly to that kind of experience in which the main purpose is to acquire and maintain a "good" object, internal as well as external. Though Ernest Jones himself has not followed up the idea of

aphanisis to the point at which it might link on to the problem of anxieties concerning internalized good objects, I feel that nevertheless his thought was tending in this direction and has widened our understanding.

7. Painters often express the feeling that their hands are only the instruments of something within them that directs their activity. But the tone of this feeling varies greatly, and indicates whether this invisible force (their internal objects) is beneficial, in harmony with the artist's personality, or persecutory, as in this example of my patient's.

8. It will be seen that these phenomena are such as are usually described as due to the super-ego. I have refrained from using this term (as well as the term "id"), as it has not been possible within the compass of this paper to discuss the relation between the concepts of internalized objects and of the super-ego (or of the id). I hope to deal with these problems in a future paper, and will remind the reader here of Melanie Klein's work on this subject, notably in *The Psycho-Analysis of Children* (1932).

9. In a paper recently published by Matte Blanco (1941), he refers explicitly to my present paper and implicitly to its whole subject-matter. In it he criticizes Melanie Klein and her collaborators—among whom he rightly associates myself—on various grounds. It is not my intention to deal here in any detail with the many inaccurate statements in his paper. I shall restrict myself to one instance only. Among other things he takes Melanie Klein to task for having ignored the ways in which the internalized objects become integrated in the ego, a criticism which, as can be seen from the literature concerned, is fallacious. The method used by Matte Blanco in his polemic is, I think, best illustrated by the fact that he quotes (p. 26)—though inaccurately—the above passage from my present paper and expresses agreement with it, yet nowhere in his paper does he acknowledge that this passage and my whole paper are a contribution towards the solution of the very problem which he accuses Melanie Klein and her school of having failed to understand. In spite of his agreement with this passage, he says (p. 18): "Attempts at further development are continually made by Melanie Klein and her followers, but the result seems to be nothing more than, to use a graphic French expression, "*piétiner sur place*", moving incessantly without ever succeeding in going forward." Further (on p. 24): "The introjected object, no matter how much divided into small pieces, no matter how many pilgrimages it makes from inside to outside and *vice versa*, will always remain what these conceptions suggest—some-

thing immobile, something outside the psyche of the individual, foreign to it, whose ultimate fate can be none other than expulsion." This may be his opinion, but my case, on the contrary, clearly illustrated the view that internal objects are far from immobile, are very much alive, and essentially a part of the subject's personality. The wish to expel them is but one reaction to one aspect of them (the persecutory). Incidentally, the fear of losing them (in their good aspects) is one of the severest anxieties human beings can experience.

References

Freud, S. (1910). Über Psychoanalyse. *Gesammelte Schriften IV*: 35.

Freud, S. (1920)[Trans 1922]. *Beyond the Pleasure Principle*, 69.

Jones, E. (1927). The early development of female sexuality. *International Journal of Psychoanalysis*, *8*: 461.

Jones, E. (1937). Love and morality. *International Journal of Psychoanalysis*, *18*: 1.

Klein, M. (1932). *The Psycho-Analysis of Children* (especially Chaps. I, VIII, IX and XI).

Klein, M. (1935). A contribution to the psychogenesis of manic-depressive states. International Journal of Psychoanalysis, 16: 145.

Klein, M. (1940). Mourning and its relation to manic-depressive states. *International Journal of Psychoanalysis*, *21*: 125.

Matte Blanco, I. (1941). On introjection and the processes of psychic metabolism. *International Journal of Psychoanalysis*, *22*: 17.

Notes on some schizoid mechanisms*

Melanie Klein

Introductory remarks

Tonight I am going to touch on a vast and relatively obscure topic, and the present paper is necessarily in the nature of preliminary notes. I had given much thought to this subject for many years, even before I came to clarify my views on the depressive processes in infancy. In the course of working out my concept of the infantile depressive position, however, the problems of the phase preceding it again forced themselves on my attention. I now wish to formulate some hypotheses at which I have arrived regarding the earlier anxieties and mechanisms.

The hypotheses I shall put forward, which relate to very early stages of development, are derived by inference from material gained in the analyses of adults and children, and some of these hypotheses seem to tally with observations familiar in psychiatric

---

* Read before the British Psycho-Analytical Society on December 4, 1946. [Reproduced, with permission, from: *International Journal of Psychoanalysis*, 1946, 27: 99–110 © Institute of Psychoanalysis, London, UK]

work. To substantiate my contentions would require an accumulation of detailed case material for which there is no room in the frame of this paper, and I hope in further contributions to fill this gap.

At the outset it will be useful to summarize briefly the conclusions regarding the earliest phases of development which I have already put forward (see particularly Klein, 1932) and (1935).

In early infancy anxieties characteristic of psychosis arise which drive the ego to develop specific defence mechanisms. In this period the fixation points for all psychotic disorders are to be found. This hypothesis led some people to believe that I regarded all infants as psychotic; but I have already dealt sufficiently with this misunderstanding on other occasions. The psychotic anxieties, mechanisms and ego defences of infancy have a profound influence on development in all its aspects, including the development of the ego, super-ego and object relations.

I have often expressed my view that object relations exist from the beginning of life, the first object being the mother's breast which is split into a good (gratifying) and bad (frustrating) breast; this splitting results in a division between love and hate. I have further suggested that the relation to the first object implies its introjection and projection, and thus from the beginning object relations are moulded by an interaction between introjection and projection, between internal and external objects and situations. These processes participate in the building up of the ego and super-ego and prepare the ground for the onset of the Oedipus complex in the second half of the first year.

From the beginning the destructive impulse is turned against the object and is first expressed in phantasied oral-sadistic attacks on the mother's breast which soon develop into onslaughts on her body by all sadistic means. The persecutory fears arising from the infant's oral-sadistic impulses to rob the mother's body of its good contents, and the anal-sadistic impulses to put his excrements into her (including the desire to enter her body in order to control her from within), are of great importance for the development of paranoia and schizophrenia.

I enumerated various typical defences of the early ego, primarily the mechanisms of splitting the object and the impulses, idealization, denial of inner and outer reality and stifling of emotions.

I also mentioned various persecutory fears, including the fear of being poisoned and devoured. Most of these phenomena—prevalent in the first few months of life—are found in the later symptomatic picture of schizophrenia.

This early period I described as the "persecutory phase", or rather "paranoid position" as I termed it later. I thus held that preceding the depressive position there is a paranoid position. If persecutory fears are very strong, and for this reason as well as others the infant cannot work through the paranoid position, then the working through of the depressive position is in turn impeded. This failure may lead to a regressive reinforcing of persecutory fears and strengthen the fixation points for severe psychoses (that is to say, the group of schizophrenias). Again the outcome of severe difficulties arising during the period of the depressive position may be manic-depressive disorders in later life. I also concluded that in less severe disturbances of development the same factors strongly influence the choice of neuroses.

While I assumed that the outcome of the depressive position depends on the working through of the preceding phase, I nevertheless attributed to the depressive position a central role in the child's early development. for with the introjection of the object as a whole the relation to the object alters fundamentally. The synthesis between the loved and hated aspects of the complete object gives rise to feelings of mourning and guilt which imply vital advances in the infant's emotional and intellectual life. This is also a crucial juncture for the choice of neurosis or psychosis. To all these conclusions I still adhere.

Some notes on Fairbairn's recent papers

In a number of recent papers (1941, 1944, 1946) Fairbairn has given much attention to the subject-matter with which I am dealing to-night. I therefore feel it necessary to clarify some essential points of agreement and disagreement between us. It will be seen that some of the conclusions which I shall present in this paper are in line with Fairbairn's conclusions, while others differ fundamentally. Fairbairn's approach is largely from the angle of ego development in relation to objects, while mine was predominantly from the angle of anxieties and their vicissitudes. He calls the earliest phase the "schizoid position" and states that it forms part of normal development and is the basis for adult schizoid and schizophrenic illness. I agree with this contention and consider his description of developmental schizoid phenomena as significant and revealing, and of great value for our understanding of schizoid behaviour and of schizophrenia. I also consider Fairbairn's view that the group of schizoid or schizophrenic disorders is much wider than has been acknowledged, as correct and important; and the particular emphasis he lays on the inherent relation between hysteria and schizophrenia deserves full attention. His term "schizoid position" seems adequate if it is meant to cover both persecutory fear and schizoid mechanisms.

I disagree—to mention first the most basic issues—with his revision of the theory of mental structure and instincts. I also disagree with his view that to begin with only the bad object is internalized—a view which seems to me to contribute to the important differences between us regarding the development of object relations as well as ego development. For I hold that the introjected good breast forms a vital part of the ego, exerts from the beginning a fundamental influence on the process of ego development and affects both ego structure and object relations. I also dissent from Fairbairn's view that "the great problem of the schizoid individual is how to love without destroying by love, whereas the great problem of the depressive individual is how to love without destroying by hate" (cf. Fairbairn, 1941, p. 271). This conclusion is in line not only with his rejecting the concept of primary instincts but also with his under-rating of the role which aggression and hatred play from the beginning of life. As a result of this approach, he does not give enough weight to the importance of early anxiety and conflict and their dynamic effects on development.

Some problems of the early ego

In the following discussion I shall single out one aspect of ego development and I shall deliberately not attempt to link it with the problems of ego development as a whole. Nor can I here touch on the relation of the ego to the id and super-ego.

We know so far little about the structure of the early ego. Some of the recent suggestions on this point have not convinced me: I have particularly in mind Glover's concept of ego nuclei and Fairbairn's theory of a central ego and two subsidiary egos. More helpful in my view is Winnicott's emphasis on the unintegration of the early ego (cf. Winnicott, 1945).[1] I would also say that the early ego lacks cohesiveness and that a tendency towards integration alternates with a tendency towards disintegration, a falling into bits. I think that these fluctuations are characteristic of the first few months of life.

We are, I think, justified in assuming that some of the functions which we know from the later ego are there in the beginning. Prominent amongst these functions is that of dealing with anxiety. I hold that anxiety arises from the operation of the Death Instinct within the organism, is felt as fear of annihilation (death) and takes the form of fear of persecution. The fear of the destructive impulse seems to attach itself at once to an object—or rather it is experienced as fear of an uncontrollable overpowering object. Other important sources of primary anxiety are the trauma of birth (separation anxiety) and frustration of bodily needs; and these experiences too are from the beginning felt to be caused by bad objects. Even if these objects are felt to be external, they become through introjection internal persecutors and thus reinforce the fear of the destructive impulse within.

The vital need to deal with anxiety forces the early ego to develop some primary mechanisms and defences. The destructive impulse is partly projected outwards (deflection of the Death Instinct) and attaches itself at once to the primary external object, the mother's breast. As Freud has pointed out, the remaining portion of the destructive impulse is to some extent bound by the libido within the organism. However, neither of these processes entirely fulfil their purpose, and therefore the anxiety of being destroyed from within remains active. It seems to me in keeping with the lack of cohesiveness that under the pressure of this threat the ego tends to fall to bits. This falling to bits appears to underlie states of disintegration in schizophrenics.

The question arises whether some active splitting processes within the ego may not enter even at a very early stage. As we know, the early ego splits the object and the relation to it in an active way, and this may imply some active splitting of the ego itself. In any case, the result of splitting is a dispersal of the destructive impulse which is felt as the source of danger. I suggest that this primary anxiety of being annihilated by a destructive force within, with the ego's specific response of falling to bits or splitting itself, may be extremely important in all schizophrenic processes.

Splitting processes in relation to the object

The destructive impulse projected outwards is first experienced as oral aggression. I believe that oral-sadistic impulses towards the mother's breast are active from the beginning of life, though with the onset of teething the cannibalistic impulses increase in strength—a factor stressed by Abraham.

In states of frustration and anxiety the oralsadistic and cannibalistic desires are reinforced, and then the infant feels that he has taken in the nipple and the breast, in bits. Thus in addition to the division between one good and one bad breast in the young infant's phantasy, the frustrating breast—attacked in oral-sadistic phantasies—is felt to be in bits; while the gratifying breast, taken in under the dominance of the sucking libido, is felt to be complete. This first internal good object acts as a focal point in the ego. It counteracts the processes of splitting and dispersal, makes for cohesiveness and integration, and is instrumental in building up the ego.[2] The infant's feeling of having inside a good and complete breast may, however, be shaken by frustration and anxiety. As a result, the division between the good and bad breast may be difficult to maintain, and the infant may feel that the good breast too is in bits.

I believe that the ego is incapable of splitting the object—internal and external—without correspondingly a splitting within the ego taking place. Therefore the phantasies and feelings about the state of the internal object influence vitally the structure of the ego. The more sadism prevails in the process of incorporating the object, and the more the object is felt to be in bits, the more the ego is in danger of being split in relation to the internalized object bits.

The processes I have described are, of course, bound up with the infant's phantasy life; and the anxieties which stimulate the mechanism of splitting are also of a phantastic nature. It is in phantasy that the infant splits the object and the self, but the effect of this phantasy is a very real one, because it leads to feelings and relations (and later on thought processes) being in fact cut off from one another.[3]

Splitting in connection with introjection and projection

I have so far particularly dealt with the mechanism of splitting as one of the earliest ego mechanisms and defences against anxiety. Introjection and projection are from the beginning of life also used in the service of this primary aim of the ego. Projection, as we know from Freud, originates from the deflection of the Death Instinct outwards and in my view helps the ego in overcoming anxiety by ridding it of danger and badness. Introjection of the good object is also used by the ego as a defence against anxiety.

Closely connected with projection and introjection are some other mechanisms. Here I am particularly concerned with the connection between splitting, idealization and denial. As regards splitting of the object, we have to remember that in states of gratification love feelings turn towards the gratifying breast, while in states of frustration hatred and persecutory anxiety attach themselves to the frustrating breast. This twofold relation, implying a division between love and hatred in relation to the object, can only be maintained by splitting the breast into its good and bad aspects.

With the splitting of the object, idealization is bound up, for the good aspects of the breast are exaggerated as a safeguard against the fear of the persecuting breast. Idealization is thus the corollary of persecutory fear, but it also springs from the power of the instinctual desires which aim at unlimited gratification and therefore create the picture of an inexhaustible and always bountiful breast— an ideal breast.

A good instance of such division is the infantile hallucinatory gratification. The main processes which come into play in idealization are operative in the hallucinatory gratification, namely the splitting of the object and the denial both of frustration and of persecution. The frustrating and persecuting object is kept widely apart from the idealized object. However, the bad object is not only kept apart from the good one but its very existence is denied as is the whole situation of frustration and the bad feelings (pain) to which frustration gives rise. This is bound up with denial of psychic reality. The denial of psychic reality becomes possible only through the feeling of omnipotence—which is characteristic of the infantile mind. Omnipotent denial of the existence of the bad object and of the painful situation is in the unconscious equal to annihilation by the destructive impulse. It is, however, not only a situation and an object which is denied and annihilated—it is an object relation which suffers this fate; and therefore a part of the ego, from which the feelings towards the object emanate, is denied and annihilated as well.

In hallucinatory gratification therefore two interrelated processes take place: the omnipotent conjuring up of the ideal object and situation, and the equally omnipotent annihilation of the bad persecutory object and the painful situation. These processes are based on splitting the object and the ego.

In passing I would mention that in this early phase splitting, denial and omnipotence play a role similar to that of repression at a later stage of ego-development. In considering the importance of the processes of denial and omnipotence at a stage which is characterized by persecutory fear and schizoid mechanisms, we may remember the delusions in schizophrenia, both of grandeur and of persecution.

So far, in dealing with persecutory fear, I have singled out the oral element. However, while the oral libido still has the lead, libidinal and aggressive impulses and phantasies from other sources come to the fore and bring about a confluence of oral, urethral and anal libidinal and aggressive desires. Also the attacks on the mother's breast develop into attacks of a similar nature on her body, which comes to be felt as it were as an extension of the breast, even before the mother can be conceived of as a complete person. The phantasied attacks on the mother follow two main lines: one is the predominantly oral impulse to suck dry, bite up, scoop out and rob the mother's body of its good contents. (I shall discuss the bearing of these impulses on the development of object relations in connection with introjection.) The other line of attack derives from the anal and urethral impulses and implies expelling dangerous substances (excrements) out of the self and into the mother. Together with these harmful excrements, expelled in hatred, split off parts of the ego are also projected on to the mother or, as I would rather call it, into the mother.[4] These excrements and bad parts of the self are meant not only to injure the object but also to control it and take possession of it. In so far as the mother comes to contain the bad parts of the self, she is not felt to be a separate individual but is felt to be the bad self.

Much of the hatred against parts of the self is now directed towards the mother. This leads to a particular kind of identification which establishes the prototype of an aggressive object relation. Also, since the projection derives from the infant's impulse to harm or to control the mother,[5] he feels her to be a persecutor. In psychotic disorders this identification of an object with the hated parts of the self contributes to the intensity of the hatred directed against other people. So far as the ego is concerned, excessive splitting off of parts of itself and expelling these into the outer world considerably weaken it. For the aggressive component of feelings and of the personality is intimately bound up in the mind with power, potency, strength, knowledge and many other desired qualities.

It is, however, not only the bad parts of the self which are expelled and projected, but also good parts of the self. Excrements then have the significance of gifts; and parts of the ego which, together with excrements, are expelled and projected into the other person represent the good, i.e. the loving parts of the self. The identification based on this type of projection again vitally influences object relations. The projection of good feelings and good parts of the self into the mother is essential for the infant's ability to develop good object relations and to integrate his ego. However, if this projective process is carried out excessively, good parts of the personality are felt to be lost to the self, and the mother becomes the ego ideal; this process, too, results in weakening and impoverishing the ego. Very soon such processes extend to other people,[6] and the result may be an extreme dependence on these external representatives of the good parts of the self. Another consequence is a fear that the capacity to love has been lost because the loved object is felt to be loved predominantly as a representative of the self.

The processes of splitting off parts of the self and projecting them into objects are thus of vital importance for normal development as well as for abnormal object relations.

The effect of introjection on object relations is equally important. The introjection of the good object, first of all mother's breast is a precondition for normal development. I have already described how the internal good breast comes to form a focal point in the ego and makes for cohesiveness of the ego. One characteristic feature of the earliest relation to the good object—internal and external—is the tendency to idealize it. In states of frustration or increased anxiety, the infant is driven to take flight to his internal idealized object as a means of escaping from persecutors. From this mechanism various serious disturbances may result: when persecutory fear is too strong, the flight to the idealized object becomes excessive, and this severely hampers ego-development and disturbs object relations. As a result the ego may be felt to be entirely subservient to and dependent on the internal object—only a shell for it. With an unassimilated idealized object there goes a feeling that the ego has no life and no value of its own.[7] I would suggest that the condition of flight to the unassimilated idealized object necessitates further splitting processes within the ego. For parts of the ego attempt to unite with the ideal object, while other parts strive to deal with the internal persecutors.

The various ways of splitting the ego and internal objects result in the feeling that the ego is in bits. This feeling amounts to a state of disintegration. In normal development, the states of disintegration which the infant experiences are transitory. Among other factors, gratification by the external good object[8] again and again helps to break through these schizoid states. The infant's capacity to overcome temporary schizoid states is in keeping with the strong elasticity and resilience of the infantile mind. If states of splitting and therefore of disintegration, which the ego is unable to overcome, occur too frequently and go on for too long, then in my view they must be regarded as a sign of schizophrenic illness in the infant, and some indications of such illness may already be seen in the first few months of life. In adult patients, states of depersonalization and of schizophrenic dissociation seem to be a regression to these infantile states of disintegration.

In my experience, excessive persecutory fears and schizoid mechanisms in early infancy may have a detrimental effect on intellectual development in its initial stages. Certain forms of mental deficiency would therefore have to be regarded as belonging to the group of schizophrenias. Accordingly, mental deficiency in children at any age should be examined in the light of a possible schizo-phrenic illness in early infancy.

I have so far described some effects of excessive introjection and projection on object relations. I am not attempting to investigate here in any detail the various factors which in some cases make for a predominance of introjective and in other cases for a predomi-nance of projective processes. As regards normal development, it may be said that the course of ego development and object relations depends on the degree to which an optimal balance between intro-jection and projection in the early stages of development can be achieved. This in turn has a bearing on the integration of the ego and the assimilation of internal objects. Even if the balance is disturbed and one or the other of these processes is excessive, there is some interaction between introjection and projection. For instance, the projection of a predominantly hostile inner world which is ruled by persecutory fears leads to the introjection—a taking back—of a hostile external world. *Vice versa*, the introjection of a distorted and hostiile external world reinforces the projection of a hostile inner world.

Another aspect of projective processes, as we have seen, implies the forceful entry into the object and control of the object by parts of the self. As a consequence, introjection may then be felt as a forceful entry from the outside into the inside, in retribution for violent projection. This may lead to the fear that not only the body but also the mind is controlled by other people in a hostile way. As a result there may be a severe disturbance in introjecting good objects—a disturbance which would impede all ego-functions as well as sexual development and may lead to an excessive withdrawal to the inner world. This withdrawal is, however, not only caused by the fear of introjecting a dangerous external world but also by the fear of inter-nal persecutors and an ensuing flight to the idealized internal object.

I have referred to the weakening and impoverishment of the ego resulting from excessive splitting and projective identification. This weakened ego, however, becomes also incapable of assimilating its internal objects, and this leads to the feeling that it is ruled by them. Again, such a weakened ego feels incapable of taking back into itself the parts which it projected into the external world. These various disturbances in the interplay between projection and introjection, which imply excessive splitting of the ego, have a detrimental effect on the relation to the inner and outer world and seem to be at the root of some forms of schizophrenia.

Schizoid object relations

To summarize now some of the disturbed object relations which are found in schizoid personalities: the violent splitting of the self and excessive projection have the effect that the person towards whom this process is directed is felt as a persecutor. Since the destructive and hated part of the self which is split off and projected is felt as a danger to the loved object and therefore gives rise to guilt, this process of projection in some ways also implies a deflection of guilt from the self on to the other person. Guilt has, however, not been done away with, and the deflected guilt is felt as an unconscious responsibility for the people who have become representatives of the aggressive part of the self.

Another typical feature of schizoid object relations is their narcissistic nature which derives from the infantile introjective and projective processes. For, as I suggested earlier, when the ego ideal is projected into another person, this object becomes predominantly loved and admired because it contains the good parts of the self. Similarly, the relation to other persons on the basis of projecting bad parts of the self into them is of a narcissistic nature because in this case as well the object strongly represents one part of the self. Both these types of a narcissistic relation to an object often show strong obsessional features. The impulse to control other people is, as we know, an essential element in obsessional neurosis. The need to control others can to some extent be explained by a deflected drive to control parts of the self. When these parts have been projected excessively into another person, they can only be controlled by controlling the other person. One root of obsessional mechanisms could thus be found in the particular identification which results from infantile projective processes. This connection may also throw some light on the obsessional element which so often enters into the tendency for reparation. For it is not only an object about whom guilt is experienced but also parts of the self which the subject is driven to repair or restore.

All these factors may lead to a compulsive tie to certain objects or—another outcome—to a shrinking from people in order to prevent both a destructive intrusion into them and the danger of retaliation by them. The fear of such dangers may show itself in various negative attitudes in object relations. For instance, one of my patients told me that people who are too much influenced by him seem to become too much like himself and he "gets tired" of seeing so much of himself.

Another characteristic of schizoid object relations is a marked artificiality and lack of spontaneity. Side by side with this goes a severe disturbance of the feeling of the self or, as I would put it, of the relation to the self. This relation, too, appears to be artificial. In other words, psychic reality and the relation to external reality are equally disturbed.

The projection of split-off parts of the self into another person essentially influences object relations, emotional life and the personality as a whole. To illustrate this contention I am going to select as an instance a more or less universal phenomenon: the feeling of loneliness and fear of parting. We know that one source of the depressive feelings accompanying parting from people can be found in the fear of the destruction of the object by the aggressive impulses directed against it. But it is more specifically the splitting and projective processes which underlie this fear. If aggressive elements in relation to the object are predominant and strongly stirred by the frustration of parting, the individual feels that the split-off components of his self, projected into the object, control this object in an aggressive and destructive way. At the same time the internal object is felt to be in the same danger of destruction as the external object in whom one part of the self is felt to be left. The result is an excessive weakening of the ego, a feeling that there is nothing to sustain it, and a corresponding dependence on people. While this description applies to neurotic individuals, I think that in minor degrees these processes are a general phenomenon.

One need hardly elaborate on the fact that some other features of schizoid object relations, which I described earlier, can also be found in minor degrees and in a less striking form in normal people—for instance shyness, lack of spontaneity or, on the other hand, a particularly intense interest in people.

In similar ways normal disturbances in thought processes can be related to the developmental schizoid position. For all of us are liable at times to a momentary impairment of logical thinking which amounts to thoughts being cut off from one another and situations being split off from one another; in fact, the ego is temporarily split.

The depressive position in relation to the schizoid position

I now wish to consider further steps in the infant's development. So far I have described the anxieties, mechanisms and defences which are characteristic for the first few months of life. With the introjection of the complete object in about the second quarter of the first year marked steps in integration are made. This implies important changes in the relation to objects. The loved and hated aspects of the mother are no longer felt to be so widely separated, and the result is an increased fear of loss, a strong feeling of guilt and states akin to mourning, because the aggressive impulses are felt to be directed against the loved object. The depressive position has come to the fore. The very experience of depressive feelings in turn has the effect of further integrating the ego, because it makes for an increased understanding of psychic reality and better perception of the external world, as well as for a greater synthesis between inner and external situations.

The drive for reparation, which comes to the fore at this stage, can be regarded as a consequence of a greater insight into psychic reality and of growing synthesis, for it shows a more realistic response to the feelings of grief, guilt and fear of loss resulting from the aggression against the loved object. Since the drive to repair or protect the injured object paves the way for more satisfactory object relations and sublimations, it in turn increases synthesis and contributes to the integration of the ego.

During the second half of the first year the infant makes the fundamental steps towards working through the depressive position. However, schizoid mechanisms still remain in force, though in a modified form and to a lesser degree, and early anxiety situations are again and again experienced in the process of modification. The working through of the persecutory and depressive positions extends over the first few years of childhood and plays an essential part in the infantile neurosis. In the course of this process, anxieties lose in strength, objects become both less idealized and less terrifying, and the ego becomes more unified. All this is interdependent with the growing perception of reality and adaptation to it.

If, however, development during the schizoid phase has not proceeded normally and the infant cannot—for internal or external reasons—cope with the impact of depressive anxieties, a vicious circle arises. For if persecutory fear, and correspondingly schizoid mechanisms, are too strong, the ego is not capable of working through the depressive position. This in turn forces the ego to regress to the schizoid position and reinforces the earlier persecutory fears and schizoid phenomena. Thus the basis is established for various forms of schizophrenia in later life; for when such a regression occurs, not only are the fixation points in the schizoid position reinforced, but there is a danger of greater states of disintegration setting in. Another outcome may be the strengthening of depressive features.

External experiences are, of course, of great importance in these developments. For instance, in the case of a patient who showed depressive and schizoid features, the analysis brought up with great vividness the early experiences in babyhood, even to the extent that in some hours physical sensations in the throat or digestive organs occurred. The patient had been suddenly weaned at four months of age because his mother fell ill. In addition, he did not see his mother for four weeks. When she returned, she found the child greatly changed. He had formerly been lively, eager for his food, interested in his surroundings. Now he seemed completely apathetic. He had accepted the substitute food fairly easily and in fact never refused food. But he did not thrive on it any more, lost weight and had a good deal of digestive trouble. It was only at the end of the first year, when other food was introduced, that he made again good physical progress.

Much light was thrown in the analysis on the influence these experiences had on his whole development. His outlook and attitudes in adult life were based on the patterns established in this early stage. For instance, we found again and again a tendency to be influenced by other people in an unselective way—in fact to take in greedily whatever was offered—together with great distrust during the process of introjection. Anxieties from various sources, constantly disturbed the processes of introjection and contributed to an increase of the greed which had been strongly repressed in infancy.

Taking the material of this analysis as a whole, I came to the conclusion that at the time when the sudden loss of the breast and of the mother occurred, the patient had already to some extent a relation to a complete good object. He had no doubt by then entered the depressive position but could not work through it successfully and the schizoid position became regressively reinforced. This expressed itself in the "apathy" which followed a period when the child had already shown a lively interest in his surroundings. The fact that he had reached the depressive position and had introjected a complete object showed in many ways in his personality. He had actually a strong capacity for love and a great longing for a good and complete object. A characteristic feature of his personality was the desire to love people and trust them, unconsciously to regain and build up again the good and complete breast which he had once possessed and lost.

Connection between schizoid and manic-depressive phenomena

Some fluctuations between the schizoid and the depressive position always occur and are part of normal development. No clear division between the two stages of development can therefore be drawn, because modification is a gradual process and the phenomena of the two positions remain for some time to some extent intermingled and interacting. In abnormal development this interaction influences, I think, the clinical picture both of some forms of schizophrenia and of manic-depressive disorders.

To illustrate this connection I shall briefly refer to some case material. I have no intention to give here a case history and am therefore only selecting some pieces of material to illustrate my point. The patient I have in mind was a pronounced manic-depressive case (diagnosed as such by more than one psychiatrist) with all the characteristics of this disorder: there was the alternation between depressive and manic states, strong suicidal tendencies leading repeatedly to suicidal attempts, and various other characteristic manic and depressive features. In the course of her analysis a stage was reached during which a noticeable improvement was achieved: the cycle became less marked but there were fundamental changes in her personality and her object relations. Productivity on various lines developed, as well as actual feelings of happiness (not of the manic type). Then, partly owing to external circumstances, another phase set in. During this last phase, which continued for several months, the patient co-operated in the analysis in a particular way. She came regularly to the analytic sessions, associated fairly freely, reported dreams and provided material for the analysis. There was, however, no emotional response to my interpretations and a good deal of contempt of them. There was very seldom any conscious confirmation of what I suggested. Yet the material by which she responded to the interpretations reflected their unconscious effect. The powerful resistance shown at this stage seemed to come from one part of the personality only, while—at the same time—another part responded to the analytic work. It was not only that parts of her personality did not co-operate with me; they did not seem to co-operate with each other, and the analysis was unable at the time to help the patient to achieve synthesis. During this stage she decided to bring the analysis to an end. To this decision external circumstances strongly contributed, and she fixed a date for the end of her analysis, in spite of my warning of the danger of a relapse.

On that particular date she reported the following dream: there was a blind man who was very worried about being blind; but he seemed to comfort himself by touching the patient's dress and finding out how it was fastened. The dress in the dream reminded her of one of her frocks which was buttoned high up to the throat. The patient gave two further associations to this dream. She said, with some resistance, that the blind man was herself; and when referring to the dress fastened up to the throat, she remarked that she had again gone into her "hide". I suggested to the patient that she unconsciously expressed in the dream that she was blind to the fact of her own illness, and that her decisions with regard to the analysis as well as to various circumstances in her life were not in accordance with her unconscious knowledge. This was also shown by her admitting that she had gone into her "hide", meaning by it that she was shutting herself off, an attitude well known to her from previous stages in her illness. Thus the unconscious insight, and even some co-operation on the conscious level (recognition that *she* was the blind man and that she had gone into her "hide"), derived from isolated parts of her personality only. Actually, the interpretation of this dream did not produce any effect and did not alter the patient's decision to bring the analysis to an end in this particular hour.[9]

At the stage preceding the breaking off of the analysis, some light was thrown on certain difficulties encountered in the course of this analysis and, as I may add, in others as well. It was the mixture of schizoid and manic-depressive features which determined the nature of her illness. For at times throughout her analysis—even at the early stage when depressive and manic states were at their height—depressive and schizoid mechanisms sometimes appeared simultaneously. There were, for instance, hours when the patient was obviously deeply depressed, full of self-reproaches and feelings of unworthiness; tears were running down her cheeks and her gestures expressed despair; and yet she said, when I interpreted these emotions, that she did not feel them at all. Whereupon she reproached herself for having no feelings at all, for being completely empty. In such hours there was also a flight of ideas, the thoughts seemed to be broken up, and their expression was disjointed.

Following the interpretation of the unconscious reasons underlying such states, there were sometimes hours in which the emotions and depressive anxieties came out fully, and at such times thoughts and speech were much more coherent.

This close connection between depressive and schizoid phenomena appeared, though in different forms, throughout her analysis but became very pronounced during the last stage preceding the breaking off which I have described.

I have already referred to the developmental connection between the schizoid and depressive positions. The question now arises whether this developmental connection is the basis for the mixture of these features in manic-depressive disorders and, as I would suggest, in schizophrenic disorders as well. If this tentative hypothesis could be proved, the conclusion would be that the groups of schizophrenic and manic-depressive disorders are more closely connected developmentally with one another than has been assumed. This would also account for the cases in which, I believe, the differential diagnosis between melancholia and schizophrenia is exceedingly difficult. I should be grateful if further light could be thrown on my hypothesis by colleagues who have had ample material for psychiatric observation.

Some schizoid defences

It is generally agreed that schizoid patients are more difficult to analyse than manic depressive types. Their withdrawn, unemotional attitude, the narcissistic elements in their object relations (to which I referred earlier), a kind of detached hostility which pervades the whole relation to the analyst create a very difficult type of resistance. I believe that it is largely the splitting processes which account for the patient's failure of contact with the analyst and for his lack of response to the analyst's interpretations. The patient himself feels estranged and far away, and this feeling corresponds to the analyst's impression that considerable parts of the patient's personality and of his emotions are not available. Patients with schizoid features may say: "I hear what you are saying. You may be right, but it has no meaning for me." Or again they say they feel they are not there. The expression "no meaning" does in such cases not imply an active rejection of the interpretation but suggests that parts of the personality and of the emotions are split off. These patients can, therefore, not deal with the interpretation; they can neither accept it nor reject it.

I shall illustrate the processes underlying such states by a piece of material taken from the analysis of a man patient. The hour I have in mind started with the patient's telling me that he felt anxiety and did not know why. He then made comparisons with people more successful and fortunate than himself. These remarks also had a reference to me. Very strong feelings of frustration, envy and grievance came to the fore. When I interpreted—to give here again only the gist of my interpretations—that these feelings were directed against the analyst and that he wanted to destroy me, his mood changed abruptly. The tone of his voice became flat, he spoke in a slow, expressionless way, and he said that he felt detached from the whole situation. He added that my interpretation seemed correct, but that it did not matter. In fact, he no longer had any wishes, and nothing was worth bothering about.

My next interpretations centred on the causes for this change of mood. I suggested that at the moment of my interpretation the danger of destroying me had become very real to him and the immediate consequence was the fear of losing me. Instead of feeling guilt and depression, which at certain stages of his analysis followed such interpretations, he now attempted to deal with these dangers by a particular method of splitting. As we know, under the pressure of ambivalence, conflict and guilt, the patient often splits the figure of the analyst; then the analyst may at certain moments be loved, at other moments hated. Or the relation to the analyst may be split in such a way that he remains the good (or bad) figure while somebody else becomes the opposite figure. But this was not the kind of splitting which occurred in this particular instance. The patient split off those parts of himself, i.e. of his ego, which he felt to be dangerous and hostile towards the analyst. He turned his destructive impulses from his object towards his ego, with the result that parts of his ego temporarily went out of existence. In unconscious phantasy this amounted to annihilation of part of his personality. The particular mechanism of turning the destructive impulse against one part of his personality, and the ensuing dispersal of emotions, kept this anxiety in a latent state.

My interpretation of these processes had the effect of again altering the patient's mood. He became emotional, said he felt like crying, was depressed, but felt more integrated; then he also expressed a feeling of hunger.[10]

Changes of mood, of course, do not always appear as dramatically within a session as in the first instance I have given in this section. But I have repeatedly found that advances in synthesis are brought about by interpretations of the specific causes for splitting. Such interpretations must deal in detail with the transference situation at that moment, including of course the connection with the past, and must contain a reference to the details of the anxiety situations which drive the ego to regress to schizoid mechanisms. The synthesis resulting from interpretations on these lines goes along with depression and anxieties from various sources. Gradually such waves of depression—followed by greater integration—lead to a lessening of schizoid phenomena and also to fundamental changes in object-relations.

The violent splitting off and destroying of one part of the personality under the pressure of anxiety and guilt is in my experience an important schizoid mechanism. I should like to quote another short instance: a woman patient dreamed that she had to deal with a wicked girl child who was determined to murder somebody. The patient tried to influence or control the child and to extort a confession from her which would have been to the child's benefit; but she was unsuccessful. I also entered into the dream and the patient felt that I might help her in dealing with the child. Then the patient strung up the child on a tree in order to frighten her and also prevent her from doing harm. When the patient was about to pull the rope and kill the child, she woke. During this part of the dream the analyst was also present but again remained inactive.

I shall give here only the essence of the conclusions I arrived at from the analysis of this dream. The patient's personality was split in the dream into two parts: the wicked and uncontrollable child on the one hand, and on the other hand the person who tried to influence and control her. The child, of course, stood also for various figures in the past, but in this context she mainly represented one part of the patient's self. Another conclusion was that the analyst was the person whom the child was going to murder; and my role in the dream was partly to prevent this murder from taking place. Killing the child—to which the patient had to resort—represented the annihilation of one part of her personality.

The question arises how the schizoid mechanism of annihilating part of the self connects with repression which, as we know, is directed against dangerous impulses. This, however, is a problem with which I cannot attempt to deal here.

Latent anxiety in schizoid patients

I have already referred to the lack of emotion which makes schizoid patients unresponsive. This goes together with an absence of anxiety. An important support for the analytic work is therefore lacking. For with other types of patients who have strong manifest and latent anxiety, the relief of anxiety derived from analytic interpretation becomes an experience which furthers their capacity to co-operate in the analysis.

This lack of anxiety in schizoid patients is only apparent. Though the schizoid mechanisms imply a dispersal of emotions including anxiety, these dispersed elements persist in the patient's mind. Such patients have a certain form of latent anxiety; it is kept latent by the particular method of dispersal. The feeling of being disintegrated, of being unable to experience emotions, of losing one's objects, is in fact the equivalent of anxiety. This becomes clearer when advance in synthesis has been made. The great relief which a patient then experiences derives from a feeling that his inner and outer world have come not only more together but back to life again. At such moments it appears in retrospect that when emotions were lacking, relations were vague and uncertain and parts of the personality were felt to be lost, everything was felt to be dead. All this is the equivalent of anxiety of a very serious nature. This anxiety, kept latent by dispersal, is to some extent experienced all along, but its form differs from the latent anxiety which we can recognize in other types of cases.

Interpretations which tend towards synthesizing the split in the ego, including the dispersal of emotions, make it possible for the anxiety gradually to be experienced as such, though for long stretches we might in fact only be able to bring the ideational contents of the anxiety together but not the affect of anxiety.

I have also found that interpretations of schizoid states make particular demands on our capacity to put the interpretations in an intellectually clear form in which the links between the conscious, pre-conscious and unconscious are established. This is, of course, always one of our aims, but it is of special importance at times when the patient's emotions are not available and we only seem to address ourselves to his intellect, however much broken up.

It is possible that the few hints I have given may to some extent apply as well to the technique of analysing schizophrenic patients.

Appendix

Freud's analysis of the Schreber case (Freud, 1911) contains a wealth of material which is very relevant to my topic but from which I shall here draw only a few conclusions.

Schreber described vividly the splitting of the soul of his physician Flechsig (his loved and persecuting figure). The "Flechsig soul" at one time introduced the system of "soul divisions" splitting into as many as forty to sixty subdivisions. These souls having multiplied till they became a "nuisance", God made a raid on them and as a result the Flechsig soul survived in "only one or two shapes". Another point which Schreber mentions is that the divisions of the Flechsig soul slowly lost both their intelligence and their power.

One of the conclusions Freud arrived at in his analysis of this case was that the persecutor was split into God and Flechsig, besides God and Flechsig also representing father and brother. In discussing the various forms of Schreber's delusion of the destruction of the world, Freud states: "In any case the end of the world was the consequence of the conflict which had broken out between him" (Schreber) "and Flechsig, or, according to the ætiology adopted in the second phase of his delusion, of the indissoluble bond which had been formed between him and God . . ." (Freud, 1911, pp. 455–456).

I would suggest, in keeping with the hypotheses put forward in my present paper, that the division of the Flechsig soul into many souls was not only a splitting of the object but also a projection of Schreber's feeling that his ego was split. I shall here only mention the connection of such splitting processes with processes of introjection. The conclusion suggests itself that God and Flechsig also represented parts of Schreber's self. The conflict between Schreber and Flechsig, to which Freud attributed a vital role in the World destruction delusion, found expression in the raid by God on the Flechsig souls. In my view this raid represents the annihilation by one part of the self of the other parts—which, as I contend, is a schizoid mechanism. The anxieties and phantasies about inner destruction and ego disintegration bound up with this mechanism are projected on to the external world and underlie the delusions of its destruction.

Regarding the processes which are at the bottom of the paranoic world catastrophe, Freud arrived at the following conclusions: "The patient has withdrawn from the persons in his environment and from the external world generally the libidinal cathexis which he has hitherto directed on to them. Thus all things have become indifferent and irrelevant to him, and have to be explained by means of a secondary rationalization as being "miracled up, cursory contraptions". The end of the world is the projection of this internal catastrophe; for his subjective world has come to an end since he has withdrawn his love from it" (Freud, 1911, pp. 456–457). This explanation concerns specifically the disturbance in object-libido and the ensuing breakdown in relation to people and to the external world. But a little further on (pp. 461–462) Freud considered another aspect of these disturbances. He said: "We can no more dismiss the possibility that disturbances of the libido may react upon the egoistic cathexes than we can overlook the *converse possibility* —namely, that *a secondary or induced disturbance of the libidinal processes may result from abnormal changes in the ego. Indeed, it is probable that processes of this kind constitute the distinctive characteristic of psychoses*" (my italics). It is particularly the possibility expressed in the last two sentences which provides the link between Freud's explanation of the world catastrophe and my hypothesis. "Abnormal changes in the ego" derive, as I have suggested in this paper, from excessive splitting processes in early infancy. These processes are inextricably linked with instinctual development, and with the anxieties to which instinctual desires give rise. In the light of Freud's later theory of the Life and Death Instincts, which replaced the concept of the egoistic and sexual instincts, disturbances in the distribution of the libido presuppose a defusion between the destructive impulse and the libido. The mechanism of one part of the ego annihilating other parts which, I suggest, underlies the world catastrophe phantasy (the raid by God on the Flechsig souls) implies a preponderance of the destructive impulse over the libido. Any disturbance in the distribution of the narcissistic libido is in turn bound up with the relation to introjected objects which (according to my work) from the beginning come to form part of the ego. The interaction between narcissistic libido and object libido corresponds thus to the interaction between the relation to introjected and external objects. If the ego and the internalized objects are felt by the infant to be in bits, an internal catastrophe is experienced which both extends to the external world and is projected on to it. Such anxiety states relating to internal catastrophe arise, according to the hypothesis put forward in my present paper, during the period of the infantile paranoid (or schizoid) position and form the basis for later schizophrenia. In Freud's view the dispositional fixation to

Dementia Præcox is found in a very early stage of development. Referring to Dementia Præcox, which Freud distinguished from Paranoia, he said: "The dispositional point of fixation must therefore be situated further back than in paranoia, and must lie somewhere at the beginning of the course of development from auto-erotism to object-love" (Freud, 1911, p. 464).

I wish to draw one more conclusion from Freud's analysis of the Schreber case. I suggest that the raid which ended in the Flechsig souls being reduced to one or two, was part of the attempt towards recovery. For the raid was to undo, one may say heal, the split in the ego by annihilating the split-off parts of the ego. As a result only one or two of the souls were left which, as we may assume, were meant to regain their intelligence and their power. This attempt towards recovery, however, was effected by very destructive means used by the ego against itself and its introjected objects.

Freud's approach to the problems of schizophrenia and paranoia has proved of fundamental importance. His Schreber paper (and here we also have to remember Abraham's paper quoted by Freud (Abraham, 1928) opened up the possibility for the understanding of psychosis and the processes underlying it.

Summary

I propose to summarize some of the conclusions presented in this paper. One of my main points was the suggestion that in the first few months of life anxiety is predominantly experienced as fear of persecution and that this contributes to certain mechanisms and defences which characterize the paranoid and schizoid positions. Outstanding among these defences is the mechanism of splitting internal and external objects, emotions and the ego. These mechanisms and defences are part of normal development and at the same time form the basis for later schizophrenic illness. I described the processes underlying identification by projection as a combination of splitting off parts of the self and projecting them on to another person, and some of the effects this identification has on normal and schizoid object relations. The onset of the depressive position is the juncture at which by regression schizoid mechanisms may be reinforced. I also suggested a close connection between the manic-depressive and schizoid disorders, based on the interaction between the infantile schizoid and depressive positions.

Notes

1. In this paper Dr Winnicott also described the pathological outcome of states of unintegration, for instance the case of a woman patient who could not distinguish between her twin sister and herself.
2. Winnicott (1945) referred to the same process from another angle when he described how integration and adaptation to reality depend essentially on the infant's experience of the mother's love and care.
3. In the discussion following the reading of this paper Clifford Scott referred to another aspect of splitting. He stressed the importance of the breaks in continuity of experiences, which imply a splitting in time rather than in space. He referred, as an instance, to the alternation between states of being asleep and states of being awake. I fully agree that splitting is not to be understood merely in terms of space and that the breaks in continuity are very essential for the understanding of schizoid mechanisms.
4. The description of such primitive processes suffers from a great handicap, for these phantasies arise at a time when the infant has not yet begun to think in words. In this paper, for instance, I am using the expression "to project into another person" because this seems to me the only way of conveying the unconscious process I am trying to describe.
5. Miss Gwen Evans, in a short unpublished communication (read to the Psycho-Analytical Society in January, 1946) gave some instances of patients in whom the following phenomena were marked: lack of sense of reality, a feeling of being divided and parts of the personality having entered the mother's body in order to rob and control her; as a consequence the mother and other people similarly attacked came to represent the patient. Miss Evans related these processes to a very primitive stage of development.
6. Clifford Scott in an unpublished paper, read to this Society a few years ago, described three inter-connected features which he came upon in a schizophrenic patient: a strong disturbance of her sense of reality, her feeling that the world round her was a cemetery, and the mechanism of putting all good parts of herself into another person—Greta Garbo—who came to stand for her self.

7. Paula Heimann (1942) described a condition in which the internal objects act as foreign bodies embedded in the self. Whilst this is more obvious with regard to the bad objects, it is true even for the good ones, if the ego is compulsively subordinated to their preservation. When the ego serves its good internal objects excessively, they are felt as a source of danger and come close to exerting a persecuting influence. Paula Heimann introduced the concept of the assimilation of the internal objects and applied it specifically to sublimation. As regards ego-development, she pointed out that such assimilation is essential for the successful exercise of ego-functions and for the achievement of independence.

8. Looked at in this light, the mother's love and understanding of the infant can be seen as the infant's greatest standby in overcoming states of disintegration and anxieties of a psychotic nature.

9. I may mention that the analysis was resumed after a break, when she felt again in danger of relapsing into a depression state.

10. The feeling of hunger indicated that the process of introjection had been set going again under the dominance of the libido. While to my first interpretation of his fear of destroying me by his aggression he had responded at once with the violent splitting off and annihilation of parts of his personality, he now experienced more fully the emotions of grief, guilt and fear of loss, as well as some relief of these depressive anxieties. The relief of anxiety resulted in the analyst again coming to stand for a good object which he could trust. Therefore the desire to introject me as a good object could come to the fore. If he could build up again the good breast inside himself, he would strengthen and integrate his ego, would be less afraid of his destructive impulses, in fact he could then preserve himself and the analyst.

References

Abraham, K. (1928)[Trans. 1942]. The psycho-sexual differences between hysteria and Dementia Præcox. *Selected Papers on Psycho-Analysis.*

Fairbairn, W. R. D. (1941). A revised psychopathology. *International Journal of Psychoanalysis,* 22: 271.

Fairbairn, W. R. D. (1944). Endopsychic structure considered in terms of object relationships. *International Journal of Psychoanalysis,* 25: 70.

Fairbairn, W. R. D. (1946). Object relationships and dynamic structure. *International Journal of Psychoanalysis,* 27: 30.

Freud, S. (1911)[Trans. 1925]. Psycho-analytic notes upon an autobio-graphical account of a case of paranoia. *Collected Papers III.*

Heimann, P. (1942). A contribution to the problem of sublimation and its relation to the processes of internalization. *International Journal of Psychoanalysis, 23:* 8–17.

Klein, M. (1932)[Trans. 1932]. *The Psycho-Analysis of Children.* London: Hogarth.

Klein, M. (1935). A contribution to the psychogenesis of manic-depressive states. *International Journal of Psychoanalysis, 16:* 45.

Winnicott, D. W. (1945). Primitive emotional development. *International Journal of Psychoanalysis, 26:* 137.